## The Needlecrafter's Computer Companion

"Will help you make the transition from curiosity and intimidation to practical application and integration of the computer into your sewing room."—Sandra Betzina, author of Power Sewing and syndicated columnist

**"The comparisons of software programs alone are worth the price of the book. Simply said, The Needlecrafter's Computer Companion is the definitive book on the subject, and will continue to be for quite some time to come."—Judith Broadhurst, author of A Woman's Guide to Online Services**

"For an entertaining, easy-reading, refreshingly opinionated reference to digital needlecrafting—software, hardware, online services, networking and more—rely on Judy Heim's book, The Needlecrafter's Computer Companion. I learned a lot."—Gail E. Brown, author of twelve sewing books, including The Ultimate Serger Answer Guide, and Gail Brown's All-New Instant Interiors

**"I am astounded by the quantity of clear and explicit computer information Judy Heim has fitted into this book... useful for anyone wanting to understand how to use and navigate the major Online Services, not just for textile and fiberarts, but for all topics...[she] obviously is comfortable with computers and knows how to explain them." —Susan C. Druding, founder of the Textile Arts Forum, Delphi, and owner of Straw Into Gold, Berkeley, CA**

"I love this book! Judy Heim has done the impossible: she's managed to solve the mysteries of the computer for the novice (or an old hand like me), while making the reader LOL (laugh out loud). The Needlecrafter's Computer Companion makes learning about the computer a treat for crafters of all kinds. Before you waste one cent on computer equipment, software or online services, buy this book—it will save you $$ and weeks of headaches."—Karen L. Maslowski, editor of Sew Up A Storm: The Newsletter for Sewing Entrepreneurs, and author of Sew Up A Storm: All the Way to the Bank!

# THE
# NEEDLECRAFTER'S
# COMPUTER COMPANION

*Hundreds of Easy Ways to Use Your Computer
for Sewing, Quilting, Cross-Stitch, Knitting & More!*

## JUDY HEIM

**NO STARCH PRESS**
SAN FRANCISCO, CALIFORNIA

Front Cover: Quilt courtesy private collection, photograph courtesy The Quilt Complex
Back Cover: Quilt courtesy Gloria Hansen
Illustration on p. 3 by Brian McMurdo, Ventana Studio

The majority of the illustrations in this book appear coutesy of Dover Publications, Inc.
Write to them at 31 East 2nd St., Mineola, NY 11501 for a free catalog.

 Printed on acid-free recycled paper.

Trademarks
Trademarked names are used throughout this book. Rather than use a trademark symbol with every
occurrence of a trademarked name, we are using the names only in an editorial fashion and to the
benefit of the trademark owner, with no intention of infringement of the trademark.

Publisher: William Pollock
Production Assistance: Vicki Friedberg
Cover Design: Cloyce Wall Design
Interior Design and Composition: Margery Cantor
Compositor: Steven Bolinger
Copyeditor: Loralee Windsor, Jerilyn Emori
Proofreader: Linda Medoff

**Library of Congress Cataloging-in-Publication Data**

Heim, Judy.
    The needlecrafter's computer companion: hundreds of easy ways to use your computer
in sewing, quilting, cross-stitch, knitting, and more / Judy Heim.
        p.   cm.
    Includes index.
    ISBN 1-886411-01-8
    1. Needlework—Data processing.   2. Computer-aided design.   3. Computer networks.   I. Title.
TT715.H45   1995
746.4'0285'416dc20                                                                94-44672

Distributed to the book trade in the United States and Canada
by Publishers Group West, 4065 Hollis, P.O. Box 8843, Emeryville, CA 94662
phone: 800-788-3123 or 510-548-4393; fax: 510-658-1834.

For information on translations or book distributors outside the United States,
please contact No Starch Press directly:
No Starch Press, 401 China Basin St., Ste. 108, San Francisco, CA 94107-2192
phone: 415-284-9900; fax: 415-284-9955; E-mail: info@nostarch.com; web site: http://www.nostarch.com

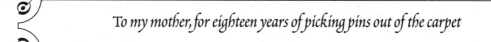

*To my mother, for eighteen years of picking pins out of the carpet*

# BRIEF CONTENTS

# CONTENTS IN DETAIL

CHAPTER **8**

**Exploring the Knitting Machine–Computer Connection  181**

CHAPTER 14

**Needlecraft Klatches Bloom on Hip America Online**   301

CHAPTER 15

**Cross-Stitchers, Quilters, and Other Fiber-Folk Have a Blast on Delphi**  319

CHAPTER 16

## Quilters Around the Globe Call GEnie Home  333

CHAPTER 17

## Microsoft Network Welcomes Quilters, Sewers, and Other Fabric Junkies  349

CHAPTER 18

## Internet Is for the Wired Crafter  353

CHAPTER 19

## A Guide to the Best Needlecraft-Related Computer Bulletin Boards  411

# ACKNOWLEDGMENTS

This book was conceived as a slim guide on how to get needlecraft information off popular computer online services. It has blossomed into something far greater. To that I owe thanks to the many sewers, quilters, doll makers, cross-stitchers, crocheters, knitters, and weavers on the Internet and computer services who offered their opinions, encouragement, and stories. Needlecrafters really are special. I continue to be touched by the generosity of their creative spirits.

I am deeply grateful to Gloria Hansen, Jamieson Forsyth, Liz Clouthier, and Ruthe Brown for their advice and contributions to the book. Had I not had the good fortune to befriend these high-tech stitching mavens, this book never would have exceeded the hundred or so pages for which it was originally planned. I'd also like to thank Jan Cabral, Penny McMorris, and Miriam Neuringer for their wit, encouragement, and advice on how best to instruct others to design quilts on a computer. Christiane Eichler generously transmitted digitized images of her tatting halfway around the world, not once, but multiple times, to reveal her secrets for how to design lace on a computer. Pat Papoure and Cozy Bendesky were reminders of how "electronic sewing bees" can transcend their purpose and can deeply affect the lives of those who join them. I would like to thank Susan Lazear and Kathy Morgret not only for their written contributions to the book and for their conversations but also for running the most incredible place in cyberspace—the CompuServe craft forums—where much of this book was researched. I am also grateful to Susan Druding and her crew in the Textile Arts Forum on Delphi for pinch-hitting with ideas and keeping me irreverent.

Others who provided reading lists, brainstorms, directions, testimonials, and scintillating conversation include Anne Browne; Karen Seymour of the Seattle Computer User's Group; Stephanie Schoelzel of the Hollywood Joint Costumers' Computer Users Group; Debs Butler; Cheryl Simmerman; Joy McFadden; Ingrid Boesel; Sigrid Piroch; Karen Maslowski; Sue Bennett; Carla Lopez; Jeanie Attenhofer; Walter Kind; Fran Grimble; and Ron Parker.

Many sewing machine and software makers went out of their way to provide test versions of their products, as well as ensure that all my technical questions were answered. Some put me in touch with customers, including professional needlework designers. All realized the risk they were taking, for my aim was not to shamelessly gush over every product, but to help consumers find a way through the thickening forest of craft software and computerized sewing and knitting machines. I thank them for so wholeheartedly supporting my efforts to help their customers become wiser, more self-assured shoppers. Hopefully, stitchers will approach high-tech needlecraft tools with less anxiety and more enthusiasm as a consequence.

My special thanks to Laura Haynie and Elvie Turien at Pfaff American; Stan Ingram, Nancy Jewell, and Debbie Nye at Viking Sewing Machine Co.; Barbara Wright at Bernina of America; Tim Plumlee of Masterstitch Designs; Angela Hay at Oxford Craft Software; Annette Scoffield and Fred Shadko at LivingSoft; Jamie Smith at Water Fountain Software; Anne Bartley at Bartley Software; Nina Antze of PCQuilt; R. Scott Horton at HobbyWare; Tony Wood at Model Systems; David Natwig at Compucraft; Phil Hisley of Computer Systems Associates; the folks at M&R Enterprise; Ricky Ford of QuiltSoft; and Janet Tombu of Morningdew Consulting. There are many others who supplied products and returned my endless calls, but whose names I've either forgotten or misplaced in the blur of talking to and exchanging E-mail with hundreds of people over the course of a year. Please forgive me, and be assured that this book couldn't have happened without your kind support.

I'd also like to thank those who provided permission to include their quotes, stories, and the digitized pictures of their craft projects that appear on various online services.

As this project sprawled like a ten-part TV miniseries out of control, Vicki Friedberg provided organization and a sure pencil that kept the pages in order. The crafty editing of Loralee Windsor and Jerilyn Emori made the words sparkle. For me one of the greatest joys of this endeavor was watching Margery Cantor's book design unfold. As I flipped through the page proofs, I always felt like a kid with a new picture book, anxious to see what would appear on the next page. Thanks to Cloyce Wall for his cover design that so beautifully portrays the marriage of technology with handicrafts. Thanks also to Lincoln Spector for his luminous technical insights.

Bill Pollock proved himself the greatest publisher in the world, revealing himself to be fluent with the sew-on kind of button as well as the mouse-clicked button on a computer screen. Were it not for his support, creativity, and shrewd editorial guidance, this book would have been just a shabby pamphlet. He turned it into something much finer than I ever dreamed. Thanks, Bill!

Throughout the project, my husband John carted page proofs and software to the post office weekly, cooked dinner almost nightly, and endeared himself with such advice as, "Why don't you take a break and spend the evening sewing while I mop the floor?" Without his help this book would still be in notecards on the floor (along with the laundry).

Perhaps, though, I owe the biggest thanks to my unofficial guardian angel over the years: Hazel, a quick-talking fairy godmother with a silver beehive and poodles, who, when I was a kid, showered me with baskets full of seam tape and darning needles big enough for little hands. She helped set it all in motion.

# INTRODUCTION

## WHY SHOULD ANYONE WHO SEWS, QUILTS, CROCHETS, CROSS-STITCHES, KNITS, TATS, OR WEAVES CARE ABOUT COMPUTERS?

❧ ☙

*Who would have guessed that you could use a personal computer to design lace patterns or that the hottest spots on the burgeoning information superhighway would be ones where sewers swap Pfaff tips?*

Back in the early '80s, when the personal computer fad hit and everyone trembled to think that if they didn't rush out and buy a home computer, their careers would perish, their recipe collections fall into disarray, and their children grow up moronic, I gave a talk on computers to a hospital charity guild. My audience consisted entirely of elderly ladies brandishing tea cups and knitting needles. I began my talk by telling them that, contrary to what they may have heard, they did not need to know anything about computers. Computers were useless to them. They had no need for a spreadsheet. Math coprocessors were probably peripheral to their lives. Despite what their well-meaning children might have told them, their homes were not going to be computerized anytime soon. Further, if they did not learn how to program in GWBasic (a popular programming language at the time), they would still be able to converse intelligently with their grandchildren for many years to come.

Eyes brightened. Several cracked smiles of jubilation and relief. After my talk, several said they were presently enrolled in a computer class, thanks to the prodding of their children, but that was going to change, thanks to my talk. They did not like computers—not at all—and they were glad to know that their time would be more profitably spent elsewhere.

Don't get me wrong, I believe knowledge is important. I believe that one should grow old learning new things. However, I also agree with Kathleen Turner's character in *Peggy Sue Got Married* when she journeys back in time to her high school days and dismisses algebra class with a huff of, "I happen to know for a fact that I will never in my future life have a need for algebra." In other words, I believe that we should spend time learning things that will prove useful to us someday.

If I were addressing that charity guild today, my talk would be entirely different. I would tell them: *Get yourselves to a computer as fast as you can! Now ladies (or gentlemen, for that matter), hup-hup!* Things have changed. The world of technology has become a different place. Indeed, it has become a very exciting place with many things to offer, even if you are a grandparent with a tea cup, knitting needles, and six grandkids.

# Your Computer May Be More Exasperating Than an 8-Year-Old with Nothing to Do, But You Can Do Many Things with It That a Few Years Ago Only Professional Textile Designers Could

*A*dmit it, few of us are truly besotted with our computers. They are irascible. They never do as they're told. They take up too much space on our desks. They do have their endearing moments, though, especially when they make themselves useful in the sewing room. Consider these things you can do with a computer:

§➥ Design elaborate quilts on screen, then let the computer calculate the fabric yardage and print out a shopping list and paper piecing templates.

§➥ Design cross-stitch charts and print them out. Or, digitize photos of your loved ones for a few bucks at the local copy shop, then "feed" them to your computer and turn them into cross-stitch charts in minutes.

§➥ Keep track of your burgeoning floss or yarn collection before it tangles into a sea of knots under the bed.

§➥ Create custom jacket, dress, and slacks sewing patterns that take into account your greatest physical assets better than store-bought patterns do.

§➥ Hook your computer to your sewing machine to custom design stitching and machine embroidery patterns.

§➥ Design that sweater covered with bowling pins that your brother Billy has always wanted. Then handknit it or, better, link your computer to a knitting machine to do the dirty work.

§➥ Design computer-generated bargello.

§➥ Correspond cheaply with stitchers around the world, even as far away as India and Japan, via E-mail. Exchange tips, patterns, and fabric with them. Attend quilt shows with them on weekends.

§➥ Tap into vast computerized libraries of stitching advice and mail order supply lists on computer services like CompuServe and Internet.

§➥ Attend virtual reality quilt shows in which digitized pictures of quilts and their makers paint themselves on your own computer screen. One such quilt is shown in Figure 1.

**Figure 1**
**A digitized picture of quilter Carol Myers and her evocative quilt "Women, Why Do You Weep?" as seen on the computer service CompuServe. Myers made the quilt to raise money for mammograms for poor women.**

**Figure 2**
It may look like something from
*2001: A Space Odyssey,* but it's
actually a computer-generated
fractal pattern that serves as the
basis for a tatted lace doily design.
German lace-designer Christiane
Eichler reveals in Chapter 7 her
secrets on how to use fractals to
design gorgeous lace.

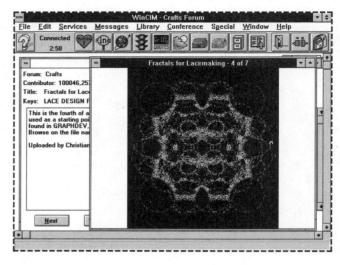

When it comes to putting that clunky box of microchips to work as a needlecraft tool, stitchers are a clever bunch. Some of us feed muslin through our computer printers to generate custom quilt labels. (Chapter 4 tells you how to do that.) Others use spreadsheets—you know, those things accountants love—to design knitting and weaving patterns. (Chapter 7 explains that.) Databases have become popular tools to track the ebb and flow of DMC floss collections (more on that in Chapter 5).

Perhaps the most innovative—and poetic—use of a computer in this increasingly computerized world of stitching involves using mathematical fractals to create patterns for tatted doilies. One such pattern is show in Figure 2. Fractals are patterns that, like a twig or a snowflake, are irregular but repeat themselves ceaselessly according to a mathematical design. James Gleick, author of the book *Chaos,* calls them "a way of seeing infinity." One can only wonder what Aunt Agatha would make of that.

## Even If You Have an Old, Crummy Computer That Your Son Left You When He Went to College, You Can Still Do Neat Things

*I*n an ideal world, all of us would own state-of-the-art Pentium PCs with high res–this's and coprocessor that's. The reality is that many of us are stuck with the Apple II that son Jonathan abandoned when he went to college. In a world where the computers grow bigger and faster every week, we are left wondering whether and how we can deploy the old Edsel to chart our cross-stitch alphabets.

In addition to explaining how to hotrod the newest Intels into lean, mean, number crunching needlepoint machines, this book will tell you how to bring the brave new world to that rusty old jalopy. You will learn how to:

- Identify what kind of computer you have and what exactly you can do with it

- Find needlecraft software that will work appropriately on it

- Get on the information highway, accelerate into the commuter lane, and have a roaring good time with other needlecrafters no matter what kind of computer you have

While this book is mostly for owners of PCs (also known as IBMs, Intels, and PC compatibles) and Macintoshes, if you own an oldie-but-goodie like a Commodore Amiga or Apple II, you'll find advice that will apply to your machine too. Whenever I uncovered needlework-related software for these machines, I've listed it along with some buying tips.

## "Migod!" She Gasped. "You're Designing Frocks on an IBM Thinkpad!"

*W*hen a friend, a nonsewer, heard I was writing this book, she was apoplectic. "Let me get this straight," she said cynically, "you're going to explain to people how to design frocks on an IBM Thinkpad?" Immediately, I pulled out an ad for a Thinkpad and tried to ascertain if that would be possible. (It would.)

Using a computer in needlecrafts is not as crazy a notion as one might think at first wink. Professional needlecraft and clothing designers have been using computers for years. An increasing number of software packages for stitchers have been popping into the stores. (At this writing, there are over twenty software packages for designing cross-stitch alone. Some are probably on the software rack in your local grocery store.) All the major sewing machine manufacturers now sell sewing machines that "interface" with PCs, letting you design stitches on the PC and then direct your sewing machine to stitch them. Most top-of-the-line knitting machines can also be linked to home computers. Computer information services like CompuServe have found, much to their surprise, that stitchers of all ages are logging on in droves each night to swap Pfaff tips, weaving patterns, and digital pictures of their crochet projects.

A revolution is occurring, and, unlike the first computer revolution, you don't need to be a gearhead to profit from it. In this book you'll find all the information you need to put your computer to work—regardless of your technical bravado or timidity—designing brilliant needlecraft projects, as well as electronically tête-à-têteing with other gracious computerized stitchers around the globe. Many techno-stitchers have selflessly contributed their own insights and experiences to the book to help you get online.

If you have problems, never fear. This book will tell you how to find other computerized stitchers who are only a phone call away and will be delighted to help you out of your quandary. So forget computerized banking, electronic stock trading, video games, and online encyclopedias: Needlework is what the information superhighway was really meant for. *Get yourself to a computer as fast as you can! Hup-hup!* I hope you enjoy your foray.

*Note: One of the challenges of writing this book came in trying to keep up with changes in the computer world. Products disappear, prices rise and fall, and computer information services are in constant flux. That's why it's so important that before buying any computer product you call the vendor and confirm pricing, support, and product features. Similarly, check all prices before signing up with any information service since their pricing plans are especially subject to change.*

*The Internet is also an ever-changing beast. Internet home pages, information, and addresses come and go with dizzying rapidity. Should it happen that you try to tap into an Internet discussion or site described in this book and receive a message reporting that it no longer exists, try sending an E-mail message to the person who maintains it (if one is listed) since the site may simply have moved. But should you get nothing but error messages while trying to connect, keep a stiff upper lip and try another site. The best way to find things on the Internet is to explore.*

# The Needlecrafter's Computer Companion

# WHAT KIND OF COMPUTER DO YOU HAVE; WHAT CAN YOU DO WITH IT; AND HOW CAN YOU BUY A COMPUTER IF YOU DON'T HAVE ONE?

*Computers are not unlike cars. A little tire-kicking and a quick visual inspection can help you determine what sort of computer you have or help you buy a new one.*

Isn't it funny how the woman of the house is often seen driving the broken-down station wagon that no one else in the family wants? Let me tell you, the same thing happens with computers. Junior heads off to college and leaves you his Precambrian Apple II. Or Pa buys a shiny new 80486 PC, and you get the old Tandy with the dysfunctional disk drive.

Many women who use computers for needlecrafts have old junkers. But an equal number of crafters have genuine hot-rod computers.

No matter which category you fall into, this chapter will help you determine where your computer resides between junker and hot-rod, and what help you can expect it to give with your needlecrafts.

If you don't have a computer yet or are in the market for a new one, at the end of this chapter you'll find advice on buying a computer to suit your needs.

## Fortunately, Some Craft Software Works on Junker Computers

While the rest of the computer world has pretty much abandoned the Sanyos, Ataris, and PCjrs that dazzled home computer buyers a decade ago, craft software makers have not forgotten that these machines still inhabit many of our family rooms. With a little ingenuity and the right software (some of it cheap), you can put that fossil to work. Even older machines can design cross-stitch and knitting patterns, catalog floss collections, and even tap into the heralded information highway to communicate with other crafters.

You'll need to be realistic though. You won't be able to use your ancient PCjr to transform digitized snapshots of your vacation in Hawaii into Fair Isle knit designs. You'll need a more up-to-date computer to do that. Nor will you be able to hook your antique to your Pfaff so that it can stitch the pictures of your Hawaiian vacation. You will also have to put a little work and ingenuity into finding the means to accomplish stitching things on an old computer (using database software to inventory fabric and floss, using a spreadsheet to design knit patterns, and so on), whereas you'll find a variety of special-purpose needlecraft software for modern machines.

## . . . But You Still May Want to Get a New Computer for Your Sewing Room

Should you splurge on a new computer? That all depends on how old and clunky your computer is. Computer models fade into obsolescence within about three years, but age alone won't tell you whether your computer is suitable. A lot depends on whether, three years ago, you bought the fastest computer available at the time or simply the cheapest. Chances are good that if your computer is older than three years it won't be able to run all the latest software. This will depend on the speed of the processor, the amount of RAM, the size of the hard disk, and its video capabilities (we'll talk more about these later). But even if your machine isn't anywhere near state of the art, you may not care (many needlecrafters don't). The machine you have now may suit your needs just fine.

Pages 3 and 4 describe the parts of a computer system. On page 5 you'll find a list of questions you should ask about your present computer, no matter how old it is, to get a feel for its capabilities. You should keep the information you uncover on file because you'll need it whenever you buy software or call software vendors for tech support.

phone line

software

modem

CD-ROM drive

CD-ROM

keyboard

monitor

floppy disk drive

eyeglasses

mouse

**Figure 1-1**
Here's a picture that shows the basic parts of a
computer. Think of it as a kind of primer. If
you're not familiar with the pieces in this picture, take a good look before going any further.

**The monitor, or screen,** lets you see into your computer's troubled soul. But when your
computer is connected to an information service, the text that scrolls over the screen is
coming from another computer. Anything you type on the screen is sent back to the service. Similarly, anything the service types to you will appear on your screen.

**The floppy disk drive** may look like a bagel slicer, but in reality it's where you insert the little floppy disks you pull from your shirt pocket. The disks contain programs or data. The
floppy drive reads the data into the computer's memory. Sometimes it copies it to the computer's permanent hard drive. Floppy drives can be temperamental. If you smoke near the
computer or there's lots of dust in the air, they may display frequent "disk error" messages.

**The hard disk** is where you keep your computer's software. It's where you store word-processing documents, marketing databases, information and software that you find on computer services and copy to your computer, and so on. As it spins, it may sound like a fingernail rubbing the lip of a champagne glass. Some hard disks make grinding noises that remind me of the killer plant in *Little Shop of Horrors,* saying "Feed me!" Some days, I would really like a plant like that on my desk.

**The CD-ROM drive** is similar in concept to the CD player you use to play music CDs. In fact, you can play those U2 CDs right on your computer as you tabulate accounting spreadsheets, and they'll sound just as awful as they do on the stereo. The music will broadcast through the computer's speakers. Computer CD-ROMs contain digitized encyclopedias and games with realistic pictures. They hold a lot of information and often display it with sound and pictures.

**The mouse,** despite its haunting similarity to a sewing machine foot pedal, does not go on the floor; it sits on a pad beside the keyboard. When you move the mouse, a small arrow, known as the "cursor," floats over the screen. Clicking one of the mouse buttons causes things to happen on the screen, like make menus appear or draw lines. My cat loves to watch the cursor flit over the screen as I move the mouse.

**The keyboard** is what you use to type commands or E-mail into your computer.

**Software** is a list of invisible instructions that comes packaged on floppy disks (or sometimes CDs). It tells your computer to behave in a certain way. For instance, it tells your computer how to help you type word-processing documents or balance your checkbook. Software is really mountains of mathematics, but you don't see them. You see only the shrink-wrapped box, the manual, the floppies, and the menus on the screen.

**A modem or fax-modem** transforms your computer's internal binary language into beeps and trills that can travel over a phone line and communicate with another computer. You need a modem to connect to computer services like CompuServe. You don't need a fax-modem unless you want to send or receive faxes in your computer.

**A phone line** is what your computer uses to talk to other computers, computer services, and even fax machines. The phone line your computer uses is no different from the phone line that you use to call your mother.

**Note:** *If you can't find the information below in your manuals or get it from the company that sold you the computer, you may be able to get it by inspecting the machine. If not, take the machine to a second-hand computer store and ask the technicians to tell you what you have. (You might ask them to estimate its value, too, just for fun.) They can also service the machine, fix anything that's broken, and suggest ways to bring it up to date, if that's possible. Computer clubs or user groups in your area are also great resources for free advice.* 

# Questions for Your Computer

Now that you're familiar with the basic parts of the computer, it's time to figure out what sort of computer you've got. Here are some questions for all types of computers.

**To what computer family does it belong?** Is it an IBM or PC compatible or an Apple II or Macintosh? (Apples and Macintoshes, made by Apple, have a multicolored apple logo on the front. Apple is only now beginning to allow companies to clone its technology. Lots of companies, including IBM, make IBM or PC compatibles.) If your machine uses DOS or Windows, it's a PC (that is, unless you happen to have a PowerMac or Power-PC). If your software has fun little folders and makes cute little beeps, or flashes a time bomb on the screen when you do something really wrong, and if it almost never crashes or gives you a problem, it's probably a Mac. If your computer is none of these it may belong to that third class of "others" like the Commodore, Amiga, Texas Instruments, or Atari.

**How much memory does it have?** Memory is measured in K (kilobyte, or thousand bytes) of RAM (random access memory). The original Apples came with an incredibly small 2K of RAM—sufficient for its time, but useless for today's software. Now it's not uncommon to buy machines with 8 to 16 MB (megabytes, or "megs"). Each megabyte equals 1000K so 8 MB is equal to 8000K of RAM. Older machines commonly have only about 620K of RAM, which will make running the new software virtually impossible.

**What kind of floppy disk drive does it have?** While your computer may not have a hard disk, it should have at least one floppy disk drive. If it doesn't, you've got an antiquity but not a truly useful computer. A floppy disk drive is, for our purposes, the slot into which you stick floppy disks. If you have a PC or compatible, your floppy drive might use either those hard plastic, little 3.5" disks, or it might need the older, larger, flat, and truly floppy 5.25" disks. Apple IIs use 5.25" floppies, while Macs require the up-to-date 3.5" disks. You'll need to know the size of the floppy drive when you order software. If the disk size is 5.25" you'll also need to know what its "density" is, or how much data it can store. If you have a PC, your floppy drives are usually called Drive A or Drive B. If you have two floppy drives, it's likely that one will be 5.25 inches and that it will be drive A. On the other hand, if you have a Mac your floppy drives won't be called anything. They just get the name of the disk you insert.

**Does it have a hard disk?** A hard disk in your computer is basically a storage place for software and files. Hard disks can hold an awful lot more than floppies—in some cases as much as 2,000 times more. And because hard disks spin a lot faster than floppies, your computer can store data on them or retrieve data from them much faster than it can with floppies. This means that software runs much faster from hard disks than from floppies.

If you have a PC with a hard disk you probably won't see it; it's inside the PC. One simple way to tell whether your PC has a hard disk is to see if you can run software when there's no floppy in the floppy drive. If so, you've got a hard disk (or a very strange computer). Your hard disk will usually be Drive C. When you first get a Mac, the hard disk is named something like Macintosh HD, but you can change it to any name you want.

**What kind of printer do you have?** If you haven't got the manual for your printer and can't remember what kind it is, here are some clues:

§➤ If your printer has a ribbon like a typewriter and prints with dots, it's a dot matrix printer. (Sometimes the dots are so small and close together that they don't look like dots, so look carefully. You might need a magnifying glass.)

§➤ If your printer has a wheel with letters on it, it's a daisy wheel printer.

§➤ Laser printers and ink jet printers can be a little difficult to tell apart. Both seem more like copy machines than printers, sucking in sheets and spitting out nicely printed pages that look typeset. Both give you nice crisp copy.

**Does it have a modem?** Modems allow your computer to send data to and from other computers and even fax machines. They can be either internal or external. There are a few simple ways to tell if you've got a modem in your computer:

§➤ If there's a phone cord plugged into the back of the computer, you've got an internal modem.

> If you spot a phone jack somewhere on the back of the computer, you've got an internal modem.

> If you spot a box sitting next to the computer with a phone cord dangling from it, that's an external modem. You should also check in the nearest closet, because many external modems turn up there.

**Does it have a mouse?** Computer mice do look a lot like sewing machine foot pedals. They roll or slide around on your desk and are one way to communicate with the software on your computer. They're usually separate from keyboards and are attached to the keyboard or the back of the computer by a cord.

## Questions for PCs or Compatibles Only

**What is the speed of your computer's CPU (central processing unit)?** The CPU is the computer's engine. The choices are 8088, 80286, 80386, 80486, or Pentium (some call this 586). The higher the number, the faster the chip. Watch the screen when the PC starts up to find out what version of CPU it has. You may have to look at the computer's box to find out more about its speed without using some special software.

**What version of the DOS operating system is installed on it?** To find out type the following at the DOS prompt:

>VER and then press the ENTER key.

The later the version, the better. The current version of DOS is version 6.*x*, where *x* stands for some number like 21 or 22, as in DOS 6.21 or 6.22.

**If Microsoft Windows is installed, what version is it?** To find out, head to the Windows Program Manager screen. Click on "Help" on the top of the screen and then click on "About Program Manager." You'll want to have at least version 3.1, since earlier versions were kind of buggy. If you've got Windows 95 you're ahead of the game—and you'll know it if you have it, because "95" will flash on the screen when you turn on the PC.

**What kind of graphics does your monitor have?** The choices are CGA, EGA, Hercules, VGA, and Super-VGA. If you have an 80386 or 80486 PC, you most likely have either VGA or Super-VGA. If the machine is older, ask yourself this question: "Is the computer a color one and do you get headaches after using it for a few hours?" If you do, you have a CGA monitor. You can't buy less than a VGA or Super-VGA monitor today; they're pretty much the standards.

## *Questions for Apple II and Macintosh Computers Only*

**What is the model or processor speed of your Macintosh?** Like the world of PCs, the Macintosh world has gone through some significant changes in the last few years. While you may have an Apple IIe or IIG around the house, these are basically nonexistent models, as far as the Mac world is concerned. The 128K and the 512K models are also obsolete and will not run any Macintosh software. So, when you think about Macintosh, think about these four processor speeds: 68000, 68020, 68030, and 68040. (The chips are commonly referred to as, e.g., the "030" or "040" chips.)

The 68000 is found on the older Macintosh machines, like the Mac Plus and the Mac SE. You've probably seen these machines around—they're all in one compact unit with a small screen. The 68020 and 68030 make up the Mac II family (x, cx, ci, si, and so on), and some of the new Performas are running on these chips as well. Some are even running the 040 chip, which is the same chip found in the Macintosh Quadras, a higher end machine.

Until the advent of the PowerMacs, the 040 chip, found in the Quadra series, was the fastest Mac chip around. Now, that's been replaced with the PowerMacs, which have a RISC-based 601 chip, and which have ushered in a completely new wave of higher powered Macintosh. This 601 chip comes in three models with three different speeds—the 6100, 7100, and 8100.

The best and most popular Macintosh for home use now is the Performa series. Mac Connection (800/800-1111) recommends the Performa 475 as a good entry level machine. The system comes complete with everything you need, though it's not a multimedia system (you can upgrade it if you like). You'll want at least 4 MB RAM in your system, which should be sufficient for most of what you do.

**What version of the Macintosh operating system is installed?** System 7.5 is the latest Macintosh operating system, a step-up from System 7.1. One of the major drawbacks of System 7.5 is that it takes up a lot of RAM (8 MB RAM is recommended). You're better off getting System 7.1, which is still available from Apple. The most common system on the Mac Plus or SE might be System 6.05 or 6.07.

To determine what System you're running, look at the menu bar that appears at the top of your screen when you turn on your machine. In the upper-left corner is the Apple icon. Click on the icon and you'll get a menu. You'll see a choice on the menu called "About this Macintosh" or "About the Finder." Click on it and you'll find the information that you need about your particular system.

**What kind of graphics does your monitor have?** You don't need to get a particular graphics card for the Mac. They all come with built-in graphics capabilities, though the older ones (like older PCs) may not be able to handle color. They also all come with built-in sound so you don't need to buy a sound card or external speakers.

# Questions to Ask When You Buy Software

It's very important that when you buy craft software for your computer you quiz the maker thoroughly on whether their package will work on your make and model of computer. Here are some questions to ask:

§➥ Has the software been specifically tested to work on the type of machine I have? If it has been tested, will it encounter any problems or limitations?

§➥ Will it work with my model of Mac or the version of PC-DOS or Windows on my machine?

§➥ Will the amount of RAM on my PC be enough to run the software without having to wait forever for it to do something?

§➥ Will I need a hard disk or mouse to use the software?

§➥ Will my graphics display (CGA, EGA, Hercules, VGA, or Super-VGA) provide sufficient graphic resolution?

§➥ Has the software been specifically tested with my model of printer?

# Special Tips for Buying and Using Needlecraft Software

eedlecraft software is in a class by itself. It's not produced by huge software companies like Microsoft. Often it's the product of home-based entrepreneurs. Many cross-stitch, knitting, and weaving design packages are the brainchildren of crafters who hire programmers to write the software for them and then write their own documentation. There are pluses and minuses to this. These companies often don't have the resources to test their products on a variety of different brands of equipment, but they usually give their customers lots of TLC in helping them get up and running. Here are some general guidelines for buying and using these sometimes unorthodox programs.

## *Before You Buy*

§ᴗ Needlecraft software is expensive. A typical cross-stitch, knitting, or sewing pattern design package costs $100 or more. Some cost as much as $300. Figure out *exactly* what you want the software to do, evaluate how much you plan to use it, and ask yourself whether you'll get your money out of it. For instance, one needlework designer I spoke with felt that, of the few programs on the market that met her specific design criteria, none printed charts that approached her high standards of camera-ready graphic quality. On the other hand, I know designers who use these same programs to design charts to sell to magazines (the magazines redesign them before printing). If you're not a professional designer and have no intention of marketing your designs, ask yourself if it wouldn't be cheaper to continue buying (instead of making) your needlecraft patterns or to revert to old-fashioned techniques like drawing on graph paper.

§ᴗ Consider whether a general-purpose drawing or painting program might be better suited to your needs. You can use programs like CorelDRAW! and Macromedia Freehand to design quilts and chart needlework. There are trade-offs (no built-in DMC colors, no quilt block libraries), but the advantages are too good to overlook. These programs give a skilled user enormous design flexibility and they are often more technically stable than special-purpose needlecraft software. (They'll work with any computer equipment and the technical support is good.) The chapters on specific crafts like cross-stitch and quilting explore this issue further.

§ᴗ Investigate shareware. Shareware is "pay if you like it" software that you can download from computer services and try before buying. You'll find cross-stitch, knitting, and weaving design software on all the major computer services and many BBSs, too. The quality of shareware will vary from program to program. Consider shareware as a way to try out different types of needlecrafting software before you go out and buy an expensive package. You should also consider shareware if you don't want to spend a lot of money on software, or if you're unsure of the features you want in a needlecraft design package. You may very well find that a particular shareware package suits you perfectly, and that you have no need for the more expensive, commercial packages.

§◆ Ask if the software vendor has specifically tested the software on your make and model of computer.

§◆ Ask if the software has won any major computer industry awards. Products that have won awards like the PC Magazine Award of Excellence tend to be very good.

§◆ Find out what kind of technical support the vendor will provide once you buy the product, and make sure that the support program sounds like a truly helpful one.

§◆ Make sure that if you don't like the software you can return it for a full refund.

§◆ If you have a PC, understand the difference between Windows software and Windows-compatible software. True Windows software runs as a full-blown Windows application, with Windows' familiar graphical interface. On the other hand, software labeled as Windows-compatible is actually DOS software that you can run from a DOS window while you're running Windows. While you can run Windows-compatible software from Windows by clicking on an icon, it's still not a Windows application. If you run and like Windows, you'll prefer true Windows software.

§◆ Craft software that was written to work with Windows 3.1 will run just fine with Windows 95.

## *After You Buy*

§◆ If you have problems with the software, like keyboard lockups, memory errors, printer problems, or weird apparitions jiggling on the screen, call the company and ask if there's a way to fix your problem. Ask about getting an updated video or mouse driver, which will fix many problems. Though few of these companies have the resources to test their products on a wide variety of computers and printers, most will go to great lengths to get their customers through any technical snafus.

୭ If the software is DOS-based, and you can't seem to get it to run, try booting up the PC with a bootable floppy disk rather than from the hard drive. This will fire up the PC, but not load any of the memory-resident programs or drivers that the PC may ordinarily run. Doing this will reduce any memory conflicts the craft software may be having with other programs, plus free up as much memory as possible. I found this was the only way to get some of the programs running.

# Buying a Computer Is Not as Hard as Buying a Car

*I*f you haven't got a computer, you'll need to buy one before you can really make use of this book. I know women who blanch at the thought of walking onto a car lot alone, but who stroll into computer stores with smug self-assurance. Maybe their self-confidence comes from the thought that if they can figure out what all those sewing machine attachments are for, buying a computer is a no-brainer. Computers also tend not to break down on a dark highway, leaving you and your family stranded in a blizzard.

There are parallels between buying a computer and buying a car. You want a computer that's as fast and powerful as possible, and you want one that is reliable. You want to set a budget and you want to stick to it. You need to do your homework before you start looking, especially since some computer vendors, just like car salesmen, *routinely* quote women prices that are higher than those they give men. (One of the computer magazines I write for finds that this happens with alarming regularity to their female price-checkers and secret shoppers.) To give you the necessary edge, you'll want to know more about the machine you're looking for and the prices than the salesperson before you even walk into a store.

Here are a few buying tips to get you in the right frame of mind.

**It doesn't matter where you buy it.** Mail-order houses and Sam's wholesale clubs are as acceptable as a computer store. But avoid geeky electronics stores run by condescending teenagers. Also avoid computer fairs that occupy the local amphitheater one weekend and are gone the next.

**Shop for brand.** Some brands, like Compaq, are known for reliability and bang for the buck. Don't compare systems. Don't say, "I can get a Blue Danube 45 MHz 80486 with a 200 MB hard disk from Joe's Wholesale for $1,399, but I can get a Red Wrecker 45 MHz 80486 with a 200 MB hard disk for $1,345 from Henry's Stop-and-Shop Appliance, so I

might as well get the Red Wrecker." In other words, don't buy the cheapest thing you can find unless you want headaches.

**Look out for restocking fees and other nonsense.** Be sure you can return any computer equipment you buy and get a full refund if it doesn't work or is unacceptable.

**Find out what, if any, support you're going to get from the seller once you buy the darn thing.** Is the store going to give you support? Or will you have to call the manufacturer directly and sit on hold for two hours waiting for some geek to spout technobabble and provide no help whatsoever? If you're new to computers, it's often helpful to deal with a local store that can provide support. And it's worth paying extra for that. Just be sure that the store does indeed have knowledgeable technicians on hand who can fix whatever's going wrong.

**Be skeptical about computer magazine product lab tests.** I've seen too many computer products that were touted as winners of all sorts of lab tests and awards but turned out to be turkeys. I do, however, highly recommend lab tests conducted by *PC World.* This is the magazine I write for, so you can accuse me of being biased if you want.

**Don't get the most awesomely fast, powerful computer on the market**—that's usually the one that's in the $3,000 to $4,000 range. Take one small and comfortable step down from that into the $1,500 to $2,000 range. That's what most people are buying, and that's where the best deals are.

**Remember that everything is open to negotiation.** Don't be afraid to bargain for lower prices and more extras. And don't be afraid to walk away if the vendor doesn't give you exactly what you want. You'd be amazed at how vendors can drop their prices to get your business.

Start the bargaining from a position of strength by making a firm, but realistic offer that's 25 percent less than what you actually plan to pay. Walk into the store at a slow time, listen to the salesperson's spiel, then say assertively, "I will give you $___ for that, that, that, and *that.*" Pick all the elements of the system yourself. Be definite about what you want.

If the salesperson tells you that's ludicrous, ask to speak to the boss. The boss will come and offer you a slightly lower price than full retail, or maybe try to sell you something cheaper (or maybe tell you to try another store), but don't be swayed. It's important that when you start the game you set a price range that you would be willing to pay and a price roof at which you'll walk away.

**Shop for a machine with a warranty of at least a year**—especially on the motherboard and disk drives, but don't buy an extended warranty. If an electronic appliance is going to break, it will probably break in the first year.

If you buy by mail, always use a credit card or order C.O.D. Never send check or cash. There are too many mail-order houses that exist only in magazine ads, waiting to take your money and never send you a computer. If you'd like to try mail-order, consider PC Connection (800/800-1111), or their counterpart, Mac Connection (800/800-1111). Their prices and selection are great, and you'll get whatever you order by the next morning.

**Check out the monitor.** Make sure everything on the screen is crystal-clear. Check the resolution of black letters against a white background. Ask to see some high-resolution black-and-white graphics. And check the quality of the colors, of course.

**Ask about manuals.** Many computers are coming without much in the way of documentation these days. Even name-brand computers like Dell and Zeos are being sold with loads of software installed on their hard disks, but no manuals explaining how to use the software. It's cheaper to sell them that way. This can be a real hardship if you're new to computers. Make sure that the computer you buy comes with manuals that include diagrams and troubleshooting advice for the motherboard, hard disk, monitor, and fax-modem, if one is installed. If the computer comes with software already installed on its hard drive, find out if you get manuals and disks for the software.

**Just because it has an Intel chip doesn't mean it's hot.** There are lots of chips in computers these days that perform as well or better than the Intel ones. One very popular manufacturer of these chips is Cyrix.

**Beware of "bundles."** Bundles are those "multimedia" PCs you see advertised on TV for a "low, low price," including all sorts of software and CDs. Usually the system is last year's technology over-priced. The software and CDs are not generally as good as they're cracked up to be, and rarely come with manuals.

**Never look back.** The prices of hardware and software are falling rapidly. It's easy to look at computer ads six months after your purchase and regret it.

For more buying tips for the first-time computer buyer, check out "How to Buy a Computer" in *Consumer Reports*, November 1994.

# The Kind of System I Would Buy for My Aunt Agatha (the One Who Tats)

OK, so I've given you all of these specifics about how to buy. But what would I buy? Well, you see I have this Aunt Agatha. She tats these great silhouettes of southern belles that she mounts on velvet. Really, the stuff of heirlooms. But I think she would enjoy using some of that mathematical fractal-generating software in designing tatting patterns. I also think she would enjoy using the software for designing stitches for her Pfaff. If I were to help her buy a computer, this is what I'd advise.

First of all, I would not let her buy an Apple. Why not? No offense to you Mac fans, but there's so much more software available for PC-compatibles, not just in needlecrafts, but all other application areas as well. And there will probably be much more on the market in the future. That said, there are certain qualities I would make sure her PC had.

## *She'll Need a Fast Processor Chip*

The processor chip is the computer's brain, and the Pentiums are presently the fastest on the market for PCs. PCs with 80486 chips are also fast and desirable. A used 80386 PC would be fine too, but I would have a knowledgeable friend check it out first. Compaqs and Microns are the best. I would avoid Packard-Bells and CompUSA PCs. I remain skeptical of IBMs because they are generally over-priced and not as state-of-the-art as other computers. I would look for a PC advertised with the fastest MHz available (that's the processor's speed) for a reasonable cost.

## *She'll Need Microsoft Windows or System 7*

Both Windows and System 7 are like NASA's Mission Control, but for computer software. With Windows, Aunt Agatha could run a bunch of different programs, like word processors and spreadsheet programs, all at once. She could also look at them on the computer's screen in different windows. All the best needlecraft software—especially cross-stitch software— is being written for Windows these days. Windows will also make Aunt Agatha's life *vastly* easier when she calls computer services to tap into the information highway. Windows comes packaged with most computers. It's what you see on a computer screen in most computer commercials. Should she get Windows 3.1 or the hot new Windows 95? If she buys a 486 or higher she should go for broke and get Windows 95. It will run all the Windows needlecraft software, even software written for the older Windows. It will also run those packages much faster than Windows 3.1. Of course, if Aunt Agatha insists on getting a Macintosh, System 7 will provide all these advantages (and will take up less of her hard disk).

## *She'll Need at Least 8 MB of RAM to Run Windows*

If Aunt Agatha runs Windows with anything less than 8 MB of RAM (16 MB if she gets Windows 95), she'll be cracking out the bottle of blackberry brandy in no time (heaven knows, that's often what I do when I run Windows on little memory). Aunt Agatha's computer should be designed so that she can easily increase the amount of RAM in it, preferably to 16 MB, in the near future. She'll need the same or perhaps a little less RAM for a Macintosh.

## *She'll Need at Least 350 MB of Hard Disk Space*

The hard disk is the place where the computer stores software and where Aunt Agatha will be storing any fractal-generated tatting designs she downloads from the Internet. And although 350 MB should be plenty of space for her (it will hold about 15,000 fractal tatted doily designs), it wouldn't hurt to get a hard disk with a couple hundred more MB if it fits in the budget. Hard drives that hold 400 to 500 MB are becoming very common, and the price difference may be almost insignificant.

## *If There's No CD-ROM, She'll Never Miss It*

These days CD-ROM drives are little more than toys for playing video games and reading CD-ROM encyclopedias that are somewhat less useful than their printed counterparts. (One of the technical editors at the computer magazine I write for is threatening to bonk me on the head with a 10-pound copy of *Computer Shopper* for saying this. Guys love these CD-ROM drives. But honestly, when you walk through many offices these days you'll be assaulted by the tinny sound of employees playing Whitney Houston CDs on their CD-ROM drives. That's about all people use them for. I think most CDs are of marginal worth.) Of course, the time may come when sewing information is available on computer CDs (in fact, as this book went to press, the Electric Quilt people were preparing a quilt block encyclopedia for possible inclusion on a CD) and Aunt Agatha will not want to miss out. Since it's almost impossible to install a CD-ROM drive in a PC that didn't come with one originally, consider a PC with a CD-ROM drive a plus.

## She Might Like a Hand-Held Scanner

If Aunt Agatha says she wants to scan family pictures to make into cross-stitch designs, or to scan magazine pictures of the *Starship Enterprise* to stitch on her Pfaff, I'd quiz her thoroughly on how often she plans to do it. If she thinks she'll use a scanner only once every six months, I'd advise her to use the scanners at the copy store, or at least to try them out before buying one.

Scanners offer a myriad of creative uses in sewing and other needlecraft design. You can use them to pull into your PC pictures from newspapers, greeting cards, even your children's drawings, and convert them to knitting, cross-stitch, sewing machine, and weaving designs. You can even use your computer printer to print them out on fabric. Scanners prices are dropping fast (for $175 you can buy a Logitech grayscale hand-held scanner, and for $200 more you can buy a color one) making them an affordable accessory on a home PC.

Buying a scanner for craft use is different from buying one for desktop publishing. For the latter you want a scanner that will bring images into your PC at high resolution. For textile use, you want images scanned at low resolution because your craft software is probably going to transform each dot, or pixel, of a picture into a stitch. That means that a 550 by 240 dot picture (a not uncommon size) will become a cross-stitch pattern with 132,000 stitches in it! Even Marilyn Leavitt-Imblum (the designer of the cross-stitch angel patterns with a bizillion stitches) would weep at that. Desktop publishing-quality scanners scan at 800 dots per inch. You want a scanner in which you can turn the resolution down to 100 dots per inch, plus some intermediate stages like 200 and 400 dots. Some scanners will let you turn the resolution down even lower.

If you buy a grayscale scanner, buy one that scans in 256 shades of gray. If you buy a color scanner, a 24-bit scanner is the ideal choice. A 24-bit scanner can provide you with up to 16 million colors, thus offering you the best color shading (although you won't need that many colors). Nevertheless, an 8-bit scanner should be just fine for most applications.

Should you buy a hand-held scanner or a flat-bed one? Flat-bed scanners are the ones that have a glass like a copy machine on which you place the picture. They run around $800 these days, and if you're a serious artist who does a lot of drawing by hand, you will appreciate how easy they are to use. For most crafters, however, a hand-held scanner is totally sufficient. And by all means, buy a scanner tray. It will make scanning easier.

> **☙ If you buy a hand-held scanner ❧**
> Get a copy of "Hand Scanning for the Textile and Craft Artist" by Susan Lazear. (Cochenille Design Studio,
> P.O. Box 4276, Encinitas, CA, 92023; phone 619/259-1698; $14 plus $2.95 for shipping and handling.)
> This little book tells you how to scan images for use in garments, knitting, and other fiber arts. It includes
> lots of tips like how to scan fabric itself and how to prepare images for the best scan possible.

## A One-Color Inkjet Printer Will Suit Her

They cost about $300 and provide crisp graphics and needlework charts, as well as sharp type that will look nice in business letters should Aunt Agatha decide to open up a home craft business. Hewlett-Packard and Canon make particularly reliable ones. For an extra $250, she could get a color inkjet, but her pension from the mitten factory imposes frugality. Dot matrixes cost about $100, but they're slow. Laser printers run from $500 to $1000. Their images are sharp and they print fast, but that might be a bit much for Aunt Aggie's needs. You can use both inkjets and laser printers to print images on fabric. Dot matrix printers won't do that, but they are great for printing quilting templates on freezer paper.

## She Absolutely, Positively Must Have a Modem

Most computer buyers think of a modem as a frill, and that's too bad because even 14,400 bps fax modems can be had for as little as $50. Stitchers will find that a modem will provide them with more hours of fun entertainment than the computer game *Doom*. With a modem you can tap into the information highway and communicate with other stitchers about Berlin work, sewing machine feed dogs, and life in general. Prodigy often runs special deals on modems, so keep an eye on those annoying ads.

*Believe me when I tell you that you will spend more time with your modem than you will spend now on all your hobbies put together. It is that addictive.* In fact, many needlecrafters report that once they discovered the joys of modeming, their spouses and children were forced to buy a second home PC so that they could use a computer once in a while.

A modem is a little device that translates the computer's internal language so that it makes sense over a phone line. Internal ones sit inside the PC, while external ones are little boxes that plug into the PC and look like they could blow up airplanes. You plug a phone cord into the modem, and then plug the other end of the cord into your phone or phone jack, and that's how your computer communicates with the rest of the world.

Any sort of modem can be used to call computer services, even the 5-pound boat-anchor-sized one still attached to my PCjr. However, for optimal comfort, buy one with the following characteristics:

 **A high "baud" rate.** *Baud,* or *bits per second* (abbreviated bps), is the term for the relative speeds at which the modem can send and receive information over a telephone line. Available speeds are 2400, 9600, 14.4K, and 28.8K bps. (The K stands for "kilo," or "thousand.") I recommend a modem with a speed of 14.4K bps, but no higher than that, because many of the higher speed modems on the market will not communicate properly with other superfast modems. Wait until the 28.8K bps modems have been on the market for about another year before you buy one. The 14.4K bps modems will be a lot cheaper anyway.

**V.32, V.32bis, V.42, V.42bis, and MNP 1 through 5.** What does this gobbledygook mean? Do you really want to know? Do you care? No, probably not. These are industry standards for transmission (sending data or information), data compression (to speed up your communication by scrunching the volume of your data), and error-correction (to get rid of errors in your computer's communication). When you buy a modem, just make sure it has all of these things. Also, make sure that V.32 and V.32bis are *certified* as industry compliant. Your modem will have a better chance of communicating properly with other modems.

> **WARNINGS!**
> If the speeds are described in the modem ad or on the box as an "effective throughput," look out! That's like saying that a laundry soap doesn't actually get clothes clean, but it does get them effectively clean. If you spot this bit of marketing fluff, look elsewhere for a modem.
>
> If you spot on the modem box V-something's that are not in the above list, be careful. Some manufacturers stuff their ads full of invented V-this's and V-that's. Don't be conned. All you need are the things listed above.

What is a *fax-modem?* Fax-modems work just like any other modem, with the difference that they can send and receive faxes. They don't use paper like regular fax machines. Rather, they take a memo or letter you've created in your word processor, and send it through the modem and over the phone line to a fax machine or another fax-modem. Your computer can also receive faxes through a fax-modem, from regular fax machines as well as other fax-modems. The computer stores the faxes electronically in a format that special fax software can display on your monitor.

Do you need a modem that can also fax? Probably not, though you might as well get one anyhow since most modems include this feature. However, if you have a home office or run a small business, you'll probably find that regular fax machines are more convenient, since they don't tie up the computer while processing and printing. If you're actually going to use the fax feature of a fax-modem, get one that is Group 3 compatible. Group 3 fax-modems will send to any fax machine. Also, be sure to get one that offers Classes 1 and 2, so that it will work with the widest range of fax software.

Some brands to consider when you buy a modem are Hayes (the Ultra and Optima lines offer good value and dependability), Microcom, Multi-Tech, and Telebit. The AT&T Dataport is also a good choice. Avoid Zoom Telephonics, Boca Research, Cardinals, Supras, Zoltixes, and Practical Peripherals. All have disturbing qualities.

Should you buy an external modem—a boxy thing that looks like an electric shaver and hangs from the PC by a cable, or an internal one—an actual circuit card that looks like a small industrialized nation (as seen from thousands of feet above), and which you insert *inside* the PC? I'm partial to externals, because they have lights that let you monitor what they're doing and whether they're connected to another computer or not. If they act up, you can simply unplug them, whereas with an internal you may have to turn off the PC. If your PC comes with two communications ports built into it (most do these days), buy an external modem. It will be so much easier to install than an internal. Just plug it into the second communications port (Com 2) on the back of your PC and you'll be ready to roll.

If your PC has just one communications port, buy an internal modem. That will give you a second communications port. Buy an internal modem with a 16550A UART chip on it. This is important. This chip will help your PC and modem to transfer data at high speed. *Do not buy a modem with a simulated 16550 UART on it!* (Cardinals have that.) It could very well mess up your life.

If you have never installed a card in your PC before, get someone else to do it with you. It's not hard, but there are tricks. A couple of tricks include grounding yourself before touching the inside of the PC and curbing the tendency to brush all the dust from inside the PC. (If your PC has inches of dust inside, as does mine, you might short out electronic components if you brush the dust around.). Watch carefully as they install the card, so that you'll know how to do it in the future. Like changing tires on a car, installing cards in a PC is something every computer owner should be able to do in a pinch. Ask them to configure the card to the second communications port. Some internal modem manuals advise that you install the card on Port 4 or 5. Ignore that.

# 2

# THE PC IN THE SEWING ROOM

*Put your PC to work on the sewing table with software that prints clothing patterns, sewing machines that hook up with PCs, and more.*

Walk into a sewing machine store these days and you'll probably spot a sewing machine hooked to a computer. Such an unlikely pairing is mind-numbing to most sewers, if not intimidating. What possible use can a sewing machine have when it's hooked to a computer?

Well, for one, computer-connected sewing machines can sew custom stitches and even embroidery designs that you "paint" on your computer and "download" to the sewing machine. You can also buy software that will print custom clothing patterns—type your measurements into the software, pick garment elements (like the shape of the collar, the cut of the sleeve, or the number of buttons down the front), and watch your PC print out a pattern tailored to your most intimate proportions.

Are these products for you? This chapter will explore that question, and introduce you to all the high-tech doo-dads available for computer-equipped sewers.

Cooking writer Laurie Colwin used to say that she shunned most kitchen gadgets, preferring only the most austere collection of cooking utensils—a few heavy-bottomed pots, some spoons, and a skillet. I know sewers who practice similar simplicity. While they're fascinated by the unfolding technological possibilities of their art, when it comes down to it what they love most is the feel of the fabric beneath their hands. They believe they can achieve self-expression as easily with a 1954 Sears Kenmore that doesn't even zig-zag as they can with a Pfaff 1475 CD with 300 decorative stitches.

You may be one of these sewers. On the other hand, you may be the kind of sewer who definitely cannot achieve self-expression without six different sewing machines, ranging from a treadle to a POEM, and including a Huskygram and at least two Pfaffs.

Whatever kind of sewer you are, you have to agree that a new age in sewing has arrived. Many of the products described in this chapter are what are called "first-generation" products: They are the first applications of a new technology to a new way of doing things. Thus they are a bit clumsy at doing it. That doesn't mean they're bad investments or that they aren't great fun to use, only that you sometimes may need a stiff upper lip and patience to use them. You also need to look beyond their advertising hype and realistically assess what they can do for you. Hopefully, this chapter will help you do that.

## You Can Use Software to Design Custom Clothing Patterns That Fit (Sometimes)

*A*t least once a day, someone posts an E-mail message online asking about software that generates custom clothing patterns. Does it work? Is it any good? Does it actually print out patterns that fit? The questions generally elicit a couple of tentative testimonials from professional dressmakers who say something like, "I've tried such-and-such a dressmaking program, and made a skirt for a customer. It fit, but I'm still experimenting."

Garment manufacturers draft pattern pieces with special CAD or "computer-aided design" software that costs thousands of dollars and often lets you view the finished garment in three dimensions. At least in concept, this software is a lot like the software that's used to design fighter planes.

The pattern software that's available for the home market at $100 to $200 a program is a lot simpler than what garment manufacturers use. You type in measurements; pick garment elements, like the shape of the bodice, the number of darts in the waist, and the collar; and then watch the software print out a pattern. This probably sounds like nirvana to anyone who's ever struggled to get a standard-sized pattern to fit them—and face it, we all have at times. But how good is the fit of the patterns that these programs produce? And what do you have to go through to get a good pattern?

"I originally approached this software with the idea that all I had to do was enter the measurements and I'd get out a tailored pattern, but it's not as simple as that," says Sue Bennett, a professional dressmaker and writer for *Threads* who evaluated dressmaking software for the magazine. "You really need to know what makes for a good fit, and whether a pattern piece is structured properly for the garment."

Bennett and I, and a battery of volunteer sewers, including Ruthe Brown, publisher of the sewing newsletter *Pface to Inter-Pface,* grappled with the three major dressmaking software packages, feeding them measurements and sewing test garments. We got sleeves that were too tight at the elbows, jacket side seams that didn't match up properly, crotches that sagged, shoulder seams that didn't line up correctly on the shoulders, and other glitches. Occasionally, we got garments that fit beautifully.

The software makers' typical response to fit snafus is to accuse the user of not taking or entering their measurements precisely enough. That is often the case. All the pattern programs provide detailed instructions for taking the special measurements that work with them. If you don't follow them vigilantly you'll most surely end up with midriff darts printed under armholes and crotch seams that fall around the knees. But often times, as Brown and sewers in Sun Cities, Arizona, found out following hours of scrupulous measuring of each other, even tape measure accuracy doesn't always help. When they tested one of the major dressmaking packages, only one of five test garments ended up fitting.

Oddly enough that did not deter them. Said Brown, "We've been wrestling with patterns for years trying to get clothes that fit properly. If I can get one software package to produce a [pattern] sloper that fits me well, I think it's worth the investment of time." Bennett felt the same way and has been using some of the packages to aid in producing custom garments for clients, sometimes with good-fitting results.

As for myself, I spent many weekends printing computer-generated patterns, taping together their jigsaw puzzle pieces, and sewing muslin test garments from them. Although my efforts weren't as ambitious as those of Brown or Bennett, I didn't get anything to fit me straight from the computer printer. While I was able to use some of the patterns as starting points to make my own custom blouse and jumper patterns, overall I found myself yearning for the comparative simplicity of assembling a Vogue pattern.

Where does that leave you?

If you're an intermediate or advanced sewer with an eye for what a good fit should be, you may find that some of these programs are worthy dressmaking tools, especially if you design clothes for a variety of body types. Too, if your size falls outside the narrow size range of commercial patterns, these programs at least have the potential to produce garments that are

**TIP**
I and millions of other sewers would be nothing but lost souls with pinking shears were it not for those valuable repositories of wisdom known as the Internet textile FAQs. Subjects addressed include these: Where can I buy fabric to sew windsocks? How do I tea-dye fabric? What are good mail-order sources for buttons, vintage fabrics, outdoor gear fabric, and so on? And how do I restore my grandma's treadle machine? For complete directions on how to get them, head to Chapter 18 on Internet.

smartly tailored, as opposed to the by-day-it's-a-muumuu-by-night-it's-a-sky-diving-target look that fills the back pages of commercial pattern books—assuming you're willing to fiddle trying to make the patterns fit.

However, if you're like one computer user who posted an E-mail message on an online service that went "My teenage daughter is learning to sew, and she likes computers. Should I purchase one of these pattern-making programs for her birthday?," the answer is an emphatic "No!" I can't imagine a better recipe for frustration.

## It Takes Special Skills to Work with These Patterns

What's the quality of the patterns that these programs generate?

First you need to print the pattern, and that can take time, depending on your printer. While my laser printer took only about 20 minutes to print the pieces of a jacket pattern, including facings and linings, it took my Reagan-era dot-matrix printer more than three hours to print the same set of pattern pieces.

Unless you have a plotter, your printer will produce segments of the pattern on standard letter-sized paper. You then need to take those segments, cut them out, and tape them together to make whole pattern pieces. Fittingly Sew is the only program that displays a map of how to tape the paper pieces together. Dress Shop prints big numbers on the pieces that makes matching them pretty easy. At the other end of the spectrum, Personal Patterns pretty much leaves you to your wits in assembling the jigsaw puzzle.

Once you assemble the pattern pieces, you may find that they lack many of the markings of commercial patterns, like centering and overlap marks. Sewing together muslin test garments of a pattern before you cut it out of more expensive fabric is de rigueur—a step you must sometimes do twice to get a good fit.

None of the packages provide anything beyond the most austere sewing directions. They remind me of turn-of-the-century commercial dress patterns, which provided little besides big pieces of tissue and left it up to the sewer to figure out what to do with them. If you plan to work with this pattern-making software, make sure that you're a sewer who doesn't blanch at sewing together garments without detailed instructions.

Finally, with the exception of those in Personal Patterns Jackets, the garment styles offered by these programs are fairly simplistic. They offer basic blouses, A-line skirts, and princess line dresses. You won't find anything from Fifth Avenue here. It's up to you to add any flourishes.

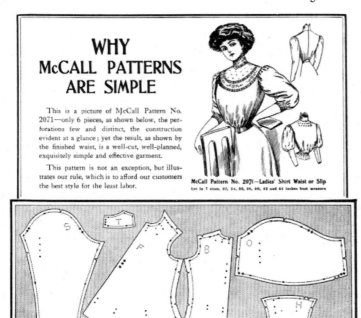

> "Computer-generated sewing patterns remind me of turn-of-the-century dress patterns that were little more than big pieces of tissue."

These products are clearly first-generation ones, with as much potential to bedazzle in the future as to frustrate in the present. Fortunately, all the manufacturers are committed to helping their customers get garments that fit, and that means a lot. And, if you're not satisfied with the software, all of the vendors promise to refund your money.

## Dress Shop 2.0 Is the Most Ambitious Pattern-Making Software Aimed at Home Sewers

*D*ress Shop is the most ambitious of the pattern-drafting programs on the market. It comes with thirty-five clothing styles that can be altered in hundreds of ways to produce hundreds of patterns. Included among the patterns are eight different styles of dresses, six styles of pants, six blouse styles, eight styles of skirts, and a fitted blazer and vest. You can customize each by selecting elements like neckline, sleeve, collar, cuff, and hem styles from pop-up menus. You can also customize darts. The styles are simple classics. You won't find the latest trend-making styles here.

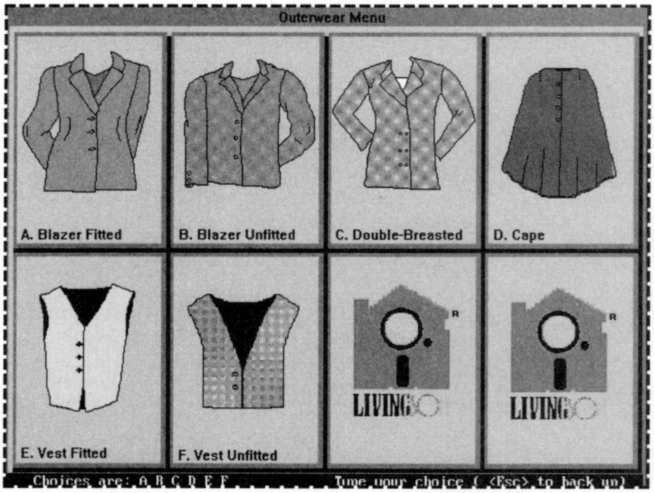

**Figure 2-1**
Dress Shop 2.0 gives you the largest selection of garment styles. You pick basic styles off a menu (this is the outerwear menu), then proceed to specify details.

Dress Shop takes your measurements and prints out easy-to-read pattern pieces that include the amount of ease you specify, as well as the amount of seam and hem allowances. It also prints facings. You can use Dress Shop to create patterns for any size woman, big or small, including pregnant women and little girls.

Dress Shop's drawback is that the first time you use it you must type in an exhausting 101 different body measurements (although if you're not built asymmetrically, you can get by with 60, but who isn't asymmetrical?). But at least they're honest: The chapter of the manual that describes how to take these measurements is entitled "This Can Get Ugly...Really Ugly."

The manual advises that you ask someone else to take the measurements, marking the measuring lines on your skin with an indelible marker so that you can compare the markings over the course of several days to make sure you got them right. It took Ruthe Brown and her crew over three hours to do the measurements on one person the first time they tried. With each person they measured, the time decreased by roughly half. LivingSoft, the publishers of Dress Shop, sells a video for $9.95 that shows you how to take the measurements accurately. Unlike the other dress-making programs, Dress Shop comes with no built-in measurements for standard sizes, so you can't cheat and just select, say, size 12 measurements (the company plans to sell add-on disks with standard sizes in the future).

Once you've leaped the measuring hurdle, you pick your garment and its style elements from easy-to-follow menus as Dress Shop paints the garment on your PC screen. Then Dress Shop goes to work for a while, calculating the dimensions of the pattern pieces. While it may take fifteen minutes or more on a 386 PC for the program to finish its calculations, the wait is worth it, for the pattern pieces print out quickly and are easy to piece together.

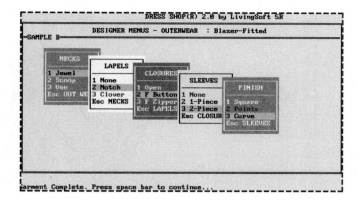

Figure 2-2
Once you select your basic garment, Dress Shop prompts you along to choose styling options like the kind of collar, sleeves, button placement, and so forth.

## *But Do the Garments Fit?*

Do the garments you get from Dress Shop fit? Our testers had mixed results. When all the members of Brown's group sewed sleeveless bodices from their measurements, only one got a top that fit, though that fit was very good. When I printed out a pattern for a pair of tailored pedal pushers (one of the example sets of measurements was nearly identical to my own, so I was lucky enough to be able to cheat), they printed out like a dream. But when I increased the thigh and rump measurements by a few inches, the pattern that printed out was downright weird. The seat of the pants increased appropriately in dimension, but the cuffs ballooned to such an extent that each was nearly an extra foot in circumference. Why would the cuffs around the shins increase if you add inches to the hips, especially when the calf and knee measurements remain the same? The front crotch seam also virtually disappeared.

The scuttlebutt among Dress Shop users on Internet is that the more symmetrical you are, the more likely you are to get patterns that fit correctly. (The one sewer in Brown's group to get a bodice to fit was the only one with a textbook symmetrical build.) Still, there are dressmakers who use Dress Shop and like it. Some sewers have found that even when patterns do print out strangely, when they sew up the patterns, they sometimes fit nicely. And most of our testers (myself included) found using the software to be an exhilarating dressmaking experience in certain respects. Fortunately, LivingSoft offers good tech support through an 800 number (our sewers found them dedicated to helping users get garments that fit), plus a money-back guarantee so you can always send the software back if it doesn't work for you.

LivingSoft
P.O. Box 1030
Janesville, CA 96114-1030
Phone: 916/253-2700 or 916/253-2703 (fax)
Price: For $79.95 you get a version of Dress Shop called the Basic Four, which includes four patterns: pants, skirt, bodice, and dress. $149.95 will get you Dress Shop 2.0, which includes the main program and the Basic Four, plus thirty-four additional patterns. You can purchase complete, single patterns for $29.95 each.
Requirements: Any PC processor from 8086 up, 524K RAM; CGA, VGA, or SVGA; DOS 3.3 or higher; hard disk; and any printer. A Mac version is planned for late 1995. Call to check availability.

You can obtain a demo of the program by sending $5 to LivingSoft or downloading it from CompuServe and many other computer services. Look for file DS2DEMO.EXE in the craft or sewing forums. You'll also find online a fact file about Dress Shop (DS2FAQ.TXT) and the company's newsletter (NEWSLT.EXE) with up-to-date information on releases and pattern additions.

## Personal Patterns 2.0 and Personal Patterns Jackets 1.0 Are More Modest Than Dress Shop, but Still Worthwhile

*P*ersonal Patterns software is more limited in scope than Dress Shop. It offers twenty different basic bodices that you can mix and match with four sleeve types (basic, gathered, bishop, and gathered short), three skirt types (straight, A-line, and high waist), and four pant styles (trouser, pleated, capri, and jean). I enjoyed using Personal Patterns because it was a simple program, and when I entered measurements it usually printed out things that fit with only minor glitches. Though the clothing styles are bland (with the exception of the pant styles, which *were* designed by a Fifth Avenue clothing designer), they can provide a launching pad for custom designing.

Personal Patterns comes with built-in measurements for women's sizes 6 to 44 (no men's sizes), and you can easily tailor these measurements to your own proportions. The program requires that you enter just thirty measurements, and these are far more fault-tolerant than those in Dress Shop. Unlike Dress Shop, Personal Patterns will not create patterns for maternity clothes. You can save measurements for all your clients in a database, and load them later to generate pattern pieces in a jiffy.

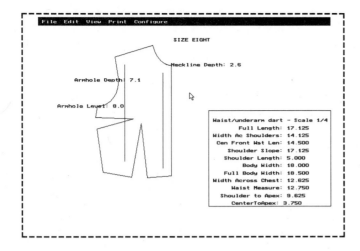

SIZE EIGHT

Neckline Depth: 2.6

Armhole Depth: 7.1

Armhole Level: 8.0

Waist/underarm dart - Scale 1/4
Full Length: 17.125
Width Ac Shoulders: 14.125
Cen Front Wst Len: 14.500
Shoulder Slope: 17.125
Shoulder Length: 5.000
Body Width: 18.000
Full Body Width: 18.500
Width Across Chest: 12.625
Waist Measure: 12.750
Shoulder to Apex: 9.625
CenterToApex: 3.750

**Figure 2-3**
Personal Patterns does a good job creating easy-to-use pattern pieces from your measurements.

Personal Patterns includes a children's module that lets you create simply styled clothes for boys and girls from 36" to 66". Standard measurements are included, but as with the adult portion of the program, you can also tailor measurements. You can generate patterns for a T-shirt, over-garment shirt, and basic front top, plus A-line pants and a skirt.

Everyone I've encountered who's used the basic Personal Patterns software agrees that the patterns it creates provide a good fit, even for nonstandard bodies. The pants patterns provide an especially well-tailored look for the gourd-shaped among us.

The Windows version of Personal Patterns offers all the adult patterns, but not the children's or jacket patterns. Once you draft a pattern, you can chage measurements and styling details like button and dart positions and the pattern will instantly redraw on the screen.

**Personal patterns jacket** A separate program, Personal Patterns Jackets, lets you create dozens of sophisticated women's suit styles tailored to custom measurements. From pull-down and pop-up menus you choose from styles that include fitted, semifitted, and boxy jackets (you can pick styles for the back and front separately). Choice of lapels includes notched, tuxedo notched, shawl, convertible, V-neckline, and jewel. You also pick button layouts (from one to four buttons and double-breasted options), sleeve type (fitted, semifitted, and boxy), and pocket style (welt or patch pocket). Jacket length is altered automatically by the program. The pant and skirt styles from the basic Personal Patterns round off the package. The emphasis of this program is style, rather than fit, according to Water Fountain Software. That means that you may have to sew up a few test garments out of muslin and get out the paper and chalk before you get a jacket that fits.

It took me less than an hour to set up both Personal Patterns and Personal Patterns Jackets, and to take and enter my measurements. It took ten minutes on a laser printer to print out a complete jacket pattern (including linings and facings), although this same task

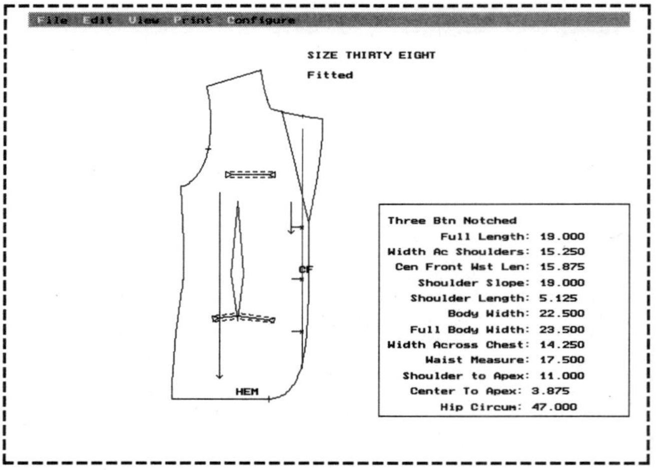

SIZE THIRTY EIGHT
Fitted

Three Btn Notched
| | |
|---|---|
| Full Length: | 19.000 |
| Width Ac Shoulders: | 15.250 |
| Cen Front Wst Len: | 15.875 |
| Shoulder Slope: | 19.000 |
| Shoulder Length: | 5.125 |
| Body Width: | 22.500 |
| Full Body Width: | 23.500 |
| Width Across Chest: | 14.250 |
| Waist Measure: | 17.500 |
| Shoulder to Apex: | 11.000 |
| Center To Apex: | 3.875 |
| Hip Circum: | 47.000 |

**Figure 2-4**
Personal Patterns Jackets lets you design a variety of jacket styles to fit your measurements. The fit occasionally leaves something to be desired in this initial version of the program, but these problems can fixed.

took all evening on my old dot-matrix printer. You don't have to print out an entire pattern, just the pieces that you want.

Jacket fit leaves something to be desired. Unfortunately, when you enter your measurements you need to manually increase the shoulder measurements to accommodate shoulder pads—(an unfortunate state of affairs, I think, and something that's not mentioned in the manual). You must also add inches to the shoulder width measurement so that the top of the sleeve cap doesn't fall on the very tip of the shoulder. Sleeve caps tend to be too narrow and elbow room is at a premium. According to Water Fountain Software, the company is working on these problems and hopes to have them rectified in a future release. In the meantime, they recommend that users use instead the sleeve cap from their basic Personal Patterns program.

I also experienced problems with front side seam edges ending up longer than their matching back side edges, even when I used the standard size measurements built into the program (this happened to me in the basic Personal Patterns program too).

The pattern pieces printed by both Personal Patterns and Personal Patterns Jackets are austere, but sufficient; like European dressmaking patterns they lack seam allowances. Also, the jackets program prints facing patterns, but the standard program doesn't—you need to create your own. You'll probably also want to create your own collars to go with patterns created with the basic Personal Patterns program, since there are only a few collar designs.

On the plus side, the manual for Personal Patterns Jackets has detailed instructions on how to sew the jackets, though the manuals for both programs could use more in the way of computer support. Because of programming glitches, the programs occasionally spit out memory overflow errors and kick you out of the software. Still, the Personal Patterns programs may be the stars of this emerging genre.

Water Fountain Software
13 E. 17th St., 3rd Floor
New York, NY 10003
Phone: 212/929-6204 or 212/929-1025
CompuServe: 71031,2656
Requirements: PC with 286 or greater processor,

*TIP*
*You can participate in lively Internet sewing-related discussions like the Wearable Arts one or the Historical Costuming discussion via your private E-mail box on whatever computer online service you subscribe to. See Chapter 18 on Internet for directions.*

640K memory, DOS 3.0 or greater; there are no plans for a Macintosh version. Windows 3.1 or later required for Windows version.
Price: $179 for Personal Patterns Classics (adult and children); $199 for Personal Patterns Jackets; or $349 for both programs; Windows version of Personal Patterns: $129.

For a demo of the basic Personal Patterns program send $10 to Water Fountain Software (Canadian orders add $3.50) or download it from an online service. Look in the sewing and craft forum libraries for the file PERSPA.EXE. For more information about Personal Patterns Jackets look for JACKET.TXT, BOXYJK.GIF, and FITJKT.GIF. The latter two files contain pictures of all the jacket styles.

## Fittingly Sew Is Pattern-Drafting Software for Advanced Sewers

*F*ittingly Sew takes a different approach to pattern design than the other two programs. It's for sophisticated sewers who are comfortable working with slopers, which are very basic patterns that represent body measurements. You create slopers based on custom measurements, then use them as the basis for designing pattern pieces. It has a thoughtful, graphical design with well-conceived tools that approach those of expensive commercial pattern design programs.

You can enter 31 basic sewing measurements, or else load up the standard measurements for misses size 6 to 20. The program displays pictures that show you how to take the measurements. Just like the other programs, Fittingly Sew lets you keep a database of measurements for your clients.

Fittingly Sew takes the measurements you enter and generates pattern pieces for an A-line skirt, single-dart skirt, pleated pants, dartless blouse, waistless dress, dress with a princess line through the shoulder, and an apron. If you want to design a blouse, for example, you'd first print out the blouse sloper, sew a muslin test, then fit it to yourself or your customer. You'd then go back into the program and fine-tune the sloper with drawing tools, and finally add to it the details that you want in the design—a jewel neckline, for example, or darts.

Fittingly Sew's drawing tools are limited; if you want to create a pattern piece from scratch, and don't want to copy a piece from an existing pattern or sloper, you must start with

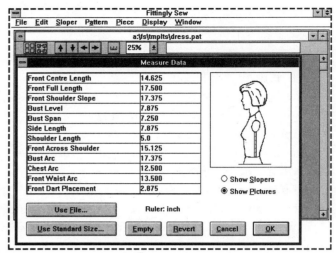

**Figure 2-5**
You can create patterns around standard misses' sizes or else enter custom measurements into Fittingly Sew. The program displays pictures that show you how to take the measurements correctly.

a rectangle and manipulate its points and angles from there. But most of the essentials are there, letting you create darts, pleats, and facings, and redesign lines and curves. You can specify your seam allowance, and the amount of ease in the pattern (minimum, medium, and maximum are the settings). You can also define your fabric space—designating fabric width, length, and fold, and manipulate your pattern pieces on the fabric. A zoom feature lets you zero in on pattern elements. Calculations can be made in inches or centimeters.

How do the garments fit? It may depend a lot on how good you are at adjusting slopers. I haven't had any problems with fit, but I know one professional dressmaker who feels that patterns produced with Fittingly Sew don't fit as well as patterns produced with Dress Shop and Personal Patterns. The only other peeve I can imagine is that you may find it easiest to use the program to generate a quick sloper tailored to your measurements, then revert to paper and chalk to adjust the pattern pieces and add design elements. For some that will be quicker than using the computer-design tools.

Fittingly Sew is the only one of the dressmaking software packages with exceptionally good documentation, but only in the computer sense. It doesn't include directions on how to sew the slopers together. But if you're a sophisticated enough sewer to use a program like this, you won't need directions.

Bartley Software, Inc.
72 Robertson Rd., Box 26122
Nepean, Ontario, Canada K2H 9R6
Phone: 800/661-5209 or 613/829-6488
Internet: 72133.3102@compuserve.com
CompuServe: 72133,3102

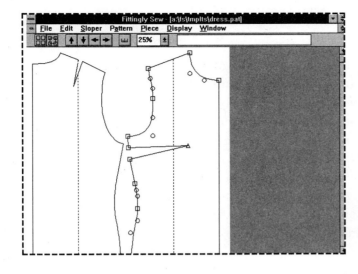

**Figure 2-6**
First you create slopers with Fittingly Sew, then use them as the basis for designing pattern pieces.

Requirements: PC version requires Windows 3.0 or later, 1 MB RAM, mouse, and hard drive; Mac version requires System 6 or 7, 2 MB RAM, and hard disk drive.
Price: $169 US (including shipping), or $199 Canadian (including shipping), plus tax.

For free demo software, call or write Bartley Software, or download the software from computer online services like CompuServe. Look in the sewing or craft forum libraries for FSDEMO.SEA and FSINFO.SEA if you're a Macintosh user, or FSWDEMO.ZIP and FSINFO.ZIP if you're a PC owner.

## *Hollywood Costumers Rely on High-Tech Wizardry to Dress Casts of Thousands*

When I studied costume design in college, one agonizing weekly ritual was the drawing workshop. As models in period costumes floated past, we sketched frantically. We were allowed just minutes to finish each drawing. (Mine always came out looking like scaly-eyed monsters stuffed in Marie Antoinette's panniers.)

Costumers must still draw fashion boards and patterns as fast as demons, but they have computer tools to help with some of the drudgery. For pattern drafting, there's Custom Patternmaker, an add-on program that works in conjunction with the popular computer-aided design program AutoCAD (AutoCAD is one of those 3-D architectural and engineering programs that they use to design Stealth bombers.) "You can use [Custom Patternmaker] to design very complex period costume patterns," says Stephanie Schoelzel, who helped develop the program at the University of California, Los Angeles. You enter the actor's measurements, then use cut and spread techniques to design the flat pattern pieces. Schoelzel claims that it cuts the pattern-making process by nearly two-thirds by eliminating the need to sew muslin mock-ups of garments. "You can take your pattern and cut right into your final fabric, and the costume will come out dead on in the fitting," she says.

Custom Patternmaker costs $1,000 and requires at least an 80386 PC with a math coprocessor. A copy of AutoCAD, version 10 (that's an old version, one that sold cheaply to students years ago) is also required; AutoCAD runs about $360 retail. Needless to say, both programs require special skills and lots of time to learn to use effectively.

Several special database programs are available for costumers to keep track of minutiae like actors' measurements, costume changes, and budgets. One is Fast Trak for Costume Breakdown and Budgeting. It costs $995 and will work on older PCs with 80286 processors and 640K RAM.

The three major costume unions in Hollywood have formed the Hollywood Joint Costumers' Computer Users Group to help wardrobe managers, designers, and costumers in the movie and TV industries better utilize computer technology. The club runs a computer lab called Hollywood Hands-On where members can go to get computer training and advice. The group is presently investigating using virtual-reality software of the kind used by movie special-effects artists to simulate in three-dimensions what garments will look like once they're sewn. This is something that was, until recently, impossible, due to the lack of any mathematical algorithms that could realistically simulate fabric draping. Still, computer scientists do not yet know how to simulate the unique draping qualities of more than a few different kinds of fabric—crisp fabrics like cottons pose a challenge to simulate by computer —so it may be a while before costumers regularly venture into virtual reality with their design pads.

For more information about the Hollywood Joint Costumers' Computer Users Group, or Custom Patternmaker or Fast Trak, call Schoelzel at 310/599-2230.

# Home Sewing Machines Link to PCs for Dazzling Effects

*I*t had to happen eventually. First, home sewing machines became computerized, with computer-like displays and decorative stitches built into memory chips inside the machine, and now some models come with a cable that connects them to the back of a home PC, just like another computer peripheral. While Detroit is finding that even macho car buyers shudder with intimidation at the thought of buying a computerized car, it's hard to comprehend the enormity of the anxiety suffered by sewers confronted by a sewing machine of beastly complexity married to an even more complex computer.

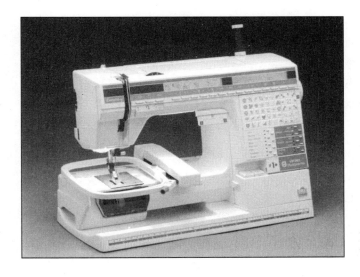

**Figure 2-7**
**The Viking #1+ sewing machine.**

I must admit, some of these sewing machines sat in my office for a week before I could summon the nerve to open their boxes. But, when I did, I found, to my relief, that the machines and their computer links were no harder to set up than a computer and its printer. And using them was more fun.

In the typical arrangement, you plug a communications cable into a socket on the back or side of the sewing machine. You plug the other end of this cable into the back of the PC in either the socket into which you'd normally plug your modem, or the one for your printer.

Special sewing software that you install on your computer lets you design your own decorative and embroidery stitches. You can even use computer clipart or scanned images from other graphics programs as the basis for your stitch design. You can create novelty stitches like you'd stitch around the edge of a petticoat or collar, or large stitch motifs for machine quilting. With the most advanced machines like the Viking #1+, you can paint multicolored, embroidered, satin-stitched pictures like the kind you used to need a dedicated embroidery machine to design. Once you've finished designing your stitches, you click on a menu choice or icon on the computer, and the design is instantly transmitted to the sewing machine's memory or to a special memory card, where it is stored even after you turn the machine off. You then use the sewing machine to stitch your design just like you'd sew any other decorative stitch. The sewing machine does not have to be plugged into the computer at this point.

The sewing machine–PC linkup offers sewers new creative opportunities. In just minutes, the design you paint on your computer screen can appear on your fabric. Some textile artists live and breathe by these machines. Home sewers find they can give projects a customized touch by embroidering school logos or religious symbols, or incorporating them into stitches.

But there are drawbacks. First, these machines are expensive. Very expensive. They retail for around $3,500, plus you must buy the computer hookup and software separately, for around $350 more. You may also need to buy additional items like memory cards to store the stitches.

Second, sewing machines that collaborate with PCs are a relatively new invention. With them come all the responsibilities of being a pioneer consumer. Sewing machine makers will hate me for saying this, but I think that neither they nor their dealers know how to provide good customer support for these computer linkups yet. Dealers know how to fix sewing machines; they've been doing that for years. But they are not computer technicians, and it is unfair to expect them to be. I've visited sewing machine stores where the mechanics inspired awe with their knowledge of buttonhole attachments, but were at loss when it came to simply booting up the PC hooked to the sewing machine in the floor display to show how it worked. (Plus, the documentation that comes with some of these sewing machine–computer linkups is ghastly. Unlike normal computer software documentation, it doesn't even provide a phone number that you can call when you run into trouble.)

Finally, designing custom stitches and embroidered pictures is tedious work. It takes time and effort to learn how to do it well, and even more time to get a stitching pattern that you like. Don't expect to take those digitized images of your prize Empress Josephine roses and be embroidering them onto your quilt within minutes after loading them into the software. Depending upon the complexity of the design you want, it may take hours of experimentation to get it right.

> *Pfaff, Viking, and Bernina all devote considerable resources to training their dealers to provide service and support for their computerized sewing machines. But I repeat, it is patently unfair to expect 75-year-old Hans, the sewing machine repairman, genius that he is, to think like Bill Gates. It can't be emphasized enough: If you buy one of these high-tech sewing machines, buy it from a reliable local dealer who will be committed to getting you the tech support you need, no matter how much the technology baffles them. Shop around for a good dealer by asking for recommendations from your local sewing guild. Be sure to buy from a dealer who offers classes on how to use the sewing machine that you buy.*

The most efficient way to learn how to use these machines is to take a class through your sewing machine dealer, or with a local club dedicated to your particular brand of sewing machine, like a Pfaff club. Your best resource for learning how to use these machines and dealing with their technicalities will be other sewers. If you already have a computerized machine, get a subscription to CompuServe, for the sewing message area in its craft forum is populated by many Pfaff, Bernina, and Viking owners. (When I posted a message asking for help understanding the Pfaff's computer link-up, I was inundated with messages from knowledgeable Pfaffies offering to help.) Prodigy's Hobby Board is also a good place to meet other Pfaffies. In fact, you'd be wise to talk to other sewers online before you buy anything!

What follows are descriptions of the computer linkups of the newest models of three leading computerized sewing machines—the Pfaff line, the Bernina, and the Viking #1+.

These are not reviews like the kind you'd find in sewing magazines. They're not intended to tell you the quality of the satin stitching or whether a particular machine is suited to heirloom sewing or machine quilting. They're simply intended to give you an idea of what it's like to work with the computer linkups for these machines and what questions to ask should you decide to buy one.

All that said, these machines are pretty amazing. If I didn't have a mortgage, I would buy one.

## Customize Your Stitches with Pfaff's PC-Designer

*T*he Pfaff 7550 and 1475 Creative Designer sewing machines can both be hooked to home computers through a cable that connects to the computer's serial port (the socket where the modem is attached). On the computer itself, you install a simple program called PC-Designer. There's a version available for Windows and one for DOS. The Windows version is far superior and the one you should purchase if your PC runs Windows 3.1 or Windows 95. (As this book goes to press, Pfaff is working on a Macintosh version. Some Pfaff dealers are providing Macintosh users with directions on how to run the PC version on a Mac in conjunction with a product called Soft PC Professional, although such a regimen is not officially sanctioned by Pfaff.)

Using the computer's mouse, you move a crosshair or cursor arrow over the screen, creating your stitch design, clicking on each point where you want the sewing machine's needle to pierce the cloth and create a stitch. These points are called "stitch points." You outline stitch points in the order in which you want the machine to sew them, starting and stopping the design in the spots where you want the needle to start and stop. In the DOS version of the software this can be an horrifically slow process, but it's fast and fun with the Windows version. A feature called "autotrace" will automatically place stitches of the length that you specify around any drawing or scanned in page that you import into the program as a black-and-white BMP file.

The DOS version lets you import TIF files (a process I had trouble with, and found the manual didn't offer enough guidance on).

**TIPS**
**Head to the Internet chapter to learn how to join the Pfabulous Pfaff Fan Club, the Bernina Fan Club, or the one for Viking owners, where you can commune in cyberspace with more computerized sewing eggheads than you ever dreamed existed.**

*Just as you can negotiate the price of a computer system, you can negotiate the price of a sewing machine. Sewing machine dealers are often given flexibility in setting their prices. It doesn't hurt to dicker or to shop around.*

You can also shrink or enlarge a stitch pattern on the fly, as well as adjust stitch length. You can click on on-screen buttons to rotate and mirror the design, as well as zoom in on stitches in the Windows version, or use pull-down menus in the DOS version to do the same.

The Pfaff system is best suited for creating outline designs in a single color, as shown in Figure 2-9. (The Viking #1+ reviewed below is best for creating multicolored machine embroidery designs). The Windows version as well as the most recent DOS version let you fill in areas of the design with a simple satin stitch by either outlining the lines between which the satin stitch will be sewed or selecting an area already outlined by stitches. PC-Designer lets you tweak stitch angle and density of satin stitches. Patterns can be as wide as 2 ⅜" and 6" long. How much satin stitch design you can store in the Pfaff sewing machine's memory is limited depending upon your machine—the Pfaff 7550 can store the largest designs— up to 8,000 stitch points. That translates into one satin stitch flower with a few leaves. Fortunately, you can store stitches that you design on your computer's hard disk or on a floppy disk instead.

One important capability that the Windows version of PC-Designer has that the DOS version lacks is the ability to "download" stitches from the Pfaff into your computer, add or delete stitches, and return them to the Pfaff. This is something that Pfaff owners have been hankering for for a long time. Another new feature in the Windows version is the ability to add letters to your stitch designs. You'll find built into the program script, block, outline, and cursive alphabets. You can also download into your computer alphabets from the Pfaff and incorporate them into stitch designs.

In the DOS version you'll find a grid that you can draw on, although some Pfaffies have found that the dimensions of the grid are slightly off, depending upon the kind of computer monitor that you have, resulting in satin stitches that are out of whack. (See the next section, "You Can Find Pfaff Computer Stitching Accessories All Over the Info Highway," for information on a program that will correct this.)

**Figure 2-8**
This paisley was designed in another graphics program, then imported into Pfaff's PC-Designer software. With your mouse, you move the crosshair and click on the stitch points where you want the sewing machine needle to pierce the cloth. It can be a laborious process in the DOS version shown here, but it's a snap in the Windows version.

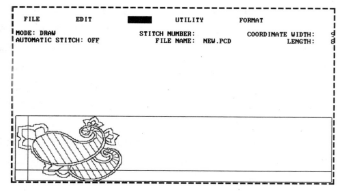

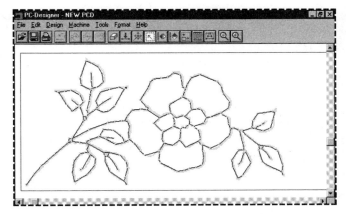

**Figure 2-9**
The Windows version of Pfaff's
PC-Designer, as shown running
in Windows 95, is a tremendous
improvement over the DOS version.
Import a black-and-white drawing,
like this rose, in BMP format, then
use the "auto trace" feature to outline
it with stitches. Use the "fade out"
tool to temporarily fade the original
drawing into the background as you
fine-tune stitch placement.

The DOS version of PC-Designer comes with a hefty 100-page manual, but its directions often leave you scratching your head. Technospeak often muddies the software. The program's main menu offers you the choice between accessing "P-Memory," "M-Memory," and "RAM-Manager." The latter "transfers a RAM file from the computer to the P- and M-Memories" according to the manual. It's mute about what P- and M- Memories are. Veteran Pfaffies may know what such things are, but the jargon can be terrifying to newcomers. The manual that comes with the Windows version of the software is better, but still afloat in jargon.

If you presently own the DOS version of PC-Designer, you would be well advised to pony up $99 to update to the Windows version.

Pfaff American Sales Corp.

610 Winters Ave.

Paramus, NJ 07653

Phone: 201/262-7211; call 800/526-0273 for name of a local authorized dealer

Requirments: PC-Designer Software 3.0 for DOS: 80286 or higher PC, DOS 3.3 or higher, 640K RAM, VGA or Hercules graphics, serial port, and Microsoft-compatible mouse. PC-Designer Software 1.0 for Windows: 80286 or higher PC, DOS 3.3 or higher, 2 megs RAM, VGA graphics, serial port, and Microsoft-compatible mouse.

Price: $3,499 for 7550, PC-Designer Software version 3 for DOS: $329; version 1.0 for Windows—$349 (if you already have the DOS version, you can update to the Windows version for $99). As this book goes to press, Pfaff is preparing 3 disks of stitch designs to use with the PC-Designer software. Pricing has not yet been determined, but the stitch designs are scrumptious.

## *You Can Find Pfaff Computer Stitching Accessories All Over the Info Highway*

A cottage industry has sprung up selling software utilities that augment the capabilities of Pfaff's PC-Designer software. StitchView is a Windows program that lets you view PC-Designer designs with the click of a mouse button. Stitch points are highly visible in color. You can print out stitches much more easily with it than you can in PC-Designer for DOS, and you can import stitch designs created with early DOS versions of PC-Designer (early versions store stitches in a different file format than the current versions).

StitchView is $15 plus $2.50 shipping from Roger Smith Software, P.O. Box 308, Mary Esther, FL, 32569. You can also download a demo version of it from CompuServe and many other computer services. Look for the file SVDMO.EXE.

Many Pfaffies upload to computer services the decorative stitches and buttonholes that they've designed with their Pfaff-computer connection, and make them available to other sewers for free. The best place to look for Pfaff stitches is in CompuServe's Fibercrafts Forum in the Sewing Library. Once you've selected the Sewing Library, search for the keyword "PFAFF" and CompuServe will display a list of files. It will include discussions, tips, and reviews of Pfaff machines, plus computerized stitches.

Don't have the time to go looking online? You can order a lovely printed catalog of the stitches you'll find on computer services and their filenames. Send $10 plus a stamped, self-addressed envelope to Disks Plus, 5312 Waits Ave., Forth Worth, TX, 76133. Include two blank formatted disks and they'll send you the stitches, too—for free.

Carla Lopez Design Studio also sells disks with Carla's floral satin stitch designs. For information send a long, stamped self-addressed envelope to 51 Mac Dougal St., Suite 196, New York, NY, 10012.

It's become standard among Pfaffies to post stitches online in ASCII or text format (this way they can even be included in E-mail messages). While the present version of PC-Designer stores stitches in binary format, early versions stored stitches in ASCII, and those are the versions that most Pfaffies use. If you have a new version of PC-Designer, you can easily convert stitches stored in text to binary format with a free utility called ConvPCD from Roger Smith Software. You'll find it online stored as file CONVPC.ZIP or CONV-PCD.ZIP.

If the problem of placing stitches close to each other in large, satin-stitched designs in DOS versions of the software has vexed you, thanks to PC-Designer's penchant to move stitches placed on its grid one to two millimeters in either direction, get a new grid for the software. ZGRID is available for $15 from Eugenia's Child, 2207 Beast Ash St., Suite 548, Goldsboro, NC, 27530-4127.

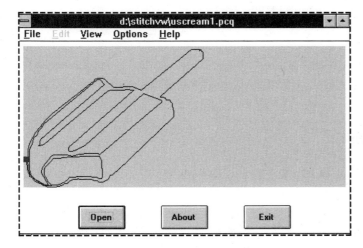

Figure 2-10
StitchView lets you view stitches designed in PC-Designer in a way that's easier on your eyes. You can also use it to print them out and convert the stitches you find online to a newer format.

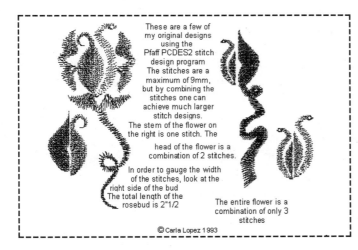

These are a few of my original designs using the Pfaff PCDES2 stitch design program
The stitches are a maximum of 9mm, but by combining the stitches one can achieve much larger stitch designs.
The stem of the flower on the right is one stitch. The head of the flower is a combination of 2 stitches.
In order to gauge the width of the stitches, look at the right side of the bud
The total length of the rosebud is 2"1/2
The entire flower is a combination of only 3 stitches
© Carla Lopez 1993

Figure 2-11
Many Pfaffies upload to CompuServe stitches that they design on their computers. This design/tutorial by textile artist Carla Lopez shows you what a really talented sewer can do with a PC–Pfaff connection.

# Bernina 1630 and 1630+ Inspiration Let You Customize Stitches in Windows

*T*he Bernina 1630 and 1630+ machine with its Bernina Designer software is quite similar in concept to the Pfaff and its PC-Designer software. You place stitches on a plain screen or grid with crosshairs, clicking with your mouse to set the stitch points. The Bernina software is nicely laid out for computer novices. You click on icons to zoom in on stitches, change stitch attributes, click rulers and grids on and off, and other such chores. Whoever designed this slick software thought of everything. It is really very easy to set up and learn to use.

With the icons and pull-down menus you can move, insert, and delete stitches, change the size of the stitch design (or portions of the design), cut and copy stitch layouts to the

Windows clipboard, and paste them into new stitch designs. You can also display multiple stitch designs simultaneously on the screen in tiled or stacked windows.

You can import into Bernina Designer any computer graphic—be it clipart, a scanned image, or a digitized picture downloaded from a computer service—and use that as the basis for a stitch design. The graphic must be in the Windows bitmap format, but you can easily convert any graphic image—TIF, GIF, or PCX—into a bitmap with Windows. It really is a snap with this program to take drawings created in another graphics program, bring them into the program, and fill them with stitches.

Stitch designs can be as large as 4" × 8", so you could conceivably design narrow quilting patterns. A wide range of zoom settings lets you view them the actual size they'll be stitched, or magnify sections to make them easier to see as you place stitches. One nice feature is the ability to click off the graphic you're working from, so that you can just see the stitches you've placed. You can also specify thread color changes, telling the sewing machine to stitch a basting stitch and stop for you to change the thread.

While Bernina Designer lets you fill areas of a design with zig-zag stitches, the areas must be square or rectangular. To fill curved areas with satin stitches you must click on each of the stitch points—right, left, right, left, and so on—to outline each stitch. It's a tedious business, and it's easy to make the stitches unbalanced. Only the Viking #1+ provides painless computerized satin stitch design.

Once you've finished your design, you transfer it to the sewing machine, which is connected to the PC via a cable hooked to the modem port. It's as simple as clicking on an icon. Once the stitch is transmitted, a picture of a PC appears on the sewing machine program screen. You select it with the track ball on the front of the sewing machine, click the sewing machine's ENTER button, and you're ready to start stitching. The software will also give you a nice clear printout of your design and your stitches numbered in the order in which they'll be stitched.

Stitches designed with the Bernina are limited to 1,600 stitch points (compare that to the Pfaff's 7550's maximum of 8,000 stitch points). The sewing machine's memory can store a maximum of 6,250 stitch points, which means that you'll probably use your PC to store stitch designs or else download them to a memory key that you insert into the sewing machine whenever you want to do the stitch. The Bernina has a separate memory that stores combinations of stitches and stitch patterns for you.

Bernina Designer includes an excellent built-in tutorial to get you started, and a pretty good software manual. However, the latter only glosses over the software's capabilities. To learn how to use this software well, you'll either need to experiment a lot or take a course. I looked at a fresh-from-the-factory version of the software and it suffered memory lockup problems that occasionally shut down the program. These problems should be corrected in the version you see in the stores. Look for software with a version number higher than 1.0 in the store, just to be on the safe side.

In addition to the sewing machine–PC connection, the Bernina also lets you design custom stitches on its tiny program screen on the face of the sewing machine, and store them in the machine's memory. Mounted on the front of the machine is a little trackball similar to the one in the bottom of most computer mice. You roll it around with your fingertips to paint stitches on the machine's screen. To place each stitch point, you press an ENTER key on the side of the sewing machine. Then you draw another stitch and press the ENTER key again. And so on. You get a total of 80 stitch points. Since the sewing machine's screen gives you a design area of about 1.5" × 2.5", you need the manual dexterity of a watchmaker to design stitches. If you have arthritis, forget it.

Bernina sells memory keys with preprogrammed stitch designs on seasonal and sports themes that you plug into the machines to display the stitches on the sewing machine's screen for stitching. These retail for around $100 each. You will probably need to buy a 9-to-25 pin serial cable adapter at Radio Shack to hook the Bernina to your computer.

I love the Bernina and its Bernina Designer software. However, for a real trip into technology heaven, take a look at the Viking described below.

Bernina of America, Inc.

3500 Thayer Court

Aurora, IL, 60504

Customer Service: 708/978-2500, 708/978-8214 (fax); call to find an authorized dealer near you.

Notice position of tape across fullest part of the bust

Position of Tape for Taking the Bust, Waist and Hip Measures

Notice position of tape on the back

NOTE :—Position of Tape slightly higher on the back for Bust Measure

Bernina Designer Software, version 1
Requirements: 386 PC or higher, Windows 3.1 or higher, VGA, 2 MB RAM (4 MB recommended), hard drive, 3.5" floppy disk drive, mouse. While a Mac version may be created on demand, the company says it's not likely to happen.
Price: $3,599 for 1630+ (all prior 1630s can be updated to a 1630+); Bernina Designer Software is approximately $350.

## Computerized Sewing Fanatics Have Their Own Newsletter

Owners of high-tech sewing machines like the Pfaff 7550 that hook to PCs will enjoy *Pface to Inter-Pface*, a quarterly newsletter devoted to explaining how to work those darn machines. It includes columns by in-the-know sewing techies like fiber artist Carla Lopez and Pfaff programming whizkid Jeannie Horton. In addition to the programmable Pfaffs, it provides support for the Bernina 1630, Viking #1+, Huskygram, and Memory Craft New Home machines. Subscriptions are $16/year. Write to Castle Ent., P.O. Box 521, Buckeye, AZ, 85326.

## Viking #1+ Is Sexy, Sexy, and Computer Stitch Designing Is a Treat

*The Viking #1+ is, quite simply, a machine to die for.*

The Viking #1+ is the first sewing machine on the market that gives home sewers the ability to design embroidered pictures of professional quality using a variety of satin fill stitches and colors. Similar to the Huskygram, a special-purpose embroidery machine, the Viking #1+ can stitch just about anything you draw on your computer screen.

You don't actually link the Viking to your PC. Instead, you hook a special embroidery card reader to the PC via its printer port. This is better than having to set the sewing machine right beside the PC to design stitches, because, as Viking advertises, you can slip the embroidery card reader into your briefcase and take it to work to use with your up-to-date office PC.

The reader copies stitch designs onto a small computer card, about half the size of a bank card, which you later slip into the sewing machine for stitching. You choose the stitch by touching a numbered touch-pad on the front of the sewing machine. Additional buttons on the touch-pad let you rotate the embroidery design, enlarge or reduce it, and sew it in mirror image. The machine also shows you where the boundaries of the design will fall on the fabric before you start stitching. Other buttons let you stop and restart the sewing process, and jump ahead in the stitching sequence, or backtrack in case the thread tangles and you need to stitch a portion of the design over again.

A computer display across the top of the machine reminds you to lower the presser foot and feed dogs, tells you the size of needle and number of the presser foot to use, and other such niceties. As the design is stitched, the machine automatically alters the stitch tension, and beeps to inform you when to change colors. (Color coding tells you what color of thread to change. It also stops and informs you if the thread breaks.)

The machine comes with a special embroidery mechanism and hoop that attaches to the back of the machine. It moves the hoop and fabric back and forth in precision motions as the design is stitched.

The software you run on your PC to design these elaborate embroideries is less elegant than the machine, but it does the job. It's DOS-based with different modules—one for designing monograms, one for prepping graphic images prior to digitizing them, another for doing the actual stitch design, and a fourth for copying the design to the card reader. All these tasks should have been integrated in one program. Further, the software violates the rules of good interface design, the art of making computers user-friendly. For instance, the same icon operates differently in different parts of the program, and odd little beeps of different frequencies dog you when you're doing things wrong, as well as when you're doing things right. And the mouse moves at different speeds in different parts of the program. When I installed it on a PC with a VGA monitor, it turned the screen green; Viking didn't know what the problem was. I found it to work fine on an SVGA monitor, though.

Then there's something called the "dongle." I first encountered the dongle in a cryptic software error message when I tried to create stitches. "No dongle attached," it blinked. Impossible! I said. I'd attached everything in the box that could be attached to a PC. I couldn't find any dongle listed in any of the Viking manuals.

It was Ruthe Brown, editor of *Pface to Inter-Pface,* who solved the mystery. She reported that owners of the Huskygram, an embroidery machine with a PC link that is the big brother of the Viking #1+, had encountered similar error messages and discovered the dongle, technically called the memo-plug, to be a weird little 24-to-24 pin connector that plugged into their PC's printer port. Searching the boxes, I found it. The dongle acts as both a software copy-protection device (the software won't work without it), and it provides additional computer-aided design capabilities to the PC.

The bafflements of the dongle and the software glitches did not annoy me much because the sewing machine is so thrilling to use. To design embroideries on your PC, you start by loading the portion of the software for preparing digitized images for stitch creation. You can import any PCX graphic, in either color or black and white. I found that I was able to import computer pictures of fairly large size and resolution, and crop, cut, paste, and color them. You can also draw on them, but the drawing tools are limited (there's no erase tool, for instance), so I think it's wiser to refine the graphic in another drawing program before importing it into the Viking software.

Once the graphic is converted to a form the software can use, you open another module of the program and begin filling in the design with stitches. The most vaunted feature of the Viking software is the variety of complex fill stitches you can easily "pour" into an area of the pattern. First, you outline the area by clicking on the points around its periphery. (Click the left mouse button and the shape will have curved sides, click the middle mouse button and the sides will be straight. Clicking the right mouse button ends the procedure and tells the computer that you're done with the area.) Once you're done, a pop-up menu gives you a choice of six stitch patterns to choose from, as well as the angle of orientation in which you want them stitched (for instance, if you're embroidering a picture of an animal, the stitches would be stitched in the same direction in which you would sketch shading lines).

**Figure 2-12**
**The Viking's PC software will let you import detailed computer graphics and photos to use as the basis for embroidery designs.**

**Figure 2-13**
Creating embroidery designs is easier with Viking's software than with the PC programs that go with other sewing machines. You can create patterns that are large and detailed, and specify a myriad of color changes as well.

You can also fill circles and boxy and irregular areas with satin stitch stitched in different directions. As with the fill patterns, you can specify density, orientation, and other stitch attributes. By clicking icons you can quickly place lines of 3mm long running stitches and 3mm long double stitches. Additional features let you specify color changes, jump stitches, zoom in on areas of a design, edit stitch points, edit color changes, change fill patterns, undo stitches, and return to the starting point of a design. At any point, you can ask the software to show you just the stitches that you've created. You can also fade the original image you imported into the software so that it's easier to see the stitches on top of it.

Viking #1+ designs can be up to 99 millimeters square with an unlimited number of color changes, although only twelve colors can be specified. The software reports the number of stitches you have created as you work on your design. In contrast to the Pfaff and Bernina machines, there is no limit to the number of stitches a design can have, although technically the memory card on which the design will be copied and later transferred to the sewing machine can hold only 120,000 stitches. Still, that's a lot. (A detailed embroidery design will have 3,500 to 5,000 stitches.) You can use the software's stitch tabulation to calculate approximately how long it will take to stitch the picture; the #1+ averages 375 to 400 stitches a minute, speed varying with the size of the stitch and the number of stitching direction changes.

Once you've finished designing, you can mirror and rotate the stitch design, as well as set its final height. You can also add lettering to it, but you must use another portion of the program to do that. You type in the letters you want embroidered, and pick a font—block, script, or baseball. (Twelve more fonts are available. They're sold separately on disks that contain three each.)

You select the letter size, which can be from ¼" to 3" high. You can also specify other options such as the amount of spacing between the letters, stitches between letters, and the orientation of the letters, such as their degree of curvature. The software displays the resulting letters on the screen. You can merge these letters with up to three designs you've created in the designing module of the program.

Once you've saved the design to your PC's hard disk, you transfer it into the sewing machine by copying it to an embroidery card in a special card reader that you attach to the PC's printer port. You then insert the embroidery card into the sewing machine.

One nifty thing about the Viking #1+ software is that you can use it to design on your PC stitch patterns for machine quilting. In fact, five designs are already included on one of the embroidery cards that come with the machine.

The documentation for the Viking and its embroidery features is truly superb. The manual I received for the software was not so good, but Viking hopes to improve it. Still, I was able to use the machine's PC link and computerized features within a short time after taking everything out of the box. Overall, this is an exceptional machine.

Viking Sewing Machine Co.

11760 Berea Rd.

Cleveland, OH 44111

800/446-2333 or 216/252-3300; 216/252-3311(fax); call for an authorized dealer near you.

Price: $3,500 for the Viking #1+

Requirements: 80286 PC (80386 with 33MHz recommended), 640K (2 megs recommended), hard disk, DOS 3.3 or later, mouse (Logitech 3-button mouse recommended), VGA (SVGA strongly recommended).

**Figure 2-14**
This design took minutes to create with canned designs and letters in the Viking #1+. However, once my husband saw it, it took me the rest of the evening to sew it on every single item of clothing in his closet.

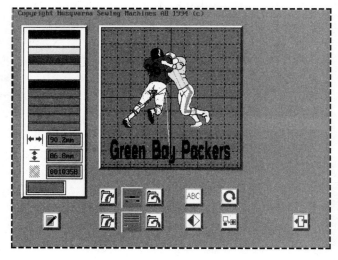

Embroidery Cards 2 and 3 are sold separately as notions for about $150. You can buy extra cassettes with 35 stitches for about $75. You can also buy additional embroidery cards (about $75), different design disks (such as Birds, Floral Corners, and Kids) for about $75, and four separate font disks, each for around $100. Prices are set by the dealers so be sure to check your local dealer for prices.

(If you're interested in buying one of these machines, it would be worth your while to call 800/358-0001 and ask for the Viking #1+ promotional video for $4 handling. It shows amazing things, like using the machine to stitch cutwork embroidery on Fabu-Leather.)

*Note: Want to get really serious about designing garments on a computer? Get a copy of "Drawing and Illustrating Garments by Computer," by Susan Lazear ($24, Cochenille Design Studio, P.O. Box 4276, Encinitas, CA, 92023, 619/259-1698). This book will introduce you to your drawing program and get you quickly sketching fashion plates on your PC. The directions are tailored for Electronic Arts' DeluxePaint and Studio/8 programs, but are general enough to apply to most other paint programs as well.*

## More Tips for Computerized Sewers

### *Use These Fashion Clipart Disks to Speed Up Your Design Time*

Cochenille Studios sells a variety of fashion clipart disks for PCs, Macs, and Amigas. Use these line drawings to speed up your design time or to preview fabrics and colors in garments. They include Fashion Garments I (25 fashion illustrations), Garments as Wearable Art (a collection of garment ensemble line drawings that follow the wearable art silhouette), Fashion Poses (mannequin illustrations of clothed models, specify the women's, men's, or children's disk), and Body Shapes (seven body shapes and 20 garments that you can embellish with color and line). All disks are $15. Specify the type of computer you have, and the disk size (3 ½" or 5 ¼").

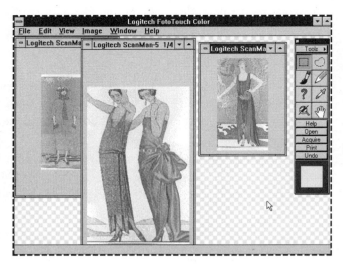

**Figure 2-15**
If you have either a color or a black-and-white hand-held scanner, try scanning in fashion plates and using them in your computer artwork or as part of your computing environment (as Windows wallpaper?). It takes only minutes, and sometimes it's just gratifying to see something on your screen other than a boring program menu.

## For Women Who Play with Dolls

**Quick steps to digitize Newt Gingrich and turn him into a puppet** Want to make a doll with a face that only a mother could love? Get out your hand-held scanner and a photo of one of your favorite faces, be it a picture of Newt in *Newsweek* or a photo of grandpa from the Civil War.

Scan only the face in the photo at a setting of 200 dots per inch. If your printer is black and white, scan the photograph in black and white. Scan it in color if your printer is a color one. Scan only the face.

Once the photo is inside your scanner's software, crop it, and if it provides the tools to do so, airbrush the bags under the eyes if you like. Or add a mustache or dimple.

You can print the photo on muslin using a laser jet or even an ink jet printer. Cut a piece of freezer paper to 8½" × 11". Iron it, shiny side down, on a piece of muslin, with the grain of fabric lined up to the long edge of the paper. Once the freezer paper is sticking to the cloth, cut the cloth to 8½" × 11" to match the freezer paper.

You can safely feed this through your computer printer. Some sewers like to set their printer to manual feed, so that the fabric doesn't twist around as it travels through the printer. I use regular feed and haven't had any problems. Just be sure to determine in advance what side of a sheet of paper the printer will print on. For instance, my laser printer prints on the bottom side of a page as it travels through, so I send the paper through upside down. (Some sewers feed fabric backed by freezer paper into copy machines, but this is more hazardous, since the fabric travels over a hot drum and that can melt the freezer paper. And copy machine toner is often not as permanent as the ink in your printer.)

Set the image by spraying it with a couple coats of Krylon Workable Fixatif No. 1306. You'll find it at any art store for about $5 to $7 per can. Spray the picture with two thorough coats, and allow it to dry between coats. Once it dries, peel the freezer paper off the back of the fabric.

Your doll face is ready to sew. If the face is black and white, consider using fabric paint to "colorize" features like cheeks and eyes, just like in old portraits that were painted in the days before the rise of color film. Fabric pens can also add subtle highlights.

You may want to experiment with your scanner software or with a drawing program like CorelDRAW! to expand or reduce the size of the photo scan to the size of the doll face you have planned. You may need to experiment with your printer's darkness setting so that it prints darker than usual.

One note of warning: Images printed on muslin with color inkjet printers sometimes fade and may even bleed. See Chapter 3 for more valuable information on using your printer to print on fabric.

**Make authentic period doll clothes with your hand-held scanner** A simple calico frock and an apron are the regulation clothing patterns you'll find in most doll patterns. What if you want to dress a doll in something more elaborate? How about a nineteenth-century bathing costume? Or a taffeta day dress? Or how about Josephine Bonaparte's wedding gown?

You can find costume design books at your library that include patterns for authentic garments from many historical periods. The patterns will be drawn to scale on a grid, and for the most part won't look too much different from the patterns you buy in the store. One such book is Blanche Payne's *History of Costume* (New York: Harper & Row, 1965).

If you have a hand-held scanner, you can scan the pattern pieces, display them in a drawing program, size them to appropriate dimensions to fit the doll, and then print them out and use them like you would any other pattern pieces. Here's how:

§ Load the software that came with your scanner, and set its scan mode to "line drawing." Set the dial on the scanner to 200 dots per inch

§ Shine a bright light on the page, so that the scanner can pick up all the fine lines. Keep the book flat as you scan, or else your scan will come out crooked.

*TIP*
*PREVENT OPTICAL MOUSE MELT-DOWN WITH THIS EASY-TO-SEW COZY*
*I once wrote a magazine story about a company that was selling fur mouse cozies that would make a computer mouse look like an actual mouse. To my astonishment, a flood of readers wrote in asking where they could buy them. That was the greatest response I have ever had to a magazine story. Here's how you can make your own fur mouse cozy: Cut a square from fake fur that's the size of your mouse, with an extra inch of fabric on all four sides. Round off the corners. Zig-zag stitch elastic cord all the way around the back side of the fur. Pull the cord to gather the fur into a bonnet, and tie the ends. With craft glue or a hot glue gun, glue felt eyes and whiskers on one end, and a string tail on the other. Slip onto your mouse. If your husband is like mine and likes to leave a high-powered desk lamp shining directly down on the optical mouse, this "mouse cozy" will actually prevent the mouse and its reflective pad from melting and welding themselves together—assuming that you have used fur that is bushy enough.*

✎  Scan one pattern piece at a time. Include any directions and the graph if you can.

✎  Once you have a scan that you like, save it as a BMP or TIF file. You'll probably want to do as much cropping and pruning of the pattern piece as you can in the photo touchup feature of your scanner software or drawing program before importing the pattern piece into a drawing program for final sizing.

✎  Import the scanned pattern pieces into a drawing program like CorelDRAW! Turn on the on-screen ruler and size the pattern pieces to the dimensions that you want. To determine how large the pattern pieces should be, measure your completed doll's chest circumference, shoulder width, shoulder-to-waist, and height. As you size the pattern pieces in your drawing program, remember to include some ease so that the garment will not fit glove tight.

✎  Once you're satisfied with the pattern pieces, print them out. It may seem like a hassle, but it takes only minutes. And it sure beats trying to reproduce those pattern pieces with a pencil and pad.

**For more tips and talk about doll and bear making, check out the doll-making message area on CompuServe** Type **GO FIBERCRAFTS** at any prompt. Join in the fun in the "ACME Babes' Lancaster Doll Progressive" on GEnie—a quirky club in which members sew individual parts of dolls then shuffle them around the country for other sewers to complete. Type **NEEDLE** at any GEnie prompt. And head to Chapter 18 for directions on how to subscribe to the elinor peace bailey E-mail fan club. You'll also find in that chapter directions on how to obtain the Internet Doll FAQ with directions for making knitted doll clothes. Finally, the knitting chapter includes information on special software for automating the creation of knitted doll and bear clothes.

# 3

# OLD-FASHIONED QUILTS FROM COMPUTERS

*It's as if computers were made for creating beautiful quilts. Special quilting software lets you design blocks and borders, then see what the finished quilt will look like. It even prints out paper templates and stencils for quilting designs, then calculates fabric yardage. And that's just the beginning!*

Phil Hisley, author of VQuilt software, says an elderly woman once accosted him at a craft show. "She accused me of ruining the art of quilting by encouraging quilters to use computers to create quilts," he says, still haunted by the memory. "She claimed it isn't quilting unless you sew blocks with paper pieces." Such old-guard quilters are the minority, however. Most have embraced computers as the most empowering design tool since the invention of the color wheel. A computer lets you test your designs before cutting into the fabric. You can flip blocks, rotate pieces, test different colors and fabric textures, add or delete borders, change quilt dimensions, and envision what the finished quilt will look like on your bed, all on your computer screen. Once you've settled on a design, the software calculates yardage, prints the blocks and paper templates—as many as you want in the blink of an eye—and even prints quilting stencils. Then, once you've completed the quilt, you can use your laser or ink-jet printer to print custom-designed quilt labels on muslin. You can also use your computer and printer to make "remembrance quilts," in which the blocks contain transfers of beloved family photos. (You'll find directions in the next chapter.)

"So why even bother sewing the quilt?" you ask. Why not let the computer just print a picture of it? Lest you fear, like the woman at the craft show, that quilt-making is getting too high tech, rest assured that beyond the initial design stages, the relationship between you and your quilt has not changed. You are still guaranteed hundreds of cozy hours with fabric piled on your lap and pins falling on the floor. Your cat will still ingest a half spool of expensive Mettler thread, and you will still forgo at least two dinner invitations so that you can crawl around on the living-room floor, basting the top to the batting. Most important, you will still enjoy that final victorious moment when you realize that a work of art has sprung from your crooked stitches, and you can tuck it around a loved one and feel happy for both of you. Isn't that what quilting is all about?

## How to Buy Quilting Software

*W*hen it comes to buying software to design quilts, you have two basic choices: You can buy special-purpose software like Electric Quilt or Quilt-Pro, or you can buy a general-purpose graphic design program like CorelDRAW! The virtue of the quilting programs is that they automate many of the design stages. They come with libraries of pre-designed blocks and borders that you can easily arrange, size, and color. They print paper templates, complete with seam allowances, and they calculate yardage. They even offer you fabric designs that you can use to visualize on your computer screen how the finished blocks will look. The people who've developed this software are experienced quilters. When you call for technical support you'll not only get computer help, you may get quilting advice as well. These software packages are relatively low priced, ranging from $40 to $110. For all they offer, they're a good deal, especially compared with other craft software.

Graphic design programs like Adobe Illustrator or CorelDRAW!, on the other hand, offer more design freedom than quilt software. If your quilt designs move beyond traditional evenly placed blocks (say with bargello designs or tessellated blocks), or if you plan to create elaborately pieced or appliquéd scenes with many different shapes, you'll find quilt-design software too restrictive. Only professional graphics software will give you the tools you need to create truly ground-breaking quilt designs. Graphics software also lets you use computer clipart, digitized photos, and your own scanned drawings as the basis of a quilt design.

## *Here's How Graphics Programs and Quilting Software Compare*

Say you want to create a bed quilt with a giant intricately pieced penguin in the center. You have a computer picture of a penguin (see Figure 4-10 in the next chapter), and you want to place it on a grid on the computer screen and "fill it" with different geometric shapes to create its feathers, beak, wings and so on. With graphics software like CorelDRAW!, you "import" your picture, and then draw quilt pieces on top of it. (see Figure 4-11 in the next chapter). (Actually, it's a little more complicated than that, but you get the idea.) You can't do this kind of designing with quilt software, because the quilt design programs generally restrict you to designing with blocks and don't allow you to import images. Although they will let you draw freehand, your drawing is restricted to simple arcs and lines.

Other disadvantages of quilt software include the fact that although the packages let you design your own blocks, some limit your ability to design borders and sashes. Also, while they usually let you design symmetrical appliqué designs, some are not suited for drawing more naturalistic appliqué patterns, like those in Baltimore album quilts.

The major drawback to graphics software is the amount of time required to learn to use it. Expect to spend at least a week playing with the package and learning its basics before you begin designing Dresden plates. Quilt-making software, on the other hand, can have you designing quilts in minutes. Also, graphics software is expensive, often costing $500 or more, whereas quilting software costs about $100; and graphics packages don't calculate yardage.

Which kind of software is for you? By far the best quilt programs are Electric Quilt and Quilt-Pro. I have never encountered a quilter who has used them who was not satisfied with their purchase. You can create scrumptious quilt designs in minutes with these programs, and they relieve you of the fiddle-faddle of measuring triangles and calculating fabric needs. You'll find commercial online services like GEnie swimming in original block designs that other quilters have created with these programs. (See Chapters 12 through 19 for discussions of the various online resources and Internet.)

Quilting software programs have a video-game–like quality. I find them as addictive as my male friends find *Doom.* I often leave the quilting programs running on my office PC all day, playing with them whenever I'm on the phone, creating drunkard's path variations until my eyes cross. I just can't leave them alone. By the same token, many quilters swear by CorelDRAW! or Adobe Illustrator and wouldn't trade them for anything. I prefer quilting software to drawing or painting software because it's simple to use, and the top-of-the-line programs like Electric Quilt come with beautiful predesigned quilt blocks. These programs easily pay for themselves just by virtue of the fact that they make me less enthusiastic about buying paper quilt patterns and books. Their ability to precisely calculate yardage needs means an end to over buying fabric too.

If you buy both a quilting program and a general-purpose drawing program, I don't think you'll be indulging yourself too much; many quilt designers use both. After all, just think of all the money your significant other spent last month on that tower computer without a power supply.

## What If You'd Rather Buy a Drawing Program?

If drawing programs are your desire, a good choice is CorelDRAW! An older release (version 3 at $149, $99 if you buy it on CD) may be sufficient for you. It's cheaper than the current version ($649) and requires less computer hardware to run (Corel Corp., 1600 Carling Ave., Ottawa, Ontario, Canada CD K1Z 8R7, 800/836-7274). Other good choices are Adobe Illustrator for $595 (Adobe Systems, 1585 Charleston Rd., Mountain View, CA, 94039 800/888-6293) or Freehand for $595 (Macromedia, 600 Townsend St., Suite 310W, San Francisco, CA 91433, 800/989-3762).

Macintosh users will like SuperPaint for $49.95 from Adobe or, at the high end, Canvas for $400 (Deneba Software, 7400 Southwest 87th Ave., Miami, FL 33173, 800/622-6827).

*Note: You'll find these programs sold at much lower prices through computer mail-order retailers like PC/Mac Connection (800/800-1111).*

## A Quilter's Drawing Needs Are Simple

As far as designing quilts is concerned, your drawing needs are simple. You want to be able to draw symmetrical blocks with precise measurements. To do this, you'll need an on-screen ruler and an adjustable grid that you can "snap" lines to, which means align them with invisible grid lines. Tools to draw a variety of geometric shapes are also helpful. You want to be able to import and export computer graphics in a variety of formats (.GIF, .TIF, and .PCX are the basics) and size them to precise dimensions. Ideally, you should be able to import and colorize "fill" patterns so that you can fill the blocks with fabric patterns. A large collection of clipart and fonts is also fun. These basic features are in most drawing programs. (An exception is the Paintbrush drawing program in Windows and Windows 95. It won't let you draw with precision because it has no on-screen ruler or grid.)

Before you buy a drawing program, find out from the manufacturer whether your computer has enough "muscle" to run it. The top-of-the-line programs often require top-of-the-line computers with lots of memory, disk capacity, and fast processors (486s or high-powered Quadras are standard for some programs). If you have an older computer, ask the software vendor if you can buy an older version of the program, one that was designed to run on your machine. Secondhand computer stores are also good places to find graphics software that runs on "oldie but goodie" computers.

## Electric Quilt 2 Is Positively Electric

*E*lectric Quilt (EQ), by Penny McMorris, host of the TV show *The Great American Quilt,* and her husband, mathematician Dean Neumann, has been the top quilt software for years, and for good reason. You can use it to quickly design beautiful quilts and blocks, color them with thousands of different fabrics, then print templates and calculate fabric requirements. You couldn't design blocks with curves with the first release of the program—a major drawback—but Electric Quilt 2 remedies that with an easy-to-use drawing feature.

You can design sashes, custom borders, plus medallion quilts with multiple borders. Most other quilt programs don't allow you to do the latter—or at least not as easily as Electric Quilt 2 does. You can even design fabric using an on-screen grid, then color the fabric with any of the millions of colors available on your computer.

To design a quilt with EQ, you might start by picking from its wide range of fabrics, from historical collections (like '50s housedress prints or the 1880 indigo collection), to contemporary ones (like the denim collection, the bandanna, or the Ashanti). You'll also find fabric collections from well-known designers like Nancy Crow. You can select the color palette in which fabrics will appear on your screen, choosing from dozens of schemes like the Andy Warhol or Paul Cezanne palettes, or the Greek pottery or Wedgewood ones. You can also mix your own colors.

Electric Quilt's "sketchbook" is where you store your fabrics, color palettes, and any block designs you choose from its library of over a thousand designs. You might place in your sketchbook, say, a log cabin block, a maple leaf, and a Mexican rose (see Figure 3-2). EQ's block collection ranges from appliqué, to traditional paper piecing, to contemporary. Or you can design your own blocks.

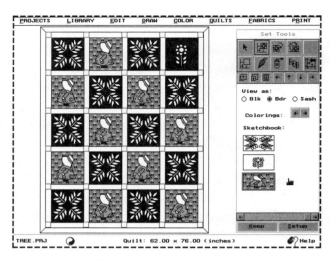

Figure 3-1
Laying out complex quilt designs is a snap with Electric Quilt. Choose from a bevy of different blocks in the library, then lay them out in your own design. Recolor different quilt areas and reposition blocks until you get the design just right.

Figure 3-2
Electric Quilt comes with a block library that includes patterns for over a thousand blocks, including many scrumptious appliqué designs like these Mexican rose variations.

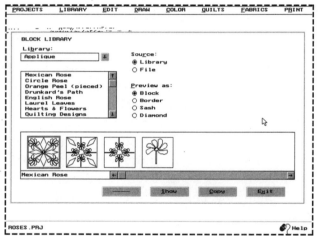

You draw pieced blocks by placing straight lines and boxes on a simple drawing grid. You draw appliqué blocks in another drawing pad that provides the bare essentials: tools for drawing Bézier lines, circles, and boxes. The drawback to this arrangement is that if you want to create pieced blocks having curved lines (like drunkard's path blocks), you must use the appliqué drawing pad. Then, when it's time to print the block, you can't print templates with ¼" seam allowances. Instead, EQ will print only a picture of the full block. Because there's no limit on block size (except when printing pieced blocks, where you'll be limited to printing out templates that fit on one printed page), you can use the appliqué sketch pad to create large appliqué designs for the center of a quilt.

You can color blocks at any stage in your design. However, it's easiest to color them before you start placing them on your quilt (see Figure 3-3). With a paintbrush tool, you fill in blocks with fabrics or with solid colors from your sketchbook palette. You can create multiple coloring variations of each block design, store them in your sketchbook, and then fill the quilt with the variations. You can also recolor all the patches and blocks once they're placed in the quilt layout.

To create the quilt itself, you specify the size of the blocks and the type of layout, whether horizontal, on-point, variable point, or baby block. You can create a layout with blocks of different sizes, as long as the blocks are of comparable ratios. For instance, some blocks could be 5" × 5" while others could be 10" × 10". You tell the program how many blocks across and long the quilt will be; you specify whether you want sashing and, if so, how wide; and you specify the width and number of borders.

Electric Quilt displays a grid of the quilt layout, which you then use to arrange blocks. You arrange the blocks by selecting them from your sketchbook, then positioning them on the quilt with the mouse pointer. You can place as many blocks on the quilt as you like, and once they're in place you can flip and rotate them.

Border styles can be mitered, corner, long vertical, long horizontal, blocks, diamonds, squares, point, and point corners. Each can be up to 25" wide and can be created with the drawing or appliqué sketchbook or by elongating one of the thousand-plus blocks in the block library. You can create sashes between blocks and quilt stencils in a similar way by drawing your own stencil patterns or using outlines of any of the blocks in the library as stencils that you can then widen or elongate to fit the quilt's dimensions. You can place the stencils on top of the design once the quilt is laid out. When you have finished, you can print out the individual quilt blocks, plus stencils, templates, and fabric requirements.

The EQ manual is one of the best I've read in years (though you'll still need to spend an evening with it in order to learn how to use the program). Computer newcomers will find it clear and full of helpful tutorials that show how to design quilts. Another nice touch in the program is its help feature. If you have a question about something on your screen, just click on it with the right mouse button and a help file pops up explaining its function. The manual doesn't include directions on everything though (there are no directions on how to delete a block from a quilt, for instance). So if you're a subscriber to any online service or have access to Internet, you'll definitely want to sign up for the EQ2 Mailing List to get answers to your questions (see Chapter 18 for directions).

*"Our guild seems to have a profusion of little old ladies sitting around comparing quilt designs on their laptops."*
— comment spotted in QuiltNet

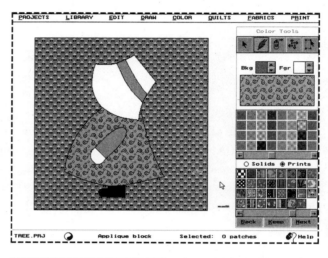

**Figure 3-3**
You can color Sunbonnet Sue—or any other blocks from EQ2's library or your own design—with thousands of different fabric designs and colors. Create multiple color variations for Sue, then save them to the sketchbook and later lay them out one by one in the quilt. It's like what you do on the floor of your living room but so much quicker and easier.

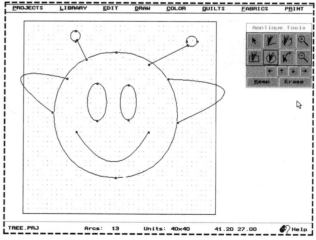

**Figure 3-4**
This lifelike portrait of my husband was created in Electric Quilt's appliqué design drawing board. However, because EQ2's design tools are limited to drawing circles, squares, straight lines, and disciplined curves, I find drawing naturalistic designs like those in Baltimore album quilts to be easier in a full-featured drawing program.

*Note: If you buy Electric Quilt, be sure to join the Electric Quilt mailing list on Internet. You'll be able to talk to hundreds of other EQ users and find out the latest hot design tips, plus get answers to technical brain-teasers. Find out more about it in Chapter 18 on Internet.*

Electric Quilt's shortcomings are the same as those of the other quilt programs. EQ won't let you design large non-block-based pieced quilts or appliqué scenes that cover an entire quilt. For these projects you'll need to use a drawing program.

The only glitch I ran into with EQ is that it has problems with some older mouse drivers (a mouse driver is a program that powers the mouse). Symptoms are smeared screens and menus that don't pop up when you double-click. Penny McMorris recommends using a mouse driver newer than 1991 and an up-to-date copy of DOS. (Some mouse manufacturers provide driver updates for free. Call the company that made your mouse and ask.) Some quilters have also experienced printing problems. If you experience these or other problems, contact The Electric Quilt Company for advice (they're very helpful). If you can't get things working, they will refund your money.

All in all, Electric Quilt 2 is a solid buy, offering more design possibilities and options than any other quilt software on the market. The company has a Macintosh version under development called MacQuilt, which should definitely be worth the wait.

The Electric Quilt Company
1039 Melrose St.
Bowling Green, OH 43402
800/356-4219
Price: $110
Requirements: 286 PC (386 or 486 recommended), DOS 5.0 or later, 640K, a hard disk, and a mouse. Not all mouse drivers are compatible. Your best bets are a 1991 or later Logitech or Microsoft mouse driver.

# How to Create Your Own Hand-Dyed Color Gradations in Electric Quilt

*by Penny McMorris*

You can create a special palette of hand-dyed color gradations to use when designing quilts in EQ. These instructions come from Edith Tanniru, owner of American Beauty Fabrics in Dewitt, NY, specialists in hand-dyed cloth.

1 In the Quilts menu choose Toolbox and then click on the RGB tool. This brings up the 12 base color chips of whatever color palette you are currently using.

2 Click on the first color chip—the one in the upper-left corner—and set the slider bars below to pure red (R = 63, G = 0, B = 0).

3 Click on the second chip—the one just below—and set the slider bars for the same red as the first chip.

4 Now, move up the green and blue sliders in equal amounts until the second chip is lightened as much as you want. (Adding the two other colors equally has the effect of adding white.) You might start by moving in units of 10, but you may want to adjust this some to get the gradation right from chip to chip.

5 Click on the third chip—the bottom one in the first column. Adjust it, then start on the second column. Always set the new chip to the color of chip one and start adjusting from there. You can make up to 12 gradations, though eight is about the maximum your eyes can distinguish. If you do six gradations, you can do two different gradation groups in one palette.

6 When your palette looks the way you want it to, click on Install and then click on OK in the Palette Installation dialog box. Choose Toolbox from the Color menu and you'll find your new color gradations ready to use.

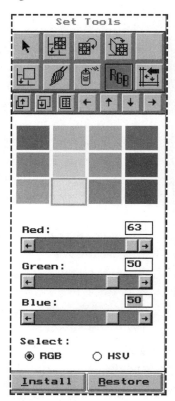

Figure 3-5
This is the RGB tool you use to create your own color palette in EQ2.

Save your new color palette as a project. (You don't need to put any blocks or quilts in the project.) If you name the project with a color name like Blue, the next time you open the Blue project you'll find your colors in the Color Toolbox. If you color blocks and quilts with this palette, save them under a name (like Blueblock), by using the SAVE AS command. By giving your project a new name, you keep your Blue color palette stored in a project of its own so that you can use it without having the file fill up with quilts and blocks.

---

**TIP**

*If you don't own a copy of Electric Quilt but would like to exchange quilt designs with users of this program or download EQ block designs from online services, get a copy of the free utility EQViewer. EQViewer lets you view Electric Quilt designs and export them to PCX format for use with other graphics programs or for printing. You'll find it online as file VQUILT.EXE (yes, the filename for the program VQuilt is the same as that for EQViewer).*

## Quilt-Pro Brings Quilt Design Heaven to Windows

*I* think I probably love Quilt-Pro as much as Electric Quilt. Quilt-Pro offers Windows users powerful design tools with an easy-to-use interface. It offers almost all the quilt design features of Electric Quilt, and it's quicker to learn, easier to use for designing pieced blocks with curved seams, and it excels in the fun factor. Bright, bold graphics and intuitive design make quilt designing with Quilt-Pro easier than playing Castle Wolfenstein 3-D.

What Quilt-Pro lacks is the ability to design quilts with more than one border (Quilt-Pro Systems hopes this will change in an upcoming release) and the ability to insert blocks into borders the way Electric Quilt does. Automatic quilt layouts are limited to horizontal and on-point, although you can do other layouts if you don't mind doing them manually. (The company hopes to offer a diagonal layout with optional sashing in the future.) Quilt-Pro also lacks Electric Quilt's rich fabric and color palettes, although its 256 colors and 250 fabric styles (that you can color) probably will be sufficient for most quilters. You can create more fabric designs by painting them with Windows' Paint or any other paint program or by using scanned images of real fabric (like those in Figure 4-6 in the next chapter).

To design a quilt, you choose a block from Quilt-Pro's library of 250 predesigned blocks, which includes everything from nine-patches to appliqué blocks. Or you can design your own. When you design pieced blocks in Electric Quilt, you do it by drawing lines. In Quilt-Pro you draw lines or curves, or you can pick patches from a radio-button menu of eleven geometric patch shapes. That means it's easier to design pieced blocks with straight lines in Electric Quilt, but easier to design ones with curved lines in Quilt-Pro (somewhat easier, for working with the curve-drawing tools can be sticky because it's hard to get curves the way you want them). When it comes to designing appliqué blocks, the two programs are roughly similar and there's no limit to how large blocks can be. Both programs allow blocks large enough to use as an appliqué center to a quilt, although border designing is narrowly limited to a single pieced or appliquéd border.

Quilt-Pro lets you color blocks with solid colors or choose from 250 fabric styles that you color yourself. The process of coloring is as simple as clicking on the patches with the paint-brush icon.

Laying out the quilt with Quilt-Pro takes only seconds. As with Electric Quilt, Quilt-Pro lets you put as many different styles of blocks in the quilt as you want, with as many blocks horizontally and vertically as you want. You specify block size, how you want the blocks arranged (the program lets you specify repeating sequences if you want), and whether you want sashing. You can then specify the width of the sashing and the border. For the border and sashing, you can choose from over a hundred pieced designs in the Quilt-Pro library, or

**Figure 3-6**
Quilt-Pro makes designing a scrap quilt even more fun than playing Core Wars. The pieced scalloped border is from Quilt-Pro's border library. Designing the blocks, laying them out, and coloring them took minutes.

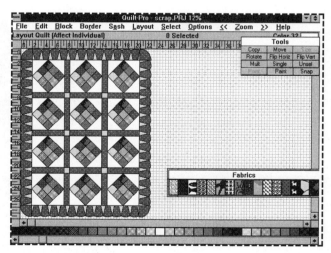

you can design your own. Once your quilt is laid out, you can easily play with color by changing, say, all the blues in the sashing, or the reds in the appliqué tulips. You can also tinker with block arrangement, sizing of blocks and borders, or anything else in the design.

A library of fifty stencils from the Stencil Company is included with Quilt-Pro. I think these look more like real quilting stencils than the block patterns used as stencils in Electric Quilt, but that's my own preference. I also find Quilt-Pro's stencils easier to see on the quilt design than the arrangement in Electric Quilt. If you don't like any of the predesigned stencils, you can draw your own in Quilt-Pro and size them to the appropriate dimensions.

Quilt-Pro, like Electric Quilt, will calculate yardage and print out blocks, templates, and stencils. I ran into several trouble spots in Quilt-Pro. Selecting and moving or copying a block or portion of a block is awkward, if not sometimes impossible. Dragging and clicking the mouse to select an area of a design is not as foolproof a procedure as it is in paint and drawing programs. In Quilt-Pro the quilt patches you select are rarely the quilt patches Quilt-Pro *thinks* you selected. Too, when you try to copy and paste a block or sections of a block to another graphics program, the entire selected area doesn't always end up in the graphics program. Finally, when you attempt to move a section of a block or design, Quilt-Pro "ungroups" the block, causing your patches to disassemble in what looks like a computer screen version of what happens when your cat walks over your quilt patches on the floor. These things make

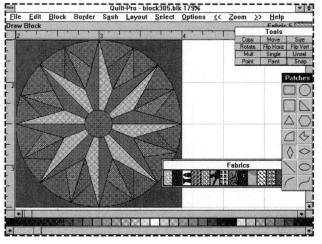

**Figure 3-7**
In Quilt-Pro, you'd design a block like the mariner's compass by using the patch pallet on the right to create circles and triangles. Then you'd color it with the fabric pallet and colors displayed on the bottom of the screen. There are 256 colors; you can click through them quickly with your mouse.

complex quilt designing awkward. Another glitch in Quilt-Pro is a conflict with Windows' screen saver. I found that if Windows' screen saver should decide to blank the screen while Quilt-Pro is painting a quilt layout (which can take a while), the program will sometimes crash. The remedy is to turn off the screen saver before running Quilt-Pro.

Which program is better, Electric Quilt or Quilt-Pro? It's tough to say, as both are exceptional programs. Because I do a lot of work with curved pieced blocks like drunkard's path and orange peel, and because I like the Stencil Company templates, I find myself drawn to Quilt-Pro. I also like Quilt-Pro's simplicity, the brightness of the blocks on the screen, and the fact that it's Windows software. On the other hand, Electric Quilt offers more design possibilities with its big block library and all the wonderful fabric and layout options. Advanced quilt designers probably will prefer it instead. You may want to buy both.

*Note: For a different perspective on Quilt-Pro, see the accompanying review of the Macintosh version by Gloria Hansen. The PC and Macintosh versions of the program are alike in most respects.*

Computer Quilter's Newsletter is a bimonthly newsletter devoted to exploring the world of quilt designing on computers. Subscriptions are $16.95 for six issues (Bon Creations, 4072 E. 22nd St., #329, Tucson, AZ 85711).

Quilt-Pro Systems
P.O. Box 560692
The Colony, TX 75056
214/625-7765

Price: $95 for PC or Macintosh version; Quilt-Pro also sells disks of quilt block, border, and fabric designs for $19.95 each; a book called *Quilt-Pro Illustrated* for $19.95 includes a catalog of quilt block designs in the program so that you can easily find the ones you're looking for without fishing through directories. You can purchase it together with one of the add-on disks for $29.95.

Requirements: PC version—386 PC or higher, Windows 3.0 or above, 4 megs RAM, hard disk, mouse, EGA or higher graphics; Macintosh version—Macintosh II or higher with System 7 or higher, 4 megs RAM, Color Quick Draw

A demonstration version is available for $5 from Quilt-Pro Systems; the $5 will be refunded if you eventually order the program directly from the company. It's also available in the quilting forum libraries on all the major online services. Look for QPDEMO.ZIP and QPDEMO.SEA.

> **TIP**
>
> Macintosh users will find that pairing Quilt-Pro with the low-cost drawing program SuperPaint will give the greatest flexibility (and fun) in designing quilts and quilt blocks. See Gloria Hansen's accompanying tips on pp. 82–83 about using a drawing program to design quilts on a Macintosh.

# Quilt-Pro 1.0 Is Top Quilt Software for Macintosh Users, but Serious Designers May Prefer a Drawing Program

QUILT-PRO for the Macintosh is similar to the version for PCs, offering a library of 250 block patterns, 750 fabrics, and 50 quilting stencils. It's easy to install—you click on the Quilt-Pro folder and the subfolders of the blocks, borders, fabric, pallets, projects, and sashes libraries are displayed. The program opens to a work area where you design your quilt with the help of a floating tool box and fabric and color palettes.

To begin a project, you specify whether you want to draw a block, border, sash, or entire quilt. Quilt-Pro can create a work area with snap-to isometric grids at any angle, and this creates an exciting wealth of design possibilities. It's as easy to create a block design based on a 60-degree grid as it is a 45-degree grid. I selected "Block" and began drawing. But rather than letting you draw with lines like a general-purpose drawing program does (and Electric Quilt for PCs does too), Quilt-Pro restricts you to creating blocks by drawing "patches."

Think of how you design when you arrange fabric pieces on a design wall; that's analogous to how you design with Quilt-Pro. A patch can be a triangle, square, rectangle, or other shape including curved pieces (created with the Bézier curve tool or arc tool which, like Judy Heim, I also found challenging to use). Although I found putting together blocks with patches awkward at first, so long as I kept the design-wall image in mind, all went well.

It's easy to place patches in blocks using the patch guidelines. These are grids of lines that appear on your work area. You create them by specifying the size and number of squares the block is divided into. For example, you'd draft a nine-patch by using patch guidelines arranged with three squares across three

rows. Because you also specify size, the guidelines are drawn the actual size. You can zoom in or out of areas of the block as you work.

Quilt-Pro's strength lies in its ability to let you quickly create quilt blocks—then duplicate, flip, rotate, or stretch them, and lay them out into a quilt top. All you need to do is open a new project, choose a layout, and open the block you wish to use. Almost immediately the screen fills with the chosen design in beautiful color. With just a few clicks of the mouse you can change colors, fabric designs, and add or delete borders and sashes. Playing "what if" games — what if the sash is red instead of blue? what if the layout is on-point?—is addictive. You can import PICT graphics, including scans, and use them as fabric fills. A color printer adds to the fun, and I had wonderful

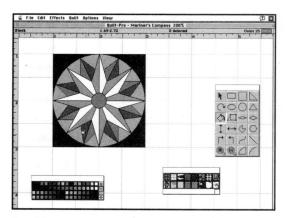

Figure 3-8

Quilt-Pro for the Macintosh is nearly identical to the version for the PC. You can design your block using any of the tools in the tool palette, then fill patches with fabrics and colors from those palettes.

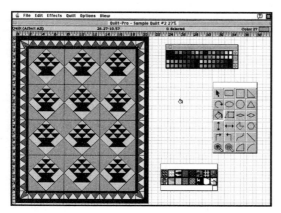

Figure 3-9

Once you lay out your quilt in Quilt-Pro for the Macintosh, it's not too late to change block colors and fabrics or experiment with borders.

results printing color quilt designs with Apple's Color Stylewriter Pro.

Quilt-Pro will print a list of the fabric yardage necessary to make the quilt, as well as print templates with squared seam-allowance points. Unfortunately, you can't print templates to a file, nor can you view them on the screen. You can't view, cut, paste, save, or rearrange which templates you want to print.

While this is an impressive program, Quilt-Pro has limitations that will lead a serious designer to want to supplement it with SuperPaint or Canvas. For instance, the current version lets you create only a single border for a quilt, so creating a medallion-style top is not easy. Working with curves is also not as fluid as with more sophisticated drawing programs. When it's time to print, you cannot adjust margins, so everything prints at the very top edge and left margin of your pages. Nor can you add text

to any design you plan to print out, and Quilt-Pro doesn't print block designs for use in flip and sew. While you can cut and paste quilt block designs into other programs, Quilt-Pro doesn't support System 7's publish and subscribe features.

The first version of the program does suffer bugs. After you group patches into a block, you can only duplicate the block once. The block then reverts to a collection of ungrouped patches. Also, I was unable to copy and paste blocks properly into other applications, like drawing programs. Whenever I tried to copy a portion of a design from Quilt-Pro, the design would break into fragments and only a portion of it would appear in the application. Quilt-Pro intends to fix those problems, so look for a release later than 1.0.

I like Quilt-Pro and am confident most quilt-makers will enjoy it too. It's not a high-end drawing/paint program, but it is the very best Macintosh-specific quilt design program currently on the market. Quilters who enjoy using traditional blocks and layouts and/or participate in block-of-the-month swaps will be in their glory with this program because it will let them pull into the program traditional designs, size them to their needs and play with colors, then print out templates and yardage needs. It's also supereasy to learn and comes with a well-written manual. This program can only get better.

GLORIA HANSEN *is a member of the NeedleArts Forum on GEnie. Her innovative quilt designs have won numerous awards and have been featured in books and magazines and on TV. She lives in Hightstown, New Jersey.*

# HOW TO CREATE FABRIC FILLS IN SUPERPAINT FOR USE IN COLORING BLOCKS IN QUILT-PRO

BY GLORIA HANSEN

Quilt-Pro is unique in that it lets you import fabric patterns created in another paint or drawing program, or fabric scanned with a hand-held scanner, into Quilt-Pro for use in coloring your quilts. Here's how to do so using the popular Macintosh program Super-Paint:

1. After starting up SuperPaint, select "Document Info" under File in the menu bar.

2. Set the width and height to 1" × 1" and then select "Okay." This will create a small page on your screen.

3. Under View select "Zoom In." (Zooming in will give you a magnified image, which I find easier to work with than the small 1"× 1" area.).

4. Either select a pattern from the preloaded ones or create one using SuperPaint's various tools (like the airbrush tool). If you select a pattern, simply use the square tool and make a small square filled with the pattern.

5. Select "Fill" under Paint in the menu bar. The entire 1" × 1" box should fill with the selected pattern. (It is important to fill the entire document.)

6. Name the document any way you wish (like "green mix 1" for example) and save it—very important—as a PICT file.

Now head to Quilt-Pro:

1. Launch Quilt-Pro and double-click on one of the fabrics in its fabric palette. Doing so will open the Open File dialog box.

2. Scroll to your saved SuperPaint file (that you created above) and select it.

You can create many different types of fabric fills in SuperPaint. For example, to create gradations of solid colors, select a solid color and lighten it (select "Lighten" under the Paint menu bar item) or darken it (select "Darken"). You can also create interesting fabric patterns using the airbrush, gradations, and other tools. Once you get started, you will be glad you kept your fabric fill files small!

---

### NOTES

*In order for PICT files to work correctly as fabric fills in Quilt-Pro, the entire document must be filled with the image. This is why I use a small document size (1"× 1"). While you can make your document whatever size you desire, keep in mind that a 1"× 1" PICT file is approximately 18K, whereas an 8 1/2"× 11" PICT file is approximately 400K. The smaller file will be much easier to work with and will take up much less hard disk space.*

*For easy access to your fabric files, place them in a new folder and move that folder into the Quilt-Pro folder. You can save a particular palette through Quilt-Pro following the directions in the manual.*

# VQuilt Is a Low-Cost Quilt Design Alternative for PCs

*V*Quilt may be your ticket if you don't need a library of a thousand quilt block designs or automatic layout of quilt blocks into isometric designs, but you want a simple design tool to occasionally create a pieced or appliqué block. Priced at only $39.95, VQuilt was designed by a middle-school math teacher as both an easy-to-use quilt design tool and a sneaky way to teach kids geometry. It's a purposely no-frills tool for quilters for whom geometric veracity has always been an elusive goal.

VQuilt lets you choose from a library of ninety blocks that includes lots of nine-patches, one appliqué, and one basket pattern. You can design your own blocks on a grid using some basic drawing tools like a pencil, a square-making tool, and a zoom feature. Freehand drawing with VQuilt is easier than with Quilt-Pro or Electric Quilt because you're not limited to using the design-style Bézier curve tools found in those programs. On the other hand, VQuilt leaves it up to you to get the curves smooth and symmetrical. You click on dots to connect lines, then color the shapes with either basic or custom-mixed colors. VQuilt has no fabric library.

To arrange the blocks into a quilt, you go to another screen where you specify block size, number of blocks, horizontal or on-point layout, and size and type of border (you're limited to either mitered or sashed). While you can lay out quilt blocks any way you like and include blocks of different styles and sizes, the blocks must be square and lined up. You can also design your own pieced or appliqué sashes and borders, even quilt stencils, but not without a hefty bit of work with the drawing tools (a process that's slowed by weak documentation on the drawing tools).When you've finished laying out the blocks, you can print your templates. VQuilt won't calculate yardage for you—an omission made purposely by the math teacher, probably as a way to get us all to think hard about those tenth grade geometry classes we skipped.

All told, VQuilt is a wonderful little program, even if you only use it to draw the geometrically perfect shapes required in block piecing. Best of all, you can give VQuilt a trial run before buying it by downloading a nearly full-featured demo version available on all the major online services. Look for the files DEMOVQLT.EXE and DEMOVQLT.TXT (on CompuServe DEMOVQ.EXE and DEMOVQ.TXT).

Computer Systems Associates
P.O. Box 129
Jarrettsville, MD 21084-9998
410/557-6871
Price: $39.95
Requirements: DOS 3.0 or greater, 500K RAM, 286 or higher, will run on 8088 (if you can stand the slow speed), hard disk, mouse

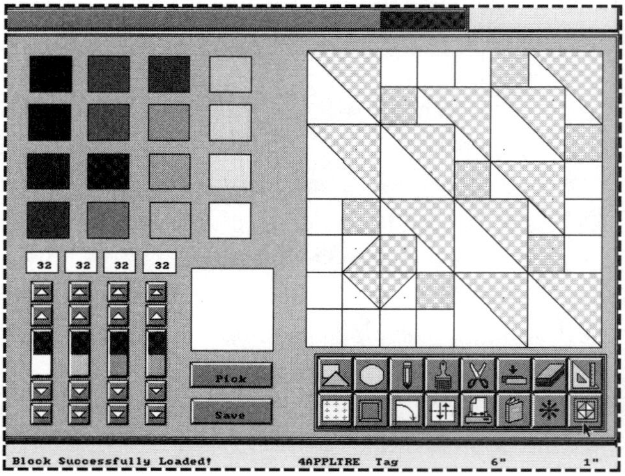

**Figure 3-10**
Designing quilt blocks with geometric precision is easy with low-cost VQuilt. This no-frills quilt design program for PCs will print block templates, but you can't use it for designing pieced sashes or borders.

# Other Quilting Software Is Available, but You May Not Like It as Much

*T*here are other quilt-designing programs for sale, but their capabilities are limited compared with the programs described in this chapter.

## PCQuilt

PCQuilt by Nina Antz (7061 Lynch Rd., Sebastopol, CA 95472; 707/823-8494). This program is available for both PCs and color Macs for $35. PCQuilt was one of the first quilt programs on the market. It includes a library of 100 block designs, but it's very limited. You can use it to design blocks with straight lines (curve drawing is not supported) and to create multiple borders, but it doesn't print templates or blocks to scale. The PC version lets you print only what's displayed on the screen, using the PRINT-SCRN key. The blocks on the screen are tiny and I found the grid hard to see. The software doesn't have a printed manual; instead, it's found in a file on the program's floppy disk.

PCQuilt is available as shareware on several computer services. For the Macintosh version, look for the file PCQUILT.SEA or PQUILT.SEA. The PC version is QUILTA.EXE.

## Quilter's Design Studio

Quilter's Design Studio by QuiltSoft (P.O. Box 19946, San Diego, CA 92159-0946; 619/583-2970) is available for both PCs and Macs for $99. It has limited features and awkward design. I found it hard to learn and not nearly as intuitive as Quilt-Pro or EQ2.

## Bargello Designer and Fabric Designer

Even though Bargello Designer and Fabric Designer are not quilt design programs like EQ, you may want to consider them, both by Discover Productions (5305 Laguna Ct., Byron, CA, 94514-9517; 510/634-6022). With Bargello Designer 2.0 you can create exquisite flame-like bargello designs using fabric and color palettes of your choosing. Take a look at Figure 3-11 to see what I mean. (You can create bargello designs with Electric Quilt and Quilt-Pro too, but you must create them manually by building different size blocks and painting them individually—a laborious process, especially if the bargello design you want to create is an elaborate one.) Bargello Designer will take "strata" of up to a dozen different fabric patterns in the colors you specify and paint them into remarkable designs on your computer screen, according to your directions. In a sense, it's a computerization of the techniques of "bargello queen" Marilyn Doheny, from her book *Bargello Tapestry Quilts.*

Unfortunately, the only way to get a bargello quilt from your PC to your sewing table is to print out a color screen to a page and then improvise with fabric and sheers.

Fabric Designer 2.0 lets you create intricate fabric patterns with custom palettes, then export them to bitmap and PCX graphic formats to use with Bargello Designer or Quilt-Pro. It includes a feature to create the most breathtaking moiré fabric patterns you will ever see on your PC screen.

Both programs were written as tools for use in teaching a bargello quilting class, which may explain some memory problems and nagging glitches as well as a lack of documentation. Hopefully, the snafus will be fixed in future releases.

The programs are $45 each and run on a PC with a 386 processor or higher and at least 2 megs of extended memory.

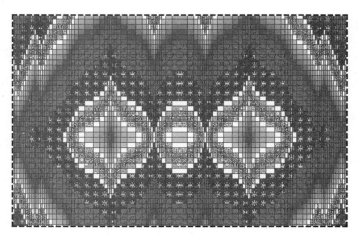

**Figure 3-11**
With Bargello Designer you can create breathtaking designs like this one for bargello quilts. Unfortunately, there's no easy way to get the quilt from your computer screen to your sewing machine.

# 4

## MORE WAYS TO USE
## YOUR COMPUTER IN QUILTING

*From printing quilt templates to transforming family photos into remembrance
quilts, your computer can serve a thousand creative uses in the sewing room.
Here are some ways your computer can speed up your quilt planning or
add a little fun and pizzazz to your projects.*

## How You Can Use a General-Purpose
## Drawing Program to Design Great Quilts

Whether you want to draw the petals of a Baltimore quilt or engineer the whorls of a modernistic one, an all-purpose drawing program like CorelDRAW! or SuperPaint can prove a more versatile tool than quilting software. But getting started can be a daunting task. What does it mean to "snap to grid"? And how can you print templates with ¼" seam allowances? Here are some tutorials from computer quilting pros to get you started.

**Figure 4-1**
Designing quilt blocks in a general-purpose drawing program is a snap. Start by setting up your on-screen grid to four grids per inch and activate the "Snap to Grid" feature. But it's not always as simple as drawing lines and coloring patches. In CorelDRAW!, you need to draw individual patches as "closed" objects in order to color them and create templates for them. See Jan Cabral's tutorial below for guidance.

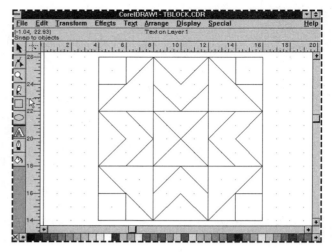

## CORELDRAW! QUILT TRICKS

*by Jan Cabral © 1995*

CorelDRAW! version 3.0 is a wonderful program for designing both traditional and contemporary quilts. While CorelDRAW! versions 4 and 5 add a few more goodies for quilters, version 3.0 has all the basic tools you need. Learning to use CorelDRAW! to design quilts takes a bit of patience. Here are some tips to get you going.

*If you buy CorelDRAW!, get a subscription to General Electric's GEnie. The NeedleArts Roundtable includes a discussion area devoted to using CorelDRAW! as a quilt design tool. Best of all, techno-quilter and Corel guru Jan Cabral is online answering new users' questions.*

## Designing and Coloring Patches

*I*f you're like most newcomers to CorelDRAW!, as soon as you install it you fire it up and draw a quilt block. When it's time to start coloring your block, though, CorelDRAW! won't let you. It will let you color the whole block but not individual patches. This is because Corel insists that you "close" any object before you fill it (or color it). For example, if you draw a 3" square and then bisect it with a diagonal line from one corner to the other, Corel will not recognize your drawing as consisting of two triangles that can be individually colored. Instead, you'll need to draw each triangle individually as a closed object. The quickest way to do this is to first draw a square, then select the square and press CTRL-V to convert its lines to curves. Now click on the Node Edit tool (second from top in the toolbar on the left-hand side of the screen) to delete one node and leave a triangle, as shown in Figure 4-2. You can create patches in other shapes using this technique.

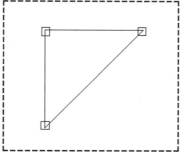

**Figure 4-2**
**To draw a triangular quilt patch, first draw a square, then select the square and press CTRL-V. Use the Node Edit tool to delete one node and leave a triangle.**

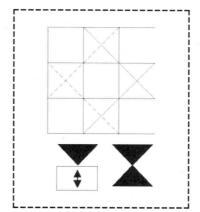

**Figure 4-3**
**Once you've closed a patch, you can duplicate it by pressing the "+" keys.**

## The Fastest Way to Draft a Block

The fastest way to draft a block is to draw it like you would with pencil and graph paper, not worrying about closing any objects. When you finish drawing the block, select the Layers Rollup tool by clicking on "Arrange/Layers Rollup." Now click on "Edit/Select All," press the right arrow in the Layers box, and click on "Move to." A fat arrow will appear asking you where you want to move the objects. Now click on "Guides" to convert the whole block to a guideline. Click on "Layer 1" to return to that layer, then turn on "Snap to Guidelines" (under Display) and you can quickly and easily make your closed pieces.

To duplicate a patch, press the "+" key; to mirror a patch, hold down the CTRL key and drag one of the center handles across itself. Tap the right mouse button before letting go to leave the original in place. (This is pretty fancy keyboard stuff and takes some practice. The trick is to hold down the CTRL key until the end.) (See Figure 4-3.)

## Printing Templates

To print templates (as in Figure 4-4), first make a duplicate of any patch using the "+" key. Move the duplicate patch to an empty space on the screen where you can work with it. Color the patch with a white fill and then click on the Outline tool. Now click on the second icon

**Figure 4-4**
To create quilting templates,
first fill your patch with white,
then give it a gray outline that's
½" larger than the patch—
half of which falls behind the
patch, giving it a ¼" outline
on the outside.

to get the Outline Rollup. Give the patch an outline with a width of .50, color it gray, and then put an X in the Behind Fill box by clicking in the box. (If you want templates with blunt corners, click on the Blunt Corners option.) Now click "Apply," and you have a template with a perfect ¼" seam allowance. Print your template by clicking on "Print/Selected Objects Only." Once you get the hang of this routine, you'll find that you can create templates from patches right inside a block layout.

## How to Design a Block-Based Quilt

*T*o design a block-based quilt, use the "CTRL/drag/click right mouse button" combination you learned earlier to lay out the blocks in your first row, then click on "Edit/Select-All" and use this same keyboard technique to make as many additional rows as you wish. Here's a timesaver: After you lay out the second row, press CTRL-R to repeat your last action and quickly duplicate the row.

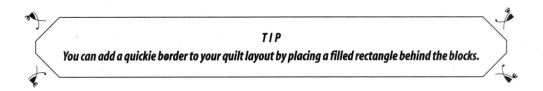

*TIP*
*You can add a quickie border to your quilt layout by placing a filled rectangle behind the blocks.*

**Figure 4-5**
You can test out quilting line designs on your
quilt layer by drawing them with CorelDRAW!,
then transferring the drawing to your quilt
design's guides layer.

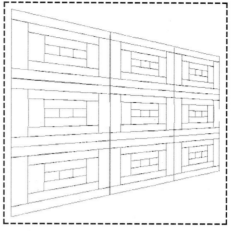

**Figure 4-6**
Courthouse Step blocks put into perspective for a three-dimensional effect.

## Designing Quilting Stencils

Here's how to design quilting lines for your quilt: First, draw your quilting design. Transfer it
to the guides layer like you did when you drafted your block. Double-click on the guides
layer in the Layers Rollup. Now select the color of your choice under Color Override.
Finally, move your design over a quilt block to see the effect.

## Printing Flip-and-Sew Blocks

You can print flip-and-sew blocks on either paper or muslin when the paper or muslin has
been ironed onto 8½" × 11" freezer paper. The flip-and-sew blocks can be distorted or put
into perspective and the ability to flip and sew will still work, although each piece becomes a
different size. Figure 4-6 shows an example of a group of Courthouse Step blocks that were
put into perspective, to give them a three-dimensional effect.

**Figure 4-7**
**Tessellated blocks are easy with a**
**drawing program like CorelDRAW!**

To create this effect, first group your blocks by selecting all of them; then press CTRL-G. Now click on "Effects/Edit Perspective." (The group should now have a dotted red line indicating the boundary of the perspective envelope.) Next, hold down both the CTRL and SHIFT keys and drag the bottom right node toward the top right node. Both nodes will move together to form a perfect perspective.

To print your three-dimensional blocks, select one block at a time and click on "Print/Selected Objects Only." If you care about the direction of the group of blocks, first do a mirror image of the entire group by clicking on "Edit/Select All." Then select "Transform, Stretch & Mirror/Horizontal Mirror" and choose "OK."

## Creating Tessellations

This same technique can be used to create tessellations, flipping and rotating the blocks so they fit together like a jigsaw puzzle.

To make the cube shown in Figure 4-7, follow these steps:

1 Make three 3" squares, as shown in Figure 4-8. Put a star from the Symbols Library into each block by pressing and holding the Text Tool to access the star icon. Then click on the block where you want the symbol to appear (select Star1 or Star2 from the list and scroll through the examples to find one you like).

80

**Figure 4-8**
**These three star-shaped blocks form the basis for the tessellated cube in Figure 4-7.**

**2** Decide which block will be the front, which will be the top, and which will be the side. Also decide whether you want to do this exercise in 30 or 45 degrees.

**3** Stretch the front and side views horizontally by the cosine of the angle of rotation (86.6% for 30 degrees or 70.7% for 45 degrees). To do this, click on "Transform" then "Stretch & Mirror," and fill in one of the two values in the Horizontal Stretch box. Click "OK."

**4** Rotate the top by 45 degrees.

**5** Skew the front view vertically by either a negative 45 or 30 degrees. Skew the side vertically by either a positive 45 or 30 degrees. To effect the skew, click on the "Select Tool" and double-click the object(s). Use the double arrow on the right-hand vertical side, and, while holding down the CTRL key to constrain it to 15-degree increments, drag the arrow until the status line shows either negative or positive 45 degrees.

**6** For the top, leave it alone for 45 degrees or stretch it horizontally 123% and vertically 71% for 30 degrees (use Transform/Stretch & Mirror and fill in the values).

**7** Now assemble your block!

*Jan Cabral teaches computer graphics to quilters nationwide. She is a consultant to Caryl Bryer Fallert and is on the Board of Directors of the Ohio chapter of the Association of CorelDRAW! Artists and Designers. She has published both a booklet and a video on CorelDRAW! for quilters. Information on these can be obtained by writing to High Tech Quilting, P.O. Box 21307, Columbus, OH 43221-0307.*

# HOW MACINTOSH USERS CAN MASTERMIND STUNNING QUILTS WITH CANVAS OR SUPERPAINT

*The beautiful quilt on the back cover of this book was designed by quilter*
*Gloria Hansen on a Macintosh Quadra. Here's how she did it.*

*by Gloria Hansen*

MY QUILT DESIGNS ARE all geometrics (I love playing with color and geometry), and for the past several years all my quilt designs have started on a Macintosh. While I'm grateful that quilt-designing programs for the Macintosh are starting to appear on the market, I have always been quite satisfied designing my quilts with general-purpose drawing programs. My favorite drawing program is Canvas, and I use it as an example here, though the lower cost SuperPaint (under $50) works just as well.

When I'm using Canvas, I begin by creating a document I call a "layout page." I set up my layout page this way: visible snap-to grids set to ⅛"; rulers displayed; the "Retain Selected" tool (from the General Preferences menu) turned on; and a custom line size of .75". (System 7 users may want to create an alias of the layout page and place it into the Apple menu items. The layout page can also be saved as a stationary item.)

I then use the line tool to draw on the layout page. Once I am happy with a segment or block design, I date and save it. I then create a series of explorations of that block in which I duplicate, rotate, distort, or add perspective to segments; eliminate or add lines; and overlap areas. Although you can create basic quilt designs on a single layer in Canvas (and in other drawing programs), I like to take advantage of the drawing program's layering ability. I treat each layer like a sheet of tracing paper, creating an exploration of a block on

it. Once I've completed a number of explorations, I can print individual layers, along with any notes I may have typed onto each. I can also print all the layers together.

In addition to exploring the line design, I sometimes tint blocks or other areas with shades of gray. When it's time to choose colors, I prefer to refine color sections away from the computer, using tracing paper, colored pencils, marking pens, and fabric. I can then refer to this paper layout to see where the different values go. Thus, a yellow might correspond to a pale gray, a purple to a darkish gray, and so on. Sometimes, in addition to using grays, I specify the placement of warm and cool colors.

Another way that I explore shading is with the bucket tool. To use the bucket tool, you must first convert the line drawing to a "bitmap" image. To do this in Canvas, select the entire drawing, group it, and then double-click on the grouped image. This will bring up an option box, with one of the choices being "Convert to bitmap." You should choose this option. Once you've converted your line drawing to a bitmap, you can use the bucket tool to quickly dump shades of gray (or color) into any area you choose.

*Note: When converting my drawings to bitmaps, I always save the original drawing, with a different file name, before converting it to a bitmap, in case I make a mistake or otherwise want to return to it. I then save any further explorations of the drawing as separate files. Another way to save your original drawing is to group the entire image and copy it onto a layer. The copy can then be converted to a bitmap, leaving the drawing in your original layer intact.*

Canvas makes it easy to adjust the size of any design by "dragging" it to the size you desire. I generally print segments to fit on paper no larger than 8½" × 11" or 8½" × 14", since anything larger will print in segments and will need to be taped together, unless the printer can accommodate larger paper. I trace the actual shapes onto template plastic and draw the sewing line onto my fabric, cutting ¼" away from that line.

Canvas makes it very easy to add a ¼" seam allowance to any shape using its parallel polygon tool. Start by double-clicking the parallel polygon tool to bring up its manager.

Now, set the parallel polygon to two lines spaced ¼" apart.

The manager allows you to customize the appearance of the lines. For example, you might make the cutting line a dashed line and the sewing line a solid line. Then simply click each point of the shape, ending with the first point, and you have a seam allowance. (For more unusual designs, I suggest having the actual drawing on one layer and tracing the templates onto another layer.)

*Note: Using these techniques you can create numerous designs in a very short time. However, finding the ones you want months later can be a chore. So, whenever I draw something that I think has potential, I type the date at the bottom of the page, save the file as the date (for example, "11/1/95 #1"), and print it. I also save a month or two's worth of drawings on a disk labeled with the date range. Later, when I come across something I want to make, I can easily find the original file.*

*Using the line drawing tool, Gloria Hansen created the schematic of the quilt "Breaking Free" that appears on the back cover of this book. She later sewed the quilt with fabrics that she painted, dyed, and airbrushed herself. The quilt won a Best of Show award in 1994 in the annual online needlecraft show on General Electric's GEnie online service. It also won first place in the 1994 American International Quilt Show in Houston in the Innovative Pieced Small Quilt division. Hansen is a member of the NeedleArts Forum on GEnie. Her innovative quilt designs have won numerous awards and have been featured in books, magazines, and on TV. She lives in Hightstown, New Jersey.*

# More Computer Quilting Tricks

No matter what kind of computer you have, or what software you use, there are nifty things you can do with your computer to aid and abet in the creation of quilts. From creating Depression-era style patch quilts with cross-stitch design shareware to designing custom quilt labels, your computer can serve a myriad of uses.

## More Ideas for Using Your Computer in Quilting

**Figure 4-9**
Creating appliqué designs with drawing programs is easy. First, turn on the program's on-screen ruler. Now specify your canvas size and then use the import feature to import a clipart or scanned image onto the canvas. Stretch the image to the size you want and then print the design on the dull side of freezer paper. If the design is larger than a letter-sized sheet, you'll need to print it across several sheets. Or use a plotter.

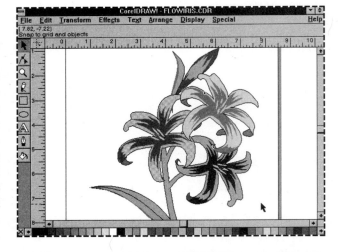

**Figure 4-10**
With drawing programs like CorelDRAW!, you can start your appliqué or pieced quilt by importing one of the clipart pictures that come with the software.

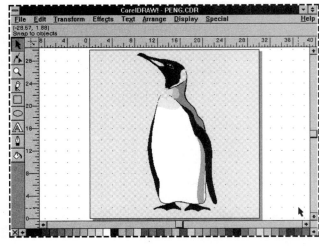

*"When you print out templates using CorelDRAW! (or other drawing programs), you can create a 1/4-inch seam allowance by filling the object with white, then selecting 'Behind Fill' and a width of .50" from the outline roll-up. Voila! You have seam allowances. I make mine light gray."—Jan Cabral*

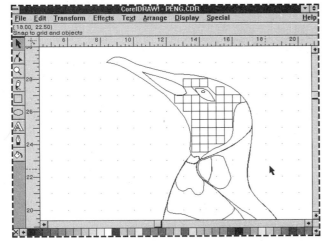

**Figure 4-11**

Here the penguin has been converted to "Wire-Frame" view. You can zoom in on features of the penguin and start drawing in blocks. Using the grid feature, you would set the grid to the size of the blocks you want, then activate the "Snap to grid" feature so that all your lines align with the grid.

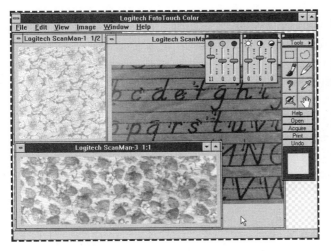

**Figure 4-12**

If you have a color scanner, you can scan fabric at 100 dots per inch and use your scan as fill patterns when you create quilt blocks in programs like Corel-DRAW! or Quilt-Pro. But you may find scanning fabric to be more trouble than it's worth. Fabric colors lose their vibrancy in the scanning process. There's still no substitute for laying the fabric all over the floor and rearranging it for hours. And frankly, I think that's more fun than transforming calicos into binary files.

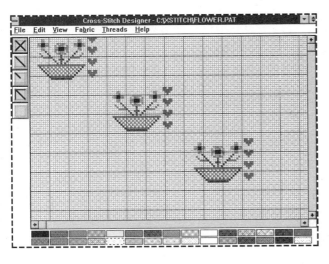

**Figure 4-13**

You don't need expensive quilt or graphics software to design old-fashioned quilts like these, with floral motifs created by joining small squares of colors. Popular during the Depression, these quilts were based on simple designs charted for cross-stitch embroidery or Berlin work. You can create your own charted quilt designs with any of the cross-stitch design software described in Chapter 5 or with Color-Knit for the Macintosh described in Chapter 7. Draw your own pattern by pointing and clicking on graph squares, or import clipart and the software will chart it for you.

# How to Ensure That Store-Bought Quilt Patterns Are Accurately Designed

*B*efore making a quilt pattern from a book or magazine, feed the piecing and template measurements into any quilt program like Electric Quilt or Quilt-Pro to see if the measurements are accurate. Often they're not!

# How to Print Templates and Appliqué Patterns on Freezer Paper

Here's what Marcy Gentry of Weatherford, Oklahoma, has to say:

*I do all my designing on a Macintosh, using SuperPaint. When I need templates, or if I'm using fusible web, I've found that a dot matrix printer like the Imagewriter prints well on the dull side of freezer paper or the paper side of fusible web. Just be sure to select a web that doesn't separate from paper immediately on handling. You can print as many templates as you need, and it's a lot more accurate than printing them once, then tracing them over and over. Using a hand-held scanner, I even scan in appliqué patterns from books, then reprint them on freezer paper. (Hint: On the Macintosh, in the page setup under options, you may have an option that says "Precision Bitmap Alignment (4% Reduction)." Make sure this option is not checked or your templates will be too small.)*

---

**TIP**

*Heirloom Stitches (626 Shadowood Lane S.E., Warren OH, 44484) sells template plastic that can be used in a laser printer. Called Templar, it's available for $8.25 for six letter-sized sheets.*

---

# How to Find an 1830 Quilt Pattern

*H*istorian Barbara Brackman's *Encyclopedia of Pieced Quilt Patterns* is considered the definitive guide to every pieced quilt pattern published between 1830 and 1970. The Electric Quilt company is putting the entire encyclopedia on disk so that you can use the block patterns with Electric Quilt or any general drawing program. The digital quilt database, called BlockBase, will be available at the end of 1995. For more information call Electric Quilt at 419/352-1134.

# How to Use Your Computer to
# Make a Remembrance Quilt with Family Photos

Quilts that include transferred images from family photos are treasures. Having photos transferred to fabric by a service bureau (at $15 to $25 per photo) can make a quilt that includes a dozen or more pictures a costly venture. Some quilters have produced impressive photo transfers by photocopying the picture onto special transfer paper, then ironing the image onto the fabric. This requires a special kind of photocopy machine (there are variations in toners, not all will transfer properly to fabric) and the transfer paper.

Here's an easy way to get a photo onto fabric using a hand-held scanner. First, you scan the photo, then you use the scanner's software to crop and size it. Finally, you reduce it to the size you want, then print your scan onto muslin with a laser or ink-jet printer. (Sorry, a dot-matrix printer won't work; but if you have one, see below for directions on how to accomplish roughly the same thing.)

**1** First, choose a photo with good contrast (strong colors that stand out from each other). Now scan only the portion you want to include in the quilt at 100 or 200 dots per inch. (See "How to Design Great Cross-Stitch on a Computer" on pages 130–131 and 135–138 for tips on how to obtain a good scan.) If you have a color scanner but a black-and-white printer, scan the photo in color anyway. Your scanner will do a much better job scanning in color than in black and white, and you can transform the scan to black and white later with the computer.

**2** Once the scan is complete, use the scanning software or a paint program to turn up its brightness and enhance its contrast. Now crop the image and reduce it to the size you

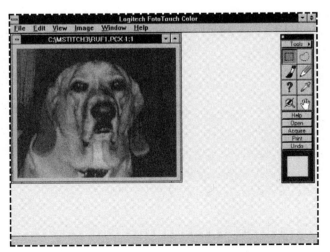

**Figure 4-14**
Once a photo is scanned, this is how it looks inside the photo touch-up software that comes with the Logitech hand-held scanner. Airbrushing the bags from my dog's chin may take me all day, but it will be worth it, for this is a mug that truly deserves to be immortalized on a quilt.

want on the quilt. You may need to experiment by printing the image on paper a few times to get it to its proper size. Depending on the software that came with your scanner, you may need to use graphics software to reduce the image. Again, the software that came with your scanner should be able to do this.

3 If you don't have a color printer, save the scan as a gray scale TIF file.

4 Now, cut a piece of freezer paper to 8½" × 11" and iron it onto a piece of prewashed muslin (100 percent cotton is best), with the shiny side to the fabric. Trim the muslin to the same size as the freezer paper.

5 You can now feed this muslin into a laser or ink-jet printer. Before you do, make sure you know which side of the paper the printer prints on. Laser printers usually flip the sheets over, so you may need to feed the muslin into the printer face down and backward. (A warning to the adventurous: In case you're tempted to feed freezer-paper-backed muslin into a copy machine, keep in mind that the heat could melt the wax on the freezer paper and damage the machine—something that's unlikely to happen in a laser printer because its heat focuses on minuscule areas of the paper. In addition, the copy machine toner may not be permanent.)

You may need to turn the printer's contrast to the darkest setting to get a good print. You'll do so either with a hardware or software control. Experiment with different settings to see what gives the best output. If the image prints too dark in areas, you may want to lighten or airbrush those areas with your scanner software's photo-paint feature, then print it out again.

6 Once your image is printed on muslin, spray it with at least two heavy coats of Krylon Workable Fixatif No. 1306, available in any art store. Be sure to let it dry between coats and to keep a window open when you spray.

> *Note: Before you print out more images or sew them into a quilt, experiment with the colorfastness of the images you're printing. The ink in some color printers will bleed when washed, or it may fade. Try hand washing, machine washing (cold water), and even dry cleaning if you think the quilt may be dry cleaned in the future. One can never tell with gifts.*

If you have an ink-jet printer, consider buying a special, colorfast ink for printing on fabric. For more information call Ramco Computer Supplies (800/522-6922) or any other vendor that specializes in printing supplies.

## What If You Have a Dot Matrix or Thermal Printer?

You can still transfer an image to fabric if you have a dot matrix or thermal printer. You'll need to buy special transfer paper that you feed through your printer. Print the photo (or other computer-generated picture) on this paper, then iron the image onto your fabric. The paper is relatively cheap—about $.78 cents per 8½" × 11" sheet—and works like a charm. It's available in both black and white and color. You can also buy special transfer sheets that work with Canon color laser copiers. For more information call Foto-Wear!, Inc., 101 Pocono Dr., Milford, PA 18337; 717/296-4709.

## What If You Don't Have a Hand-Held Scanner?

If you have a CD-ROM drive, consider having your family photos put on a CD. It's not as expensive as you think. Once the photos are on a digital disk, you can display them on your computer's screen with any graphics program, then crop, edit, and print them just as if you had scanned them.

The only requirement is that your CD-ROM drive be moderately up to date (it needs to be a multisession, double-speed drive; old single-session drives won't work). Your photos should be either negatives, slides, or still undeveloped. It's pricey to have prints scanned to CDs (about $10 each).

Advanced Digital Imaging (112 E. Olive St., Fort Collins, CO 80524; 800/888-3686) charges from $.65 to $1.35 per image to transfer photos to CDs. The lower price is for undeveloped film, with processing charges added on. (All photos on the roll will be transferred to a CD.) The higher price is for developed negatives or slides. There's a $15 minimum. Call them and ask for a brochure before sending photos.

## What If You Don't Have a CD-ROM Drive Either?

You can have your photos put on a floppy disk instead. A copy shop can scan them but the price is high ($9 to $12 for each photo). Try a film development store instead. Seattle Film Works (1260 16th Ave., W., Seattle, WA 98119; 800/445-3348) will transfer a roll of 24 negatives to a floppy disk for $11.95 plus $1.45 shipping. They'll also transfer prints to floppies for bargain-basement prices. Ask for a brochure before you order, and be sure to specify disk size and type when you do.

Another possibility is renting a hand-held scanner to scan photos yourself. You can rent one from a graphics arts or copy store for about $25 an hour.

For more information get a copy of Jean Ray Laury's book *Imagery on Fabric* (C&T Publishing, 1992), available from Clotilde's (800/772-2891).

## How to Create Quilt Labels on Your Computer

You can use the techniques just described to create some truly innovative quilt labels with your computer (see Figure 4-15). To do so, first design the label in any drawing program or word processor. Then, after printing test samples to ensure they're the proper size, print the labels on muslin backed by freezer paper. (Use your drawing program or word processor's copy command to place two labels on a letter-sized sheet.) Finally, spray the printed labels with two coats of Fixatif and let them dry before cutting them out.

An advantage of making labels this way is that you can include clipart pictures of angels, penguins, cats, or whatever you want. You can also frame them with the beautiful clipart borders that come with many graphic design programs or that you design.

For the words on your label you can use letters from the many specialty typefaces (fonts) available for Macintoshes and PCs. You'll find these fonts on graphic arts disks and online in the desktop publishing forums of computer services. There are fonts in which letters are formed of Egyptian characters, dinosaurs, fairies, Halloween characters, and much more. You'll also find fonts for foreign alphabets.

Once you download the fonts and decompress them, you install them in Windows 3.1 by heading to the Main group in the Program Manager, double-clicking on the "Control Panel" icon, and then double-clicking on the "Fonts" icon. Now, click on "Add" and click to the drive and directory where the fonts are located. When you've located the font you want to install, click on the name of the font and then click "OK." Windows should now copy the font to its font directory and make it available to all your Windows applications.

If you have Windows 95, open the Fonts folder by clicking on "My Computer," then "Control Panel," then "Fonts." On the File menu, click "Install New Font." Click the drive and folder that contain the fonts you want to add. Double-click the icon for the font you want to add.

To use your newly loaded font, head to your application and choose "Font" the way you normally would. You should find your new font(s) listed.

**Figure 4-15**
This quilt label was created with a clipart border. I added a scanned image of a rubber stamp (it's a little girl shrieking at the sight of a bumblebee). I scanned the image at 100 dots per inch with the "Line Art" setting. I could have used a downloaded lettering font from CompuServe, but I prefer these simple letters. The label is ready to be printed on muslin.

To install fonts into DOS applications like WordPerfect for DOS, you'll need to check the manual for that software. (Installing new fonts under DOS isn't as easy as it is with Windows, and the procedure varies from application to application.)

If you have a Macintosh, add new fonts to the system folder by dragging the font's icon to a closed system folder. The system will prompt you with a dialog box that identifies the item being moved as a font and asks if you want it stored in the folder. Click "Yes."

Here are some intriguing shareware fonts that make especially nice quilt labels. You can download all of them from the desktop publishing forums on computer services with an average registration fee of $20 each. The filenames in brackets following the description of each font are the filenames that you should search for online.

> **Note:** For many of these special fonts you'll need to specify a large point size like 36 or 48 so they'll print legibly. You'll probably also want to make them print "Bold." If, after specifying a large point size and bold type, the letters still print light on muslin, turn up the darkness on your printer.
>
> If you're running Windows 3.1, you may find that some of the elaborate fonts you've installed won't print when they're enlarged. To fix this, open up Windows' settings file, WIN.INI, in your word processor. You'll find it in the main Windows directory. Find the line [**TrueType**]. Directly beneath it type **outlinethreshold** = 70 and save WIN.INI as a pure text file. Now exit and reload Windows. 🐀

## TRUETYPE FONTS FOR PCS

Isla Bella: a fairy woodcut alphabet [BELATT.ZIP]

Halloween: letters formed of Halloween characters [HAL_TT.ZIP]

ToonTime: cartoon-style letters [TOONTM.ZIP]

Celtic: Celtic-style lettering [CELTPS.ZIP]

Balloons: letters formed of balloons [BLOONS.EXE]

Fairies: images of fairies by nineteenth-century artists [FAERTT.ZIP]

Metropolitan: lettering used on Paris metro signs in the 1900s [METRTT.ZIP]

Flintstone: Flintstone-style lettering [FLINT_.EXE]

Rickshaw: Chinese-style letters [RICK_T.EXE]

## TRUETYPE FONTS FOR MACINTOSHES

Lilith: alphabet formed of vines and flowers [LILH.SEA or LLII.SEA for a lighter version]

Tango: German-Italian art nouveau alphabet formed of "tall charming men in tuxedos" (this one is actually a Postscript font) [TANGTT.SIT]

Isla Bella: fairy woodcut alphabet [BELATT.SIT]

African Ornaments: alphabet with African motifs [AFONRNT.SIT]

Halloween: alphabet formed of ghosts and goblins [HALWT1.SIT]

Metropolitan: alphabet from Paris Metro signs of the 1900s [METRTT.SIT]

ToonTime: cartoon-style alphabet [TOONTM.SIT]

Harlequin: another art nouveau alphabet [HARLTT.SIT]

# These Programs Turn Your Computer into a Quilting Buddy

*T*he problem with computers is they're not warm and fuzzy. They straddle your desk, stoic and chunky, like R2D2's lumpish brother. You can give your computer a bit of quilting hominess with several software utilities available on services like CompuServe.

## *Quilting Gewgaws for PCs*

### USING WINDOWS' WALLPAPER PATTERNS

If you're a Windows user, you can change Windows' boring wallpaper patterns into quilt blocks with a collection of festive patterns found in a free utility available on CompuServe as QWLTPAPR.ZIP (see Figure 4-16). Download the file QWLTPAPR.ZIP and copy it into Windows' main directory. Now, uncompress it by typing its filename.

If you're running Windows 3.1, head to the Main window, found in Program Manager. Click on the "Control Panel" icon, then click on the "Desktop" icon. Near the bottom of the menu that appears you'll see the word "Wallpaper." Click on the down arrow beneath it and a list of files will appear. Click on a filename that begins with a Q (which should be one of the quilt patterns). Now, make sure that the circle next to "Tile" is turned on (it should be black in the center; if not, click on it). Finally, click your way back to the Program Manager and you're all set. Simply reload Windows and—voila! Quilt blocks everywhere.

*Note: If you want to preview the quilt patterns, you can display them in Windows Paint or any other paint program.*

If you're running Windows 95, click "My Computer," then "Control Panel," then "Display." Select the "Background" notecard. At the bottom right-hand side of the screen you'll spot a list of items under the heading "Wallpaper." Click on a filename that begins with a Q (which should be one of the quilt patterns). Windows 95 will display the patterns on screen for you to preview. When you find one you like, click "Apply" and then click "OK."

### FREE QUILTING ICONS

You'll also find special quilting icons available online for free. Imagine being able to load Microsoft Excel by clicking on a Moon Over the Mountain quilt block, or firing up Word by clicking on a Lily Pool. Look for the file QUILTS.EXE online.

If you're running Windows 3.1, to install the icons copy the file to your Windows directory and type **QUILTS** to unpack it. Now head back to the Program Manager, or the program group where the icon you want to change resides, and with your mouse highlight the icon you want to change by clicking on it just once. In Program Manager click the "File/Properties/Change" icon. Click "Browse" and head to Windows' main directory. Click "ICO File" to display the icon files. When the icon you want is displayed, click "OK," then click your way back through the screens by clicking "OK" each time.

If you're running Windows 95, click "My Computer/Explore." Click through the directory tree to the application whose icon you want to change. On the top menu bar click "File/Properties," then click "Shortcut." At the bottom of the screen click the button that says "Change Icon." Click "Browse" to browse through icon files. You can click through directories until you find the icon you want. When it's displayed, click "OK."

### A QUILT SCREEN SAVER

Quilts is a screen saver for PCs that will dance quilting patterns over your computer screen when you leave your PC unattended. This will prevent "burn in" or the shadow of frozen menus etching themselves permanently into the monitor's phosphor. You'll find it online as QUILTS.EXE. It's also shareware, so if you use it send $20 to Cascoloy Software, 4528 36th St. N.E., Seattle, WA 98105. You can order it for an additional $4 shipping.

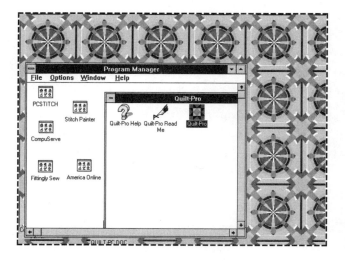

**Figure 4-16**
Transform Windows' ho-hum existence with quilt wallpaper patterns, available on many computer online services and oh so easy to install.

# *Quilting Doodads for Macintoshes*

### A QUILT SCREEN SAVER

Patchwork-9 is a screen saver module for use with the After Dark screen saver program. Patchwork-9 displays up to ten quilting block patterns that you can choose from a selection of two hundred. It's available for $40 from Meta Theory, 1678 Shattuck Ave., #243-A, Berkeley, CA 94709, 510/540-0822; Internet: MetaTheory@aol.com.

### A YARDAGE CALCULATOR

Quilter's Aid is a $5 shareware hypercard stack that will calculate fabric yardage for quilt designs with up to six fabrics. You'll find it online as QUILTX.SEA, or you can write to Little Patches, 154 S. Via Lucia, Alamo, CA 94507.

### CREATING DESKTOP PATTERNS

If you use System 7.5, it's easy to create a new desktop pattern using quilt designs. Create a quilt design in any drawing program (or Quilt-Pro), then copy it and paste it into the control panel called Desktop Patterns.

### CREATING QUILTING ICONS

Creating quilting icons is also easy. Create your quilt design icon in any drawing program, then copy it with the clipboard. Highlight the icon you want to change by clicking on it just once. Choose "Get Info."(Command-I). In the information box that appears, click to highlight the icon that appears in the upper-left. Now paste in the new icon (Command-V). To return your original icon, click the icon in the Get Info box, then cut it (Command-X).

Find out what happened to quilters on GEnie when they sewed Norman Schwartzkopf a patriot quilt. Discover how CompuServe quilters swap fabrics, blocks, and notions. Learn how you can join kimono "bale parties" with quilters on Prodigy. See the chapters on these services for more information.

# Morphing Sunbonnet Sue

We all know her, Sunbonnet Sue, the ageless cutie with the big bonnet whose profile has graced more American quilts than that of George Washington. Haven't you ever wondered who Sunbonnet Sue really is? She always keeps her face hidden, like a fugitive on the lam, even when she's feeding chickens.

Then there's Sunbonnet's boy-toy Overall Bill. A dour fellow who also keeps his face hidden, he slouches beneath a straw hat that looks like it was smashed by a tractor. Bill only appears in Sunbonnet Sue quilts at square dances. You never see him feeding chickens, or packing the picnic lunch, or even stringing daisies with Sue. And he clearly can't dance. He always looks like he's reaching out, waiting for someone to hang a coat on him. He looks like he's afraid that any minute federal officials will break in the door and arrest both of them for cow-tipping.

Computers can tell us more about Sunbonnet Sue than we'd ever want to know. Through complex computer imaging and analysis we can slice away the calico veneers and discover what secret desires motivate Ms. Sunbonnet to do such inexplicable things as feed chickens with fastidious care when most women would just throw a pan of feed out the door, or string daisies together when it would be so much easier to buy fake ones at Kmart and hot-glue them together.

In an attempt to uncover the real Sunbonnet Sue, I used a sophisticated computer animation technique called "morphing." Morphing is a staple of such movies as *Terminator 2* and of TV political campaigns in which humans are transformed into space aliens. A morphing transformation, in which the facial features of one person liquidly melt into those of another, is supposed to pictorially reveal the alternate universe lurking in the heart.

You'll find software to do your own morphing on all the computer services. I downloaded some and found that all the programs were written by intense-sounding programmers who ended their documentation with "Party on!" I also found that all the programs provided the identical illustration of morphing: a picture of a woman transforming into a cheetah.

You start a morph animation by drawing something called a "morph-mesh" on top of your picture. In this case I drew a morph-mesh on Sunbonnet Sue (see Figure 4-17). To my delight, I found that the morph-mesh was almost identical to many of the stitches I design with Pfaff's PC-Designer software. In fact, I found that I was able to move easily between the two programs, morph-meshing one minute, Pfaffing the next. I only occasionally got confused.

Once my morph-mesh was done, the morphing began. The screen flashed. It flickered. The PC beeped as if it were startled by something. I thought it had crashed, but a second

> *It was Alfred Hitchcock! Sunbonnet Sue had morphed seamlessly into the profile of Alfred Hitchcock! The little devil! Even while she was feeding chickens! I was stunned.*

later Sunbonnet Sue appeared. She was slowly metamorphosing into . . . a high forehead . . . a black suit jacket in profile . . . a big nose. (See Figure 4-18.)

My own Sunbonnet Sue quilt blocks started to make sense. The maniacally jagged appliqué lines. The missing pieces I would find years later moments before setting off on a train for Berlin. The *Psycho*-like meandering of the Wonder Under. And the inexplicable appearances of a portly stranger looming in the shadows of my washday scene blocks. It was all so terrible but so true.

Never again will Sunbonnet Sue seem like the innocent cutie she once did. Perhaps this is a good thing. I was getting tired of her relentlessly cheery facade, of her tireless chicken feeding, and, in quilts of recent years, of her ability to do aerobics in a sunbonnet.

Who knows, maybe Overall Bill harbors secret desires too—like playing the sax or joining the men's movement.

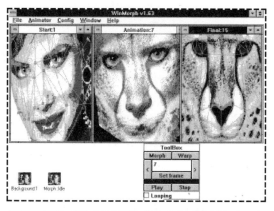

**Figure 4-17**
In the computer animation technique of morphing, the features of one image melt into those of another. A woman changing into a cheetah is the stock example used in every morphing program on the market.

**Figure 4-18**
A morph-mesh has been applied to Sunbonnet Sue. Amazingly, it looks like the stitches I design with the Pfaff. Once the process is complete, she has morphed into . . . omigod, Alfred Hitchcock!

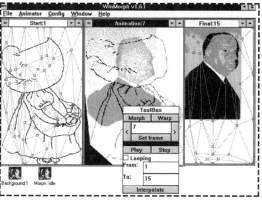

# 5

# HIGH-TECH TOYS FOR CROSS-STITCHERS AND OTHER EMBROIDERERS

*Embroiderers can put their computers to use with software for designing cross-stitch charts, programs to catalog floss, and more.*

mong the oldest of needlecrafts, embroidery probably predates weaving since it's likely that our ancestors experimented with decorative stitches as they sewed together animal hides. Today's embroiderers have more high-tech toys available to them than any other needle artist. At the high end you'll find professional-quality embroidery machines, like Viking's Huskygram, that hook to a PC. They let you design your picture on the PC's screen and then download it for the embroidery machine to stitch. A growing number of sewing machines, like the Viking #1+ and the Pfaff, similarly link to a PC so that you can design machine-embroidered pictures on the computer and then download them to your sewing machine. The Viking will sew multicolored embroidery designs that are as elaborate and lustrous as those on any store-bought garment. Even though these machines

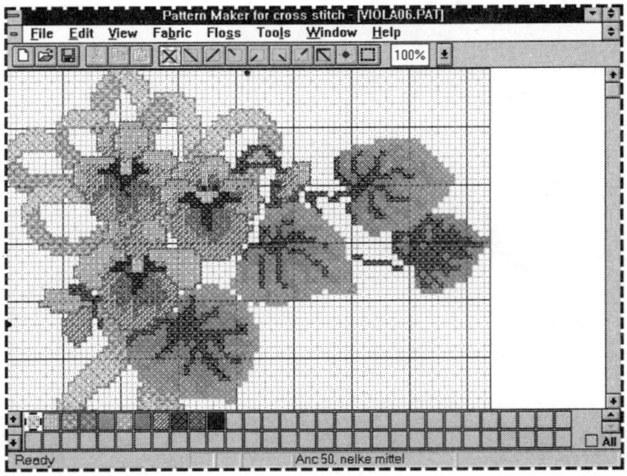

**Figure 5-1**
There are many wonderful programs for designing cross-stitch on a home computer. You don't have to be a talented artist or spend a lot of money to create beautiful designs.

cost thousands of dollars, their popularity is growing among home sewers. See Chapter 2 for more details about them.

This chapter, however, is dedicated to exploring computer tools for hand embroiderers like cross-stitchers, crewel workers, and Hardanger devotees. You'll find a virtual sea of software for designing cross-stitch charts on your computer screen. You'll find software to transform scanned and digitized family photos into cross-stitch charts and then print the charts with symbols and the proper DMC or Anchor floss colors. You'll even find software that will track your burgeoning inventory of thread, charts, and beads before all those DMC colors tangle into one big knot under your bed. Type in the floss and fabric requirements for a project, and these programs will scan your supplies inventory and print out a shopping list.

This chapter will also show you how to use spreadsheet software to catalog floss and print custom graph paper for needlework design, how to transform clipart into crewel designs, and how to use your computer to chart embroidery designs for sweaters. In fact, you can do a lot with your computer to make your needlework shine, and you don't need to buy expensive software to do it.

## Secrets to Buying Good Cross-Stitch Software

*T*here are oodles of programs on the market for designing cross-stitch patterns. The number seems to grow daily, and the programs seem to get better with each passing month.

The best cross-stitch design programs give you a palette of the complete DMC and Anchor floss colors and let you paint your design on a grid. They let you fill the squares with color and/or a symbol of your choice to represent the color. This procedure is similar to working with graph paper and colored pencils but much easier. Erasing misplaced symbols is easier than with a pencil, and, believe it or not, a computer monitor is usually easier on the eyes than a pencil-marked page.

The better programs provide ways to signify backstitches, quarter stitches, and French knots in your pattern. Using "paint" tools, you can zoom in on the image and flip, rotate, cut, paste, or mirror portions of the design. You can print out the design in color (if you have a color printer) or with symbols. The program will also print out a symbol key. The best programs convert clipart and scanned photos to charts and let you use elements of other computer graphics in your design.

The programs vary a lot in the features they give you to work with and how well they perform. Some convert clipart and scanned photos to charts better than others. Others provide a grid and tools to paint on it that are easier to use and to see. Some chart with better looking symbols. Some print more professional-looking charts. And so on. Here are some things to look for in a cross-stitch program:

**Do you prefer to design by filling squares on a grid or by freehand drawing on a page?** Most cross-stitch programs allow you to draw your initial design in a drawing program, then import it into the cross-stitch program and place it on the grid. MasterStitch Designs' CrossStitch Designer, on the other hand, gives you a blank screen to draw and color and converts the design into a chart when you're done. I prefer the freedom of the first approach because it gives more control over the initial design (paint programs have more professional drawing tools than CrossStitch Designer) and over the ultimate placement and sizing of the design on a grid.

**How well does the cross-stitch software chart clipart, scanned photos, downloaded computer pictures, and drawings from other graphics software?** And how easy is it to do? Even expensive cross-stitch programs don't handle imported images perfectly all the time. Some turn subtle pinks into ghastly electric blues and wreak other color distortions on your picture. Some "mush" lines and features together, turning that subtly hued picture of your cat into a cartoon painted of just a few shades of black and brown. Others turn each pixel of a computer image into a single cross-stitch, producing humongous charts containing tens of thousands of stitches even when you cropped the image tightly before importing it.

Image importing is a hassle in some programs. They may put you through extra steps at the DOS prompt (copying the graphics file to a specific subdirectory, for instance). They may subject you to primitive cropping

> **TIP**
> *You can chat via E-mail with literally thousands of other friendly cross-stitchers on Prodigy, CompuServe, GEnie, and other online services. Swap patterns, compare floss collections, and participate in round robins, in which samplers are mailed around the country so that dozens of stitchers can work on them, just like in an old-fashioned sewing bee. Find out how to join the stitching sisters of cyberspace by checking out the chapters on computer online services.*

routines that lock up the computer if the image is too large. Some chart the picture but don't bother to assign DMC or Anchor floss colors to the chart; others assign colors automatically. Some don't let you move or size the picture on the grid once you import it. You need to ask the software vendor about all of these things before you buy.

Ideally, cross-stitch software should let you import PCX images (standard paint-program–generated pictures), GIF images (pictures you download from CompuServe), and BMP pictures (Windows-generated graphics). Few let you import all of these types of images; most import just PCX ones. Utilities are available that convert a computer picture from one image to another (some good ones are recommended in Chapter 6), but doing so adds one more step to the design process.

**What does the software's printed pattern look like?** Will you be able to read it without a magnifying glass? Will the pattern print out on one or two neatly organized sheets, or will it print as some illegible, multipage blueprint that you'll need to paste together? If you have a dot matrix printer, will the charts print legibly? Professional designers like to be able to adjust the thickness of the thread and the thickness of the grid lines in their final printout to make the pattern as easy to read as possible. Presently only one program lets you do that (Hobby-Ware's Pattern Maker, described on page 111), but more programs will include this feature in the near future.

**Will the software work optimally with your computer configuration?** If you have a mouse, you'll definitely want software that lets you draw with a mouse. If your PC runs Windows, you'll probably want software that is Windows based (not just DOS software that is advertised as "working under Windows"; that is an entirely different thing). Working with graphics is much easier with Windows than with DOS. This isn't an issue with Macintoshes because they have always excelled over PCs at working with graphics.

Make sure, too, that the cross-stitch software supports the highest-resolution video mode that your computer offers. If you have a Super-VGA monitor, you don't want a program that will display only in lower resolution CGA or EGA. Look for software that specifically supports Super-VGA or whatever is the highest resolution on your monitor.

Check to make sure the software supports your printer too. Most of these packages have not been tested on a wide variety of printers. If you have a color printer, you want software that will let you print patterns in color.

Some programs that are advertised as being able to work with a 286 or 386 PC run so slowly on these lower powered machines that they're unusable. Check the software reviews in this chapter to make sure the program will run suitably on your PC.

Does the software let you export designs into a standard graphics format, like PCX, so that you can use your designs with other art programs or with desktop publishing software (an important consideration for budding designers)? Although this feature is less important than others, it is handy for store owners and designers who plan to use patterns to create store flyers or camera-ready copy to take to a printer.

**What "grid acrobatics" does the program support?** Can you resize a grid once you've completed a design, reducing the chart's dimensions or expanding them on the fly? Most programs won't let you do this. Can you make grid squares higher than they are wide, for graphing duplicate stitches, or are you stuck with perfectly square squares? You won't find this feature in most programs either.

**Are the palette and grid size adequate for your needs?** Most cross-stitch programs limit you to 60 to 120 colors in a design, and most limit grids to 150 to 300 squares vertically and horizontally. That translates into roughly a 10" × 20" strip of Aida, which may be too small for your needs.

**Can you choose the background color of your design?** Many programs limit you to painting on a white canvas with a black grid. Other programs provide a choice of an off-white or black canvas. Some go so far as to let you design on a canvas of any DMC or Anchor color of your choosing.

**Will the program let you place on your design quarter and half stitches, French knots, and backstitches?** Can the backstitches be any color you want? Most programs restrict you to creating backstitches in black or brown. Some let you paint them in a small assortment of colors. Some let you use the entire DMC or Anchor spectrum. Some don't let you put them in your design at all!

**Does the software come with a library of predesigned images and alphabets that you can use with little fuss?** Sadly, most don't. This is an odd state of affairs, I think, because most general graphics software comes packed with disks full of clipart and examples of art that can be created with the program.

**Does the software fully support the thread palette you use?** The popular Oxford Craft programs provide only limited support for DMC thread, since Anchor helped develop the programs. Few programs support J&P Coats thread. You should ask whether the software supports all the current colors in the brand of thread that you use. Thread manufacturers are constantly adding to their list of colors. If the software doesn't support the full color line for your thread, ask if the vendor will send you a free update when they do.

# You Might Consider Buying a Drawing Program Too

*I*f you don't have one already, you should consider buying a drawing program that will let you crop and manipulate pictures before importing them into a cross-stitch program. Not only is it often easier to draw original designs in a drawing program than in a cross-stitch program, but you may need one to prep clipart, scanned images, or downloaded pictures before putting them on a chart.

When you import a scanned image or piece of computer art into a cross-stitch design, the software often converts each pixel of the design into a stitch. If your computer picture is large and of a high resolution (as most digitized images are), you can end up with a cross-stitch pattern of 20,000 stitches. A drawing program will let you trim the image down before changing it into cross-stitches. It also allows you to fine-tune any image prior to converting it into a chart.

## *Your Drawing Program Needn't Be Fancy*

Almost any drawing program will suffice, even the Paint program that comes with Windows or Windows 95 (if you can't find it, check the "Accessories" group). If you have a hand-held scanner, check to see if it comes with graphics software to crop images. If so, that software may be sufficient for cropping and manipulating images. If none of the foregoing are options, and if you own a PC, consider the lower power versions 3 or 4 of CorelDRAW! ($149, $99 if you buy it on CD; Corel Systems Corp., 1600 Carling Ave., Ottawa, Ontario K1Z 8R7, Canada, 800/836-3729 or 613/728-8200). The current version costs $649. Macintosh users will love SuperPaint ($49.95 from Adobe Systems, Inc., 1585 Charleston Rd., Mountain View, CA 94039, 800/888-6293).

Other favorites for both Macintosh and PCs are Freehand ($595 from Macromedia, 600 Townsend St., Suite 310W, San Francisco, CA 91433, 800/989-3762) and Adobe Illustrator ($595 from Adobe Systems, Inc., 1585 Charleston Rd., Mountain View, CA 94043, 800/888-6293), and CorelDRAW!, version 5 for PCs only. At the high end for Macintosh users, a popular program is Canvas ($400 from Deneba Software, 7400 Southwest 87th Ave., Miami, FL 33173, 800/622-6827). (Note: You'll find these programs sold at much lower prices through computer mail-order retailers.)

At the very, very high end of drawing programs, both Mac and PC professional artists swear by Fractal Design Painter (Fractal Design

Corp., 335 Spreckels Dr., Suite F, Aptos, CA 95003, 408/688-8800). It offers a wide array of image editing and painting techniques and can be used with a graphics tablet—a touch-sensitive tablet that hooks to the computer and lets you draw with a stylus instead of a mouse.

## Start Your Shopping for Cross-Stitch Software by Investigating Shareware

*I*f you scan the ads for cross-stitch design software in any of the cross-stitch magazines, the first thing that will leap out is the high price of these products. They range from $60 to $300. These prices may be no problem if you're a professional needlework designer or if you expect to spend a lot of time designing charts. If you're an occasional cross-stitch artist, though, $250 for software may seem as extravagant as feeding the cat beluga caviar. Thankfully, there are other options: shareware and do-it-yourself.

You'll find shareware cross-stitch programs ranging from $20 to $40 on all the major online services, as well as Internet (although you'll need to hunt to find them there). You can also obtain them for a small fee by writing the authors. While admittedly some of these programs aren't wonderful, some out perform retail software.

If you're running Windows 3.1 or Windows 95, the best shareware for you is HobbyWare's Pattern Maker, also called Cross-Stitch Designer. In the spring 1995 release of this classic you'll find features that you won't find in retail products costing many times more.

If you're a DOS-bound PC user, try Bill Love's $39 X-STITCH for PCs. I think it's nearly as good as the best commercial programs on the market. Like retail programs, Love's will even convert family photos to a chart—and it does a reasonably good job. There's a Windows version of the program, but the DOS one is better.

If you have an older PC (like an 8088) or old Tandy (like a 1000), try CompuStitch by John George. It's a limited program, but it may be all you need for charting alphabets or simple designs. You'll learn more about these programs later in this chapter.

I haven't spotted any shareware cross-stitch programs for Macintoshes or old Apples. That doesn't mean some aren't materializing right now on the info highway. If you're a Macintosh user, be sure to look before you head to the store.

*Note:* *Why is cross-stitch software so expensive? When you buy a package, you'll probably end up calling the manufacturer at least once with technical questions. That tech advice costs vendors money to provide. If an employee spends twenty minutes on the phone with each customer, the manufacturer's payroll costs can add up.*

## TIP

The Seattle Textile Computer Users' Group sells several disks containing shareware cross-stitch software, including some of the programs mentioned in this chapter. The disks are available for $4 each from STCUG, P.O. Box 17506, Seattle, WA 98107. For PCs specify disk size (3.5" or 5.25"). Ask for IBM Disk #11 (3.5" size only) and IBM Disk #15 (mention that you want the cross-stitch disks just in case the disk numbering has changed). For Macintosh users, Macintosh Disk #1 offers general-purpose charting software that can be used to create cross-stitch graphs.

# Only If You're Not Satisfied with Shareware Should You Investigate Commercial Software

*I*f you decide you're not happy with any of the shareware candidates, then you should investigate the higher-priced commercial programs advertised in cross-stitch magazines. My first pick is the retail version of the HobbyWare shareware program previously mentioned; it's called Pattern Maker. The low-end version, at $59.95, is a best buy for home computer users, providing a wide range of sophisticated design tools in a very user-friendly Windows environment. You can import BMP, PCX, and Windows metafile graphics into charts; the program performs the computer-graphic-to-chart transformations moderately well.

Professional designers will find their best tool to be HobbyWare's Pattern Maker Pro, at $119.95. Also a Windows program, it offers features that designers have asked for that aren't available in other programs yet, like the ability to fine-tune the appearance of grids, symbols, and threads in the printed pattern and to preview it before printing. It also lets you display multiple patterns on the screen in multiple views (symbol, color, and stitch), cut and paste between them, and easily import a wide assortment of graphic types. Its only faux pas is that it doesn't transform digitized photos and drawings to charts quite as well as the pricier Oxford Craft programs or MasterStitch's CrossStitch Designer.

PC users who insist on sticking to DOS will find their best value in Oxford Craft's X-Stitch Designer line of programs, ranging from $49.95 to $249.95. They're pricey, especially since you need to buy extra utilities for the low-end DOS version—like the utility to import PCX graphics ($29.95) or the one to increase the number of colors you can use in the budget version of the program ($10). X-Stitch Designer imports color images well, with only occasional hiccups, and provides a wide variety of professional-level design tools.

MasterStitch's CrossStitch Designer and its Color ImageImport companion program are DOS-based programs that the professional will appreciate for their ability to transform a photo into a chart with crisp detail. It does this considerably better than any of the other programs. Its drawback is that it doesn't let you chart quarter or half-stitches or backstitching, nor can you size the imported photo to a chart of your own dimensions (it picks the chart size for you).

Macintosh owners will find their best buy in Compucraft's Stitch Crafts for $150, while owners of old Apples will enjoy Stitch Grapher for $49.95. You'll find more details on all these products later in this chapter.

The only commercial program I found difficult to work with was Davis Computer Service's $120 EasyGrapher for PCs (800/231-3480). It requires that you use a keyboard rather than a mouse to place elements on a chart, a cumbersome process.

*Note: Even if you're not averse to the idea of splurging $250 on cross-stitch software, you should start your shopping by giving low-cost shareware programs a spin. They'll give you an idea of the kind of features you want in a design program, and they may end up being all you really need.* ❧

# If You Don't Want to Buy Anything at All, There's Still Hope for You

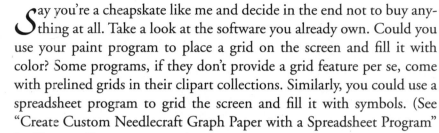

*S*ay you're a cheapskate like me and decide in the end not to buy anything at all. Take a look at the software you already own. Could you use your paint program to place a grid on the screen and fill it with color? Some programs, if they don't provide a grid feature per se, come with prelined grids in their clipart collections. Similarly, you could use a spreadsheet program to grid the screen and fill it with symbols. (See "Create Custom Needlecraft Graph Paper with a Spreadsheet Program" in Chapter 6.)

And why not use that database software you already own, be it Paradox, FileMaker, Access, or HyperCard, to create a floss and materials database? If you don't have such a database, download a low-cost shareware one from CompuServe or another online service. (Jim Button's ButtonFile will work on any PC, no matter how ancient. It's called PC-File in really ancient permutations. I still have a copy of it on my 486 PC and like it, even though people make fun of me for it.) For directions, see the section on creating a DMC thread catalog on page 128.

These programs won't provide you with all the conveniences of cross-stitch–specific software (like built-in DMC and Anchor databases and symbol charts) but they're worth exploring.

*"The eye that directs a needle in the meshes of embroidery will equally well bisect a star with the spider web of the micrometer— Maria Mitchell (1818–1889), American astronomer and mathematician"— spotted as part of the signature to an E-mail message in QuiltNet*

**TIP**
**To learn how to get the invaluable "Internet Cross-Stitch Frequently Asked Questions File (or FAQ)" that answers such eternal questions as "Won't tea dyeing leave acid in my sampler that will cause it to deteriorate a hundred years from now?," head to Chapter 18.**

# What About Charting Other Stitches Like Hardanger? Or Embroidery for Sweaters?

*A*ll the cross-stitch design programs suffer one serious drawback as far as some professional needlework designers are concerned: None allows you to chart the kloster blocks of increasingly popular Hardanger or other satin or specialty stitches that embroiderers like to combine with cross-stitch. (Rumor has it that new programs are in the works that will do this.)

Until something new comes on the market, try Cochenille's Stitch Painter Gold. Stitch Painter is not a cross-stitch design program in the ordinary sense. It was designed for charting patterns for a wide variety of needlecrafts, including knitting, crochet, and needlepoint, as well as cross-stitch. Consequently, it lacks some design features that cross-stitchers like, such as the ability to chart backstitch and French knots on top of or beside grid squares filled by cross-stitch symbols. Nor does it include a DMC or Anchor color palette, and it will only import photos or clipart in two colors. It's also pricey at $85 to $165, depending on the version you buy. However, it's an excellent program overall, and you can use it to chart Hardanger and other satin and flat stitches on an adjustable grid. A built-in palette of cross-stitch charting symbols lets you incorporate cross-stitches into your design too.

Duplicate-stitch designers will love Stitch Painter Gold because you can place cross-stitch symbols on customized grids that approximate the dimensions of knit stitches. You can even make your graph *look* like knit stitches. Sweater designs, as you know, need to be graphed on a grid with slightly rectangular "squares" because knit stitches are not perfectly square. The only cross-stitch programs that presently let you modify grid size for designing duplicate stitch are the HobbyWare ones.

See Chapter 7 for a full description of Stitch Painter. Stitch Painter Gold is available for PCs, Macintoshes, and Amigas for $165 (Cochenille Design Studio, P.O. Box 4276, Encinitas, CA 92023, 619/259-1698).

Davis Computer Service's EasyGrapher Specialty for PCs will chart Hardanger and

> **TIP**
> **When you use cross-stitch software to design a chart, have your box of floss at hand. The DMC or Anchor colors represented on the computer screen will not be close in tone to what's in your floss box.**

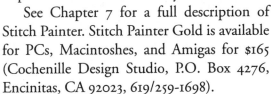

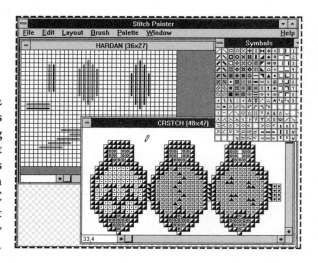

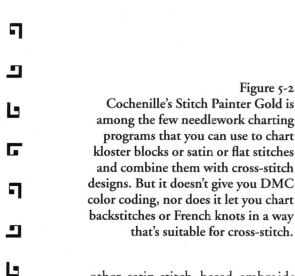

Figure 5-2
Cochenille's Stitch Painter Gold is among the few needlework charting programs that you can use to chart kloster blocks or satin or flat stitches and combine them with cross-stitch designs. But it doesn't give you DMC color coding, nor does it let you chart backstitches or French knots in a way that's suitable for cross-stitch.

other satin-stitch–based embroidery stitches ($99, P.O. Box 750141, New Orleans, LA 70175, 800/231-3480). It doesn't chart cross-stitch, though; and as more than one designer has pointed out, the charts it prints may be suitable for submitting to magazines, but they're not camera-ready for use in needlework brochures. You can find a demo version of the program on many online services. Look for a file named EGSZIP.EXE.

What about graphing Hardanger and specialty stitches in a drawing program like Macromedia Freehand? You can do it, but it won't be worth the bother. General-purpose drawing programs simply don't provide the tools for charting needlework easily.

## Cross-Stitch Picks and Pans: Choosing the Design Software That's Best for You

Does it seem overwhelming—all this talk of importing images and adjusting grids? All you want to do is stitch Xs on fabric, you say. Surely, choosing a software package to help you do that cannot be hard. No, it's not. Here are capsule reviews of the leading cross-stitch programs, with the lowdown on what they'll do for you—and what they do badly. I tested all on a variety of PCs including 286s, 386s, and 486s, with a variety of graphic standards (EGA, VGA, Super-VGA), and two different printers (dot matrix and laser). I also interviewed professional designers and hobbyists about their preferences and experiences. I've listed the products in the order in which I suggest you consider them, depending on your computer hardware.

## *HobbyWare Products Are Hands-Down Winners for Windows Users*

HobbyWare stunned the computer world when its original cross-stitch program, Cross-Stitch Designer, proved to be one of the most popular shareware programs ever. Now HobbyWare's shareware is even better, and the company is selling two outstanding retail versions as well.

Pattern Maker and Pattern Maker Pro (the retail versions) exploit Windows' graphical environment to give cross-stitch designers many of the tools that regular graphic artists find in their graphics software but that have been slow to appear in the cross-stitch world: the ability to display multiple canvases on the screen and to cut and paste elements between them, easy import of graphics in a variety of formats, and complete control over printed designs.

**These programs have everything you need** Designers have the entire DMC and Anchor floss lines to play with (Pattern Maker Pro offers J&P Coats as well) and can use a canvas of any color, with dimensions of nearly limitless size. All the editing tools you need are in buttons and pull-down menus, including cut, copy, paste, flip, and rotate. The screen is easy to see, and multiple levels of zoom let you focus in on areas of the design as well as step back for a broader view. As you work, you can view your design-in-progress in stitches, full color, or symbols. A symbol editor lets you assign symbols to colors and print symbols in any of your Windows fonts—a feature not found in other programs.

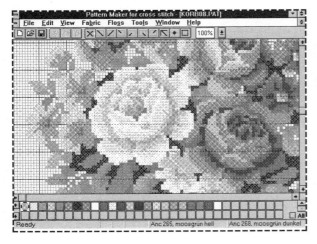

**Figure 5-3**
Designing beautiful cross-stitch is fun in Pattern Maker. Easy-to-use zoom features, adjustable color and symbol palettes, and fast clipart import will take your artistry to new heights.

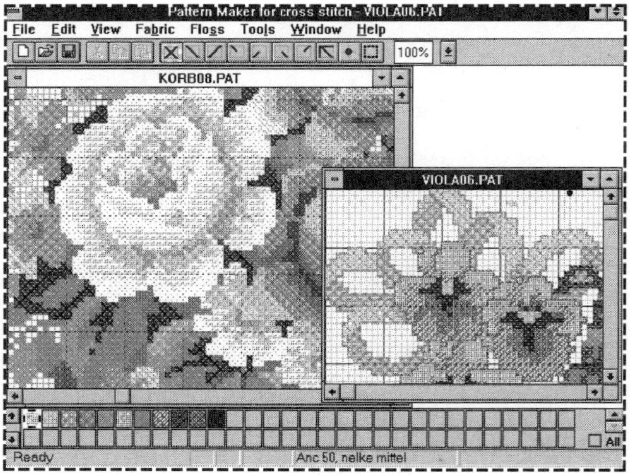

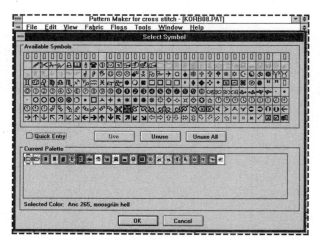

**Figure 5-4**
With Pattern Maker you can display multiple patterns on your screen and cut and paste between them.

**Figure 5-5**
A highly advanced symbol palette in Pattern Maker Pro lets you assign symbols to colors, as well as print symbols in different fonts, to make your charts as easy on the eyes as possible—features fussy designers will appreciate.

Because professional designers are fussy when it comes to the look of their printed designs, HobbyWare has paid attention and has provided ways to spruce up the look of that final printout. You can tell the program how thick you want backstitch and French knots to appear on the pattern. You can specify the thickness of the grid and whether you want solid, dotted, or dashed lines. You can set up the grid for the rectangular squares used to chart duplicate stitches as well. You can also preview your pattern before printing it out in color or black and white. None of these features is available in other programs. Pattern Maker programs also create a report of statistics on your design, including how many stitches it contains in each color and how much floss will be required of each color (you can tell the program how many strands you'll be stitching with).

**It swallowed the creature from the Black Lagoon** Incorporating clipart or other digitized graphics in your design is easier with Pattern Maker than with any of the other cross-stitch programs. You can import images you've cropped or spruced up in other graphics programs through the Windows clipboard, or you can use the special import feature to import BMP, PCX, GIF, or Windows metafiles into your chart. (The lower end versions import a smaller selection of these.) Unlike some of the other programs, you can tell Pattern Maker how large or small you want the image to be (how many graph squares it will cover); then once it's on the canvas, you can move it and reposition it to your heart's content. You can also use multiple clipart images in a design.

Its import feature, compared to that of some other programs, is adequate. Its ability to handle images that are too large is superb. When fed images that were too large, other cross-stitch programs choked, either turning the chart into a mishmash of color or locking up the computer and forcing a reboot. Pattern Maker never lost its cool, even when handed scans of monstrous proportions.

The downside? Pattern Maker is not quite as good at turning clipart or photos into charts as the Oxford programs. And it's nowhere near as good as MasterStitch's CrossStitch Designer. When I fed it a black-and-white photo of the Creature from the Black Lagoon, it came up with an all-black chart. When I fed it a scan of an old German painting of a librarian, it produced an unrecognizable swirl of browns. But when I fed it a photo of a cat, puss looked great. And when I fed it a photo of some roses, they came out looking like roses.

If you're a professional designer, I strongly recommend the $119.95 Pattern Maker Pro. Home computer users should take a look at the $35 shareware version. The shareware restricts you to designing with 45 colors of DMC floss. It will only import bitmaps and doesn't include the snazzy printout or report features, nor will it let you view charts in multiple views. For most stitchers these limitations will prove no inconvenience. Should you decide you want a little more, go for the $59.95 retail Pattern Maker. It provides PCX and metafile import, designing in up to 60 colors, an Anchor palette, and multiple chart views. (The company has no plans to create a Macintosh version.)

HobbyWare
9686 Spruce Lane
Fishers, IN 46038
Phone: 800/768-6257 or 317/595-0565
Price: Pattern Maker Pro is $119.95; Pattern Maker is $59.95; the shareware version is $35
Requirements: 386 (DX recommended) or later PC, Windows 3.1 or greater, mouse, VGA or Super-VGA monitor, 4 megs RAM

CompuServe: 71543,1504
HobbyWare can also be contacted through their technical support forum in the Needle-arts Roundtable on GEnie. Type **needle** at any prompt.
Filename: CSD40.ZIP (known as Cross-Stitch Designer)

## *DOS Devotees and Owners of Old PCs Should Test-Drive Bill Love's Shareware*

If you're hooked on DOS, or if you have an older 80286 PC with a less-than-up-to-date graphics monitor, you'll find your best buy in the $40 shareware gem X-STITCH. It gives you most of the tools of expensive programs, plus it has a special talent at turning GIF images into cross-stitch designs.

You can define your canvas up to 320 stitches square (it will calculate the design size when you tell it how many stitches there will be per inch in the fabric you plan to use). You pick your floss colors from the entire DMC palette (Anchor is not supported), using up to 62 colors in the chart. You can also choose one of 16 colors as a canvas color. You place stitches on the canvas by clicking on squares with your mouse. The stitches look like actual cross-stitches, and when you zoom out, X-STITCH displays, with 3D-like realism, what your design will look like once it's stitched. Some stitchers find this hard to see, while others love the effect. You can cut, paste, and move parts of your design as well as rotate and duplicate them.

X-STITCH imports GIF images onto the canvas with what I think is the best GIF-import feature in both the shareware and commercial worlds. It's much better than the Hobbycraft programs at interpreting imported colors. Of the dozen digitized photos I fed it, it converted most flawlessly. (O.K., a few colors were out of whack, and it really did a job on the scan of the old German painting, turning the elderly librarian into shamrock green streaks. It also reduced the number of colors in the picture to 16. But then, none of these programs is perfect.)

Once you've transformed a digitized photo to a chart, X-STITCH will let you shrink it and even cut, paste, mirror, and duplicate elements of the design. You can change the colors of stitches and add back, quarter, and half stitches as well as French knots. The symbol editor lets you view the chart in symbol form and change any symbols that might not be easy to see. Finally, the charts' X-STITCH prints are among the most legible of any of the charting software. Look at this program before you buy anything!

**A Windows version is available too** Bill Love also sells a Windows version called X-STITCH Windows Pattern Design Software. It's an impressive program, and many stitchers love it (I find the HobbyWare shareware slightly better). If you're in the market for a low-cost

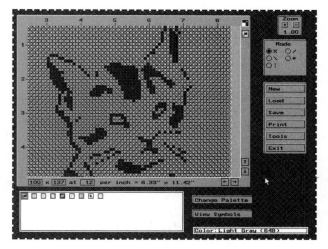

**Figure 5-6**
Turning computer clipart into cross-stitch charts is easy with X-STITCH. It also does a good job transforming photos to cross-stitch charts.

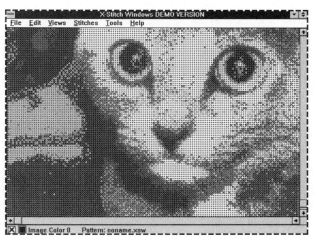

**Figure 5-7**
A photo of Jessica the cat was scanned and converted to a cross-stitch chart of humongous proportions with X-STITCH Windows Pattern Design.

cross-stitch design program that enables you to click on grid squares with DMC colors and to specify backstitches, X-STITCH is a pleasant enough program. It also lets you import images through the Windows' clipboard, usually keeping the lines of the design crisp and the colors true to their originals (although the DOS version of the program does a better job).

A drawback is that it won't tell you which DMC colors correspond to which colors on the chart. You have to get out the box of floss and figure this out for yourself. It also translates an image's pixels into stitches in a one-to-one ratio. This means you'll need to crop down the size of your image before importing it or else you'll be stuck with a chart so huge not even your Great Aunt Lizzy, the cross-stitching demon, could finish it in her lifetime. Figure 5-7 shows a photo of a tabby that was converted to a chart that suffers this problem.

Nonetheless, this is a good program; and if you're a Windows user, it's certainly one you should try.

Pilgrim Works
P.O. Box 16615
Greenville, SC 29606
Price: Both versions are $39 each
Requirements: DOS version—80286, 80386, or 80486 PC; DOS 3.3 or greater; 512K RAM; VGA, EGA, or Hercules monitor; Microsoft-compatible mouse. Windows version—Windows 3.1 or greater, VGA or Super-VGA, mouse
CompuServe: 70451,2255
Filename: XSZIP.ZIP is DOS version; XSWIN.ZIP is Windows version

## *PCStitch for Windows Is Another Good Buy*

Next to HobbyWare's Pattern Maker Pro, PCStitch for Windows, by M&R Enterprises, is my second favorite among the retail programs. At $79.95 it's also one of the cheapest. Within minutes of installing it, I was able to transform hand-scanned images of all the human and animal members of my household into dazzling charts.

PCStitch lets you paste a digitized image into a selected section of your chart and design the rest by hand or paste in more images. You can then move, rotate, recolor, and generally touch up the picture once it's in the chart. The chart can be any size that you designate, up to 500 × 500 stitches, and can contain whatever number of thread colors you specify, up to 64 colors. The program automatically converts the colors of the image to either DMC, Anchor, or J&P Coats thread numbers. PCStitch accepts GIF, TIF, PCX, and Windows bitmap images, so you won't have to spend time converting files between these different formats. A preview feature lets you view the image before you import it into the chart (a feature also found in Pattern Maker but strangely left out of the other programs).

*"I like PCStitch best because it's Windows based, easy to operate, and I can review the whole pattern rather than just sections. I can work on sections, then pan out and get a full view. PCStitch does need some work with importing pictures, but whenever I mention a problem to M&R Enterprises they're right on it. I've used CrossStitch Designer because it gives me color printouts, but it's more cumbersome to use." —Christi McNeil, Bremerton, Washington; cross-stitch designer of custom-design charts of houses, wedding invitations, lighthouses*

**It's easy to use and the documentation is good** Designing from scratch with PCStitch is a snap. Using the mouse, you draw in full, back, outline, quarter, and half stitches. With the zoom features you can quickly zero in on a chart section. PCStitch is easy to learn and its documentation is good (although spare). It prints in color and it works well on both a 386 and 486 PC.

On the downside, PCStitch doesn't offer some of the frills of Pattern Maker or Oxford Craft's X-Stitch Designer series, like a symbol editor or the ability to paint backstitches in color. And while PCStitch gives you eight canvas colors, they're pretty garish colors—like cyan and magenta. Its photo import feature is pretty good, although it doesn't import with as much artistic subtlety as the Oxford programs, or even the shareware program X-STITCH. And it's not as good as the MasterStitch product. When I imported a picture of a cat, for instance, PCStitch colored the eye with bright orange and lemon yellow, while the Oxford products used a more subtle combination of three shades of light gold and pumpkin. However, you may decide, like me, that three shades of light gold aren't worth paying extra for. On the other hand, I know professional artists who'd disagree.

Drawbacks not withstanding, PCStitch is still one of the best deals for the average cross-stitch hobbyist.

M&R Enterprises
P.O. Box 9403, Dept. 505
Wright Brothers Branch
Dayton, OH 45409
Phone: 800/800-8517 or 513/263-4122
Price: $79.95
Requirements: 80386 or 80486, Windows 3.1 or later, 2 megs RAM

## *Oxford Craft's Programs Are Great but Pricey*

Oxford Craft sells a complete line of Windows and DOS cross-stitch programs for PCs. They're superb, full-featured programs that are worth considering if you're a professional designer, because their photo and clipart import feature is one of the best. If you're chained to DOS, have a 386 or better PC, and you don't like Love's shareware X-STITCH, you may find your cross-stitch solution in Oxford's low-end products. Windows home computer users will probably want to pass because these programs are costly.

Oxford's programs all look and work essentially the same but offer different levels of capabilities. For instance, the basic $49.95 DOS program gives you a select palette of 64 Anchor or DMC colors to design with, and you can use 16 of those colors in a chart (you can change this preselected palette but need an extra $10 utility to do it). The high-end Windows version at $499.95 gives you the full color palettes of the Anchor and DMC thread lines. Similarly, your canvas is restricted to 200 × 120 stitches in the low-end programs, while the high-end ones give you a canvas of 300 × 300 stitches.

Zoom capabilities are limited in the lower-end programs too, as is the ability to design backstitch in more than one color. The high-end programs let you design backstitch in up to 8 colors, and in different widths, and give you a wide range of tools to do so. The high-end programs also let you view your completed chart on 18 or more colors of Aida, while you're limited to a standard white or black canvas in the low-end programs.

**X-Stitch Designer gives you a grid to fill** You design charts in X-Stitch Designer much like in the other cross-stitch programs, clicking on grid squares to fill them with full, half, and quarter stitches in colors in the DMC, Anchor, Red Heart, and Madeira floss lines (the last two thread brands are only available in the high-end programs). You use editing tools to cut, paste, copy, turn, and move elements of the design. In addition, you can reduce or enlarge sections of your design (something not found in other cross-stitch programs) and blanket designated areas with color. The high-end programs give you fill patterns—like checker-board, cross-hatch, and diagonal—to fill selected areas with, another feature not found in other programs.

Once you're finished designing a pattern, X-Stitch Designer will calculate how much floss you need in the different colors, then print out an exceptionally professional-looking chart coded across several pages. You can print the chart in black-and-white symbols or color ones. Although you can edit the appearance of symbols, you can't view a chart in symbol form before printing. And, unlike Pattern Maker, it doesn't let you adjust the grid and stitch widths on your chart.

**X-Stitch Designer excels at subtlety in image import** The X-Stitch Designer programs' PCX image import feature is one of the best (the low-end DOS program lacks this feature, but you can add it to the program with an extra $29.95 utility). When it converts computer art into color charts, it preserves their artistic subtleties, getting lines, shadow, and color gradations just right. This feature sets it apart from other programs that, when converting art to cross-stitch charts, sometimes produce garish color interpretations or wash out shadowing. MasterStitch's CrossStitch Designer, described next, is the only program that does image import better, but it's not nearly as full featured a cross-stitch design program as the Oxford programs.

X-Stitch Designer's main drawback is that when you convert a photo or clipart to a chart, it will only assign Anchor floss colors to the picture's colors. There's no way to change the default to DMC colors, nor globally change the chart to DMC colors once the clipart is imported. The reason for this is that X-Stitch is endorsed by Anchor, the British thread company that funded its development. In response to complaints from U.S. consumers, Oxford is considering adding instructions to the documentation that will enable customers to change the Anchor default to other brands of thread. In the meantime, you'll need to use an Anchor-DMC conversion chart to convert your chart thread list to DMC or J&P Coats.

I generally got gorgeous conversions of photos and clipart to color charts, although features occasionally washed out. For instance, when I tried to import a charcoal drawing of a flower in shades of gray into a chart, X-Stitch Designer converted it into black-and-white squares, while X-STITCH and PCStitch had no problem charting all the shades. This can sometimes be corrected in Oxford's programs, as well as other cross-stitch programs, by brightening the photo and enhancing its contrast with a graphics manipulation program before importing it into the cross-stitch software.

**X-Stitch Designer has some drawbacks** In the DOS versions you must exit the program and run a separate utility program to convert the clipart or photo to a chart (which means you're limited to one imported image per chart). You must also run a separate program to print charts. Surprisingly, the Windows version of the program even requires that you print with a separate program. There's also a separate program (another $19.95) to scale the design and print in color. It would be better if all these programs were integrated.

While both the Windows and DOS versions of X-Stitch Designer are advertised as working on any PC-compatible, I found that for the Windows version a 486 or Pentium with SVGA is absolutely essential. (In fact, it ran sluggish on my 486.) Eight megabytes of memory is also helpful. Otherwise, you'll be plagued by agonizingly slow screen repaints and memory lockups. The DOS version works best on a 386, but again, lots of memory is essential. And SVGA helps.

One more issue worth noting is tech support. X-Stitch Designer is produced in Britain, and that's where its programmers are. To obtain support, you call the 800-number of the distributor (in California), and the British programmers will call you back. Or you can fax or call Britain directly. Due to time differences, it may take a day or longer to get your questions answered.

For the hobbyist needlecrafter, the $49.95 DOS version of X-Stitch Designer may be too limited with its 16-threads/64-color palette limitation. Also, the need to buy an extra utility to give the program clipart import adds $29.95. Similarly, the low-end Windows program at $64.95 is expensive in light of its limitations. If you're a professional, the high-end DOS and Windows versions at $249.94 and $499.95 will be more to your liking, but the prices are steep, especially in light of what's available in other programs. Be sure to call the company and ask for a brochure detailing the features of the different versions before you buy.

Oxford presently sells three design programs for the Macintosh that are similar to the PC versions, but they're being retooled. The company is also working on a version for the Power Mac.

Figure 5-8
When this "killer" scan of a painting of an elderly librarian in subtle shades of browns was imported into X-Stitch Designer, the software did an admirable job of transforming it into a chart. (Only MasterStitch's CrossStitch Designer did better.) But it would only chart it with Anchor floss colors.

Oxford Craft Software
P.O. Box 208
Bonsall, CA 92003
In U.S.: 800/995-0420, 619/723-6196 (fax)
In U.K.: (0993) 779274; (0993) 702048 (fax)
Requirements: Windows versions—386 processor (486 or Pentium preferred), SVGA, 2 megs RAM, Windows 3.1. DOS versions: 386 processor (will run on 286 but not recommended), VGA, hard disk, mouse. Macintosh versions: System 7, hard disk, 256-color screen and printer, 3.5" drive
Price: Windows versions—Standard version $64.95, Intermediate version $129.95, Enhanced version $249.95, Premium Plus $499.95. DOS versions—Basic version $49.95, plus $29.95 for image-import utility disk, $10 for Color Charts utility to modify basic set of DMC colors used, $19.95 for utility to scale printed charts. Semiprofessional version $189.95 (includes all features of the utilities that accompany the Basic version). Professional version $249.95. Pattern libraries for all versions available for $45.95 to $49.95. Macintosh versions—Basic version $59.95, Semiprofessional version $199.95, Professional version $269.95.

*Note: Unfortunately, you can't take a chart you design in one cross-stitch program and fine-tune it in another. The programs all use their own proprietary file formats to store charts.*

## CrossStitch Designer Tops All at Photo Import for PCs

CrossStitch Designer and its companion utility, Color ImageImport, offer the best photo-to-chart conversion of any cross-stitch program on the market. It was the only one that turned my scan of an old German painting into a chart I actually wanted to stitch—and which I am doing so almost at this very moment! It gave the elderly librarian's facial features subtle colorings, whereas the Oxford Craft programs turned his face into a single-toned tan cloud. All the other programs turned the picture, originally painted in subtle hues of browns, parchments, and yellows, into streaks of red, blobs of brown, and smears that looked like a child's hand-pats in the mud.

I am particularly amazed by the number of small businesses this product has spawned. These businesses run the gamut from artists who transform paintings of historical landmarks into charts to ma-and-pa shops that sell charts of high-school mascots and logos. And CrossStitch Designer customers speak well of this product. Many people I spoke with said they had tried other cross-stitch programs, but couldn't get them working right, in part due to their own newness to PCs. They found in the company president, Tim Plumlee, a devoted ally who goes to great lengths to help customers get their software and PC up and running. I couldn't help but be impressed by the enthusiasm Plumlee's customers have for him and his product.

> "I have no computer background and I still don't know much about computers, but within a very short time I was able to turn out drawings and images with the Master-Stitch program. I started out by scanning in images that I had painted myself. The image was basically camera ready. I jockeyed the symbols around and edited out some extra images. Within two months we had our first chart ready for publishing. The charts we do are quite complicated Victorian things. I never would have done them if I didn't have this program."—Walter Kind, Kind Stitchworks, Seattle, Washington

**CrossStitch Designer is unique, quirky** CrossStitch Designer is unlike any program on the market, from the way you design charts to the charts it prints out. To design a chart, you're given a blank screen, not a grid, on which you draw freehand with colors representing the DMC threads. The printed chart has 40 × 40 stitch segments on individual pages with symbol and color keys on each, so that you can slip them into your needlework bag and stitch them a page at a time. You don't have to grapple with a huge chart.

It has drawbacks. It doesn't support Anchor or J&P Coats threads, and there's no way to signify back, half, or quarter stitches—a significant omission. The program could use work in the error-handling department (it freezes the PC when it's not happy), and the PCX import feature is not conveniently integrated into the design program, which makes for some hamfisted moments at the DOS prompt. Plumlee promises that all these things will be fixed in an upcoming Windows version. Even with these drawbacks, I found myself using the program again and again.

**It gives you basic drawing tools to design with** Designing with CrossStitch Designer is like drawing in a general-purpose computer drawing program. It gives you a pencil tool for freehand drawing; a spray can for dotting areas with color; an eyedropper for applying hints of color; tools for drawing lines, rectangles, curves, circles, ovals, and polygons; and tools for copying, moving, and flipping design elements. If your design has more curves than straight lines, this is a more natural way to design than clicking on squares. If you want to create geometric patterns or alphabets you can zoom in on the portion of the design where you want to place the item, and fill the grid with colors. When you're done painting, CrossStitch Designer prints out a symbol pattern with a very professional look, similar to those found in craft magazines. Unfortunately, it only prints in black and white. Your pattern is standardized to a 200 × 190 stitch grid; you can't specify a grid of a different size. This limits your grid to a stitching area of approximately 14" × 13". Also, there is no symbol editor or way to view the chart in symbol form before printing it, although you can change the symbols that are assigned to different colors to give your chart contrast.

CrossStitch Designer is selective about the type of images it will convert to charts. You need to spend some time prepping the image before importing it with Color ImageImport, reducing its pixels and size. But this is true of all the cross-stitch programs. It can also take the program a long time to convert the photo to a chart (Color ImageImport took twenty-five minutes to generate a chart on a 386 PC but only about seven minutes on a 486).

If you have ambitions to turn artwork or photos into salable cross-stitch charts, this is one program you'll want to buy.

**Figure 5-9**
**MasterStitch's CrossStitch Designer**
**is the very best of all the programs**
**at converting photos to charts.**

MasterStitch Designs, Inc.
P.O. Box 6283
Kent, WA 98064-6283
Phone: 206/413-1054 or 206/850-3302
Price: CrossStitch Designer $119.95, Color ImageImport $49.95
Requirements: 286 PC or higher, 640K RAM, Microsoft-compatible 2-button mouse, VGA or SVGA, hard drive. If you have an old PC XT with a low-density disk drive, MasterStitch will be glad to supply disks for it. Please call.

*Note: If you like the idea of being able to draw your cross-stitch designs on a blank screen with "computer crayons" (as opposed to scrupulously filling in squares on a grid), take a look at the $25 shareware program Patterns Unlimited. It's a simple DOS-based program that will run on a 286 PC (although it requires VGA and mouse). It was originally intended for designing knits, but it's well suited to cross-stitch. It doesn't give you DMC colors to paint with, and it likes to decide for you the size of the grid it will graph designs to, but it may hook you with its simplicity. It also imports PCX graphics. Look for PATTUNLM.ZIP online, or write Personalized Productions, 1055 Westaire Way, Ann Arbor, MI 48103; or CompuServe 71431,2013; or "Lieverj" on America Online.* ✍

## Compucrafts' Software Is Perfect for Macintosh Folk and Owners of Old Apples and PCs

If you're a Macintosh owner, or if you own one of those original Apple IIs, Compucrafts has some great software for you. If you're running a PC as old as an 8088 (the original IBM PC), Stitch Grapher may be the one for you.

**If you're a Macintosh user** Stitch Crafts for the Macintosh ($150) is professional-quality design software that will work on any Mac except for the original Macintosh 512. It gives you three different grid styles on which you can design with any of the DMC colors, plus it lets you create your own grid. You can draw outline stitches; view charts in symbol, color, and silhouette mode; and you can freehand draw and cut and paste. You can also import photos and clipart in PICT format through the Macintosh clipboard. (You design in color unless you have a Macintosh older than a Mac II, in which case you'll see only symbols.)

**If you use an old Apple**  Stitch Grapher for the Apple II is a bargain at $49.95. It runs on the Apple II Plus, IIe, and II98. It's a simple program, which suits the simplicity of the Apple II, and it lets you design only in monochrome, using symbols to represent colors. Yet, in spite of these limitations, several professional designers use it to produce charts for magazines. It requires DOS 3.3.

**If you use an old PC**  Owners of old PCs may find the cross-stitch program of their dreams in the $49.95 Stitch Grapher for IBM-compatibles. It runs on PCs dating all the way back to the original 8088 IBM PC (around 1984 or so), which run CGA or Hercules graphics. It requires at least DOS 3.1, a relatively late version of DOS for an old IBM. While the program requires no mouse or hard disk, its 512K RAM memory requirement may seem steep for an old computer. Designing is done with symbols.

*Note: Compucraft does sell a design program for more modern PCs, but its programmer, David Natwig, asked that it not be reviewed because it's dated. He's at work on a new version, Stitch Grapher Plus for Windows, priced at about $150, which should be out by the time this book is published. It will include tools for drawing half, quarter, and three-quarter stitches, as well as French knots and satin stitches. Rather than limit a pattern to 50 colors/symbols as previous versions of the program do, the new Stitch Grapher will allow users to create designs with up to 120 colors. It will support Anchor, DMC, and J&P Coats palettes and also import clipart and photos through the Windows clipboard.* ✍

When you buy any of these programs, you'll get a guarantee that allows you to upgrade to a better Compucrafts cross-stitch program for a price minus the cost of your original purchase.

Compucrafts
P.O. Box 6326
Lincoln Center, MA 01773-6326
Phone: 508/263-8007; 508/264-0619 (fax)
Price: Stitch Crafts for the Macintosh $150, Stitch Grapher for Apple IIs $49.95, Stitch Grapher for IBM-compatibles $49.95. Estimated price of the promised Stitch Grapher Plus for Windows is $150.

Requirements: Macintosh versions—(Stitch Crafts) any Macintosh except the original Macintosh 512. Apple versions—(Stitch Grapher) Apple II Plus, IIe, and II98, and DOS 3.3. DOS and Windows versions—(Stitch Grapher) 8088 IBM PC (the original PC) or higher, CGA or Hercules graphics, DOS 3.1, 512K RAM. Stitch Grapher Plus for Windows is promised and may be out by the time you read this book.

## *CompuStitch Is Great If You Own a Really Old PC and All You Want to Do Is Draw a Pineapple or Two*

CompuStitch is a simple DOS-based program that lets you design cross-stitch patterns in color on just about any species of PC running versions of DOS as old as 3.0. There's even a version of CompuStitch that will run on a Tandy 1000 (a real dinosaur by contemporary standards).

Use your mouse to click on squares on a grid and fill them with the DMC color of your choice. (Sorry, but if your PC uses CGA or EGA video, you get just three colors.) Your cross-stitch pattern can be as large as 180 × 180 stitches, which is about a one-foot-square piece of Aida cloth. You can draw backstitches, quarter stitches, and French knots. You can also cut and paste elements of your design, move them around, flip or rotate them, and even export them into a different design. When you print out your pattern, CompuStitch also prints out a handy shopping list of floss colors.

CompuStitch is a great program for those of us who don't have much interest in doing more than graphing out an alphabet or maybe a pineapple or two. The serious designer will find the program limiting, because it won't import digitized images or clipart, it won't interface with other graphics software, and it limits your drawing to clicking on squares.

Printing your patterns with CompuStitch is no fun either. When I tried to print my ABCs and pineapples, CompuStitch first printed a big DMC chart and then printed thirty-six pages of fishy looking letters, numbers, and symbols that looked like secret code. The idea behind these pages was that I tape them all together and stitch from the resulting pattern. Right. It would have been easier to stitch the pattern directly from the computer screen.

Still, if you have an older PC, and your design needs are modest, using CompuStitch is easier than shading in squares on graph paper. It's shareware too, so you can try before you buy. It's cheap at $20.

CompuStitch
John George, Jr.
Rt. 3, Box 607
Altoona, PA 16601-9413

Requirements: Mouse optional, any printer that supports compressed printing, DOS 3.0 or higher, CGA, EGA, or VGA monitor
Filename: CSTVGA.EXE for VGA version, CSTCGA.EXE for EGA/CGA version. For the Tandy version mail $20 to the author.
Price: $20

# This Software Lets You Easily Catalog Floss and Charts

*I*f you love to be organized but don't always have the time to be, a cross-stitch supply inventory program can prove an invaluable friend. The following three programs will let you keep a database of the DMC and/or Anchor floss colors that you own. All of the programs circulate as shareware on CompuServe and many other computer services. Unfortunately for Macintosh and Amiga people, they're all for PCs.

## *DMC Inventory*

DMC Inventory is a simple program that records the number of DMC colors you have on hand and prints out a table listing them. The author, Ken Saloranta, tested it on an 80386 PC with a dot-matrix printer mimicking IBM ProPrinter, and makes no claims about its suitability for other PCs or printers. It will probably work fine on an 80286 PC too. It can be had for $10 from Ken Saloranta, 8 Lomond Dr., Apt. 1106, Toronto, Ontario M8X 2W3, Canada (CompuServe: 70621,3202). You'll find it on computer services stored as file DMCINV.ZIP.

## *DMC Database Management*

DMC Database Management is more sophisticated than DMC Inventory. Key in the color numbers of the floss you own, then type in the color numbers needed for projects. DMC Database will print out a shopping list. It also prints labels for the floss. It's available for $10, from Richard Robishaw, 7890 Rt. 46, Orwell, OH 44076. You'll find it on computer services as file DMCINV.ZIP. It requires a PC with at least an 80286 chip and a hard drive.

## *CrossMagic*

My favorite inventory program is CrossMagic. CrossMagic lets you keep an inventory of both DMC and Anchor colors (a conversion utility lets you translate between the two), as well as Balger filaments, Krenik metallics, DMC Flower thread, and Balger ribbon. Color descriptions and numbers for all are already included in the database (which is not the case with some of the other programs), so all you have to do is key in the number of skeins of each that you have. Figure 5-10 shows the materials menu.

CrossMagic lets you inventory any other thread or filament you have. You can also inventory fabrics, beads, and other materials, as well as charts and their requirements. You can even inventory your needles. Cross-Magic will print shopping lists for individual charts and print inventory reports. An evenweave conversion utility tells you how large your design will be and helps you calculate how much fabric you'll need for it.

**These databases will help keep your DMC floss under control.**

You can buy the full version of CrossMagic for $30 from Model Systems, P.O. Box 40047, Glenfield, Auckland, New Zealand, phone 09-366-7471. Order it in the United States at 800/242-4775 or contact Model Systems at CompuServe ID 100240,1477.

A demonstration version of CrossMagic is available on most computer services as XMAGIC.ZIP or XMAG20.ZIP. The demo has all the features of the commercial version except that it will only store data on ten cross-stitch charts. You can also buy the demo by sending $5, in check or bank draft, directly to Model Systems. Please specify the disk size (5.25" or 3.5") that your PC uses.

CrossMagic requires an 80286 PC or higher, 640K RAM, color CGA or better video, and an Epson or IBM ProPrinter compatible printer.

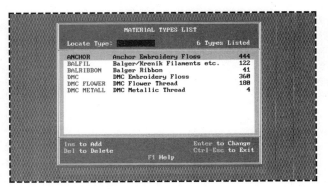

**Figure 5-10**
**The CrossMagic floss and materials inventory program keeps track of your DMC collection and your Balger filaments and Flower thread.**

# *Create Your Own DMC Thread Catalog with Spreadsheet or Database Software*

You can use literally any spreadsheet or database software to create your own floss catalog, even an old copy of Lotus 1-2-3. You can set it up not only to catalog floss but to print project shopping lists like the programs previously described.

Microsoft Works, which comes with many PCs you buy these days, includes both a mini-spreadsheet program and database software; either works just fine. If you don't own a spreadsheet or database program, look on computer services for a shareware one to download. If you have an oldie-but-goodie PC, look for the minidatabase program PC-File by Buttonware (P.O. Box 96058, Bellevue, WA 98009, 206/865-0773). It's stored online as PCFILE.ZIP. A good spreadsheet program is the $20 Alite/R (Trius, Inc., 231 Sutton St., Suite 2D-3, P.O. Box 249, North Andover, MA 01845, 508/794-9377). You'll find it online as ALITE.EXE.

Figure 5-11 shows how a floss database is set up in Microsoft Excel. The process is identical for other spreadsheet programs.

To set up this same sort of catalog in database software, you set up separate fields for floss color numbers, number of skeins, and location. Then you type in all your floss numbers, how many skeins you own of each, and the project they're stored with. When you're ready to generate a shopping list, type **need** in the skein field for each floss color you don't have. Then, use the database's search feature to search all the fields for "need."

**Figure 5-11**
**You can use a spreadsheet program like Microsoft Excel to create your own thread database. Label the first column DMC or Anchor, label a second column Skeins, and a third Location. In the first column type in the complete list of thread numbers. In the second, record how many skeins of each that you own. In the third column type the name of the project that they're stored with. When you need to buy floss for a new project, type "need" in the skein field for any floss number you don't have. After you're done, use the search column feature to search for all cells containing the word "need." Use the report feature to generate and print out a list of all the floss colors you need to buy.**

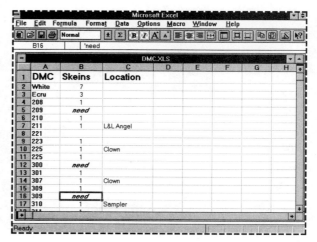

# 6

## HOW TO DESIGN GREAT
## CROSS-STITCH CHARTS ON A COMPUTER

*Whether you use shareware or commercial cross-stitch design software, here are
some tips on using clipart, scanners, and other computer tools for creating original
charts for cross-stitch, crewel, and other forms of embroidery.*

The first step in designing cross-stitch charts on your computer is buying cross-stitch
design software. The second step is learning to use it effectively. Mouse-clicking on
squares to fill a grid with color is fun, but soon you'll be yearning to transform hand
sketches and family photos into cross-stitch charts. You'll also want to take clipart that you
download from computer services like CompuServe and incorporate it into your stitch designs.

You can do all these things with most of the cross-stitch programs described in Chapter 5.
Even low-cost shareware ones will let you import art—photos too—into charts. This chapter
explains the techniques for doing this and reveals some secrets from professional needlework

designers. In addition, you'll learn about low-cost shareware programs that will graph down-loaded computer images into cross-stitch charts.

# Should You Buy a Scanner?

*W*ith a scanner hooked to your computer, you can scan family photos, noncopyrighted art from books, and your own drawings (or your child's) and bring them into your computer so that you can manipulate the images in drawing and cross-stitch programs or incorporate them in word-processing and desktop-publishing documents. Scanners are loads of fun, and their prices have dropped enough to make them a comfortable indulgence for many home computer owners. You can buy a color hand-held scanner for $200 to $300 and a black-and-white one for under $100.

While a hand-held scanner will probably be all you need, flatbed scanners are also available. Preferred by some professional cross-stitch designers, they cost from about $300 to $3,000 and up. Flatbed scanners look and work like photocopy machines: You lay your picture on the glass to scan it. Flatbed scanners can scan a much larger area at one time than hand-held scanners can, and the scans don't end up peppered with "artifacts" caused by jerky hand scanning. While flat-bed scanners are particularly good for digitizing large pictures, many professionals use hand-held scanners. A hand-held scanner will probably meet your needs.

## *Special Considerations for Buying Scanners for Cross-Stitch*

Because color is so important in cross-stitch, you'll want a color scanner, unless you don't mind coloring each square on your design by hand. Either an 8-bit or 24-bit scanner will do. A 24-bit scanner is preferable, however, because it will digitize with a palette of 16 million colors (an 8-bit scanner uses only 256 colors). The 24-bit scanner gives more subtle color since it digitizes with so many more colors.

For scanning photos to use in cross-stitch design, you want a scanner on which you can turn the resolution down very low, because most cross-stitch software translates each dot of a computer graphic into a single cross-stitch. That means that the number of dots per inch (dpi) from the scanner equals the number of stitches per inch on the canvas of your finished cross-stitch design.

If you scan at too high a resolution (for instance 200 dpi or more), you'll end up with a chart containing millions of stitches. (Or else your cross-stitch software will cough and die.) Typical low settings on Logitech scanners are 100 and 200 dpi, but ideally you want a scanner that scans at even lower resolutions. The IBM Easy Option Scanner, for instance, scans at resolutions as low as 10 dpi. Try to get a scanner that lets you turn the resolution down to at least 50 dpi. (See Chapter 1 for more recommendations on buying a scanner.)

## *There Are Options If You'd Rather Not Buy a Scanner*

If you don't think you'd get enough use out of a hand-held scanner to justify the price, consider renting one for those special jobs like transforming that wedding picture of your grandparents into a chart. Look in the Yellow Pages under "Printers" for stores that call themselves "service bureaus." There you can rent a scanner workstation by the hour, and the staff will be willing to show you how to use it. Some photocopy and print shops also rent scanners by the hour. If you can't find a scanner, call a design firm in your area and ask them where they have images scanned.

If none of these options appeals to you, you can take your photos to a photocopy shop to be scanned, at about $9 to $12 per scan. The drawback is that you can't scan the photo over and over and test it out in your cross-stitch software, without having to pay for each scan.

*Note: Always call first and find out if the photocopy shop can provide the type of scan you need according to the directions in this chapter. I visited several copy shops, and when I presented their personnel with a photo and list of relatively simple directions for a scan, they said "Huh? What do you mean, 24 bits?" Some shops charge as much as $2 to $3 extra for a diskette, so bring your own.* ৯✍

# How to Turn a Computer Graphic into a Cross-Stitch Chart

*W*hile the exact procedure for transforming a computer picture into a cross-stitch chart differs with the cross-stitch charting program you're using, your starting point will always be a GIF, TIF, or PCX image that you either create with a scanner or download from a computer service.

You'll first need to crop the image in a graphics program, like a drawing or photo/paint program (see Figure 6-1), or the software that came with your scanner. If your cross-stitch software is DOS based, you'll then need to save that cropped image in the graphics file format the charting program requires and copy it to the subdirectory on your hard disk where your cross-stitch software resides. Next, fire up your cross-stitch software and load the graphic into a chart with the "import" command. (Some programs require that you convert the image to a chart with a special utility before importing it into the charting software.)

If your cross-stitch software is Windows or Macintosh based, the process is easier. Using the square-shaped cropping tool in your graphics program, cut out the portion of the image that you want to chart and copy it to the Windows clipboard (this will probably happen automatically as soon as you cut the image). Now, switch to your cross-stitch software and, using its "Edit/Paste Image" command, bring the image into the program (see Figure 6-2). (Note that some cross-stitch programs don't support clipboard import but instead offer a feature on their File menu called something like "Import.")

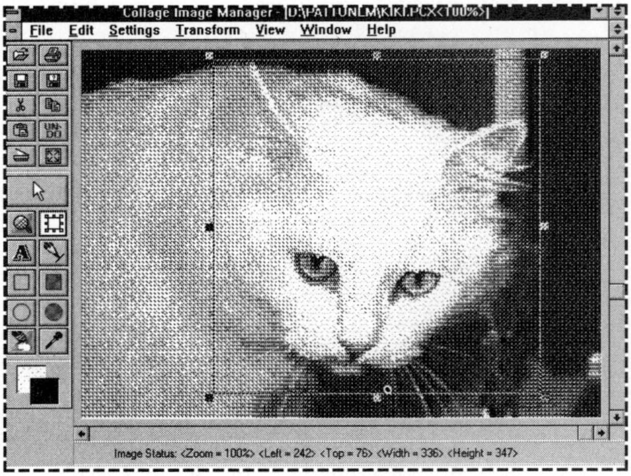

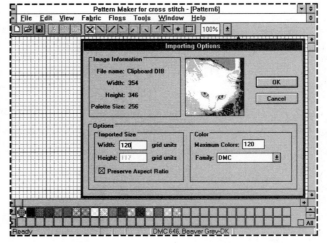

**Figure 6-1**
Before importing a graphic image into a cross-stitch chart, crop it in a graphics program so that it's not too big for the chart.

**Figure 6-2**
If your cross-stitch software is Windows based, like HobbyWare's Pattern Maker or Oxford Craft's X-Stitch Designer, you can easily import the graphic into a chart using Windows' clipboard or the cross-stitch software's import feature. The software may prompt you for the size of the chart and the number of colors you want in it.

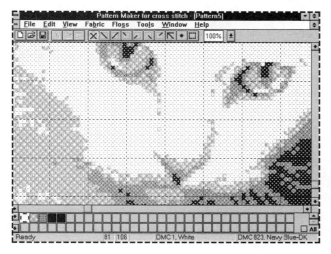

**Figure 6-3**
**If your cross-stitch software's import feature is good like HobbyWare's Pattern Maker, the resulting chart will retain the subtle coloring and texture of the original graphic.**

## *Use a Shareware Utility to Convert Your Image and Crop It*

Depending on the demands of your cross-stitch software, you may sometimes need to convert computer pictures to different graphics formats—from a PCX to a TIF file, for example. There are lots of shareware utilities on computer services that will get the job done, and some will even let you crop the image.

A favorite among PC users is Paint Shop Pro, available online as shareware PSP*x*.ZIP (the *x* will vary with the latest version number), or directly from the publisher for $69 plus shipping (JASC, Inc., 10901 Red Circle Dr., Suite 340, Minnetonka, MN 55343, 612/930-9171). Another favorite is Graphics Workshop, found online as GWSWIN.ZIP for the Windows version or GRFWRK.ZIP for the DOS version. You can order it for $40 from Alchemy MindWorks (P.O. Box 500, Beeton, Ontario L0G 1A0, Canada, 905/729-4969).

## How to Find Computer Clipart
## and Other Pictures to Use in Cross-Stitch Designs

*U*nfortunately, you can't just take any picture from a magazine or book and transform it into a cross-stitch design, especially if you plan to sell the pattern. Most graphic images are copyrighted, which means that someone owns them and you can't use them without obtaining permission and sometimes paying a fee.

Walt Disney is probably the most vigilant copyright protector in the craft world. For years the Disney folk refused to license Mickey and Minnie to pattern companies, despite nationwide letter-writing campaigns by crafters (some of these were organized on Prodigy). Disney feared that once the characters were transformed into cross-stitch and knitting designs, it would lose control over and, hence, ownership of these valuable characters, especially if stitchers began mass-producing them and selling the products at craft shows. (Disney has recently relented and has begun marketing its own line of cross-stitch kits, with the designs cleverly drawn so that the characters can't easily be pirated into other craft designs.)

Copyright is a hot issue in the craft world, and you'll want to avoid infringing on anyone's copyright when you design. The solution is to use clipart. Clipart is drawings and photos, often from old books or advertisements, that either aren't copyrighted or the copyright has expired.

Most graphics and paint programs these days come with large collections of computer clipart that you can freely incorporate into designs you create on your computer. For sources of clipart, your best bet is to check the back pages of PC or Macintosh magazines, especially those that cater to desktop publishers, small presses, or graphic artists. You'll find advertisements for companies that will send you tens, hundreds, even thousands of pieces of clipart, royalty-free, on one CD-ROM for a fee. These collections are always changing, and companies seem to go in and out of business daily, so call for catalogs.

Another excellent source of clipart for owners of hand-held scanners is the Dover line of black-and-white clipart books. Subjects range from flowers to animals, to children, to Aztec and architectural designs. Many books are filled with Victorian art, those charming pen-and-ink drawings like the ones that adorn this book.

Dover clipart books can be found in many bookstores and at any art store, or you can get a free catalog by writing Dover Publications, Inc. (31 E. 2nd St., Mineola, NY 11501, 516/294-7000 or fax 516/742-5049). While you're at it, ask for their craft catalog too.

What about the pictures you can download from computer services? CompuServe and GEnie are treasure troves of computer art. In the different forum libraries you'll find everything from digitized photos of family pets to gorgeous computer graphics. You'll also find computerized images of cartoon characters—many of which are in fact copyright violations. While you can download all of these graphics files to your computer, you may not be able to use some of these pictures in cross-stitch designs if they're copyrighted and you don't have permission from the author. In fact, you should assume that any computer graphic you download is copyrighted, even if there's no notice in the description. If you want to use the image in a design, ask the person who originally posted it on the service. The uploader's computer ID will be listed on the service in the description of the picture. If the person who posted it doesn't own the graphic or seems vague when you inquire as to who does, don't use it. (Head to the chapters on the different online services for directions on how to find clipart on them.)

# Turn Family Photos and Artwork into Cross-Stitch Charts Whether or Not You Own a Scanner

*Y*ou've probably seen the ads in craft magazines for services that will convert your photos into cross-stitch charts for $20 to $30 a piece. You can perform this bit of magic yourself with a hand-held scanner and most of the cross-stitch design programs described in Chapter 5. In fact, if you've purchased some of the low-cost shareware cross-stitch programs you download from online services, you can get results just as dazzling as the professionals. If you don't have your own scanner, try renting one at a service bureau as recommended earlier in this chapter.

Here are some tips for using a scanner to digitize photos and artwork, with special thanks to Tim Plumlee of MasterStitch Designs:

1 Start by choosing a photo or piece of art with good contrast and crisp lines. Faces should be well lit and have few shadows so they will scan cleanly. Always clean up the original photo or picture as much as possible before scanning and be sure to erase any stray pencil lines. Make sure it's flat; if it's a newspaper image, iron it.

2 Find out what graphics format the cross-stitch software you're using requires (PCX, TIF, GIF, or BMP) so that you can make sure that the output you get from the copy shop or service bureau is delivered in the correct format. Tell them what format you'll need. If the cross-stitch software reads TIF files, tell them you want the file in uncompressed TIF format.

3 Make sure that the face of the scanner is free of lint and dust to avoid adding dirt to your scan. Now, turn down the resolution on the scanner. (This may freak out the copy shops, which usually want to give you the highest possible resolution.) Think of the dots-per-inch setting as comparable to stitches per inch. Say you have a 4" × 4" picture you want to transform to an 8" × 8" chart to be worked on 14-count (14 stitches per inch) Aida. You'd want to scan at 28 dots per inch. If the scanner's resolution setting doesn't go down that low, don't worry; just ask them to turn it down to the lowest setting. You can always use the scanner's software to decrease the resolution once the image is scanned and in the computer. (If you do this, don't decrease the resolution too much, because the software reduces resolution by arbitrarily hacking, say, every tenth line from the image, distorting your image and its shading in the process. This is why it's preferable to scan at a low resolution to begin with.)

4    Scan the photo at either an 8- or 24-bit setting. A setting of 8 bits means that 8 computer bits will be used to designate each dot of color and that the scanner has the potential to create up to 256 colors. A 24-bit setting means that the scanner will use 24 computer bits to describe each dot of color in a picture and that it has the potential to create up to 16 million colors.

If you're scanning at home, scan the image with a 24-bit setting. You'll get the best color shading at 24 bits, plus you'll be able to use the high-resolution editing features of your scanning software or stand-alone graphics software to spruce up the picture before turning it into a cross-stitch chart. If you get your photo scanned at a copy shop, ask them to scan at 8 bits instead. The reason is that you take the scanned 24-bit image and reduce it to a 256-color, or 8-bit, one (to reduce the 16 million colors to a more manageable 256 colors, since there are not 16 million colors in the DMC or Anchor floss lines). You'll do this with graphics software once the image is scanned. Your copy shop probably won't be able to handle this added complexity, so for simplicity's sake ask them to scan it at 8 bits/256 colors right off the bat.

**TIP**

*If you have a hand-held scanner, get one of those $35 scanning trays, available at office and computer stores, to hold the image and help you scan in a straight line. If you don't have a scanning tray, use a ruler to make sure you scan in a straight path.*

5    If the photo is glossy or on textured paper, you'll need to make adjustments. If it's glossy, you may want to reduce the light in the area directly around the scanner or lower the scanner's contrast setting. Scanning near a bright light, or with a light shining into the scanner's window, will cause streaking and washed-out details. If the photo is either glossy or on textured paper, try placing a clear matte plastic

*Note:* *Once you've scanned your photo, you'll need to reduce that image to an 8-bit one with 256 colors—using the scanner's software—because your cross-stitch software won't be able to handle 16 million colors. This may seem contrary to the tenets of desktop publishing (which are to scan at high resolution and store the image with millions of colors), but you'll ultimately get the best image if you scan at a low resolution with the most colors possible, then store it as a 256-color image. Remember, your cross-stitch software has to siphon that image into 390 DMC thread colors.* ❧

film over it. Similarly, cover small objects with a plastic sheet to hold them in place while you scan. If the photo's contrast is weak, try turning up the scanner's contrast dial slightly.

6    If you have a 24-bit scanner at home, scan your photo at 24 bits and scan just the portion you want. Scanning an entire picture will result in an image too large to be processed by most cross-stitch programs. Once the picture is scanned, save it in the graphics format that the cross-stitch software you're using requires, usually PCX or TIF format. Once the scan is complete, use your stand-alone graphics software or the software that came with your scanner to crop the picture to a manageable size that your cross-stitch software can accommodate. While you'll need to check your software's manual for the exact size, a typical dimension is 320 pixels wide by 200 pixels high.

7    Once your scan is complete and in the proper file format, reduce the number of colors used in the scan from 24-bit, 16 million colors, to 8-bit or 256 colors.

8    If the picture originally was scanned at 8 bits, before you save it, use the graphics or scanner software to crop the picture down to the dimensions your cross-stitch software wants. Again, remember that pixels translate to stitches per inches; so if you want the design to be 100 × 200 stitches, save the file as 100 × 200 pixels. Check your software manual for guidance. A typical maximum canvas size is 320 × 200 pixels, but you'll probably want your design to be smaller.

**TIP**
*If your scanner scans with a red light, it may have a hard time seeing the color red and may interpret it as white or pink. Similarly, if your scanner has a green light, it may have a hard time with greens. To remedy this, try putting a yellow clear plastic sheet over the photo or artwork, or experiment by turning up the scanner's contrast dial. If scans created with a hand-held scanner suffer from shade variations between strips, you need to calibrate the scanner. Refer to the scanner's software manual for directions.*

9    Now, use your scanning software or graphics program to clean up the image as much as you can, before importing it into the cross-stitch program. Use the software's "sharpen feature" to sharpen the image by about 10 percent. This will make individual pixels appear more defined and will prevent details of the picture from being lost or washed over with a single color when the picture is imported into a cross-stitch chart. Also, increase the brightness and contrast if such features are available in your scanner or graphics software. This can make a world of difference in how well the picture translates into a chart. Some graphics software packages, like Adobe Photoshop (which comes with many scanners), will even let you airbrush portions of the photo or adjust colors, as well as generally clean it up.

Be sure to use the zoom feature of the scanner software to focus in on and delete any "artifacts" or errant black spots that scanning may have introduced into the image.

*Note:  Don't feel bad if you have to import the photo into your cross-stitch software several times before getting a good chart. Sometimes the proportions of your photo may inadvertently have been stretched. Reimporting should solve the problem.*

Once you are satisfied with the way the photo is placed on a chart, you can further adjust the DMC colors of your chart. Pay particular attention to tones and shading in faces, as the range of available flesh tone colors in DMC floss is woefully limited.

Scanning photos is much easier than these directions make it seem. Honest! Try it once. You'll find it a simple, addictive process that takes just minutes.

## Several Shareware Programs Convert Computer Pictures to Cross-Stitch Charts in One Fell Swoop

*Y*ou'll find several little shareware utilities floating around computer services that will let you convert GIF or PCX computer pictures into cross-stitch charts, though they won't let you paint or design graphs. They merely take a digitized picture and convert it into a stitching chart complete with DMC color symbols.

The most popular is PCXCCS, a DOS-based PC program for transforming PCX pictures into charts. It's the successor to another popular utility called GIF2XTS, which turns GIFs into charts. Both programs let you crop and scale the image, add rows and columns, and then print out a black-and-white chart. They work well with the simple color combinations found in cartoons, clipart, and small graphic images but can trip up when fed large, complex pictures.

While these programs are fun to play with, I personally prefer using some of the shareware charting programs described in Chapter 5.

Chris O'Donnell
P.O. Box 113
Middlebury, CT 06762
Phone: 203/758-1451
Price: $40 each
Requirements: PC 640K RAM, EGA or VGA monitor, additional 300K XMS, EMS or virtual memory required for PCXCCS
CompuServe: 70431,1427
Filename: PCXCCS.EXE and GIFXTS.ZIP

## Take Crewel to High-Tech Heights

*B*lack-and-white clipart can be the start of gorgeous crewel designs. The clipart that comes on CDs packed in drawing programs like CorelDRAW! is wonderful for crewel. You'll find cupids, cornucopias, floral swags and edges, and art nouveau borders. Transforming them into crewel patterns takes minutes.

To create a crewel design from clipart, first set up your drawing program so that the ruler is visible on the screen and the snap-to-grid feature is activated. Set the page size to match the letter size of 8.5" × 11" if that's the size of the paper in your printer tray. (I also like to set the page to display in landscape mode, which makes it easier to see and arrange shapes on the computer screen.)

Bring the clipart onto the page by using the drawing program's import feature. Once you've imported the image, you can size it and place it where you want it using your mouse. You can use "copy" and "paste" to replicate portions of the image (the borders in Figure 6-4 are actually three individual pieces of art), and you can import more clipart as you build your design.

Once you've completed your design, you'll need to transfer it to your fabric. To do so, print the design and then transfer it to the canvas with embroidery transfer paper, available by mail order from Clotilde's (800/772-2891). If the fabric is thin, like muslin, a better way to transfer the design is to tape the design to a sunny window or clear-topped glass table with a light beneath. Now tape the fabric on top of the design and then lightly trace over the design with a sharp pencil.

Scanned images also make great embroidery designs. (I once scanned the silver-work on an antique purse, brushed it up in an image-editing program, then turned its whorls into a

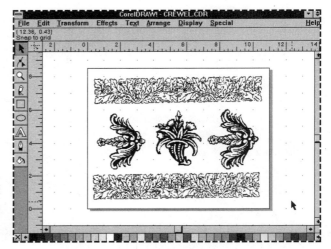

Figure 6-4
The black-and-white clipart that
comes with many graphics programs
can be an unending source of inspiration for crewel.

stitching design.) If the picture is black and white, scan it at 200 dots per inch (lower resolution settings create grainy images), and make sure your scanning software is set for black-and-white line art.

*Note: You can use this design transfer technique to make designs for other kinds of embroidery, too, like red work or backstitch embroidery.*

## Create Custom Needlecraft Graph Paper with a Spreadsheet Program

*Y*ou can use a spreadsheet program like Microsoft Excel to create and print custom graph paper for those days when you prefer to design cross-stitch with pencils. This is especially handy if you need that sometimes-hard-to-find graph paper with slightly rectangular grids on which you draw duplicate stitch or cross-stitch designs for sweaters.

I've used Microsoft's Excel as an example, but you should be able to follow a similar procedure to create graph paper with any spreadsheet program. If it doesn't work the first time, try it again. It will!

To create graph paper with Microsoft Excel 5.0 for Windows, begin by opening a new file (see Figure 6-6). Highlight with your mouse an area 50 squares horizontal (A to BB) by 100 squares vertical. Now click on "Format/Row Height" and enter 5. Click on "Format/Column Width" and enter .5 for square grids or .75 for rectangular ones. To print out the graph paper, head to "File/Page Setup" and click on "Cell Gridlines."

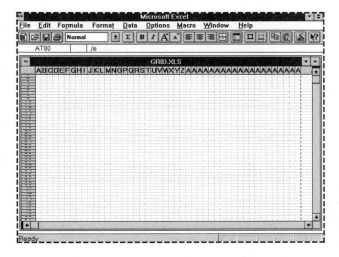

Figure 6-5
This is what your screen will look like if you use Excel to create custom graph paper.

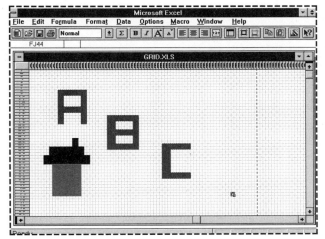

Figure 6-6
You can use spreadsheet programs like Excel to chart cross-stitch patterns on your computer screen, but this can be time consuming. It's also nearly impossible to draw curves. (The atomic-looking blob in the bottom left-hand corner is supposed to be a house.)

Before you print, there is one important thing you must do: Type in a character—any character—in the very bottom right-hand square of your grid so that Excel thinks it is actually a spreadsheet and worthy of printing. Once you've done that, head to "File/Print" to print out. These directions print an easy-to-work-with 50 × 100 grid on an HP Laserjet. You may have to experiment with the number of squares in the grid so that it prints out nicely on one page on your printer.

You can also use your spreadsheet software to graph cross-stitch patterns right on the computer screen, as in Figure 6-6. To do so, fill the spreadsheet cells by typing in characters or numerals, just as if the cells were graph paper squares. You can use the cell fill patterns too, like those found in Excel in the Format/Patterns/Pattern menu, which are similar to the square-shading patterns in some cross-stitch programs. You can fill individual squares or, with your mouse, select an area of spreadsheet cells and fill them with the pattern. This is time consuming, though, and you may prefer to stick to drawing on graph paper.

# 7

## AMAZING FEATS OF STAR-TREK–LIKE COMPUTER WIZARDRY INVOLVING YARN

*Whether you knit, crochet, tat, needlepoint, or weave, there is software to help you create spectacular garments and charted designs. These packages are so astounding you'll swear you've been whisked into the twenty-second century!*

ow do you think garments are created on the *Enterprise?*" was the topic of a recent discussion among knitters on Internet. Star voyagers on the ship in *Star Trek: The Next Generation* have at their disposal an amazing machine called the replicator. Press a few buttons, and the replicator clones any garment, foodstuff, or office supply item that it is fed.*

---

\* My husband, who is a Trekkie, maintains that the *Enterprise* replicator is not very good at cloning organic materials. For instance, while it may be able to duplicate a slice of strawberry-rhubarb pie, it will probably come out tasting a bit plastic. Similarly, when it clones an Aran knit sweater, it comes out looking like a wrinkled fiberglass sheet with ribbing attached. This is what he says, anyway. Since my husband spends 75 percent of his life in the Star Trek discussion groups on Internet, and the other 25 percent watching reruns of the show, I believe that, if he's not correct, he's at least given the matter a lot of thought.

This trick can leave fiber artists puzzled. If citizens of the twenty-fourth century have replicators at their disposal, does anyone bother to knit, weave, crochet, or tat? And if so, how? You'll find at least part of the answer in this chapter.

Some of the computer software available for knitters is so amazing you'll think you have been transported to the days of starships and replicators. Feed it garment measurements, tell it the yarn you'll be using and the gauge, and it will print out knitting directions lickety-split. Or draw the pieces of the garment on the screen with computer-aided design tools, fill them with color and elaborate geometric patterns, then watch as the knitting machine you have hooked to your computer knits the sweater for you, the computer displaying the rows of stitches on its screen as each one is knit. You can also knit the sweater by hand, with the computer helping you along.

Crocheters can use stitch-painting software to grid patterns for filet crochet, or they can use fractal software that paints lacy flowers on their screen that they can use as the basis for breathtaking original lace designs. Needlepointers will find software that graphs needlepoint designs so quickly and beautifully there's no need to buy another pricey painted canvas again. Weavers have a plethora of weave-design and loom-control software available to them.

This future is just unfolding, but already it looks like members of the twenty-fourth century will not only still enjoy the feel of yarn, shuttles, and needles in their hands, but will deploy high-tech tools in ways that will help them achieve even greater artistic satisfaction with those ancient implements. And some of those tools are available now.

> **TIP**
> Internet is a favorite haunt of weavers. You'll meet other weavers in the Usenet discussion group rec.crafts.textiles, as well as in the weavers' mailing list. Head to the chapter on Internet for more information. Several computer bulletin boards around the country also are maintained by and for weavers. Read the BBS chapter to learn more about them.

## The Wide World of Knitting Software

*F*our types of software are available for knitters: software that calculates sweater patterns, software that designs garments, stitch-painting software, and software to do tasks like calculate yarn needs.

Software that calculates sweater patterns has you feed it your measurements; select the kind of collar, sleeves, and sweater style you want; then it prints a custom pattern for the gauge you give it. You can use these programs for generating simple patterns for both hand and machine knitting or for adjusting store-bought patterns to custom sizing. The programs are relatively inexpensive, usually costing from $15 to $60, and you can find several available as shareware.

More sophisticated knitting software, like KnitKing's Design-A-Knit, lets you design the shape of knit garments on the computer screen and add color patterns to the garment. These programs, which run hundreds of dollars, often boast spectacular graphics that show your sweater in multiple views on the computer screen, or being knit row by row. While you can use some of these products to create hand-knitting patterns, the software is intended to be used with particular brands of knitting machines. You hook your electronic knitting machine to your computer, and the computer directs the knitting of the sweater you designed. Chapter 8 covers the knitting machine–computer connection in more detail.

Stitch-painting software puts a grid on your screen that you use to paint knit designs. You can use the software to graph not only knit patterns, but also other yarn-based textiles—such as needlepoint, crochet, and rugs. You create the design on screen, then you print it and follow it like a traditional graphed knit design. Several programs suitable for graphing knits are sold as shareware. The top-of-the-line program, Cochenille's Stitch Painter, lets you save your designs in formats you can use with knit-styling programs like Design-A-Knit or other machine-knitting software.

Finally, various utility programs for knitters let you create graph paper for charting knit designs with pencils, keep track of your yarn stash, or calculate how much yarn you'll need for a project.

**TIP**
*Where do knitters hang out when they go online? On Internet the most popular knitting coffee klatch is the KnitNet mailing list, which most knitters appear to tap into from their office computers. CompuServe's knitting discussion area in its Fibercrafts Forum is another favorite spot for both hand and machine knitters. Perhaps best of all is the Fibercrafts Forum library of information files and patterns. It's full of patterns and tutorials for Design-A-Knit, Passap knitting machines, and much more. Delphi is also a great spot to meet other machine knitters (and get hard-to-find technical advice for that irascible knitting machine). See the chapters on these online services for more advice on tapping in.*

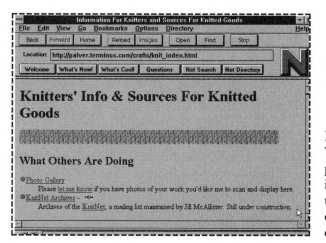

**Figure 7-1**
The easiest way to reach all the knitting patterns and databases on the Internet is to aim your World Wide Web crawler to the page dubbed "Diana's Knitting on the Web." It's at http://palver.foundation.tricon.com/crafts/

## SOFTWARE THAT CONJURES SWEATER PATTERNS

*By Elizabeth Clouthier*

Have you ever lingered in front of a rack of knitting patterns, looking for a certain sweater—one with dolman sleeves, perhaps, or a baggy raglan with a boat neck? You couldn't find it, so you settled for a pattern of a ho-hum cardigan or else went home and created your own with a calculator and pencil.

A growing number of software packages can help you create your own sweater patterns. You type in measurements and then choose elements of the garment, like the type of sleeve, the neckline, the collar, and the length. You then knit a sample swatch with the yarn you plan to use, then type in its gauge. After a bit of calculation, the software comes up with knitting instructions that take you from cast-on to armhole shaping, tell you how much yarn you'll need, and even provide you with scale drawings of what the finished knit garment pieces should look like. All you need to do is spend about fifteen minutes entering data.

Don't confuse these programs with the kind that let your computer interface with an electronic knitting machine and tell the machine what to knit. Those software programs are covered in the next chapter. The programs reviewed here print knitting patterns that you print and follow as you knit just like you would a traditional knitting pamphlet. Some of these programs generate patterns for knitting machines, as well as for hand knitters. They also come in handy for quickly adjusting store-bought patterns to your gauge and sizing preferences.

## Are These Knitting Programs Worth Buying?

How good are these computer-generated patterns? As good as anything you'd generate by hand with a calculator. (Since the number crunching that goes into knit patterns is simple, it's hard to screw up.) Be advised that none of these programs lets you work surface design into a sweater pattern or generate instructions for color changes. Only a few will adjust patterns to accommodate knit designs like cables or special repeating stitches. Most assume that you will be using one gauge throughout a sweater, although a few accommodate different gauges for ribbing. In addition, the graphics in these programs are not particularly dazzling. Although some of the Windows-based programs draw outlines of sweaters and pattern pieces on your screen, some of the DOS-based ones won't.

Most of these pattern-writing programs range from $40 to $90. For many knitters that's a lot of money. Is it worth it? That's a tough question, and it figured strongly in my judgment of the programs. For each review I asked myself: "Would I pay money for this?" Often the answer was no. I feel comfortable with my calculator and would rather put the $40–$90 toward yarn.

The best buys in knit software, as in other categories of craft software, can be found among shareware programs. Knitnotes for Windows is only $14.95 and has many of the capabilities of $70 programs. Knitware Sweater Design for DOS is $40 and brings with it all the bang of programs twice that price. Plus you can try these programs before buying.

Elizabeth Clouthier calls herself "a compulsive knitter, adequate spinner, and wanna-be weaver." A mathematician by training, she supports her yarn habit with her chosen trade of computer programming. She has found her spiritual home in midcoastal Maine and shares it with husband Tom, daughter Cait, Foamy the cat, and Gusthewonderpuppy.

*Note: The world of knit software is PC dominated; most of the programs reviewed here are for PCs. Products that are also available in Macintosh or Amiga versions are noted in the "Requirements" section at the end of each review.*

## Design-A-Pattern for Windows

*It's good for machine knitters, but its patterns are austere.*

Design-A-Pattern for Windows is a knit pattern-generating program geared for machine knitters who want to produce a variety of fitted garments. There are four versions of the program: one for sweaters, another for skirts and pants, one for darted tops, and one to create vests. Each is $75. (There are also four versions available for DOS.) All the programs work similarly: You first pick your garment from a pull-down menu, then choose style elements like neck style, sleeve length, and so on. You choose from a list of standard women's, misses', men's, and children's sizes (or enter custom measurements), then Design-A-Pattern displays each of the pieces on the screen and calculates a pattern for it. It lets you create instructions for knitting garments vertically or sideways.

Installation is simple, but the manual is overwhelming. Only four pages are devoted to explaining how to run both DOS and Windows versions of the program. The rest is concerned with how to knit a sample swatch (to determine gauge) and how to take body measurements. The program has the annoying habit of asking you to enter a digit from the software registration number each time you load it. (The registration number is listed in the manual.) The number it asks for is different each time, so you have to look it up. I found that you can hit every number, 1 through 9, until the program accepts one. What a pointless exercise.

## It Has Many Garment Options and Is Easy to Use

Design-A-Pattern is pleasant to use. In the sweater version you can choose from drop shoulder, raglan with both curved and straight seam, saddle shoulder, set-in with cap, angled or square seam, gusset insert, and sideways. For necklines you can choose from V, notch-V, square, boat, adjustable crew, tab-front crew. In the darted tops version, you can choose from curved set-in, angled set-in, tunic top, sun top, sun top with bra, asymmetric top, double breasted, and crossover front. The vest version of the program gives you boleros, and also vests having bottoms that are concave, convex, pointed, or rounded. The skirts and pants module lets you choose from A-line, gored, hip yoke, scallop hem, and sideways skirts, as well as briefs, culottes, shorts, and slacks.

Once you've chosen your garment, you can select a standard size that ranges from women's 38–50, misses' 6–18, men's 34–50, and children's 2–18. You must add your own ease to garment patterns that you create, and neither manual nor program offers much help in figuring out how to do that. You can also create patterns from custom measurements, but the number of measurements you must enter is overwhelming: You need to enter eighteen for a sweater, including upper arm, mid arm, wrist, and so forth. When I design patterns using my calculator, I never need more than chest and sleeve measurements.

Finally, you type in gauge and machine-knitting information (tensions, number of needles). The program requires that you enter the latter even if you plan to knit by hand, another annoyance. I found that if I didn't set the maximum needles number large enough, the program wouldn't come up with my pattern.

## The Patterns Are Definitely for Machine Knitters

Once all the data is entered, you can view the pattern pieces and adjust measurements accordingly (see Figure 7-2). When I generated a sweater for a standard size 14, I ended up with a pattern that measured a meager 36" across the chest. I needed to check all the measurements and add some ease.

When you're finished tweaking, the program comes up with instructions that are austere, to say the least. They consist of a table that includes row number, number of stitches, and the stop/start needle. Any text instructions pertain only to machine-knitting techniques like when to scrap, rehang, and so forth. The instructions are sufficient for machine knitters, but hand knitters who don't like math will find them frustrating to translate.

You can also print out outlines of the pattern pieces to scale, with a stitch-by-stitch or inch-by-inch grid. The versions of the program for darted tops and vests let you take your pattern pieces and their grid into Windows' Paint and apply some surface design.

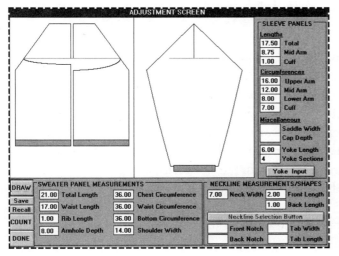

Figure 7-2
Design-A-Pattern displays individual pattern pieces and lets you tweak their measurements. It doesn't like to add ease, though, so be sure to add your own. This is the intriguingly named "Sun Top With Bra" pattern from the "Darted Tops" module.

Home machine knitters might find Design-A-Pattern worthwhile, assuming they're content with one $75 module. The production knitter will find more value in a full-featured program like Design-A-Knit. Keep in mind, too, that if you feel at home calculating patterns with a pencil and calculator, you'll probably find the program and all the body measurements it requires too fussy. Similarly, if you just need to change a gauge or neckline in a pattern occasionally, you don't need this program.

Ileen's Needle Nook
4106 W. Ely Rd.
Hannibal, MO 63401-2539
Phone: 314/221-9456
Price: $75 for each program, or $140 for 2, $195 for 3, or $240 for 4
Requirements: PC with 80386 or higher, VGA monitor, Windows 3.1

## Knitnotes 1.0

*Here's a dandy low-cost program for hand and machine knitters.*

*T*his nifty little shareware flat-knit sweater-pattern calculator has been winning raves from knitters on Internet. You enter your measurements and gauge, select your garment options, then Knitnotes draws the garment pieces and calculates a pattern for you to print. It creates patterns that can be used by both hand and machine knitters, but it's for experienced knitters only. It's a no-frills program that won't calculate how much yarn you'll need for a project or accommodate color/texture designs in a pattern, but for $14.95 it can't be beat.

From pull-down menus you choose from pullover, cardigan, or vest patterns with drop shoulders or set-in sleeves. For collars you're limited to crew, V-neck, and cut/knit. You're limited to one pattern for the sleeves, but you can specify length and size of armhole.

Built-in sizes include women's 32–50 (with 4" added for ease) and men's 34–50 (with no ease added). You can adjust the dimensions of sweater pieces by specifying chest width, neckline, and sleeve measurements. The program is intelligent enough to, say, automatically adjust armhole depth when you change sleeve width but not smart enough to keep you from entering outrageous dimensions. It happily drew a schematic for me when I specified a 25" long V-neck on a 22" long sweater!

You also specify gauge (the program wisely asks for gauges for both the main knitting and ribbing, something its higher priced peers don't always do) and choose from hand- or machine-knitting options. If you're a machine knitter, you enter the number of needles on your machine, and the program sensibly checks that there are enough needles on your machine to knit the gauge. It will warn you if your sweater will not fit.

## *It's Fun to Use—but for Experienced Knitters*

Once you're done entering measurements, Knitnotes calculates the pattern. You can pop into a graphics screen to view the fruits of your work: Knitnotes draws outlines of the sweater pieces, and it lists knitting particulars like gauge, measurement of the pieces, and abbreviated knitting instructions along the bottom, as shown in Figure 7-3. An experienced knitter will have little problem knitting a sweater from just this information. You can't edit this screen, but you can easily hop back to the first screen and alter, recalculate, and instruct the program to redraw pattern pieces.

The only problem I had with Knitnotes (and one other knitters have also had) is that it refuses to print patterns for certain computer-printer configurations. Since it stores patterns to disk in binary format, you can't simply display the pattern in your word processor and print it out as a text file. This problem will hopefully be remedied in future versions (its author has been creating and distributing new versions at a furious rate, in response to feedback from knitters online).

The program's only documentation is a tiny text file that addresses a few basic capabilities of the program. But Knitnotes is straightforward enough to install and use that most computer users won't have problems with it. When you register the program, you get an instruction booklet and a new version that includes children's sizes, measurements in centimeters and inches, and the ability to print out row-by-row instructions for sleeve increases or decreases.

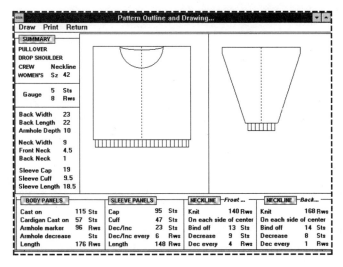

| SUMMARY | | | |
|---|---|---|---|
| **PULLOVER** | | | |
| **DROP SHOULDER** | | | |
| **CREW** | Neckline | | |
| **WOMEN'S** | Sz 42 | | |
| Gauge | 5 Sts | | |
| | 8 Rws | | |
| Back Width | 23 | | |
| Back Length | 22 | | |
| Armhole Depth | 10 | | |
| Neck Width | 9 | | |
| Front Neck | 4.5 | | |
| Back Neck | 1 | | |
| Sleeve Cap | 19 | | |
| Sleeve Cuff | 9.5 | | |
| Sleeve Length | 18.5 | | |

| BODY PANELS | | SLEEVE PANELS | | NECKLINE *Front ...* | | NECKLINE *Back...* | |
|---|---|---|---|---|---|---|---|
| Cast on | 115 Sts | Cap | 95 Sts | Knit | 140 Rws | Knit | 168 Rws |
| Cardigan Cast on | 57 Sts | Cuff | 47 Sts | On each side of center | | On each side of center | |
| Armhole marker | 96 Rws | Dec/Inc | 23 Sts | Bind off | 13 Sts | Bind off | 14 Sts |
| Armhole decrease | Sts | Dec/Inc every | 6 Rws | Decrease | 9 Sts | Decrease | 8 Sts |
| Length | 176 Rws | Length | 148 Rws | Dec every | 4 Rws | Dec every | 1 Rws |

**Figure 7-3**
Once you choose your sweater features and enter measurements, Knitnotes draws a schematic of the garment pieces and displays abbreviated knitting instructions.

Judith Hiam
129 Revere Rd.
Grand Island, NY 14072
Phone: 716/773-7524
Price: $14.95; after you register, upgrades are $5.95
Requirements: PC-compatible with Windows 3.0 or higher, 80386 or higher, VGA, and DOS 3.1 or higher
Filename: KNITNO.ZIP

# Knit One 2.1

*Use it to adjust store-bought patterns to size and gauge preferences.*

You type a knit pattern into Knit One and it automatically adjusts the directions to your size and gauge preferences. Unfortunately, Knit One demands a lot of typing and time to effect its simple pattern transformations. That, and a steep $79.95 price tag, make it a dubious buy.

Also, Knit One's installation doesn't work well. I won't go into details of all the fooling around I went through to get it running. Suffice it to say that a new computer user will not be amused by the situation.

## Typing in Patterns Is a Lot of Work

You type into this DOS-based program the gauge and finished dimensions of your original pattern, followed by the desired dimensions. Knit One will adjust any knit pattern from sweaters to mittens to moccasins, should you care to knit them.

The program works by searching for key words like "sts" and "inches" and translating the numbers associated with them based on a proportion. You must type in stitching information for two sizes of a pattern. For instance, you need to type **cast on (240, 260) sts.** If you just type in **cast on 240 sts,** the program won't work.

As you type, your pattern appears on the left side of the screen, and the translated version appears on the right. I found it was easiest to type one pattern step per line, for it's when you press ENTER that Knit One performs the translation. The process of typing in the pattern requires concentration because you must mentally convert the pattern from the terminology it is written in to the terminology Knit One requires. What a lot of work! The program will not recalculate correctly if the range of values in a pattern step is not represented in the correct order. Nor will the program recalculate how many times to repeat a decrease row (for instance, "decrease every 4th row"). Also, it will not take into account color and texture variations in a pattern and adjust them accordingly.

## Its Pattern Transformations Aren't Bad, but Its Price Is High

The finished pattern prints out in a sprawl across multiple pages and includes the original pattern you typed into the program. The sweater pattern directions Knit One created in one of my tests were nearly identical to the directions for that particular sweater size in the pattern book—not a bad translation feat. However, considering all the typing required, not to mention the high price, I prefer my calculator and pencil.

Penelope Craft Programs, Inc.
P.O. Box 1204
Maywood, NJ 07607
Phone: 201/368-8379
Price: $79.95
Requirements: Any PC running DOS 3.3 or later, 192K RAM; Macintosh Plus or higher, 384K RAM

# Knitware Sweater Design and Knitware Tops/Vests Design 1.33

*These programs provide more low-cost shareware gold for hand and machine knitters.*

*T*he Knitware products are solid, no-nonsense programs for creating text-only knit patterns for hand and machine knitting. They're simple to use, they come with good manuals, and one of the programs—Sweater Design—is available as shareware, so you can try before buying.

Sweater Design ($40) starts by asking you to enter your design preferences: measurement units (centimeter or inches), knitting method (hand or machine), needle size and type (metric, Canadian, or U.S.) or knitting machine type (the latter entry is just to remind you which machine you have designed the pattern for). You can also tell Sweater Design if you plan to knit a portion of the sweater by hand rather than machine (like the ribbing or sweater body) or vice versa, and it will generate a pattern accordingly. Any of these preferences can be easily changed for each sweater you design.

After this, Sweater Design prompts you along with questions and lists of choices about the sweater you want. If you like, you can enter the planned start date for the project and a completion date (a prospect that may strike some as amusing), as well as washing instructions for the yarn. You choose from standard chest sizes 30" to 48" for women, 32" to 52" for men, or 20" to 32" for children. Or you can enter custom sizing for up to nine sweater measurements. Unlike some of the other programs, it won't create patterns adjusted to accommodate repeating patterns or stitch designs.

You can choose from pullover or cardigan style, specify any of four lengths (waist, regular, hip, or coat/tunic), and choose from sleeve types: drop-shoulder, set-in, or raglan. For the latter, you can choose from only two lengths: three-fourths and long. Necklines can be crew, V, square, scoop, butted boat, or overlapped boat. (Unlike other programs reviewed, you can't specify different front and back necklines.) Collars can be single, double, rolled edge, cowl, turtleneck, or shawl. As you can see, there are enough options to keep you knitting for a long time.

## *There Are a Few Quirks, but They Are Good Patterns Overall*

One of your options is ease. You can choose from skin tight, to tight, moderate, comfortable, and oversized/coat. Unfortunately, neither program nor documentation explains what factors are used to calculate these ease settings; so if you enter custom sizing, you won't learn the dimensions of the sweater's finished chest until a screen appears much later at the end of the pattern-generating routine. However, I didn't spot any ease problems with the measurements I tried; the ease seemed to be in line with current style conventions.

One bugbear I ran into is that when I accidentally pressed the down arrow on one of the garment style screens, the program would not let me back up to change my erroneous entries. This happened several times. The manufacturer says they are in the process of correcting this.

Once you've made all your garment choices, Knitware calculates a pattern, which you can save to a file or print out. Hand-knitting patterns are easy to follow and include measurements of the finished garment. Machine-knitting patterns are equally concise, although they don't include row-by-row summaries of the needles in use like patterns generated with Style & Chart by Lucy Morton (reviewed on page 156). The manual offers additional knitting advice and techniques. When Sweater Design prints to a file, it gives the file an obscure name that you must hunt for, then promptly rename, or it will write over the file the next time you save a sweater pattern.

You can display schematics of sweater pieces, but you can't print them directly (you need to use a screen-capture utility, which is not included in the program). The screens don't list measurements of the individual pieces, though I found that flipping back and forth between the schematic and measurement screens gave me confirmation of some of my alterations.

Alterations are not a no-brainer with Knitware. The user's manual states that not all measurement relationships are checked, but it doesn't say which ones are not. Thus, you should verify all sweater measurements. For instance, the program erred when I changed a sweater's finished chest size; the back width remained unchanged. Standard sweater calculation routines always change the back when you change the chest measurements.

The program will calculate how much yarn you need for the sweater, but only if you first figure out how many rows/stitches one ball of your yarn will produce at the desired gauge—a chore you might not want to contemplate.

## *The Tops/Vest Version Works Similarly*

The Tops/Vest Design program ($40) is nearly identical to Sweater Design except that it gives you two basic garment types: a top described as "lightweight and close-fitting" and a vest that is "heavier and looser." You can choose from three sleeve styles—short-sleeved, cap-sleeved, and inset—and, unlike with Sweater Design, you can choose a style for the back neck that's different from the front. The program is not shareware.

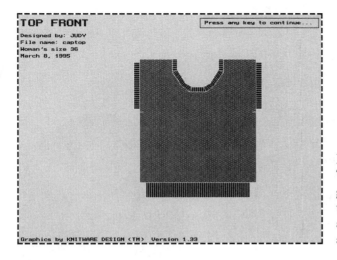

Figure 7-4
The Knitware pattern-creation programs will draw your sweater, but they don't include measurements for sweater pieces on the screen. This is a top created with Tops/Vest Design.

Installation of both programs was easy—although their screen colors are annoying. Overall, the Knitware programs are useful and solid. If you're an avid knitter, you'll get your money's worth out of at least one.

## Knitware Doll & Bear Clothes Design 1.4

*Sweater patterns for Care Bears, trolls, and Raggedy Ann can be yours in minutes.*

*I*f you like to outfit Teddy with knits as fashionable as the ones you create for the rest of the family, you'll love Knitware Doll & Bear Clothes Design. Lest you blanch at its $45 price tag, consider this: It offers more garment styles than just about any other knitwear design program, including straight, flared, and ruffled skirts; skirt and pullover dress styles (with lacing at the waist); trouser styles that include straight, bell-bottomed, legging, and suspender styles; and of course pullovers in a variety of formats that include drop shoulders and ribbing. (Sorry, no cardigan option is available.)

For sizing, you can choose from eighteen standard doll sizes—including nine bear sizes like Pooh Bears, Care Bears, musical bears, and fat bears. Cabbage Patch dolls, Raggedy Anns, and troll dolls (two sizes) are covered, as is Barbie. You can also generate patterns for Wrinkled Dogs and Wrinkled Elephants. If you can't find something that fits, you can customize sizing by adjusting a selection of measurements as thorough as those provided for Knitware's sweater pattern–generating programs. You can even specify ease. Thorough documentation helps you through the designing stages.

In most other ways, the program is nearly identical to other Knitware programs. You can generate patterns for both hand and machine knitting, and you can display and print schematics of the pattern pieces.

The next time your daughter wakes you in the middle of the night to tell you her Cabbage Patch doll is cold, just fire up this program. You'll be done knitting doll-sized, Nordic-style leggings in no time.

Morningdew Consulting Services Ltd.

7604 Morningdew Rd.

R.R. #5

Victoria, B.C.

V8X 4M6, Canada

Phone: 604/652-4097

Internet: ue773@freenet.victoria.bc.ca

Price: Sweater Design, $40; Tops/Vest Design, $40; $70 for both; Doll & Bear Clothes Design, $45

Requirements: 286 PC or higher, 384K, DOS 3.0 or later, VGA recommended

Filename: KWS.ZIP

*Note: See Chapter 18 for directions on how to find doll and bear clothes knit patterns on Internet. Be sure to join the Internet Ragdoll Mailing List to meet other toy makers in cyberspace.*

## Style & Chart 2.1 by Lucy Morton

*These patterns are great for hand and machine knitters but suffer grievous interface.*

*I*f your computer is a vintage one—say, a Commodore 64 or 128—or one of the original IBM PCs or compatibles, Style & Chart may delight you with the easy-to-follow custom flat-knit sweater directions it creates for hand and machine knitters. If your PC is any newer, the program may leave you scowling at its pre-Cambrian user interface that asks the same questions over and over and lacks menus.

On the plus side, Style & Chart offers some sophisticated styling options for flat-knit sweaters that go beyond the "do you want a pullover or cardigan?" approach of other sweater programs. For instance, you can create patterns for sweaters with curved side seams and specify the type of edges you want on the bottom of sweater and sleeves—crocheted edges, for instance, or sewed hems, or noncurling knit stitches like seed stitches. You can create patterns for pullovers, cardigans, and jackets in a wide range of sizes for men, women, and children using either standard sizes or custom sizing.

You can choose from square, round, and V necks; straight, pointed, and ribbed collars or neckbands; cap, drop, wide, or raglan sleeves; and all these styles can be fitted, straight, short, or long. The program also gives you more choices of the kind of front band you want (knit on, picked up, ribbing, and nonstretch knit stitch are among the choices) than other programs. Patterns make accommodations for fancy pattern stitching.

## The Patterns It Prints Are Easy to Follow

The program prints separate directions for hand and machine knitters. Both are easy to follow, with lots of plain English (Judy Heim claims she found them the least intimidating of the patterns produced by the programs reviewed). The knitting machine patterns include row-by-row summaries so you can keep track of where your knitting machine is in the pattern.

The downside is that Style & Chart has an interface that harkens back to the days when PCs tried to emulate insurance company mainframes. Each time you load the program, you must tell it what kind of monitor you have, how you want the program to display, and whether you want to save your pattern to disk or print it (there's no way to save the settings). It then prompts you along, asking you to enter fitting information, style choices, and whatnot. Once you've typed in responses, it generates charts of the garment and pattern pieces, and they're not bad. The drawback is that the only way to print them is to use a third-party utility program to capture screens and print them later. Fortunately, printing pattern directions is a more straightforward procedure.

While the patterns it generates are good, going back and changing the sweater or the fitting details to fine-tune the pattern is a pain. Once, while trying to save a pattern to disk, I typed in a name that Style & Chart didn't like, so it issued a programming error and then dumped me out to DOS. "What happened to my pattern?" I cried. Although the slim manual includes a glossary of knitting terms, it includes little advice about installing or running the program.

Lucy Morton is a fine and savvy knitter and has created a program that is a distillation of her wisdom, but users of today's computers may find the interface too off-putting to justify the $90 price.

Cochenille Design Studio
P.O. Box 4276
Encinitas, CA 92023
Phone: 619/259-1698
Price: $90 for complete program; $55 for single module, such as women's, men's, or children's patterns
Requirements: Any PC-compatible with 256K RAM or more, no graphics card required; any Amiga or Commodore

**Figure 7-5**
**Style & Chart by Lucy Morton offers sophisticated sweater styling options and easy-to-follow charts for hand and machine knitters, but the interface is not for the timid.**

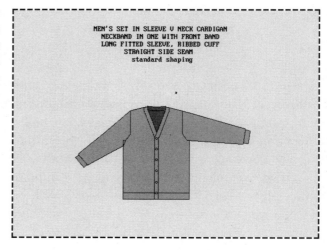

MEN'S SET IN SLEEVE U NECK CARDIGAN
NECKBAND IN ONE WITH FRONT BAND
LONG FITTED SLEEVE, RIBBED CUFF
STRAIGHT SIDE SEAM
standard shaping

*Note: You can purchase an additional program to use with Style & Chart that will let you take a sweater designed with Style & Chart, overlay a pixel-per-stitch graph on it, and use it with any paint program to design knit patterns on the sweater. You still need a screen-capture utility to save the design to a graphics file, though. The Style & Chart Stitch Graphing Utility is available just for the PC version of Style & Chart and is $10 when purchased with Style & Chart, $20 if purchased separately.*

# Sweater 101 on Disk 2

*This program is pricey but good for hand knitters who are just starting to calculate their own patterns.*

*H*ere's a frustration-free tool for creating very basic flat-knit sweater patterns in standard sizes. It's based on Cheryl Brunette's book *Sweater 101*. You choose your style (pullover or cardigan; with drop-shoulder, set-in, or raglan sleeves; crew or V neck), pick a size (women's 30–50, men's 34–50, and children's 6 months to 12 years), and specify your gauge. Sweater 101 prints a pattern of about two pages with text and schematics. It will estimate the yarn you need for the project without requiring you to rip a swatch, like other programs do.

The predefined sizes are appropriate to body measurements—the woman's size based on a 36" chest produced a sweater with a 38" finished chest. Altering measurements of pattern pieces is easy, although I found that changing the armhole depth did not alter the sleeve width and vice versa, a troubling faux pas. You can enter four body measurements and sleeve lengths into the software, but the manual explicitly states that these are for the user's reference and that the program only uses chest size to calculate the sweater pattern.

## *Knitters Who Like to Adjust Patterns Will Like It*

Installation is easy and on-screen help is good, so the program's limited documentation is not a big drawback. Disadvantages are that the interface isn't intuitive, and not much mouse support is offered. For instance, it took me several minutes to figure out that to view sweater pieces, one must scroll down from the entry screen. Because the program is DOS based, screens are not pretty like the Windows programs are.

The printed row-by-row instructions are concise, although peculiar—the right-justification formatting of numbers makes them hard to read. You can print schematics of pattern pieces.

Sweater 101's $59.95 price seems high considering its archaic interface and the fact that it offers few bells and whistles. Still, it's a suitable tool for hand knitters just taking that first bold step out of store-bought patterns into the world of calculating their own. To that end, excerpts from Brunette's book are included in the program. Knitters who like to do a lot of rejiggering of patterns will like it too, but I'd be wary of using it to generate anything but standard-sized patterns in light of the arm-hole problem described earlier.

Patternworks
P.O. Box 1690
Poughkeepsie, NY 12601
Phone: 800/438-5464 or 914/462-8000

Price: $59.95
Requirements: PC with 512K, DOS 3.3 or greater

# The Sweater Workshop for Windows 1.1

*This program is designed for knitting raglans in the round, but you may want to buy the book version instead.*

*T*his is a computerized version of techniques in Jacqueline Fee's book *Sweater Workshop* for creating the "perfect raglan sweater" in the round. If you don't mind the $69.95 price tag, you'll find it a good value if you knit a lot of raglans this way. Otherwise, you may want to buy the book instead. I was disappointed that the software didn't offer pictures of the styling and shaping options found in the book, but that's my only major complaint with the program. Overall, I found it easy to use and much simpler than crunching out a basic gauge change by hand. I would prefer using it to a calculator.

The manual is spare, limited to basic installation instructions and a walk-through of how to calculate a pattern for a sample sweater. But it should be sufficient for most users. You start by choosing your sweater shape (pullover or cardigan) and neckline (seven choices including hooded and placket). You get four choices of sleeve style (fitted through fuller), and you can choose one of six raglan decrease methods. (The built-in help handily describes the methods and their best applications.) You then enter your gauge and choose your finished chest size. The program includes no standard, predefined sizes. All sizing is based on desired finished chest size, utilizing Elizabeth Zimmermann's EZ Percentage System for calculating sweater proportions based on finished chest size.

The program calculates button spacing after you have specified the number of buttons, how far they will be placed from top and bottom, and the length of the sweater from the underarm. You can specify the number of stitches in a repeating pattern, and Sweater Workshop will adjust your pattern accordingly, prompting you to find out if you want to make the sweater larger or smaller to accommodate the pattern. Whenever you make a menu choice, a picture of a sheep materializes on the bottom of The Gauge Page (see Figure 7-6) in what is clearly a knitter motivational ploy. (The program also advises you to stick to knitting with natural fibers when it prompts you for the kind of yarn you'll be using. I was tempted to tap in "virgin acrylic" just to see what would happen but was afraid the sheep would disappear.) Also shown on The Gauge Page are the choices you've made and some of Sweater Workshop's calculations, such as number of stitches to cast on.

The program prints the kinds of patterns that hand knitters are familiar with: thorough but not chatty. However, they can span as many as seven pages, listing every single decrease

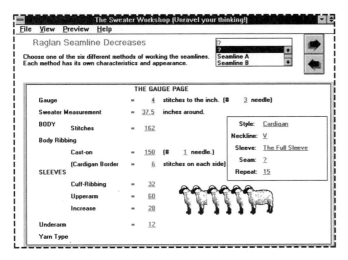

Figure 7-6
Sweater Workshop prompts you in a straightforward manner for things like chest size and number of buttons, then displays your choices and some of its calculations in its Gauge Page.

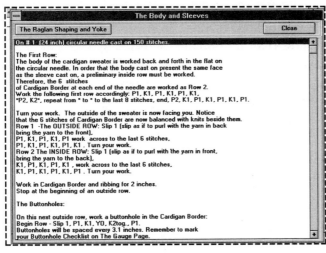

Figure 7-7
With Sweater Workshop you can preview the pattern for your raglan before printing it out. Hand knitters will find its patterns easy to follow.

in a check-off list, an option I would like to skip. The graphic printouts of the sweater itself are nothing but generic sketches showing the body knit in the round, how to join the sleeves to the body, and how to work the yoke. Overall, Sweater Workshop is a solid value for raglan fans—assuming you don't mind the sticker price.

Patternworks
P.O. Box 1690
Poughkeepsie, NY 12601
Phone: 800/438-5464 or 914/462-8000
Price: $69.95
Requirements: IBM-compatible running Windows 3.1

# Sweater Maker 1.2

*This shareware pattern maker is for machine knitters.*

Sweater Maker is a quick and simple program to use. You choose your size, specify your rib and row gauge and tension, and choose your pullover options from choices on one central menu, and it prints a pattern for machine knitting. But its style options are limited: You choose from either a set-in or drop shoulder; and for neck you get a choice of crew, V, crew with placket, and deep crew. The program lacks some of those nifty machine-knitting options that Design-A-Pattern gives you, such as the ability to knit pieces sideways. It displays schematics of sweater pieces on the screen, which you can print out. But when it came time for me to print them, the software and the Laserjet IIIp staged a war, and the software, the printer, and the computer died. The directions it prints are jargony and confusing.

On the plus side, it includes a wide range of built-in men's, women's, and children's sizes, and you can customize sizing by a dozen different measurements, including problem fitting areas like back shoulder width, armhole depth, and sleeve-to-underarm length. However, there's no way to specify ease except for chest. The program is shareware, though, with a request that you pay "whatever you think it's worth."

Seedling Software
8 Hillcrest Heights Lane
Mount Vernon, IA 52314
Price: $49.95 or "whatever you think it's worth"
Requirements: Any PC-compatible with 256K; Hercules, CGA, EGA, or VGA graphics
Filename: SWMAKER.EXE

**Figure 7-8**
You can buy sweater patterns on the Internet's World Wide Web. Aim your Web crawler to http://usa.net/spider/fhs/0thswtr.html.

## SOFTWARE FOR GRAPHING KNITS, NEEDLEPOINT, AND OTHER CHARTED DESIGNS

If you're like me, you loath pulling out graph paper and toiling with colored pencils to chart a knit design, even if it's a simple one like a snowflake for the back of mittens. You scowl when it comes time to trace a detailed pencil sketch onto graph paper so that you can transform it into a multicolored needlepoint design or elaborate sweater design. A growing genre of programs is designed to rid your life of those messy pages full of pencil erasings. They put a graph on your computer screen and give you a color palette and drawing tools to fill in the squares. It goes without saying that drawing with them is easier than with graph paper because you can make changes so quickly. They also print charts that are a joy to follow.

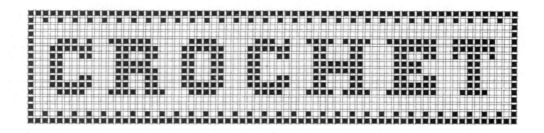

## Use Low-Cost Cross-Stitch Shareware to Design Knits, Crochet, and Other Graphed Needlework

Programs designed specifically for charting cross-stitch are covered in detail in Chapter 5. They differ from the programs designed for charting knits in that their palette consists of the hundreds of colors of DMC and Anchor floss. More significantly, their grids are perfect squares, not the slightly rectangular squares needed to chart knits. For a low-cost PC program that can be used for designing knits (or crochet), you may want to try HobbyWare's Pattern Maker, a cross-stitch program, or the shareware version by the same name, that does use rectangular grid squares. At $35 for the shareware version, or $59.95 for the low-end version, this may be your best buy.

If needlepoint canvas designing is your game, any cross-stitch design program will prove an ideal charting mechanism. It will give you all the tools you need, from color-art importing to large canvas size. While needlepoint wool isn't available in as many colors as cross-stitch thread is, it never hurts to have a large color palette to work with when you're charting. Head to Chapter 5 for more information.

## Low-Cost Knit Charting Shareware Is Available for Macintosh Users

While there's a paucity of cross-stitch software for the Macintosh (and what's available is expensive), there is a $15 Macintosh program for charting knit designs. Called ColorKnit, it gives you a grid, drawing tools that include a paintbrush and bucket, plus tools to cut, paste, and rotate portions of your design. You can design with up to twenty colors. If your Macintosh is a black-and-white one, you can choose from a palette of twenty patterns to draw with. You can even see what the design will look like once it's knitted. ColorKnit is available on most online services. It exports images to PICT files but won't import clipart.

E&P Ware
Paul Duffy
71 Oxford St.
Somerville, MA 02143
Price: $15
Internet: epware@world.std.com or 72521.417@compuserve.com
Filename: COLKNT.SEA

## Cochenille's Stitch Painter 2.0 Is Superb for Graphing Knits, Crochet Patterns, More

The best textile charting software is Cochenille's Stitch Painter, available for PCs running Windows and for Macintoshes. Among the many things that make this program special is the wide selection of professional-looking symbols and textures it gives you to graph designs with, along with the high quality of its printed graphs. Its graphs of knit designs are particularly beautiful. You can use knit stitch–like symbols, together with fiery colors, to make your graphs both visually arresting and easy to follow. The charts of crochet

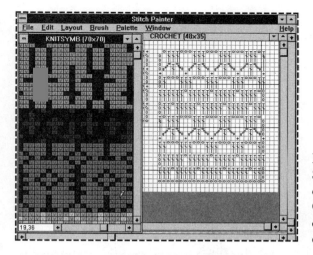

Figure 7-9
Stitch Painter is wonderful for charting knits, as well as crochet. On the left is a charted knit design. On the right is a filet crochet pattern.

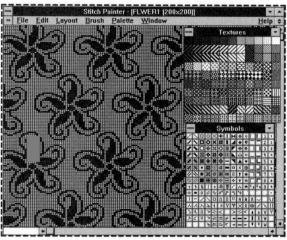

Figure 7-10
Stitch Painter is perfect for working with the geometric patterns of knits and other textile designs. You can paint your designs in color or use the texture or needlework symbol palettes.

patterns (like filet crochet) look the spitting image of the kind you see in magazines. If you're a professional textile designer who cares about looking good, this is the program for you.

Stitch Painter's other strength lies in the tools it provides for working with geometric and repeating designs, like those in knits. For instance, you can create custom "brushes" that will fill areas on your chart with repeating designs you create, and you can save those brushes to use in other designs.

You can also export knit designs to formats that will work with high-end knit design software packages like Design-A-Knit, Creation 6, and System 90's Intoshape. Formats include PCX, DAK, S90, CUT, LBM, and BBM.

## *Stitch Painter Is Easy to Use*

Stitch Painter is very intuitive. You fill graph squares with color, textures, needlework symbols, or all three. Drawing tools include paintbrush, eye dropper, a line and arc drawer, and square and ellipse tools that can be used to outline areas on the grid with a selected color, texture, or symbol, or to fill the area. You can flip and rotate elements of your design. You can also incorporate lettering from any installed font.

You can set grid squares to any dimensions. You can also set major grid lines (the dark lines dividing grid regions by, say, 10 × 10 squares) and can readjust the gridding dimensions of images on the fly (something you won't find in any other graphing software, even cross-stitch software). You can make the grid disappear, which is helpful when shaping knit designs. Multiple levels of zoom let you focus in on portions of a design or view the whole design from a distance.

You can display multiple designs on the screen simultaneously and cut and paste between them. You can import bitmaps into your design (such as clipart and scanned images) but only if the image is black and white. You can also "mix" your own colors to augment those in Stitch Painter's 46-color palette. Stitch Painter will calculate the number of stitches in each color or symbol so you can estimate how much yarn you'll need for a project.

## *Machine Knitters and Serious Designers*
## *Will Like Stitch Painter the Most*

Stitch Painter has two versions: the "gold" version for $165 and the "standard" version for $85. The most notable difference is that the standard version lacks the symbol and texture palettes. It also lacks some extras—it doesn't calculate stitches, for instance.

If you're merely looking for a program to help graph the brim of a stocking cap, the Stitch Painter programs may be overkill; you're better off using shareware cross-stitch software. But if you're a professional textile designer, an avid machine knitter, or are looking for a knit graphing program to use with Design-A-Knit or any other high-end knit designing software, you should give Stitch Painter a look.

Cochenille Design Studio
P.O. Box 4276
Encinitas, CA 92023
Phone: 619/259-1698
Price: $165 for "gold" version, $85 for "standard" version

Requirements: For PC version—386 or higher, VGA or SVGA, Windows 3.1 or greater, 4 megs RAM. For Macintosh version—Macintosh Plus or higher, System 6 or higher. There is also a version available for the Amiga that differs slightly from the Macintosh and PC versions.

You can find demo versions of Stitch Painter available online. Look for SPDEMO.ZIP for the PC version and STCHPA.SEA for the Macintosh version.

## Software for Knitting's Mundane Chores

$S$hareware programs to inventory yarn and print graph paper on your computer printer occasionally pop up on online services. I prefer to use spreadsheet software for these chores, since most computers today have spreadsheet software installed on them. If yours doesn't, you can find low-cost spreadsheet shareware programs on any online service. (See the cross-stitch chapter for directions on how to use spreadsheet software to create custom graph paper and to inventory materials.)

One nifty commercial program you may want to consider, especially if you're a prolific machine knitter or shop owner, is Yarn Calc by Patternworks (P.O. Box 1690, Poughkeepsie, NY 12601, 914/462-8000 or 800/438-5464). This $39.95 program for any PC with 512K RAM calculates how much yarn you'll need for any project, from sweaters to afghans. The project can be one color, have color repeats or isolated motifs, and have multiple textures.

To use the program, you knit, crochet, or weave a swatch—then type in the number of strands used, the yards or weight of the yarn, and the gauge information. When working with color, you tell the program whether the pattern consists of stripes, triangles, circles, squares, or rectangles and their sizes. You pick the project type (choices are afghan, scarf, dress, blanket, skirt, socks, mittens, and hat) and type in its finished dimensions (for instance, for hats you'd type in circumference and height). Yarn Calc will tell you how much yarn you'll need and how much it will cost.

### SOFTWARE FOR WEAVERS

There are hundreds of software packages for weavers, both commercial and shareware ones. Here are some to get you started.

*Note: If you're a weaver, you owe it to yourself to get online with CompuServe. You'll find a wealth of weaving information in the Fibercrafts Forum, ranging from texts discussing dyeing issues to lists of spinning and weaving magazines. You'll find a list of dye plant sources (look for file DYEPLT. TIP), a compilation of legends of spinning and weaving (LEGEND. THD), a program for calculating warp and weft thread needs for projects (YARNCA. TXT), and tips for adjusting Ashford wheels (ASHADJ. TIP). You'll also find digitized images of textiles. You'll meet lots of other weavers online and can participate in some of their offbeat activities, like the pet hair swap. Head to Chapter 12 for more information.*

## Fiberworks PCW Is a Favorite for PCs

*M*any weavers with PCs like Fiberworks PCW. It's a general-purpose weaving design program that lets you draw on a computer screen what weavers have always graphed out tediously with colored pencils and graph paper. Fiberworks sells optional modules that give the program loom control. You can set up drawdowns for up to thirty-two shafts and sixty-four treadles. Designs can be up to 2400 warp ends and 4800 picks and can have sixteen colors. You can view designs on the computer screen as drawdowns, color and weave, interlacement, rep/warp faced, weft faced, bound weave, or double layer. You can view the back of the weave as well as the front. A fabric-analysis feature lets you pick apart a design thread by thread.

You can download a free demo of this DOS-based program from most online services. In the weaving file libraries look for a file with the letters PCW, PCWDEM, or PCWDEMO.

Fiberworks
27 Suffolk St., West
Guelph, Ontario N1H 2H9, Canada
Phone: 519/822-5988
Price: $170 (without loom control); $35 extra for loom control for Cyrefco Compu-Marche, J-COMP, SLIPS, or Schacht COMBBY; $85 extra for loom control for AVL Compu-Dobby
Requirements: Any PC-compatible with 512K RAM (640K recommended for loom-control options), DOS 2.0 or higher, one floppy drive, optional mouse. If your PC has no graphics adapter, or uses CGA or EGA, request the standard version. If your PC has VGA or SVGA, request the enhanced version.

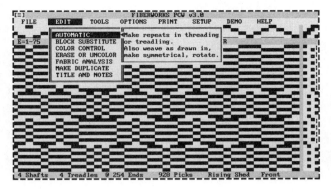

**Figure 7-11**
Fiberworks PCW is a capable and sophisticated program that will work on just about any PC. Plus, you can use it to control a wide variety of looms.

## Weave for Windows Is a Low-Cost Alternative

*I*f you blanch at Fiberwork's $170 price tag, and aren't interested in software that will control your loom, Weave for Windows may prove a good alternative. It's not as sophisticated as Fiberworks PCW, but weavers seem to have fun with it. It also provides the added benefit of letting you copy drafts and drawdowns to the Windows clipboard and use them in other applications (like your word processor when you create weaving guild newsletters). You can download a wonderful demo of it from most online services. The file name to look for is WV_DEM.EXE.

Shuttleworks
16018 Spring Forest Dr.
Houston, TX 77059
Price: $55
Requirements: 386 PC or later, EGA or higher graphics, Windows 3.1 or later

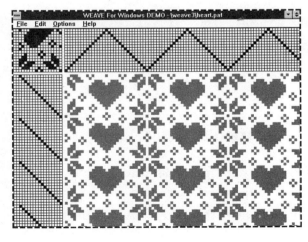

**Figure 7-12**
You can download a demo of Weave for Windows from most computer online services. It's a fun, graphical program that you can use to design drawdowns.

# Free Weaving Programs Are Available for DOS

*T*wo free weaving programs that will run on just about any PC in existence are available on many computer services. You can use them for simple designing. Weave lets you create designs of up to 1,023 warp or weft threads and up to 16 treadles or 16 shanks. It's stored online as file EZWEAV.ZIP. If you can't find it, try sending E-mail to the Internet address: keister@poincare.phys.cmu.edu.

WeaveView is another design program worth looking at. You can use it to do color drawdowns of various weaves. It requires a VGA monitor but will work with only 256K of memory. If you're a commercial weaver, you must register the program for $10. You can find it online as file WEAVIE.EXE. You can also write William K. Stark, 1441 McLaren Dr., Carmichael, CA 95608.

# Macintosh Users Like Swiftweave

*S*wiftweave is a high-end drawdown program for the Macintosh that can be used to control AVL looms or any electronic loom with a SLIPS interface. You can create repeating patterns quickly and view the drawdowns in various scales. You can also analyze a design's threading and vary the thickness of selected threads. You can view designs with the threads outlined. The program will accommodate up to 256 harnesses.

AVL Looms
601 Orange St.
Chico, CA 95928
Phone: 800/626-9615
Price: $300; you can get a demo for $25, which will be credited toward the program if you buy it (there's a demo available online, but it's a very old version)
Requirements: Any Macintosh with 4 megs RAM and System 7

# EasyWeave Is a Low-Cost Alternative for Macintoshes

*E*asyWeave is billed as an entry-level design program for home weavers. Its design tools include a pencil for clicking on and off dark squares of fabric elements, like threading, tie-up, treadling, and peg plan; and a crayon for coloring warp and weft. It supports up to 32

harnesses and 32 treadles and warp and weft lengths up to 600 threads. There's a Tromp-as-Writ option to make treadling duplicate threading. Additional tools make it easy to create straight repeats, mirrored repeats, and other variations in weaving elements (threading, treadling, peg plan) and in warp and weft color assignment. Printing options include threading, treadling, or whole drawdown in two grid sizes.

EasyWeave supports three Dobby loom drivers, including AVL Compu-Dobby and Cartridge, SLIPS (for Schacht COMBBY), and the Macomber Air Dobby. It can also be used to create unique computer-generated designs and color weaves.

Designer Software
500 S. Salina St., 6th Floor
Syracuse, NY 13202 or
P.O. Box 6351
Syracuse NY 13217-6351
Phone 800/490-0118 or 315/422-0118
Internet: weavemaker@aol.com
Price: $145, loom drivers $75 extra. A free demo will be mailed out on request; the demo will be online in the future.
Requirements: Macintosh SE or higher, 5 megs RAM, System 6 or higher, black-and-white or color monitor

## WeaveDraft Is Budget Shareware for the Macintosh

WeaveDraft will design patterns of up to nine colors for looms with up to eight shafts and eight pedals. It can draft sample patterns 36 squares wide and 20 squares high. It's very easy to use; just point and click to change threading, tie-up, or pedaling.

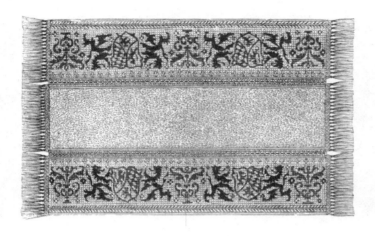

Nick Gammon
P.O. Box 124
Ivanhoe, VIC 3079, Australia
Internet: 100033.1340@compuserve.com or nick@connexus.apana.org.au
Filename: WVEDR1.SEA
Price: $20
Requirements: Any Macintosh, either color or black-and-white

## More Information on Weaving Software

You'll find reviews of weaving software in these magazines:

*Computer Textile Exchange*
Abracadata, P.O. Box 2440, Eugene, OR 97402, 503/342-3030

*Handwoven*
Interweave Press, 201 East Fourth St., Loveland, CO 80537-9977, 303/669-7672

*Weaver's*
Golden Fleece Publications, 824 W. 10th St., Sioux Falls, SD 57101, 605/ 338-2450

*Shuttle, Spindle & Dyepot*
121 Mountain Ave., B101, Bloomfield, CT 06002

"Let's Get Cookin': Recipe for a Computer," by Sigrid Piroch, *Weaver's*, issue 17 (2nd Quarter, 1992), pp. 8–9.

"Hook Your Loom to a Computer," by Sigrid Piroch, *Computer Textile Exchange*, vol. III, no. 1 (Spring 1991), p. 506.

## Spinners Join Hands in Cyberspace

*I*f you're a hand spinner, you owe it to yourself to join the National Electronic Spinning Guild, an informal organization of about one hundred spinners who keep in touch on various online services and Internet. The group publishes a hefty bimonthly newsletter in which members relate the goings on in their lives. They teach each other to spin, exchange fibers, and hold annual retreats dubbed "Bent Nail." To join, send an Internet message to Jamieson Forsyth at JamiesonF@delphi.com. In return, you'll receive the newsletters as electronic messages on whatever online service you subscribe to. If you're not online, the newsletters will be sent to you by regular U.S. mail.

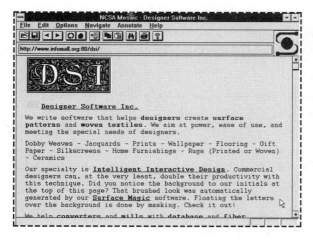

**Figure 7-13**
**You can log on to the Designer Software World Wide Web home page at http://www.infomall.org/dsi to learn more about EasyWeave and other high-end software products for professional designers and textile artists.**

*Yes, even on the info highway you can find crochet patterns for cat toys and Barbie doll wedding gowns. You'll find them in an electronic library called the FidoNet Craft Distribution Network. See the chapter on computer bulletin boards and the chapter on Internet for directions on how to tap in.*

# LAUNCH LACE MAKING INTO
# THE SPACE AGE WITH FRACTALS

*W*hen you think about it, lace and mathematics are a natural pairing. Mathematics tells us things about the universe with its symmetries; lace does too. The frost patterns on windows are reflected in the stars, and the mightiest ebb of a spinning galaxy is mirrored in the gentle swirl over the surface of a pond. If we look around us, we see endless patterns; and while we can use mathematics to describe them, lace likewise shows us their symmetries.

*Fractals are a form of mathematical equation that, when allowed to dance over a computer screen, paints lacy designs that may start as cobwebs, bloom into peacock eyes, and at the next moment explode into fierce galaxies. Their animated, random patterns have been described as the geometry of life. In the following article lacemaker Christiane Eichler follows fractals from their initial inspiration for her lace designs along the path to their implementation in thread. She explains how you can be similarly inspired by this lifelike computer graphic, whether you're a tatter, crocheter, or bobbin-lace maker.*

*Free and low-cost fractal software is available for literally every make and model of computer, and you can find it on all the computer online services. Because these programs have been around since the dawn of home computers, if your computer has a graphics adapter, you can find fractal software that will run on it.*

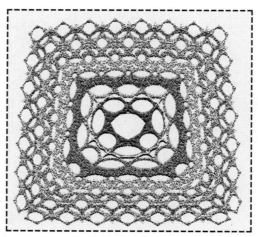

Figure 7-14
Fractal-generating software can provide endless inspiration for lace makers. It's not hard to imagine this as a tatted antimacassar. It was designed by Christiane Eichler of Cologne, Germany.

# Spinning Fractals into Tatted Doilies

*by Christiane Eichler*

Several years ago I visited a friend I had met through CompuServe. He showed me a fascinating program that painted lacy designs on a computer screen. The designs were called *fractals,* and were created by putting into motion a complex computer algorithm called Hop-along Fractal. As I watched the lacy designs swirling over the screen, changing colors, sprouting picots like in tatting, blossoming with lushness one minute, rotating into delicate webs the next, I wondered: Would it be possible to use these as the basis of tatting designs?

I exchanged E-mail with the programmer who had written the program (HOP: Fractals in Motion), and eventually I purchased the popular PC drawing program CorelDRAW! After some experimentation with both programs, I found a way to take lace from the computer screen and reproduce it with a tatting shuttle and thread.

## First Step:
### Run a Fractal Program

First, you must run some kind of fractal-generating program. I like Fractals in Motion. As it runs, painting lacy designs on your screen, pick ones you like and save their parameters to your hard disk. That way, you can later "play" the same fractal again and take screen snapshots or experiment with fractal parameters without losing the original design that you liked. You should let the fractal

program run for a while, because even fractals that start out looking dull can later blossom in beautiful ways. Here's how to generate fractals that are well suited for use as the basis of lace designs.

৯ Keep the picture from being distorted by rotation. Most fractal-generating programs will have a "Rotation" setting (in HOP it's found in the Mathematical Parameters section of the program). Turn it off. You see from Figure 7-15 that the "doily" isn't parallel to the picture surface. Designing is easier from a pattern that's not tilted.

৯ Set the pixel shape to the "Circle" setting and other pixel attributes to very conventional parameters (in HOP, these parameters are found on the Graphic Effects page). The settings you should make are: Set "Elliptic" to off; turn off "Oscillate"; set "Fill" to solid; turn "Reflection" off. Similarly, turn off "Connect," "Shadow," and "Grid"; set "Twinkle" to 0. Other settings will result in fuzzy, nonlacy pictures or else will slow down the picture's animation.

৯ I prefer setting the fractal background to black (so it's easy to see the lace) and using a rainbow palette without stripes for the fractals themselves, which will make it easy to later manipulate the picture with a paint program. Several such palettes are built into HOP.

৯ If you're a registered user of the HOP program, you'll find a setting page called Tuning Hop. Some suggested settings that will cause the program to generate lacelike fractals are: Patterns only = 0 %, Rotation = 0 %, Slow Pixels = 0 %, Shadows = 0 %, Black background = 100 %.

## Second Step:
### Take Screen Shots

Once the fractal program is in motion and lacy pictures are flowering over your screen, you'll need to make screen shots of the ones you like. You can use either the screen-shot feature of your fractal-generating program (if one is built in) or else a screen-shot utility, either purchased from a store or downloaded from a computer online service. I recommend that you take the screen shots in GIF format so they're easy to work with in your

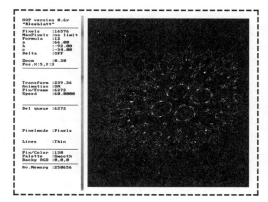

**Figure 7-15**
This fractal, generated with a fractal-generating program like Fractals in Motion, can be your starting point for creating beautiful lace designs.

drawing program later and retain their vibrancy. I also recommend that you avoid taking screen shots in the fractal program mode that displays the fractal's parameters (no need for mathematics cluttering up your lace screen).

Take as many screen shots as you like. I recommend taking multiple snapshots of moving fractals that you like. You should also write down the fractal parameters for each shot. This will help you identify your screen shots later and perhaps get even better shots of the same fractals.

Now that you have a collection of fractal screen shots, and your hard disk is full, you'll need to sift through them with a GIF-viewing utility and decide which to use for your lace design (see Figure 7-16). Be sure to copy the others to floppies or a back-up tape for later use.

### Third Step:
### Prep the Fractal in an Image Program

Once you've chosen a fractal, you'll need to prep it in an image-manipulation program. (I like to use Corel's PhotoPaint, which is found in CorelDRAW!) The smaller the image the easier it will be to handle in your drawing program. Now, invert the fractal (Figure 7-16). This will change the black background to a white one, with the fractal painted in colored pixels. Do not change the picture to black and white or grayscale. It is easier to

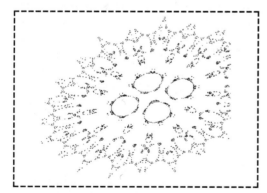

**Figure 7-16**
Once you've chosen your fractal, you need to invert the image from design-on-black to design-on-white in your graphics program to make it easier to work with.

draw on colored pixels. Save the image and head to your drawing program.

### Actual Lace Design Starts
### in a Drawing Program

Every drawing program is different, but most let you create drawings in different levels (importing images into one level, for example, and drawing on them in another level). Essentially, you want to import your fractal design into one level, then lock the level so you can't change it. In another level, you would draw a rough sketch of the fractal's outlines, then connect them with lines according to the lace-making technique you plan to use (Figure 7-17). In CorelDRAW! you would start the process by opening the Level roll-up menu. You would create a new level called, say, "bitmap," and import your fractal design onto this level.

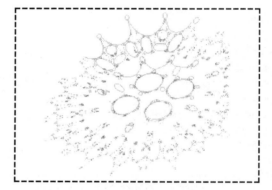

**Figure 7-17**
Start to draw your lace design in your drawing program by connecting the dots in the fractal.

As you are drawing your lace design, you will need to improvise a bit, guessing where lines should go when the pixels don't create a clear enough picture. This is where your creativity comes in. You can change the design to find your vision. When you are through sketching, you can discard the original fractal from the picture (Figure 7-18). You would do this by first unlocking that level and then deleting the level "bitmap" from the Level roll-up menu.

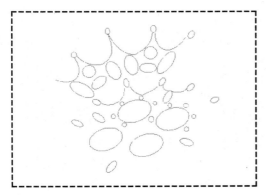

**Figure 7-18**
This is what your doily design looks like when you discard the fractal layer after you're through drawing.

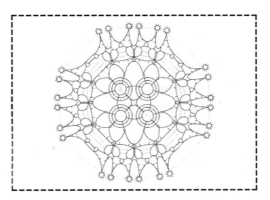

**Figure 7-19**
Use the drawing program's mirroring tools to replicate the motif of your lace and make your doily nicely symmetrical.

Now you can enhance your lace sketch with colors or thicker lines or with other technical information for creating the lace. I draw thick lines to show where chains and rings are and finer lines to depict parts of the lace connected by picots or pieces of bare thread without knots. I add color to show which parts of the design should go into which row. When you have finished drawing, print your sketch.

### Get Out Your Shuttle

It's time to get out your thread and shuttle. You tat from your printed fractal sketch. As you tat, jot on the sketch, with a pencil, the number of stitches, picots, joins, and so forth, so you can remember what you've done (see Figure 7-20). Don't forget to write down tips you've discovered to overcome difficulties.

In the lace in Figure 7-21, I tried to keep as close to the original fractal as possible. As you tat, however, you may want to change the structure of the design. Sometimes the limits of lace making will force you to change the pattern too. Never feel obligated to stick to the original fractal design, for it is nothing but a starting point for your own inspiration.

### You Can Create a Pattern for Others to Follow

Once the tatting is done, you can draw a chart of your pattern using CorelDRAW! or whatever drawing program you like (see Figure 7-20). I recommend that you use the auxiliary line features and catch functions. That way you can draw not only vertical and horizontal lines but every other kind of line, curve, or oval onto the auxiliary-line level to keep your drawing tidy. For doilies the rotation function is wonderful. You draw just one repetition of your pattern, place the rotation centerpoint at the middle of your pattern, rotate with the Keep Original function on, and then use the Repeat function until you get a round doily.

Europeans prefer their lace designs to be charted in the schematic fashion just described, although Americans prefer patterns with words. Lately, though, schematized lace patterns like this seem to be catching on in the United States.

### Use a Scanner to Make Your Pattern

If you have a scanner, there is one more way to graph your pattern: Scan your lace with medium pixel density

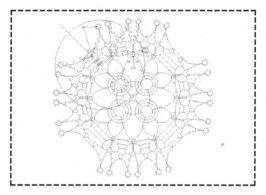

**Figure 7-20**
As you tat, keep note of the number of stitches, picots, and joins used to create the design.

**Figure 7-21**
Here is the finished product. Who would have guessed that this delicate hand-worked design sprang from a computer-generated mathematical image?

and import the image into your drawing program just as you would a fractal picture. You can trace over the image with the drawing tools just as you did with the fractal design.

HOP: Fractals in Motion
Randall Scott
1013 Mondale Pl.
Las Cruces, NM 88005
Registration: $30
Requirements: PC with 490K, EGA, VGA, or Super-VGA monitor
Filename: HOPZIP.EXE

Color Fractal Generator
John A. Schlack
406 Newgate Court, Apt. A1
Andalusia, PA 19020
70252.143@compuserve.com
Registration: $15
Requirements: Color Macintosh with System 7 or later; Power Macintosh or Macintosh with math co-processor recommended
Filename: CFG221.SEA

*Christiane Eichler works as a translator in Cologne, Germany. She is married and has two young children. She began lacemaking with crochet in her teens. She attributes the friendly support of Crafts Forum members on CompuServe with helping her teach herself to tat. Today she designs many of her patterns herself, and has published several in the newsletters of the Deutsche Spitzengilde (German Lace Guild) and the Ring of Tatters in England. She makes lace through crochet, knitting, and tatting and hopes to learn other lace-making techniques in the future.*

## Seattle Textile Computer Users' Group
## Puts Home Computers to Surprising Uses

ost computer users' clubs are comprised of staid button-down types who sit patiently through long demonstrations of spreadsheet programs. The Seattle Textile Computer Users' Group has been known to demonstrate Lotus 1-2-3, but they don't show members how to calculate spreadsheet rows. Rather, they teach them how to use spreadsheets to chart knitting designs. When they demonstrate laser printers, it's not paper that gets printed, but fabric. When they talk about "PC peripherals," they're as likely to be referring to knitting machines and looms as they are to printers and scanners.

The Seattle Textile Computer Users' Group (STCUG) has been pioneering an unlikely trail between home computers and textiles for half a decade. The club started as an informal support group for people trying to use computers to do textile design, says president Karen Seymour, a weaver who runs a Seattle computer training center. "Computers are still macho. We wanted to provide a place for fiber artists to exchange information and feel free to ask all those dumb questions about computers that they may be afraid to ask other places."

In a short time membership grew to over a hundred people in the Seattle area and over three hundred world-wide. Members hail from as far away as Scotland, The Netherlands, Japan, and the Philippines. Some are textile industry professionals, using personal computers to design fabric, garments, and home furnishings, but most are needlecraft devotees who simply want to use the abandoned computer in the basement to accomplish needleart-related feats. Not surprisingly, the group's most popular yearly seminar is the one devoted to helping new members figure out what kind of computer they have and what they can do with it.

For $18 a year members get a bimonthly newsletter called *Fiberbits*, packed with tech tips and software reviews on craft-related software ranging from quilting and cross-stitch design

software for home PC users to weaving software for professionals. They also receive a 60-page resource guide listing names and addresses of vendors of craft software and computer craft products. Members are eligible for discounts on select computer hardware.

At meetings, members may try their hand at using popular craft programs (like Electric Quilt) for designing, or test new computerized sewing machines. At one meeting they designed and sewed blouses using the three major pattern drafting programs. "Then we put them on the models and laughed at them," says Seymour, adding, "The packages have probably improved by now. All this software is constantly evolving."

One of the club's most popular attractions is its software library. The club sells seventeen disks of shareware and software demos for PCs, including ones for cross-stitch, needlework charting, weaving, and pattern drafting. Three Macintosh disks are also available. The disks are a bargain at $4 each. You can write the STCUG at P.O. Box 70234, Bellevue, WA 98007.

There's a similar club in England called the Computer Textile Design Group. Write Dee Chester, 12 Le Brun Rd., Eastbourne, England BN21 2HZ. A subscription to the quarterly newsletter is £35.

## *The Poor Man's Graphic Scan*

Here's a tip from the Seattle Textile Computer Users' Group: If you can't afford a hand-held scanner, try this simple technique to get a hand drawing or clipart drawing from a book or newspaper into your computer. Trace the picture onto a clear plastic transparency or piece of waxed paper. When you're done, load your paint software and tape the drawing on your computer screen. Now trace it using your mouse and the drawing tool. Save it in the graphic format that your needlework charting software uses. Now you can import your drawing into that software as if it were another piece of computer clipart.

If you have a fax modem, you can try a variation of this technique by faxing the drawing to your PC from a fax machine at a local copy store (for about $2). The drawing may arrive with blurred lines, so you'll need to darken them with your paint program. You'll also have to find a way to cut and paste it from your fax software into your drawing program in order to save it in a standard graphic format. Head to Chapter 6 for directions on using a hand-held scanner to create images suitable for use in textile designs.

# 8

## EXPLORING THE KNITTING MACHINE–COMPUTER CONNECTION

*There's a new movement afoot in knitting. More and more knitters are teaming their knitting machine with their home computer to create unique sweater designs that they couldn't knit otherwise. Here's how you can do it too.*

I f you're tired of clicking needles together, or if you dream of bringing automation to your knitting to produce sweaters faster or of richer designs than you have in the past, why not take the plunge and buy a knitting machine? Knitting machines offer several levels of automation beyond simply knitting the yarn into stitches. If you buy a basic mechanical one, like a Bond Incredible Sweater Machine, you can create patterns for it using many of the sweater pattern–generating programs described in Chapter 7. Of course, you'll need to manipulate the knitting machine by hand—the "old-fashioned" way—according to your pattern's instructions. Alternatively, you can buy a more sophisticated electronic knitting machine, like a Studio, that you can hook to your computer. Once connected, these more sophisticated machines will let you design the garment on the computer screen, add motifs and other color patterns, and then download the pattern to the knitting machine, or let the computer direct the machine in its knitting.

## An Expensive Proposition

*B*efore you whip out your credit card, be warned that knitting automation does not come cheaply. Knitting machines can run from $1,000 to $4,000 or more. Then you'll need accessories, like ribbers, and those can add considerably to the cost. If you plan to hook the knitting machine to your computer, you'll also need software to design your sweaters and their fabric, to the tune of another $400 to $500.

## Get Wired Before You End Up in Knots

*B*efore you buy a knitting machine, or software/hardware product to link your present machine to your computer, do as much research as possible. Buying a knitting machine is a complicated and expensive purchase not to be taken lightly. Your most important source of information will be other machine knitters, not magazines. The two best places to talk to other computerized machine knitters are the Fibercrafts Forum on CompuServe and the Textile Arts Forum on Delphi. The knitting mailing lists on Internet are also good places to go for recommendations. The knitting guild in your community is another resource; ask members about their experiences with local knitting machine dealers.

Make sure you buy your knitting machine and its computer linkup accessories from a reputable local dealer whom you can count on to provide lots of technical support and training classes so that you can get the most out of your equipment. (These machines can be hard to master and the fact that their manuals are often translated from another language, like Japanese or Swiss, doesn't help.) Horror stories abound about machine knitters left stranded by indifferent manufacturers and dealers not up to the task of providing the technical help their customers require to get their knitting machine and its software working. When you shop, always take someone with you to provide objectivity, whether it's another knitter or your spouse. Beware of offers that seem too good to be true or knitting machines sold far below their list price—you probably won't get the support you need. Be warned that, as in any equipment business, there are sharks who may tap your wallet for overpriced repairs and unnecessary machine upgrades.

# MARRY YOUR KNITTING MACHINE TO A COMPUTER

—BY SUSAN LAZEAR

IMAGINE WHAT IT would be like if your knitting machine could serve as a special kind of computer printer. You could design a sweater on your computer, and instead of printing a pattern, you could send your design to your knitting machine, which would knit the sweater. You could wake up each morning with a new idea for a sweater and by nightfall have the finished garment in your hands.

Many knitters find that by marrying their knitting machine to a computer they discover in themselves an artistry they never knew existed. They can design large, complicated, and vibrant knit patterns more easily on a computer than on a knitting machine alone. Even those who can't draw find that a hand-held scanner and a paint program can turn them into master knit designers in no time. (This was the case with me. One of the great joys in my life was discovering—thanks to a computer—that I could design knits and even had a talent for it.)

When you marry a knitting machine to a computer, you can design large complex designs within an hour that would have proved daunting tasks had you tried to draw them on graph paper or Mylar plastic sheets. And because you don't have to manually input each stitch into the knitting machine, you can take your garment from conception to mannequin within a day, relying on the computer to transfer the stitch data to the knitting machine in seconds.

Yes, mastering the tricks of using a computer to design knits does take a bit of learning, but the payback is tremendous. Even if you are new to computers, you'll find designing knits on your screen a simple process. Neophyte computer users are often amazed to find that when they are using that new computer to do something that truly interests them, like designing Fair Isles, they become computer whizzes in no time.

## THERE ARE FOUR KINDS OF KNITTING MACHINES— FOUR DIFFERENT WAYS TO COMPUTERIZE KNIT DESIGN

A knitting machine consists of a row, or "bed" of needles, each of which holds a stitch that is knit as you push the machine's carriage across the bed. One pass of the carriage over the needles is like knitting an entire row on hand knitting needles. The machine knows the pattern to knit by reading a punch card, a Mylar card, or in the case of electronic knitting machines, by getting instructions from a personal computer or other electronic device. You can also manually feed a knitting machine the particulars of a pattern, but that takes time. As the machine knits, its needles move to one of two possible positions, creating color changes and slip or tuck stitches, and so forth.

Beginning machine knitters usually buy inexpensive manual knitting machines, which require that they do much of the work of moving stitches, changing colors, and so on. If you own a manual knitting machine, as opposed to an electronic one, you'll need to get your design from the computer to the knitting machine by reading a computer printout as you manipulate the machine. You can't automate the process as you can with electronic knitting machines, though you still can design your sweater using a computer and many of the software packages described in this chapter.

Punch-card knitting machines are the next step up from manual ones. With punch-card machines you design your sweater on a computer. Then, using a graph as your guide, you punch the pattern onto a 24- or 40-stitch card with a special tool that works almost like a paper punch. As the machine knits, you follow a computer printout to prompt color changes and special operations like hand cabling and bobbles.

Mylar card–driven electronic knitting machines, like punch-card knitting machines, require that you transfer the data for your pattern to Mylar cards by drawing on the cards with a special lead pencil. You then feed the cards into a reader on the knitting machine and the machine stitches the design from there. Again, as with the punch-card machines, special hand manipulations need to be documented on a graph or printout. While you still need to shape your piece, the machine knows what to do with the patterning of the stitches.

The next step up from card-based machines are electronic knitting machines that hook directly to your computer, typically through a cable or hardware box. These machines take their pattern information directly from a personal computer or other electronic attachment. An electronic knitting machine is the fastest and least tedious way to get your pattern from the computer to the knitting machine and is a great way to transfer large patterns. The software that you use to shape your sweater, establish the gauge, and even paint the knit pattern and specify color changes can either be purchased with the knitting machine and computer linkup or bought separately.

## WHERE TO START SHOPPING FOR A KNITTING
## MACHINE TO HOOK TO YOUR COMPUTER

The price of knitting machines goes hand in hand with their ability: The more expensive machines produce more types of knits with greater versatility than the less expensive ones. The four major brands of knitting machines sold in the United States are Studio/Singer, Brother/KnitKing, Passap, and Bond. Studio/Singer machines, imported from Silver in Japan, offer a wide range of electronic and nonelectronic options. They are unlike other machines, because their electronics are modular; rather than occupying a part of the needle bed, they reside in a separate box. For this reason you can purchase different needle beds to outfit the machine and accommodate different yarns. Presently, Studio/Singer machines are available in four different beds/gauges: bulky, intermediate (similar to hand knit), standard, and fine gauge.

Brother and KnitKing machines, both imported from Brother in Japan, offer a wide range of manual and electronic machines. In addition to their bulky and standard-gauge machines, Brother also sells a semi-industrial model called the CK35. The CK35 comes with a motor, a color changer on each side, and an attached ribber, making it an ideal machine for the knitter planning to go into small-scale production.

The fourth brand of knitting machine available in the United States is Passap of Switzerland. Passap sells two kinds of knitting machines: a small plastic one and a double-bed electronic one.

In addition to the knitting machines just described, all the knitting machine companies sell plastic machines for beginners. If you're buying your first knitting machine, it would be wise to consider buying a plastic one, because it will give you a chance to determine whether you like machine knitting before you invest a lot of money in an expensive machine. If you choose to consider the plastic machines first, take a look at any of the models produced by the major manufacturers. One feature to note when auditioning machines is that some require you to manually feed them yarn while others include feed mechanisms; those with feed mechanisms are more desirable.

When you buy a knitting machine, you should choose one that suits your particular artistic personality. For instance, because I enjoy the design phase the most, I like a machine that gets me through the knitting quickly and comes up with a finished garment without a lot of fuss. (I'm a sucker for automation.)

When you visit a knitting machine dealer, ask these questions:

1 What kind of fabrics can this machine knit and with what weights of yarn?

2 Will I be able to use the machine with my computer and how? Will I need to purchase extra accessories to complete the knit-machine-to-computer linkup?

3 What can this knitting machine do that others can't?

4 What can it do that others can?

5 What other knitting machines does this particular manufacturer sell? Does the company have a good history of supporting its machines and developing new products that enhance the machines in its line?

6 What sort of accessories can I buy for the machine?

7 What kind of support will you, as a dealer, provide?

Bear in mind that you can approach knitting in several ways with a knitting machine. For example, you can knit shaped garments (whereby you cast stitches on and bind them off to shape your sweater), or you can knit flat yardage, then cut sweater pieces from it and sew them up. (I like to knit yardage, then fuse the back of the fabric with lightweight fusible knit interfacing. After that, I deal with the knit as though it were any other fabric, cutting into it and easily sewing together vests and hats.) You can also use a combination approach, knitting the unshaped garment and its ribbing separately, then cutting out the neckline and sewing on the ribbing—a production knitting shortcut.

*Note: Knitting machines knit a wide variety of fabrics, including plain knit, knit/purl combinations, Fair Isle, slip, tuck, weaving, plaiting, double bed jacquard, hand-manipulated stitches such as cables and traveling stitches, lace, and thread lace. Look for pictures of each of these fabrics in the knitting-machine manuals or knit design books. The first time I shopped for a knitting machine I found that scrutinizing pictures of the fabrics the machines could knit went a long way in helping me determine the machine for me.* ✑

## BUYING THE KNITTING
## MACHINE-TO-COMPUTER LINKUP

Once you've purchased your knitting machine, you'll need to buy the hardware to link it to your computer so that you can use software to design sweaters. The two types of links you're likely to encounter are electronic box-cable combinations and plain cables. The box-cable configuration generally provides a greater level of safety because it has fuses that, in a well-designed box, absorb errant electrical pulses that may wreak havoc on your computer. The Bit Knitter product I currently sell is a box-and-cable combination. It works with the Brother KnitKing 910, 930, 940, 950i, and soon the 965i, as well as all the current Studio/Singer models and Passaps. (Computer linkups, like the Creation 6 for Passap machines, generally consist of just cables with accompanying software.)

Aside from the nature of the hardware hookup for your machine, your most important consideration when you shop for a computer-ready knitting machine should be its accompanying design software. The two major aspects of the software to consider are its garment-shaping capabilities and its fabric-design features. Design software generally lets you create garments either by picking elements, such as collar or sleeve type or length, or by drawing individual sweater pieces on the screen. Once you've made your selections or completed your drawing, you'll set your gauge and, ideally, be able to view your garment pieces to scale on the screen.

Designing the knit fabric itself with knitting machine software is like drawing with crayons on electronic graph paper. The software will generally let you paint repeat patterns that fill the whole garment, or create a large design that wraps itself around a garment or fills a designated garment space. (For creating wraparound designs, you will need software that lets you place a picture of the front and back of the garment next to each other on the screen as you design. Figure 8-1 shows such a garment, designed in Cochenille's Stitch Painter.)

When weighing the fabric-design capabilities of the different software packages, look for these features:

§➤ **The ability to mix custom colors.** You'll want to be able to mix your own colors so that you can see your yarn colors accurately on the computer screen and can make design decisions without having to knit swatches.

§➤ **The ability to import graphic images.** You should be able to import clip-art and scanned images and place them on a grid to use as either repeating

Figure 8-1
This sweater design was created by taking garment silhouettes from the Cochenille program Garment Styler and importing them into Stitch Painter. A scanned image was then imported into Stitch Painter and placed on the sweater, wrapping around the front and back.

designs or single motifs. You should be able to control the size of the image as you import it, magnifying or reducing it on either your grid or your sweater piece.

୫୭ **The ability to mirror, flip, rotate, move, and multiply the image on your sweater or grid.**

୫୭ **Windows rather than DOS-based software.** Windows makes it easier to manipulate images because it uses a clipboard to cut and paste them. However, at present most sweater-design software is DOS based.

୫୭ **The ability to save motifs in a library to use later in other sweaters.**

୫୭ **Software with a symbols or textures palette.** If you like to do hand manipulations or if you want clear printouts of your knit fabric design from a black-and-white printer, you'll need software with a symbols or textures palette.

୫୭ **Copy protection that's easy to live with.** Some programs, especially European ones, require that a key or cable be inserted into one of the computer's ports whenever you want to use the software.

Look for software that prints row-by-row instruction summaries, showing the number of needles that are worked. This makes knitting foolproof. If the phone rings, you won't lose track of where you are in the pattern, since you can easily check the row counter on the knitting machine and see how many needles are at work and match it to the row counter on the computer screen or in the printed pattern. If you own a garment-shaping accessory for your knitting machine, you'll also

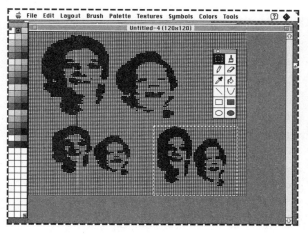

**Figure 8-2**
I scanned photos of my sons, then imported them as silhouettes into Stitch Painter, where they were transformed to a stitch-for-stitch design. I then resized them into smaller designs, ready to be knitted into a sweater.

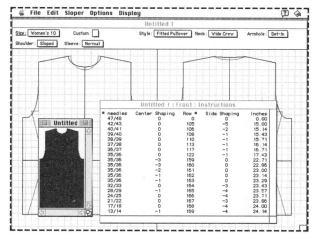

**Figure 8-3**
With Cochenille's Garment Styler you use your computer to design knits or garments for the loom by entering body measurements or choosing from standard sizes for women or men.

want to be able to print a schematic of your garment design to scale. You can feed this printout through the shaping device and shape your garment by watching the printout move through it as the machine knits. Another way to knit shaped garments with your computer is to watch your monitor as you knit. You can do this whether you hand knit or machine knit. Your computer prompts you to bind off or add stitches. As you knit, you may choose to watch the numeric instructions or watch the shaping taking place on the graphed garment. Some software will let you add memos or other notes to the pattern as you go.

## DON'T BE AFRAID TO TRY IT

The idea of linking a knitting machine to a home computer may seem overwhelming, but don't be intimidated. Thousands of knitters are doing it, and they're finding that they can easily create garments that they couldn't knit before, either by hand or by machine, and with a speed and ease that is immensely satisfying to the creative soul. You have to try it!

*Susan Lazear is a knit designer, instructor, and software developer. With her company, Cochenille Design Studio, she designs software and products for computerized knit and textile design. Her products include Bit Knitter and Stitch Painter. She is the author of numerous books on designing knits on computers, including The Pixel-per-Stitch Technique of Design and Designing Repeat Patterns by Computer, both available from Cochenille. She is married, has two sons, and lives in La Costa, California.*

## Buying the Software for the Knitting Machine–Computer Connection

*The following sections were written by Jamieson Forsyth, a "fiberholic and computer addict" who spins, dyes, quilts, and machine knits. She spent seventeen years working in different areas of the computer industry before moving to Coventry, Connecticut. She is married and has a five-year-old son. In addition to her fiber and computer interests, she also raises angora rabbits. You can find her on many online services going by the handle CyberFyberOtter.*

Buying the knitting machine is the easy part. (If you need help, see the accompanying chart titled "Choosing a Knit Machine to Hook to Your Computer.") Once you've got the machine, you need to buy sweater-design software to run on your PC. (Sorry Macintosh fans, none is presently available for the Macintosh, although we heard whispers about packages under development.)

Sweater-design software allows you to style garments and design multicolored motifs, both large and small, to knit into your garment. You then take your design, hook your knitting machine to your PC, and either download the computer-generated pattern into the knitting machine or let the PC direct the machine's knitting.

## CHOOSING A KNITTING MACHINE TO HOOK TO YOUR COMPUTER

| Brand of Knitting Machine | Passap E6000 | Brother/KnitKing | Studios | Bond Incredible Sweater Machine |
|---|---|---|---|---|
| Software It Can Be Used With | Design-A-Knit Creation 6 | Design-A-Knit System 90 | Design-A-Knit System 90 | This machines has no electronics, but you can use it with Design-A-Knit if you don't mind manual needle selection. |
| Fabrics It Can Knit Well | Good on double bed-fabrics, double bed tucks, jacquards, pintucks, nopps. | Does well on traditional Fair Isle, lace, knitweaving. | Does well on traditional Fair Isle, lace, knitweaving, but also has wonderful electronic intarsia ability. | If doing hand-manipulated stitches, cables, and textured patterns appeal to you, or you want to do some limited Fair Isles, this machine is an inexpensive way to go. |
| Special Talents | Does excellent front-bed-to-back-bed transfers. The beds are set at a perfect upside-down pitch, which makes it easy to do circular tucks, circular Fair Isles, and cross-bed transfers. | Has an optional garter carriage for knit-purl combinations in one color for Aran and gansey sweaters. The Pattern Program Designer, for creating designs on a TV screen that you can download to a knit machine, is interchangeable between the 930, 940, 965, and 270 models (they are bulky). | Has a good range of intermodular machines with electronics that can be hooked to the PE1 design accessory. | This machine gives you more of a hand-knitted look than other knitting machines. |
| Disadvantages | Lace, knit-weaving, or Fair Isles can be done, but not as well or as easily as on the Japanese machines. Difficult to do shaping unless you stick to cut and sew. | Some knitters find its double-bed fabrics limiting. The transfer carriage can be used to transfer stitches from the bottom to the top bed, but not vice versa. However, the garter carriage solves some of that problem. | Accessories for these machines are expensive, and you need to buy a lot of them to give the machines the capabilities you want. | Less automation than other machines. |

Not all sweater-design software works with all brands of knitting machines, and not all are good at all tasks. Some make it easy to design garments but tough to create motifs, while others suffer the reverse problem. Too, all these programs were written overseas and, consequently, pose challenges to American knitters and computer users. These hurdles range from the use of metric measurements, to poorly translated manuals, to quirky copy-protection schemes, to sometimes abysmal tech support. Still, even though these programs can be trying, and learning to use them effectively can require a forklift full of patience, their popularity among knitters is growing. The reason is probably that, in spite of their difficulties, once mastered they provide knitters with a level of creative freedom unrivaled by any tool since the spinning wheel.

## Design-A-Knit 5 Is Popular for Designing Multicolored Garments for Machine or Hand Knitting

*D*esign-A-Knit (more commonly referred to simply as DAK) is the most popular of the knit-design programs, because it's so versatile. You can use it to design knits for both hand and machine knitting, and it works with a wide variety of knitting machines (including KnitKing/Brother Electronics, Studio Electronics, and Passap E6000s). DAK lets you either hook your PC directly to your knitting machine for DAK to direct the knitting, or you can download the pattern you create with DAK into your knitting machine. DAK's "knit" feature lets you watch as your garment is stitched row by row on the computer screen, while you or your knitting machine knit it—a pretty snazzy feature. It prints both hand and machine knitting instructions, as well as punch cards and Mylar cards.

> *Note: See the review of the program Stitch Painter in Chapter 7. Many machine knitters use Stitch Painter to create motifs and other designs to use with Design-A-Knit and Creation 6.*

DAK's drawbacks include the fact that it's sometimes not intuitive and learning it can take some serious study. Its user interface can become tiresome, as it requires endless pulling down of menus. Also, because of its copy protection, you can only install DAK twice on your computer. If your hard disk crashes, if you get a new computer, or if you run a hard disk utility and the program is somehow mangled, you may exhaust the software's two lives and possibly be forced to buy another copy. (Knitcraft says their policy regarding such situations is to "work with customers on a need basis.") Therefore, before running hard disk utilities, like disk defragmenters or compression or scanning utilities, you should first uninstall DAK and then reinstall it in order to protect against using up its lives. Another drawback is a bug in the raglan shaping feature that makes the feature quite impossible to use. Knitters end up making raglan garments out of a book rather than trying to use this portion of the program.

## *Choose Built-In Styling Elements or Draw Your Own Designs*

Installing DAK is easy because, unlike other knitting machine programs, it has no cables or special computer settings to mess with. To design a sweater you start with the Shaping menu, where you enter gauges (for both main and ribbing) and select from standard sweater styles and sizes or enter custom sizing information. The standard sizes included in the program run from children's 12 months to 14 years, women's sizes 6 to 22, and men's sizes 34 to 44. You'll find king and queen sizes all the way up to a 60-inch bust and 70-inch hips. (Check the measurements for the standard sizes carefully and add ease where needed, as the dimensions for some of these sizes are snug.) You can adjust the measurements for chest, hip, wrist, upper arm (a heaven-sent for those of us with middle-aged arms!), nape to wrist, nape to garment bottom, and length.

Once you've finished with the Shaping menu, you choose styling elements from a selection of garment styles or use drawing tools to create your own sweater pieces. Built-in styles include cardigan jackets for men or women, skirts, vests for men or women, sleeveless pullover, and basic sweater styles that include raglan, saddle, set-in and straight sleeves, and polo, square, straight, and V necks. DAK's garment-design tools, though tricky to use, let you draw, size, and rotate garment pieces on the screen (as you can see in Figure 8-5).

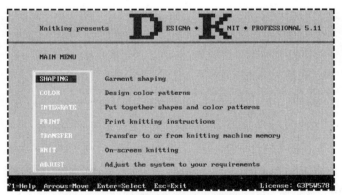

**Figure 8-4**
**All Design-A-Knit functions are easily accessible from this self-explanatory introductory menu.**

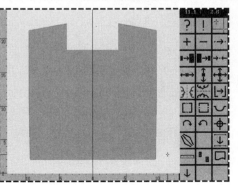

**Figure 8-5**
Design-A-Knit gives you drawing tools to design garment pieces on your computer screen. But you may rather learn Vulcan than grok these!

DAK lets you copy into your design garment pieces from other sweaters that you've designed, while the Exact feature allows you to adjust the exact stitch layout of your garment. You can create a range of garment sizes for any sweater that you've created.

## You Can Design Elaborate Color Motifs to Knit into Sweaters

When you design color patterns with DAK, you can design and store knit designs apart from sweaters so that you can use any motif pattern with any sweater (another aspect of DAK that takes time to master). You can also incorporate computer graphics into your pattern as PCX files. As you design, DAK displays your motif as knit stitches in the editing window, so you don't have to guess what your colors will look like when knit. When you import PCX images or portions of other patterns, you can tile and resize the imports by adjusting the size of a box surrounding the image. You can also change the size of imported PCX files by adjusting the tension gauge of your garment.

DAK's drawing tools include line, square, rectangle, circle, and ellipse. A grid, that you can turn on and off as you edit, is provided to help you draw. Once you've finished fine-tuning your motif, you can lay it out by specifying the number of repeats you want in the pattern. You can then expand, shuffle, and rotate it; insert or delete whole row columns or stitch rows; make the pattern wider or taller; and use the Pairs feature to make jacquard pair separations.

You select yarn colors in DAK with its Woolbox function, which gives you 256 editable colors. (Although you can use up to 50 colors in one design, when you print it, your best bet will be to use only the 16 default colors to avoid muddy-looking printouts.) In addition to the Woolbox, the Yarn menu lets you delete extraneous yarn colors or vary the colors, a fun way to rotate colors and discover new color combinations. This same feature also shows you what the knitted fabric looks like.

**Figure 8-6**
**Design-A-Knit displays your motif as knit stitches. You can take this single motif and multiply it, resize it, or manipulate it to create repeating designs.**

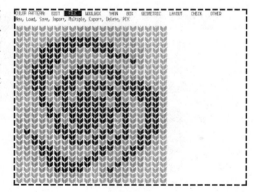

You can add lettering to your sweater design using any of four different typestyles (if you do add lettering, be sure to add rows to the sweater or you might type right over your motif). A Cut and Sew feature places a cutout of the garment piece directly on your motif repeats, then fills the outside with a plain color so you know exactly where to cut and sew the fabric when you've finished knitting.

Other necessary functions include a feature to check the number of colors used per row, a floats feature that checks to see that there aren't too many floats for fingers to get caught on, and a jacquard checker that will check and automatically correct errors. An "info" feature keeps track of your garment's specs, including its gauge, number of motifs in a row, number of motif rows, and so on.

*Note: The primary criticism users have of DAK's motif editing feature is that the mouse doesn't behave as much like a mouse as it should. Say you want to change the color of a line. It's too easy to end up with lines of the new color all over your design if you're not careful. The problem is exacerbated when a design is huge, because the mouse gets lost and can cause havoc in unlikely places.*

One nice feature in DAK is its ability to export your motifs into other art or knitting programs as PCX files. All you need to do is open your design, type its name with a PCX extension, and store it in a special DAK subdirectory called PCX. I often use this feature to take designs I like from the Brother/KnitKing repertoire and import them into Passap's Creation 6 knitting-machine software. You need to use a graphics conversion program like HiJack to save them in the pure 16 EGA colors though, or you'll get an unholy mess: A blue-green will be transformed into a blue-and-green checkerboard pixel design that will be impossible to later edit. One bug is that the number of rows in the PCX file must be divisible by eight or DAK adds extra stitches and rows. For instance, say you design a 63-row by 32-stitch repeat and save it as a PCX file. DAK will add one extra row to your design. If your numbers are further off—say 67 and 37—DAK may draw solid black lines. (You can, however, edit these imperfections out with your paint program.)

## The Fun Part Is Putting Motif and Sweater Together

Once you've finished both your motif and sweater designs, DAK displays them on the screen. Using the arrow keys, you then position outlines of the garment pieces on the fabric. At the press of a mouse button, DAK "cuts" the pattern piece. You can edit the final garment piece if there are extra stitches or repeats that you don't want.

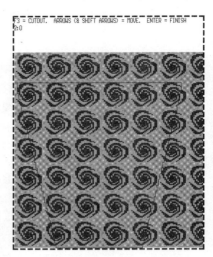

Figure 8-7
Using arrow keys, you position
individual sweater pieces on
your motif fabric as you want
them knit.

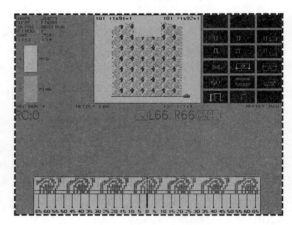

Figure 8-8
Design-A-Knit displays the
sweater piece with color
motifs as it's being knit. A
row-by-row display ensures
you'll never lose your place.
Chimes sound when it's time
to change colors.

You can transfer both pieces and integrated garment patterns from a Brother/KnitKing
knitting machine into your computer so that you can add color motifs to them with DAK.
DAK's Knitting feature displays your garment pieces on the computer as they're knit row by
row. If you want to print a pattern instead, you can tell DAK whether to reverse printouts or
print for punch card or Mylars. Unfortunately, DAK doesn't support some of the latest models of printers, so you may encounter intensely frustrating printing problems or not be able
to print at all.

> **TIP**
> *A number of professional Design-A-Knit users
> hang out on CompuServe, making it an excellent
> place to go to get answers to questions you can't
> get from your dealer.*

As this book goes to press, a Windows version was about to be released. DAK has traditionally been the program most recommended for machine knitters just getting started with a knitting machine-to-PC linkup. That was in part due to a starter version of the program that was available for $260 (that version is no longer available). It's true that DAK is easy to use and there are many sweater designs available for use with it. Personally, though, I prefer System 90, described next.

Knitcraft Inc.
500 N. Dodgion Ave.
Independence, MO 64050-3023
Phone: 800/521-4912
Price: $379.95;
Requirements: PC-compatible with 286 or higher, 1 meg RAM, VGA, 2 floppies or hard drive

You can find a slide-show demo of the program online stored as file DKDEMO.ZIP.

## System 90 Intoshape Makes Garment Styling So Easy It Will Become a Good Friend

System 90 Intoshape is my favorite garment-design program. While it's not as feature packed as Design-A-Knit, I find it easier to use (even though all measurements are in millimeters, which many American knitters dislike). It comes with cables so that you can hook it

> System 90 was the first knitting machine software ever written, authored over twenty years ago by Clwyd Technics, the industrial arm of a college in Wales. The school wrote the program as part of its search for industries it could computerize. A Brother knitting machine dealer in Clwyd lent the college knitting machines. All profits from the sale of System 90 now go to the school. Unfortunately, not many knitting machine dealers sell System 90. However, the American distributor, Northwest Knitting Supplies, Inc., is a helpful company, and that means a lot in this crazy industry.

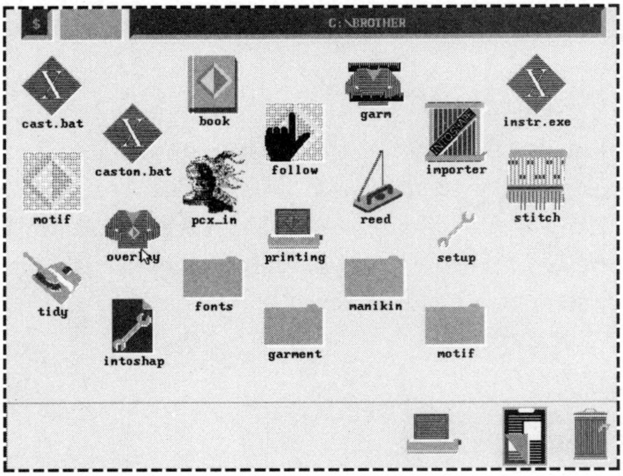

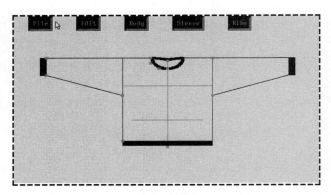

**Figure 8-9**
System 90 Intoshape is a very user-friendly program that you can use to design and download knit patterns to Brother and Studio electronic knitting machines.

**Figure 8-10**
You adjust shaping of knit garment pieces in System 90 by moving the "points" shown in the garment outline. For instance, you would lengthen the sweater by pulling down the points of the hem.

to Brother or Studio knitting machines. You can also use it to print instructions for machine and hand knitting sweaters.

System 90 comes with ready-made jumper, cardigan, and raglan designs. You begin by choosing size and ease, after which the program displays individual pieces of the garment. You're given a number of garment pieces to choose from, such as a selection of sweater fronts. When you pick one, System 90 draws it on a "mannequin" of horizontal lines. You then choose other garment pieces, such as neckline, sleeves (options are drop shoulder, slightly set in, very set in, and kimono), back piece, and neckline and ribbing. Once the garment design is complete, you can adjust the garment by moving the points that make up an outline of the garment on your screen. For example, if you want to eliminate step decreases from drop shoulder sweaters you would click on the points, as shown in Figure 8-10, and redraw it as a straight-edged drop shoulder.

If you don't want to use System 90's ready-made patterns, you can design individual garment pieces from scratch. To do so, you pick a garment piece from the menu, and the program displays its outline with anywhere from 4 to 20 points that you can stretch and reshape. Stitch gauge can be specified at any time in the garment shaping or motif design, and you can always resize garment pieces by changing your stitch gauge.

## *You Design Motifs by Drawing on a Grid or Importing PCX Graphics*

Because System 90 runs with a program called DOS MetaShell, it has a Windows-like interface that makes designing motifs easy. Still, the program's motif creation tools aren't as intuitive as they should be. (That's why I like to use Creation 6 (described next) for pattern and motif design, then import my designs into System 90 to create the sweater.) You draw your motif on a large grid, using the usual computer drawing tools, like paint buckets and lines. System 90's drawing features are similar to those in older DOS programs, which is something many knitters like because they're easy to use. It gives you only 16 default colors to paint with, though these can be edited to some extent. System 90 doesn't offer scanner support, though you can import PCX graphics into motifs.

You can display as many motifs on the screen as you wish and, while you're working on the large grid, System 90 displays a smaller version of the motif in the corner of the screen so that you can see your design from a more macro perspective. You can put text into your motif designs, in any of four typefaces. Once you have finished your motif, you pick the colors and stitch that you will be using—whether Fair Isle, slip stitch, main bed jacquard, designer or regular jacquard—a part of the program that some knitters find confusing. (Note that it can be difficult to set the colors in the regular jacquard, but don't give up.)

## *The Features for Placing Motifs on Garments Are My Favorite*

When it's time to overlay your motif on garment pieces, you can choose to position it over the entire garment, with a brick fill or in the shape of a cross, a diagonal X, three in a row, or three down. After you have finished, if you have a half or quarter of a motif that you don't want, you can use the drawing tools to delete it. You can also easily edit the motif once you place it on the garment. (In Design-A-Knit, by comparison, you must edit motifs stitch by arduous stitch.)

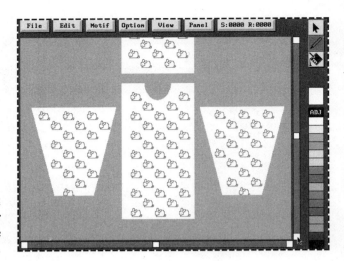

**Figure 8-11**
The features in System 90 for
placing motifs on garments are
some of the easiest to use.

## System 90 Is Very Versatile

System 90 will print templates, as well as machine and hand knitting instructions. It's my favorite program for generating hand-knitting instructions, especially since you can export garment designs in PCX files for use with other graphics programs.

One of System 90's particularly unique features is its ability to print garments, motifs, and patterns from Windows (something none of the other programs can do). This makes printing almost foolproof, and if you have an offbeat printer model, you're more likely to be able to print to it than with DOS-based programs (by contrast, neither Design-A-Knit nor Creation 6 includes drivers for my printer, an Epson 720 Stylus). If you have an older version of System 90, you can buy this Windows printing utility for $10.

Installing System 90 is simple, but be aware that the program is copy protected and comes with only one "life" per disk. (If you're running older versions of DOS, you should uninstall System 90 before you run hard-disk utilities.) Should you accidentally deep-six System 90, Northwest Knitting will send you a new copy for free if you send them your original disk. Program updates are reasonably priced at $10 each, and Northwest Knitting will go to great lengths to help you through technical glitches.

System 90's knitting portion simultaneously displays your design and the needle bed (see Figure 8-12). You hook the System 90 cable to your knitting machine, follow the directions, and knit away.

System 90 comes in a version that will work with either an electronic Studio or a Brother 930, 940, or 965I. You can buy an additional cable to hook it to the Brother Pattern Program Designer, which works in conjunction with the above-mentioned Brother machines, as well as the 270 (the Brother Bulky Electronic).

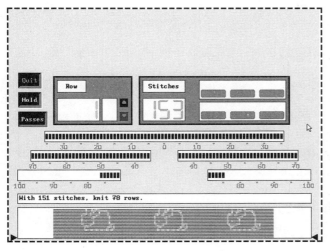

**Figure 8-12**
System 90 Intoshape displays both the design and needle bed while your knitting machine knits. Indicators keep you abreast of the row and stitches, and also your position in the pattern.

Overall, System 90 is a wonderful deal and a program you'll find valuable for years to come.

Northwest Knitting Supplies, Inc.

219 S. 50th

Tacoma, WA 98408

Phone: 206/472-4554; 206/472-4744 (fax)

Price: $398 for software and cable to work with either Brother or Studio knitting machines. For an additional $119 you can upgrade the software to work with both flavors of knitting machines; software upgrades are $10.

Requirements: PC-compatible with 286 or higher, DOS 3.0 or later, 590K RAM, color VGA, hard drive, mouse, one serial port

## Creation 6 Lets You Create Knit Designs with Paint-Program Features, but It's Tough to Install

Passap's PC-based sweater-design software, Creation 6, works with their model E6000 knitting machine. It works like a paint program: You use tools like paint buckets and line, square, and circle drawing tools to create multicolored knit designs. It's one of the only knit-design programs that works with scanners, letting you turn photographs or art into large or small motifs. It's not a true garment-design program, however, because it won't let you create garment shaping easily, although you can do so in a crude way.

## A Horror to Configure!

Creation 6's greatest drawback is that it's a beast to install (see the section titled "Muster von Diskette Holen?" Anyone?). A hint of what you're in for comes on the photocopied setup page packaged with the software, which advises: "The best time to start setting up your computer for use with the E6000 machine is before you buy it." It then tells you how to set your modem and printer ports for the software to work. I've heard of knitters who bought computers to use with their Passap knitting machine, then had to return them and buy another to use with Creation 6. On top of that, the manual is a hideous affair—several books have been written in an effort to augment it. The one that Passap sells, "Creation 6: Basic Training," is only marginally helpful.

## Paint Tools Make Motif Creation Supereasy

Once you get Creation 6 running, it's one of the easiest knitting machine–specific programs to use. You draw and color your design with simple paint tools, and you can easily cut and paste, reduce, enlarge, and repeat elements of your design. When you use its magnifying glass tool, your design is enlarged on a grid, allowing you to correct or change colors stitch by stitch. You can enter your specific knitting technique (using the numbers of the techniques like double-bed jacquard and Fair Isle that are programmed into the Passap E600 console), then zoom in to see how much or little distortion of your color design will be present for your various Fair Isle and jacquard garments. As a further tie-in to the E6000 console, Creation 6 includes symbols that match the E6000's programming instructions, including those for flipping, rotating, and mirroring designs. The program also includes all the patterns built into the E6000.

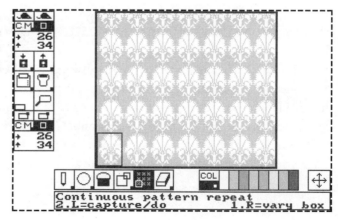

**Figure 8-13**
**Creation 6 is the easiest of the knitting machine programs to use to design motifs.**

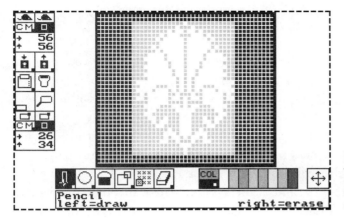

**Figure 8-14**
You can zoom in on elements of your fabric design in Creation 6 and adjust the design stitch by stitch.

Another splendid feature is that you can make global color changes, like changing a black-on-red motif to a red-on-black one with a single mouse click. Or, if you want to change a red to match your yarn more closely, you simply click on a color icon and move the color bars to match the color you want. You can save special palettes for each design to use later when you want to work on the design. Another useful capability is that you can switch colors on the fly, a feature that's especially helpful when you're creating fantasy Fair Isles or blister jacquards.

## Some Elements of the Software Demand Diligence to Master

One glitch in the program is that the default palette contains 10 different blacks, which are impossible to tell apart. The danger here is that, should you accidentally use a different black from the one you've been using, you could end up with a multicolor design when you just intended say black and white. Another problem is that the program's screen color is not pure white. Passap designed this so that the screen would be easy on the eyes. However, the off-white screen prints out as gray, no matter how you set your printer. If you want white print-outs, you must custom design a new palette that contains pure white and then apply that palette to your screen.

The program has other quirks that bedevil first-time users, and the manual is mum about how to deal with them. For instance, most newcomers to the program can't figure out how to store a design that's larger than their computer screen.

Designing garments in Creation 6 can also require a computer nerd's diligence to master, although some knit designers do beautiful things with it. When designing with the program, you first use the square and ellipse icons to shape the garment body, neck, sleeves, and so on;

then you tell the program how many rows you'll need to knit. Once you finish your pattern, you download it to your Passap through a cable that connects the PC to the knitting machine. (This cable also serves as a copy-protection key, and the program will not work unless it is plugged in.)

If you decide to buy Creation 6, your greatest concern should be whether it will work with your present computer, since it's a picky program hardware-wise. For example, there are only two scanners sold in the U.S. that will work with it (the Logitech DEXXA and 32 for DOS), and its list of supported video cards and printers is antiquated. If you do purchase it, you should make friends with the knowledgeable machine knitters on Delphi, America Online, or the machine knitters' mailing list on Internet, because Passap's tech support leaves a lot to be desired.

PASSAP Machines, Inc.
271 West 2950, South
Salt Lake City, UT 84115
Phone: 801/485-2777
Price: $499
Requirements: 386DX33 PC-compatible or higher, 4 megs RAM, VGA, mouse, DOS 5.0 or higher, Passap E6000 knitting machine

---

**BIT KNITTER LETS YOU HOOK YOUR AMIGA OR MACINTOSH TO YOUR KNITTING MACHINE**

Bit Knitter, from Cochenille Studios, was one of the first products available for hooking a home computer to a knitting machine. It's a cable/hardware-box configuration that lets you hook a PC-compatible, Amiga, or Macintosh to a Studio/Singer, Brother/KnitKing, or Passap electronic knitting machine. You design your garment and motif design in any paint program and download it to the knitting machine (which can be a bit roundabout, because you don't get the features for automating garment design that you do in some of the more sophisticated knitting programs, like Design-A-Knit). Still, Bit Knitter ($250 from Cochenille Design Studio, 619/259-1698) is your only choice if you own an Amiga or Macintosh.

# "MUSTER VON DISKETTE HOLEN?" ANYONE?

*How a leading knitting machine software product turned Judy Heim, a mild-mannered knitter, into a frustrated Luddite*

Editors at the computer magazines I write for tease that if I can't get something to work, no one will be able to. After many years of computer product testing, I think I've met my match. I had been warned that setting up Creation 6, the software for designing knits for the Passap knitting machine, was sometimes no easy task, but it wasn't until I flipped open the manual to confront English peppered with foreign phrases like "Introduire disquette 2" and gibberish like "acquaint yourself with the technical terms of your devices" that I realized I was up against a challenge.

Technical challenges energize me. I pried the diskettes out of their peculiar girding in the box (glued beneath a multilingual licensing agreement cross-referenced with a page in the manual) with anticipation. Creation 6 has some bizarre requirements. For instance, it requires that you set up your modem, mouse, printer, and scanner (if you have one) to use particular communications ports, and it requires that those ports be configured to use specific interrupts within the computer, (IRQs), something you must fish inside your computer to change. Ridiculous! The IRQ setup it uses is a standard one, but should your computer deviate (and there's no way to change it, as is the case with some popular computers like Gateways), you won't be able to run Creation 6.

Not surprisingly, when I installed Creation 6, I couldn't get it to work (even with the correct IRQ settings). With some futzing, I got it running in German. But when I reconfigured it to run in English (one of many idiotic steps in the installation process), my mouse wouldn't work.

When I called Passap's technical-support number, the technician was polite (he insisted on calling me back to save me long-distance charges), but stymied. After consultation with a co-worker, he advised me to get a new mouse driver (a small program that activates the mouse). He added that maybe I should buy a new mouse too. Before hanging up, I asked him if it was possible to install Creation 6 on a hard drive named D: instead of the C: it required. He said it was, but he didn't know how.

Because I have a number of mice lying around, I tried them all, along with several different drivers, but still couldn't get Creation 6 working in English. I wasn't surprised. I had been skeptical of the advice. These days mouse drivers are fairly standard things, and it's almost unheard of for a program not to work with them all. And the mouse did work when I loaded the program in German.

I called Passap's tech-support team back (this time they did not call me back). They were stumped. "Our suggestion is you learn German," the tech said, only half joking. He said the problem was probably a software bug and promised to mail me a new copy of Creation 6.

# 9

## THE VERY BEST THING YOU CAN DO
## WITH YOUR COMPUTER
## IS GET ON THE INFORMATION HIGHWAY

*Software for printing sewing patterns and designing
quilts is great, but when you get down to it,
nothing is so sweet as the companionship of fellow stitchers.*

Just as rotary cutters revolutionized quilt-making, computers are revolutionizing the way needlecrafters socialize and exchange tips. All over the country, throughout the web of computer services and networks that has come to be known as the information highway, stitchers have created their own private places. Each night tens of thousands of needlecrafters exchange tips about quilting, sewing, cross-stitching, knitting, weaving, and every other craft—all via their computers. Just like members of more traditional needlecraft guilds, they swap quilt blocks, fabrics, and buttons; work on charity craft projects together; send each other reviews of the newest craft books; chat about patterns; and swap pictures of projects. They also talk about their lives. They do this all through their home computers.

These electronic craft guilds, as you might call them, have swept the information highway with the gusto of a political movement. The consumer computer service CompuServe estimates that about sixty thousand crafters visit their craft forum in any six-month period, posting an average of 1,200 electronic messages per day. It's by far one of the most popular, and profitable, areas of the service. Prodigy and General Electric's GEnie have also found that electronic sewing, quilting, and cross-stitch guilds are among their services' hottest draws, a surprise to many since these services marketed themselves for years by touting futuristic features like home banking and shopping.

## Merge a Ladies' Club with a Computer Service and You Have an Electronic Craft Guild

Services like Prodigy and CompuServe offer a socialization experience that's hard to replicate in any other way in our society. That's why they can be so valuable to you as a needlecrafter. They can offer you friends, conversation with other stitchers at all hours of the night or day, and information and advice you'll find nowhere else. They can also be prime sources for fabric, buttons, thread, and computer software for crafts.

What is a computer service? It's really nothing but a big computer, or computer network, that you tap into with your computer and modem. You call it over an ordinary phone line, just like you'd make a normal phone call, except that your computer dials the number. When you connect to the other computer, you hear the "tweet-tweet-whoosh" of your modem and its modem agreeing to talk to each other, and then some kind of special menu appears on your computer's screen. You're connected. The services' menus are often pictorial and they show a number of pictures, or icons, depending on the service and the area that you've entered. For example, your screen may display a shopping cart icon to signify electronic shopping (point at it with your computer mouse, click a button, and you enter the electronic "mall"). Or it may show a plane icon to point the way to travel information like the main menu for CompuServe does in Figure 9-1.

You'll find three basic types of services and information on a computer service: electronic mail, or E-mail, which is a message you type on your computer and send to a friend (or anyone) on the service, or on other computer services or networks; libraries of information like stock prices or news stories, also known as databases; and public forums on specific topics

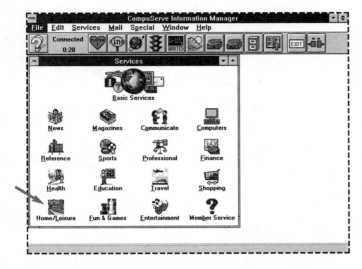

Figure 9-1
To get to the craft area on
CompuServe, click on the
picture of a house labeled
Home/Leisure.

like needlecrafts, parenting, or pet care. Public forums are essentially collections of E-mail messages on a chosen topic that anyone can read. It's these public forums that have become so popular with crafters.

## Computer Services Offer Something for Every Kind of Needlecrafter

*W*ho logs into these forums or guilds? Everyone you can imagine. From crocheting retirees in Florida trailer parks to military wives in Germany, from college students who tap in from college computer labs to mothers with small children. Many professional women find that the online guilds provide them with a needed break from the stresses of the day. Thousands of textile professionals also rely on them for news, product information, and advice.

Julia Benson, a computer science instructor, as well as a busy mother and weaver, says that the CompuServe craft forum has changed her life. "I've logged on at 5 a.m., unable to sleep, and found warmth and laughter to cheer me up," says Benson. "I've logged on at the end of a bad day when everyone's dumped on me, and suddenly the world looked less bleak. I've logged on in the middle of a blizzard, unable to get further from my house than the end of the driveway, and found others to share blizzard stories with." She adds, "Despite the crowded world we live in, so many of us feel very alone much of the time. As craftspeople, we may feel alone more than the average person, for we have an artistic obsession and no one to share our enthusiasm and vision with. The little community we've built here [on CompuServe] is an antidote to that."

Debbie Moyes, an American fiber artist who found herself alone in Singapore when her husband's job took them to the Far East and he was frequently traveling, relies on Compu-Serve's craft forum for a daily dose of friendship and talk with stitchers back home. "I have not found many people here in Singapore who share my addiction to wonderful fabrics," she says, "so I was quite lonely. Being online, I can talk with others who share my interests. My husband's phone calls and my few minutes on CompuServe are the highlights of my day!"

## How Do You Get Information from a Computer Service?

Online services provide many different forums. For needlecrafters, these will be called things like Crafts, Home/Leisure, Interests/Hobbies, and so on. These forums are organized by topic, typically, Sewing, Quilting, Cross-Stitch, Cross-Stitch and Pulled-thread Embroideries, Knitting, Weaving, and Textiles. These topics are then further broken down into groups of related messages, called threads, like the sample threads from the knitting topic area on America Online shown in Figure 9-2. Threads get "spun" like this: You type an E-mail message asking, say, "Which is your favorite iron cleaner?" and "post" it. In other words, you make it public on a computer service. Dozens, possibly hundreds of sewers will type in replies, providing testimonial for a favorite product or a method to remove gunk from the bottom of your Rowenta. This is a message thread.

**Figure 9-2**
Knitters discuss a wide variety of topics on America Online, and these are organized into "message threads" on specific subjects.

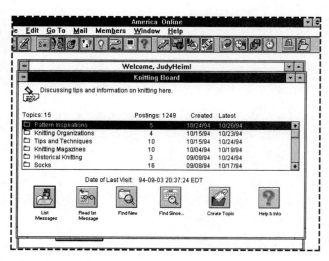

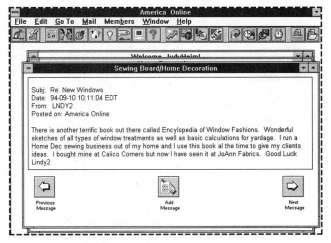

**Figure 9-3**
In this public E-mail message on America Online, a sewer responds to another sewer's request for ideas on sewing window treatments. There are many more such messages in this "thread."

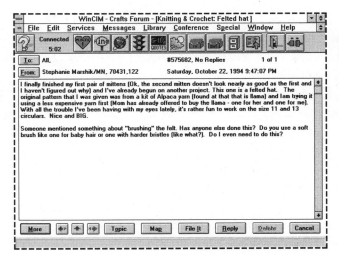

**Figure 9-4**
Mittens, felted hats, and alpaca yarn are among the many topics you'll find discussed by knitters on CompuServe. Be warned: The service hosts a long-time feud between hand knitters and machine knitters.

## *Threads Are Always Changing and Forums Are Supportive Places to Be*

The quilting topics on computer services typically have several hundred message threads going at any one time. The threads change from day to day, depending on what participants are writing about. They range in topics from "Liquid Thread: How to Use It?" to "Bowtie Quilts."

Threads inevitably veer off into discussions of things other than the topic at hand (something people who run the services tolerate either a little or not at all). That iron topic, for example, may mutate into a discussion of serger thread, tracing paper, and eventually, what hamburger stands everyone likes to stop at while driving to the quilt show at Paducah. (Depending upon the online service, this conversation drift is either tolerated, encouraged, or banned. Sometimes forum leaders will retitle the subjects of the message to more appropriately reflect their content, or else move the messages to a more fitting area of the service.)

Stories and anecdotes about crafters' personal lives spill into the craft E-mail. Crafters talk about their husbands, children, and jobs. They console each other on miscarriages and breast cancer. They often discuss things women dare not discuss in any other part of the growing web of online services that has come to be known as "cyberspace." The sense of friendship and community among crafters in these forums is strong. On all the services you'll find continuing message threads in which crafters plan to get together for lunch, sewing festivals, and even getaway weekends.

When Hurricane Andrew hit Florida, sewers on Prodigy raided their sewing closets to send homeless sewers packages of notions. When Mississippi flood waters buried the Midwest, quilters on GEnie raised $14,000 to help Midwestern quilters restore their tools and fabric stashes.

Husbands also get into the act. Cherry Jackson, a quilter in Melbourne, Australia, says that her computer-holic husband of 24 years helps her download messages from American quilters on CompuServe. "It has helped us have another common interest," she says. Lurking Joe is the nickname of a husband-mascot on the GEnie quilt forum. ("Lurkers" are people who read electronic messages but are too shy to post any of their own.) Lurking Joe spent hours online each week helping crafters with their computer problems. When he was stricken with cancer, the quilters got together and—what else?—stitched him a quilt.

> "It's really fascinating because when you finally get to meet these people whom you've exchanged messages with, you sit down and talk to them and it's like you've known them your whole life," says Anne Browne, an administrative assistant in Freeport, Maine, who helps run CompuServe's craft forum.
>
> "The unconditional support that everyone gives everyone to do the work that they're doing is unbelievable," marvels Jody McFadden of Sacramento, California, who runs the Needlearts Roundtable on General Electric's GEnie. "It's something that you can't get in an offline guild."

## There's a Treasure Trove of Free and Nearly Free Crafting Information in the Craft Forums' Libraries

In addition to public E-mail discussions, craft forums also house "libraries" of information. These libraries are like databases except that they're more of a hodgepodge of collected and related things, while a true database is regimented in organization. Message forums typically

> *Note: When crafters get online for the first time, they are sometimes disappointed to discover that there are not many sewing or knitting patterns in these libraries. You'll find a few, but commercial patterns cannot be distributed through computer services because they are copyrighted. I guarantee that any disappointment will be short-lived once you discover all the other information that's available online.*

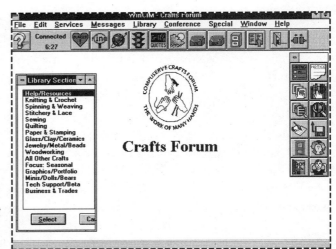

Figure 9-5
In this list of libraries on Compu-
Serve you'll find thousands of
computer files with information
and software for your needlecrafts.

Figure 9-6
The Stitchery & Lace Library on
CompuServe offers hundreds of
files dealing with embroidery,
tatting, and lace making. Next to
the file's name is a brief description
of what's in the file and the date
it was posted on the service.

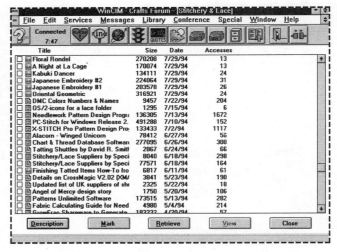

have many libraries. The subject of each parallels the subjects in the messages. Figure 9-5 shows a list of libraries in the craft forum on CompuServe. Each library has thousands of computer files with information and software for all needlecrafting interests. One library might hold advice on running a craft business, while another holds digitized pictures of subscribers' projects. Still another might tell you where to find the best and cheapest muslin in Alabama.

The content of these libraries is truly eclectic. They contain information you won't find anywhere else. Some samples: directions on how to clean old lace, techniques for sewing bowtie quilts, an organic chemist's advice on setting dye in fabrics, and directions on how to make yo-yo jackets. You'll also find lists of fabric, yarn, and button suppliers; mail-order sources for rare and vintage fabrics; popular specialty stores around the country to visit while you're on vacation; other computer users' reviews of craft magazines and books; discussions of the latest sewing or quilting technique that some member may have learned in a class; free how-to tutorials that other crafters have written and posted out of the generosity of their hearts; computerized knitting and quilting designs for use with popular software; and much more.

There are thousands of such information files. Few public libraries offer a fraction of the craft information you'll find on computer services. And it's all up to date too.

You can read these articles on your computer screen while you're connected to the online service, or else transfer the entire article to your computer to read later or print out. Just like you do in a public library, you can search these electronic libraries by subject. You can look for all the articles labeled "tatted angels" or "cat quilt blocks." Or you can just browse by scrolling through descriptions of what's in each file as in Figure 9-6. Reading and copying these files to your computer can easily become a delightful addiction. I'll tell you more about all of this later in Chapter 11.

## *Crafters Can Even "CB" with Each Other*

It's called "computer CBing" or "chatting." Your PC is connected to a computer service, and you're blithely typing in an E-mail message or scrolling through a library list, when a message pops onto your screen.

*"Nan: Hiya!"* Who is Nan? You have never heard of Nan. Gamely, you click on the computer conference button, and type back, *"Hi. Are you a cross-stitcher too?"*

Nan types back, *"No, I weave."* Then she adds, *"I also do macramé sometimes. I am really into macramé."*

*"You too!"* you gasp, typing faster. *"I like to make plant hangers out of hemp."*

And so it goes. You type something to Nan, she types something back. Your conversation scrolls over the computer screen like dialog in a script to a play. The conversation is in "real time" in the sense that it's happening now. It's not delayed in the sense that you write Nan an E-mail message, and she replies to it later at her convenience.

Of course, the above exchange is—what do they call schoolgirl samplers in which the horses are bigger than the houses?—*naive*. In reality, you are more likely to receive a chat request like, *"Ramblin' Dude: Speak to me, babe!"* And when you ignore it, the pest persists: *"Ramblin' Dude: Do you have blond hair?"*

Fortunately, such interruptions are easy to ignore. On some online services, you can even set your account so that people cannot bug you with chat requests. (A necessity if your children are calling the service, because chat requests are sometimes sexual in nature.)

Computer chatting can be found in most needlecraft forums, and it has evolved into some interesting events. Two evenings a week, the National Online Quilters on Delphi stage two- to three-hour gabfests where a dozen or more participants converse via keyboard about their projects, their peeves, and their lives. One member compares it to the "bitch and stitch" soirees of their mothers.

The Needlearts Roundtable on GEnie holds weekly seminars in which a needlearts expert teaches a hobby or technique. You buy the designated supplies in advance like you do when you take a course at a craft store. But you sit at your computer keyboard with your materials and follow the instructions as they scroll across the computer screen. You and the other students type questions to the instructor, and the instructor types the replies. You can read everything that anyone in the class types, and you can capture all the conversation to your computer's disk and read it or print it later.

The services also invite "guest speakers" to monthly CB forums. Some recent guests on online services have included experts on the use of video digitizing in textile design, well-known quilt designers, representatives of craft book publishers, and experts on turning your craft hobby into a business. The guests converse via keyboard with an unseen crowd, answering their questions, typing observations about their art. These forums can become lively, with audience members flooding guests with questions faster than they can type answers.

## You Need Very Little Computer Expertise to Use These Services Because Everyone Will Be Eager to Help

Honestly, you need little if any computer expertise to use and enjoy computer online services. Remember, seven-year-olds tap into them all the time. So do members of Congress. If you're still not convinced, be aware that many women feel more comfortable posting technical computer questions in needlecraft forums than they do in other parts of a service, because they can be assured that other women will go to extraordinary lengths to help them, and no one will dare laugh at them.

In fact, laughing at another's plight is probably the greatest sin anyone can commit in these forums, and the surest way to be hounded out. Compare this to the football discussion group on Internet in which *not* laughing at another's predicament is considered a character flaw. In fact, whenever someone is foolish enough to post a computer question in that raucous forum, other computer users heckle them into oblivion. They also feed them erroneous advice like "To fix that problem all you need to do is type **C:format**," which will reformat their computer's hard disk and thus obliterate all the data on it. This does *not* happen in needlecraft forums.

Feel free to post as many computer questions as you wish in these forums. Subscribers will not just give you sound advice but also sympathize profusely with you.

## You May Have Heard About Sexual Harassment in Cyberspace, but This Does Not Happen in Needlecraft Forums

TV tabloid news programs fill the air with stories about "online stalkers," stalkers on computer services who harass innocent victims just like stalkers in real life. *Newsweek* trumpeted how the information highway is a hostile place for women in a cover story titled "Men, Women and Computers" in May 1994. It described the computer world as full of poorly socialized men spouting sexist epithets and picking fights with each other. *Working Women* chimed agreement that the online world is a rude place for women.

Is this the kind of thing you can expect to run into if you read and answer messages about sewing and quilting on computer services? *Not at all.* If the rest of the information highway is a Wild West world, the stitching guilds that we crafters have created with our computers are old girls' clubs (sorry, guys, but that's the way it is). Women, and men too, go to great lengths to treat each other graciously. They frequently mail each other seam tape, quilt blocks, yarn, and old patterns. Rarely does anyone get mad at anyone else, and when somebody does, others rush to quell the flames. It is a genteel world straight out of a Victorian painting, except for the computers.

For instance, a young woman in Chicago recently wrote a message on CompuServe asking for advice on making a bridal gown. She was swamped with E-mail replies, some correspondents telling her which fabric stores to check out in her city, which pattern lines to investigate, and which swatch collections to mail away for. One woman told her the story of how, when she was born, her father was fighting in Vietnam and sent his wife 23 yards of Chinese dragon-embossed silk to celebrate the birth. She related the details of how they hired a seamstress and sewed the silk into a wedding gown. Everyone told the original message writer that, as she sewed her own gown, she should write details and upload digitized pictures if she could, and they would offer her sewing advice.

This is the kind of world you are entering. No one will ever, ever pick on you or laugh at you. If they did they would find 500 women with razor-sharp rotary cutters all over them immediately.

## How Much Is This Going to Cost You?

*D*epending upon how often you call a computer service, it may cost you anywhere from a few dollars a month, to $20 or $30, or even more. No, it's not cheap, but you can keep your bills low by calling in the evening, using special software to minimize your time online, and other stratagems.

The consumer computer services typically charge a monthly subscription fee under $10, either billed to your credit card or automatically withdrawn from your checking account each month. They may also charge hourly fees depending on what kind of information you access on their service. Luckily, crafting forums are one of the lower-priced items on the services, costing from $3 to $5 an hour to read.

If you live in a small town, you may have to pay a few dollars an hour extra to call the service through a special computer long-distance service. Or you may have to call the computer

In the online needlework forums you won't find the kind of bravado and posturing that you will on many other services.

service using your regular long-distance carrier, and that will also add to the cost of accessing the craft forums.

But don't despair. Whether you live in a small town or big one, in Appendix A you'll find surefire ways of cutting your access bills. It also includes explanations of the kinds of charges you'll find on your computer service bills and a list of questions pertaining to fees and telephone access in your area that you should ask a computer service before signing up.

## *Stitchers' Favorite Computer Services Tend to Change as the Prices Change*

Needlecrafters tend to be more price conscious than other computer service users. Consequently, the services they like best often change with the services' price fluctuations. Prodigy was popular a few years back, but when the service increased its prices, many of its quilters and cross-stitchers fled to low-cost GEnie. Here, in a nutshell, is the lowdown on which computer services crafters like best these days. Future chapters will tell you more about each service, what makes each unique, and how to sign up and use them to your best advantage.

☙ **CompuServe** No matter if you're a Pfaffie or a spinner, you gotta subscribe. CompuServe's humongous population of crafters, plus its big libraries, make it the place where you'll learn the most and make the most friends. Its prices may seem high, but automation software will keep your bills closer to those of budget rival GEnie.

🖎 **General Electric's GEnie**   While GEnie is the cheapest service, it's hard to use. Still, lots of quilters, stitchers, and sewers call it home. Many subscribe to both CompuServe and GEnie.

🖎 **America Online**   AOL is sexy looking, easy-to-use, and it's popular with the MTV crowd (in fact, MTV is online). Although there are some crafters online, there aren't as many as on other services. The service's advertised prices are low, but its response time (how long it takes America Online to respond to commands that you enter in your computer) is so slow that you'll rack up big bills in no time. Pass on it if needlecraft is your only interest. Try it if you're interested in tapping into the Internet or if you think that your family might like it.

🖎 **Prodigy**   If you've never been online before, Prodigy is a good place to start. It's designed like a video game so even three-year-olds can call and run up big online bills. Lots of sewers, quilters, cross-stitchers, and other crafters are online, but you won't find as strong a sense of community as you do on CompuServe or GEnie. The ads that always flash on the bottom of the screen drive some crafters batty.

🖎 **Delphi Internet Services**   Delphi is as low-cost as GEnie and equally trying to use. Several tight-knit handiwork communities have sprung up on Delphi. Though they don't have as many members as other services, their members are friendly and chatty.

**Internet**   This is the not-for-profit web of government, university, and corporate computers that you hear so much about. You can tap into the Internet in varying fashions from all the services listed above and from independent, local services in your area. Figure 9-8 shows how to read the Internet sewing conversations from America Online. The needlecraft-related discussion groups that swirl through the Internet are very different from those on the major commercial online services. Most of the people in them are textile professionals, artists, and stitchers affiliated with universities. While you won't find the sense of community on the Internet that you do on commercial services, the conversations (which are sometimes artsy in nature) are valuable and fascinating. You'll also find that the Internet offers information on fabric techniques and products that you never knew existed.

My favorites? CompuServe (I can get any question answered there), Internet (the things you read are amazing), and Prodigy (I love the video-game screens).

# SETTING UP EVERYTHING
# TO COMMUNICATE WITH CRAFTERS
# AROUND THE WORLD AND CALLING A
# COMPUTER SERVICE FOR THE FIRST TIME

*Computers and modems are very simple appliances and far
easier to learn to use than a Pfaff or a knitting machine.*

If you can thread a serger, you'll find it a snap setting up your PC to join an electronic craft guild. The most daunting part will be hooking your PC to a modem. (See Chapter 1 for modem-buying tips and setup advice.) Remember that a modem is nothing more than a device that picks up the phone, dials a number, and lets your computer talk to another far-off computer. That distant computer could be one that runs a sprawling global information service like CompuServe, or the home computer in someone's rec room that runs an electronic bulletin board. They're the same thing to your modem. When you're done reading databases or typing E-mail, you tell the modem to hang up and it does.

In most instances, all you need to do to get your computer communicating with other computers is to plug the phone cord into the modem, type another computer's phone number, press RETURN, and you're cruising the information highway. The communications software on the market today—especially the packages tailored to calling individual services like

CompuServe, Prodigy, or America Online—handle most of the minutiae of setup for you. This proprietary software tests and configures your modem, and even finds the best phone number for you to dial. All you need to do is to run the software's install or setup routine to copy it to your PC's hard disk.

## Everyone's Afraid of Botching It the First Time, but There's Really Nothing to Be Worried About

*I*'m someone who is always tentative about trying a new stitching technique or attempting to work with a new pattern or fiber. I'm afraid that I'll botch it or that it's beyond my skills. One of the things I love most about online services is that when I log on and type an E-mail message about my concerns, a chorus of caring and supportive women responds, urging me on and giving me the confidence to try it. Often my fears about botching it are unwarranted, but when they're not, that chorus of women is still there telling me what I did wrong and how to fix it. The support is incredible. You'll find the same support when you try something new with your computer.

The women who run the craft and needleart forums on CompuServe and GEnie try to ensure that every visitor who writes an E-mail message asking for computer help gets a response. Sandy Wheeler, the official "tech angel" on GEnie, has been known to spend countless hours on the phone talking crafters through their problems dialing and connecting to the service. That's pretty amazing, because you don't get that kind of help many other places, not even in the online tech support forums for major computer manufacturers or the online service's tech support number. What's more, Sandy and the other tech angels who provide this advice don't get paid for their time. Many pay for the time they spend online just like you and I do.

**Tech angels online ensure that crafters get the help they need.**

*The needlearts forum on GEnie has designated tech angels to assist floundering callers. These self-sacrificing volunteers will even telephone you to help figure out what you are doing wrong and get you online.*

# You Should Find Out a Few Things
# About Your Modem and Setup Before You Go Online

*T*he easiest way to get online is to call the services and ask for their free startup kits. This software makes these services extremely easy to use. Prodigy is the easiest to call and should be your first choice if you're a novice. Steering around this service is just like playing a video game. There's also a large family of crafters online.

You can also use the software that came with your modem, or any general-purpose software like Procomm Plus, to call CompuServe, Delphi, or GEnie, or any of the bulletin boards listed in Chapter 19. You won't be able to use it to call America Online or Prodigy, however; you'll need special software for these services. Calling a computer service with an all-purpose communications package is harder than using one specially tailored for the service because you need to figure out what commands to type once you get connected to the service. The software won't know. But don't let that deter you. Remember, you can never mess anything up, on either your own computer or the computer service, by experimenting.

Most communications software these days sets itself up and even configures your modem for you. Gone are the days when you had to figure out what N-8-1 meant. Once you get communications software, you won't have to do a lot besides run the installation routine. When you slip that floppy disk into the slot on the front of your PC and type the applicable install commands, or double-click that Installer icon on your Mac, the software copies itself to your PC's hard disk (see Figure 1-1). Your PC's hard disk is like a record—you know, one of those old 33⅓ rpm ones on which Elvis songs were originally released. It stores software and computer files like word-processing

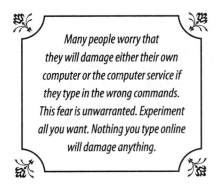

*Many people worry that they will damage either their own computer or the computer service if they type in the wrong commands. This fear is unwarranted. Experiment all you want. Nothing you type online will damage anything.*

documents and spreadsheets. When it's done copying, you remove the floppy disk from the PC, open the software's icon or enter the commands that the directions tell you to type, and the PC loads into its memory the software that now resides on your hard disk. Now you're ready to rock 'n' roll.

Although you probably won't have to do much to the software to get it to call the online service, it may ask you for these things:

🖝 **What brand of modem you have.** Some communications software figures it out by itself by running a few invisible tests on your modem. Others will show you a list of modem brands. If it's a good day, your modem will be among them. All you have to do is tell the software which one it is. If your modem is not on the list, or if you don't know what type of modem you have (a common problem if you bought a PC with an internal modem—the manufacturer may not even know), try selecting an entry containing the word "generic" and whatever Vs your modem has (V.42, V.32, etc.). Or, select "Hayes compatible." If all else fails, select "Hayes compatible 2400 bps modem," even if your modem is faster than 2400 bps. You can always set the modem's higher speed in the software's phone list or dialing directory.

🖝 **Which communications port the modem is connected to.** Don't know? If you have a mouse connected to your PC, the modem is probably on Com Port 2. If your PC is hooked to an office computer network, it may be Port 3 or 4. On a Mac, the modem should be attached to the telephone port (labeled with an icon that looks like a phone receiver), but it might be attached to the printer port. Check the icon above or below the port. You can always experiment. If the modem is an external one, the Terminal Ready

> The most common reason for communications software failing to talk to a modem is that the communications port is set wrong. It can be set wrong in the software (it may be set to Com 1, when the modem is actually hooked to Com 2), or, if the modem is inside your PC, its switches may not be set so that it's communicating through the proper computer port. If you can't get your communications software to work, check with whoever installed the modem to make sure that the modem is set to use the proper communications port.

(or TR) light will flash (assuming the modem has one, many don't) if the communications software is talking to the modem. You can also type, right on the communications software's terminal screen (that's the big blank screen), **AT**, and ENTER. That's the command to get the modem's attention. If an "OK" appears in response, the communications software and modem are talking to each other and everything's working.

☛ **How fast your modem is.** This is where computer black magic comes in. Your modem is described on its box as 2400 bps, 9600 bps, 14.4K bps, or 28.8K bps. (Bps stands for "bits per second.") That's the top speed at which your modem can shuffle computer bits down the phone line to the computer service. For Prodigy and America Online software, select the top speed that's listed on the installation screen at which your modem can communicate.

Modem settings in Windows 95 are handled by a universal modem-driver called "Unimodem." This makes life easy because Windows 95 takes care of modem settings for you—plus tells the communications software how to work with the modem. To install a modem in Windows 95 click on Start/Settings/Control Panel, then click on the Add New Harware icon. If your modem is already installed, you can find out how it's set up by heading to the Control Panel and Clicking on the telephone icon labeled "Modem."

If you bought your modem second-hand and can't get it to work with the communications software, poke around in the software's modem setup screens until you find a long string of program commands that begins with **AT** and looks like a program compiler drooled on the screen. It might look something like this: **ATE1Q0V1X4&C1&D2S7=60S11=55S0=0^M**. This may take some fishing. Directly after the **AT**, type into the string **&F**, as in **AT&F**. If you see a Z anywhere in the string of commands, erase it. Don't erase anything else in the string. Save these settings with the communications software's Save command (if it doesn't have one, don't sweat it). Now exit the program and then reload it. This will return the modem to its original factory settings

## *Some Communications Software Keeps Its Own Phone Book*

If you're installing all-purpose communications software, you may spot somewhere in the program a list of phone numbers for computer services like Dow Jones-News Retrieval or CompuServe. This is called the dialing directory. This is where you set your modem's speed for calling services. You'll see a bps rate listed next to each phone number. That's the speed the modem will use to call that service.

Most communications software today comes with all the entries in their dialing directory set to 56K bps. "Wait a minute!" you say. Most modems' top speed is 14.4K bps. True, but this 56K bps speed is the speed at which *your computer and modem* will talk to each other. The modem will still talk to the computer service at its top speed, be it 2400 bps or 14.4K bps. The speed at which your modem and computer talk to each other is called the *port speed*. It's set higher than the telephone line speed so that when your modem uses its built-in data compression (remember those Vs?), your computer can process all that incoming information at a speed that's fast enough to prevent traffic jams.

Yes, it is confusing. Here's what I do when I call a bulletin board or service for the first time: I set that speed entry to 2400 bps, even if my modem is much faster. Modems often have an easier time connecting at 2400 bps than at faster speeds, so I can be assured of connecting with that first call. Plus it gives me a chance to log on to the service and find out what its rates are; some services charge extra per hour for connecting to them at speeds higher than 2400 bps. After I hang up, I can always go back into the dialing directory and boost the modem's speed to 14.4K or 56K bps, or whatever. I always experiment with what will work the best when I call that particular service. Different settings work better for different services.

When you buy a modem, don't bother reading the whole manual. If it's got step-by-step instructions for setting up the modem and making a call, follow them, but the rest will probably be incomprehensible. Similarly, avoid calling the modem manufacturer's tech support number. If anybody ever answers the phone, they will probably have just come from a Klingon summer language camp and be unable to sustain conversation in any known human speech pattern. (Actually, of course, some tech support people try to be helpful, but they *do* tend to talk jargon.)

# Calling a Computer Information Service for the First Time May Be the Most Memorable Experience You Have Using a Computer

The procedures for calling a computer service for the first time will differ depending on the communications software you use. With Prodigy, CompuServe, and America Online software, you may enter a sign-up number and perhaps a user ID (that's a unique name or number that the service will use to keep track of you) that comes printed on your startup kit. Then the software will log you onto the service, register you, and ask you for the credit card number to which it will bill your online charges. It may retrieve from the service a local telephone number you can use to call the service in the future, hang up, and log you back onto the service by using that number.

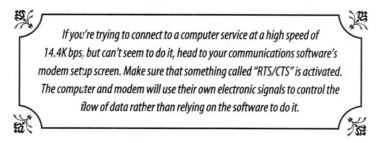

If you're using all-purpose communications software—you know, Procomm Plus—you need to do a little work. You type the service's modem or data phone number into the software's dialing directory (that list of phone numbers), highlight the number, and press ENTER or RETURN.

If you have an external modem, you'll hear the modem beep out the phone number through its speaker. You'll hear the tweet of a distant modem, followed by the trills of the modems trying to negotiate a connection. You'll hear a "whoosh" if they successfully connect. Silence will follow. If you're using all-purpose communications software, the screen will go blank. What to do next? Press ENTER, unless you have instructions to do otherwise. That should bring up the service's menus, and you should be able to find your way around the computer service from there.

How do you know your modem is connected to the computer service? The pictures on the screen may change and show you, for example, the news headlines for the day. Or the computer may beep or trill. In some instances you'll see a "Connect" message. Tucked in some discreet corner of the screen you may spot a little picture of a phone showing the receiver off the hook, or a more obscure picture of two modem cables connected. If you're running Microsoft Windows, a small hourglass may appear on your screen. That's the Windows symbol telling you to wait, your computer is busy. In this case the modem is waiting for something from the online service.

Similarly, how do you know when you've lost the connection? Sometimes a discreet message will flash "Connection Lost" or "Carrier Lost" or "Remote Computer Disconnected." What went wrong? Sometimes the connection is lost because there's noise on the phone line. Sometimes the computer service is having problems. Don't assume it's your fault; just try again. And again and again.

If, after four or five tries, you still can't connect, lower your modem's speed to 2400 bps, or even 1200 bps, by going into the software's setup screens and adjusting the speed setting. If you still can't connect at the lower speeds, wait a little while before trying again—maybe fifteen minutes, or even an hour. Sometimes in the evening, when lots of people are calling computer services, you may have problems connecting to certain services, especially Prodigy, CompuServe, and America Online. If you call back later and still can't connect, telephone the online service's tech support number, if there is one.

> If you're trying to connect to a computer service at a high speed of 14.4K bps, but can't seem to do it, head to your communications software's modem setup screen. Make sure that something called "RTS/CTS" is activated. The computer and modem will use their own electronic signals to control the flow of data rather than relying on the software to do it.

## *Don't Be Afraid to Act Like a Tourist Once You're Online*

Once your modem is connected to a computer service, you can stroll around the service by typing in commands or using your mouse to point the cursor at objects on your PC screen and clicking on them. Click on the newspaper to read the day's headlines, for instance. Or click on the picture of the woman doing aerobics to get to the databases and public discussion groups about that. (Yes, we all want to do that, don't we?)

The commands you type or issue with your mouse are sent to that far-off computer on the other end of the phone connection. The computer acts on these and sends back information or E-mail. Think of a genie in a bottle—the analogy General Electric was thinking of when it chose the name for its computer service. You type commands, and with almost magical intuition, the computer service does your bidding.

When you connect to a computer service for the first time, the best thing to do is explore like a tourist. Click on the images that interest you. You can't hurt anything by fooling around. And don't feel self-conscious if you don't know what you're doing. The other half-million consumers who call the service probably don't either.

In addition to the craft clubs, you'll probably find other things online that will interest you, like current affairs discussions, book clubs, ask-the-vet public conferences, and support groups for just about any problem or illness imaginable. Unfortunately, once you find your way to the needlecraft forums, you won't have time for any of those.

## *Don't Be Shy About Jerking the Phone Cord from the Modem If That's What It Takes to Get the Computer Off the Phone*

In some of the software for calling computer services it is not obvious where the hang-up button is. Frankly, the services do not want you to disconnect and end the cash flow from you to them. But, rest assured that there is in every communications software package a button or method for hanging up. If you can't find it (we'll go into more detail on this later), remember that you can always close up the software, unplug the phone cord from the modem, or turn it off if it has an on/off switch. No harm will come of it. And sometimes it's the simplest way to get the computer off the phone.

# The Gentle Art of Electronic Conversation

Oh wouldn't we all love to have the time to write our friends finely calligraphied letters on stationery festooned with doves and roses? The art of correspondence as the Victorians knew it is, alas, practically dead. Computer mail has taken its place.

E-mail is the fast food of written correspondence. While E-mail may seem rude, with its bits and bytes and lack of wax-sealed envelopes, sending E-mail is ever so much more fun than the laborious letter writing our grandmothers knew. You can type a letter on your computer, send it to a friend on the other side of the world, and within minutes receive a reply. Of course, you can't bundle the letters together with silk ribbons and store them at the bottom of your sewing basket as a memorial to a dear friendship. Not unless you print them out first.

Electronic mail is, quite simply, a message that you type on your computer and send to a friend via a computer online service. Your friend reads the message on her computer, and, with just a few keystrokes, she writes a reply to send to your computer. While you can compose E-mail in a word-processing program, the easiest way to send E-mail is either to type your message while you're online and then send it, or to compose it offline using your telecomm software or the service's front-end software and then connect to the service and send it.

Just as with a paper letter, you can send E-mail to anyone with an E-mail address, whether it's on your computer service, a different service, or the Internet. Just as you could with paper mail, you can even send E-mail to companies or universities that have E-mail addresses.

You can do other tricks with E-mail as well, like carbon copying an E-mail message to others, or forwarding a message you receive to a third person. You can save E-mail to your computer's hard disk or print it.

More and more people these days are using E-mail to keep in touch with their children at college, their brothers and sisters at military bases overseas, and even their spouses while at work. (A common question I hear is "How can my husband and I exchange E-mail during the day from our respective places of work?" The answer is "If both of you work in an office where the computer network is connected to a major computer service or Internet, it's usually simple to do.") Typing a note into your computer is quicker than pulling out the stamps and envelopes, and gratification is immediate because the recipient often receives your message in minutes, and may reply just as fast.

You'll find software that automates the quick sending of mail, and I highly recommend that you buy it. You'll find both generic and service-specific software. Most of these packages let you type messages offline, and then they automatically log onto the computer, post the message, download any waiting E-mail, and log off. These packages will save you barrels of money in online fees too. Chapters on the respective services discuss this software in detail.

One of the amazing things about E-mail is that it makes it so easy to share confidences with people you have never met. Someone you know only by a cryptic E-mail address of POLLY54@PORCUPINE.COM can become a fast friend sight unseen. For instance, today in my E-mail box there is a letter from a sewer in Japan who relates that because the Japanese live in such tiny quarters, they don't sew large quilts, but prefer to stick to small, hand-pieced projects like handbags and placemats. There is one from a librarian in Philadelphia who has sent me the most damning review imaginable of a wearable arts book. There is a message from a needle-artist in Michigan offering advice on how I can fix a botched appliqué floral by festooning the errant petals with silk ribbon embroidery. I have never met any of these people, but I would gladly invite them into my home.

## Cyberspace Etiquette Is Not Much Different
## from Real-Life Sewing Guild Etiquette

E-mail is infamous for bringing out the worst in people, but that's not necessarily true in the electronic needlecraft forums. In fact, several of the forum managers have mentioned how remarkable it is that participants are so polite to each other. "People don't act so nice in person in guild meetings," said one cynically.

**Don't flame others in public or private E-mail.** The verb *flame* is technospeak for verbally attacking someone in E-mail for an opinion or behavior you don't agree with. When someone flames another, there's a chain reaction. Other people flame you, you flame them back, suddenly everyone is fighting. While flaming is a regular feature of the Internet football conference (where the concept of head butting takes on whole new dimensions), fiber art conferences have a low level of tolerance for such childishness.

**Never distribute or upload copyrighted material to the service.** This includes copyrighted patterns, instructions, software, or articles from magazines. Copyrighted materials may be distributed electronically to others only with the author's permission.

**Never send unsolicited public or private E-mail advertising a commercial service or product.** Sending computer junk mail is considered the pinnacle of online gaucherie. People have to pay for their time online, and often they pay fees based on the amount of E-mail they receive. So, advertising your product by writing messages about it in public forums wastes their money. Most online services will boot you off if you do it. If your product is mentioned in the course of public discussion, it is of course permissible, even desirable, for you to participate in the conversation. But outright selling online is a no-no.

**Try to keep your public messages related to the topic in the message subject line.** This rule, which is one of the cardinal laws of most computer online services, is followed and enforced to varying degrees, depending on which needlework forum you tap into. While those who run the sewing forum on CompuServe demand strict compliance to it, messages in the National Online Quilters forum on Delphi rarely relate to the subject, or quilting in general, for that matter. The rule of thumb is this: Try to get a sense of the kinds of messages others are writing before jumping into the conversation.

**Never be afraid to ask questions, no matter how silly they may seem.** Everyone was or is in the same boat as you. Never be afraid to post a public message asking for help with your computer. No one will make fun of you. You will not embarrass yourself. The gracious crafters of the needleworker forums will offer you all the help they can. And you may even make friends this way.

**Read any applicable help files before requesting help from the management.** It takes a lot of time to help modem callers out of their technical predicaments. Remember that most of the people who manage online needlecraft forums are volunteers. Try to help yourself before sending them an S.O.S.

**Don't give people who run the service a hard time.** This is true for commercial services, but it is especially true for small, private online services like computer bulletin boards. Many bulletin boards are run from someone's family room, and you should behave as if you're entering someone's home. Always use your best manners, and if it's a free service, be sure to leave a thank-you note before logging off.

*"We're not getting old, we're reaching mythic stature."*

*—*

*Spotted at the tail end of an E-mail posted in the historical costume mailing list on Internet.*

## *Needlework Hieroglyphics in E-Mail*

Habitués of online needlework forums have developed a shorthand to signify certain words they use over and over. Here are some acronyms, abbreviations, and symbols you'll run into online. Most are unique to the needlecraft forums, but some can be found in other electronic forums too.

**BD**   Birthday. Online needlecrafters like to exchange birthday gifts and talk about what sewing goodies they got on their birthday.

**BTW**   By the way.

**CS&CC**  This is the abbreviation for Cross-Stitch & Country Crafts magazine.

**DH**   Dear Husband.

**DMC**   The embroidery floss by the French manufacturer of the same name.

**FOM**   Fabric of the month—the fabric that everyone is exchanging or talking about.

**<G> or <g>**   The writer is grinning.

**IMHO**   In my humble opinion…

**LOL**   The writer is laughing out loud.

**OTOH**   On the other hand…

**Q**   Quilting or something quilt related.

**ROFL**   The writer is rolling on the floor laughing.

**RR**   Round robins. Sewers, quilters, or cross-stitchers will pass a project around the country through U.S. mail, each stitching on it a bit and then mailing it to the next sewer on the list.

**UFOs**   Unfinished objects. All those hooked rug projects that fill up the guest room closet.

**<smile> and <sob!>**   Anything typed in triangular brackets signifies the writer's emotion, either seriously or jokingly. These are the two most common manifestations of this practice.

**X**   A single cross-stitch. Sometimes writers will fill up a message with Xs to pass along a design or instructions.

**Xstitch**     Cross-stitching.

**<VBG>**     Writer is sporting a Very Big Grin.

**Wearables**     Wearable art; any clothing that you make that is truly a work of art.

**:-)**     The infamous "smiley." Tilt your head sideways and you'll see it. It's supposed to represent someone smiling or grinning. Smileys, also called "emoticons," and their many variations (8-) and ;-> for example) are inserted into messages to signify the writer's subtle shifts of emotion. Just like the yellow smiley face buttons, some people love them, and some see in them the decline of civilization as we know it.

## *How Private Is Private E-Mail?*

The commercial online services will assure you that any message you send from your private E-mail box to another subscriber's private E-mail box is immune to prying eyes. All guard their E-mail systems in varying ways, including keeping hardware and software for the online service in locked rooms, requiring that employees enter passwords to access sensitive areas of the system, and keeping tape backups in vaults. However, when pressed, all the services admit that it is possible for technicians to read just about any message on the system.

How likely is it that someone will read your private E-mail? Not very, since hundreds of thousands of E-mail messages flow through these systems daily. Still, it is not a good idea to write anything in an E-mail message that could potentially destroy your personal life or career. This is especially true on Internet, where private mail bounces through computers all across the country (if not around the world) before it reaches its destination.

## Keeping Your Hands Fit at the Keyboard

*M*any needlecrafters suffer gnarled, painful hands, twisted by arthritis or throbbing from carpal tunnel syndrome. The repeated hand motions of their craft are partially to blame, but often a computer is the main culprit. A needlecrafter may pound his or her knuckles over a keyboard all day at work and then pick up knitting needles to relax at night. The results can be devastating.

All the electronic craft forums are filled with needlecrafters suffering hand disorders. It's surprising the number of people you'll meet who have endured multiple surgeries to alleviate the pain of carpal tunnel syndrome. If you are in this league, you'll find support groups online in the needlecraft forums on CompuServe and GEnie. (In fact, if your hands suffer from carpal tunnel or any repetitive stress disorder, post a message in just about any craft forum and you'll get dozens of messages of advice.)

Here are some tips to keep your hands healthy at the computer:

**Get an adjustable chair, preferably one with arm rests.** Position the monitor at eye level. If glare greets your eyes, get a glare screen and proper lighting so you don't squint or bend over the machine. Your desk and keyboard should be positioned low so that your fingers hang over the keys. You don't want to rest your wrists on the disk. In general, you want to avoid putting weight on the undersides of the wrist. And remember what Sister Carmine told you: Good posture will help you avoid many problems in life.

**Try to become as mouseable as possible.** Use software in which most commands are entered, not by typing in commands but by pointing and clicking. Microsoft Word is preferable to WordPerfect, while Procomm Plus for Windows is better than Procomm for DOS, and of course, all Mac software is mouse oriented. At the same time, too much mousing can give you "mouse finger," or even "mouse shoulder." So learn those keyboard shortcuts and try to switch back and forth. Mouse pads with built-in wrist supports provide some relief.

**Take frequent breaks from the computer.** Please don't answer 90 E-mail messages at one sitting. If your hands or wrist start to get sore, rest.

**Don't underestimate the benefits of regular exercise, especially if you're an arthritis sufferer.** Even a low-key fitness regimen can do wonders in preventing joints and tendons from swelling.

> Do those special ergonometric devices like split keyboards and desk wrist supports help? For some people, yes. It depends upon your working style. I know one woman who cuts Dr. Scholl's shoe pads into tiny pieces and sticks them on her keyboard keys. Whatever works for you!

**If you start to feel pain in your hands or arms, *rest immediately* and change your style of computer use.** Cut down on the E-mail, talk to your employer and doctor. Talk to other computer users too. Repetitive movement injuries are not easy to treat and, if left untreated, can play havoc with your life. (One editor I know can't even pick up her child anymore.)

**Fingerless, elasticized gloves provide considerable relief to many arthritis and carpal tunnel sufferers.** Several years ago, while I was writing a story on Handez gloves, New England Therapeutic shipped me a bunch and I passed them out to friends to try. Every single one of them has since become a devoted wearer. You can find the gloves at craft stores or order them for $19.95 from Patternworks at 800/438-5464.

## Text Versus Binary, or E-mail Versus Software

*E*lectronic mail is stored in what's called text or ASCII form. Computer software, on the other hand, is stored in a different form called a *binary file.* The main difference, as far as we're concerned, is in the methods of copying information to your computer.

When you want to copy an E-mail message to your computer's hard disk, you issue a simple capture command, and your computer snatches the message off the computer service and scribbles it on its disk, where you can read it later with your word processor.

When you want to copy software from the computer service onto your PC, the process is more involved. You must do something called a *file transfer* with a *protocol* that will ensure that the file arrives at your PC intact and without any errors. Otherwise, you may not be able to run the software on your PC. If you try to read a binary file with your word processor you'll see nothing but gibberish.

> *Note: Sometimes software or binary files are attached to E-mail messages so they can be transferred automatically to your PC. If you should be sent an E-mail message with such an attachment, your communications software will tell you.* ๑◣

## Some Additional Tips

◞ Your PC cannot contract a computer virus simply by reading E-mail or participating in online needlecraft forums.

◞ When calling a computer service for the first time, especially if it's a computer bulletin board, call early in the evening before most people go to sleep. That way, if you dial a wrong number, or if the service or BBS (bulletin board system) has been disconnected, you're less apt to wake someone who will likely pick up the phone and scream in fear at the sound of a modem trilling at them in the middle of the night.

🙿 When a bulletin board or online service asks you to type in a password, never use something other people might guess, like the name of your computer, your town or street, your own name, or the name of your dog.

🙿 Never use the same password on two different services. It's best to use some randomly chosen word paired with a number or two, like BUGGY4.

🙿 It's O.K. to pick up the phone when your modem is connected to a computer service. It may temporarily cause weird characters to spill over your computer's screen (that's why you don't want to do it), but it will not wreak permanent damage on either your computer or the computer service.

🙿 As silly as it may sound, if something goes wrong, don't panic until after you check to make sure that everything is plugged in right. Especially the phone cords. It's easy to get phone cords plugged into the wrong jacks.

🙿 If your modem shares the phone with other members of the house, put an end to the annoyance of teenagers picking up an extension while your computer is on the phone with a little $15 Y-plug, available at most office stores. Stick it into your phone jack, and if someone picks up an extension while the PC is on the phone, their phone will be effectively dead. You'll find it at most office supply stores.

🙿 If your PC runs Microsoft Windows 3.1 or earlier, never keep more than one communications program loaded at a time. Before you call a computer service, quit any fax software or Windows Terminal. Otherwise, you'll get an error message like "Communications port busy" or "Could not initialize port." To find out what if any communications software is loaded, point to the square at the top left corner of the computer screen with your mouse. Click the left mouse button. In the menu that appears, point to and click on "Switch to..." In the "Task List" you'll find all the programs that are currently loaded. On Macs running System 7 you point to the icon at the top right corner of the screen and press the mouse button to see which programs are loaded. If a communications program is in the list, drag down to select it and then choose Quit from the File menu.

🙿 A user ID, sometimes known as a logon or user name, is a string of characters that a computer service assigns to you to keep track of who you are. A screen name, which is the name that appears on the screen when you type in a message to others, is usually different. A screen name is your real name, a nickname, or some variation that you have chosen for others to identify you online.

↩ If you call a computer bulletin board or online service using all-purpose communications software, and you have no idea what to type or do once your modem connects to the service, hit ENTER. That should bring up the service's menus, and you can find your way around from there. You may have to press ENTER twice or more to get a menu.

↩ Get your PC off the phone during thunderstorms. Unplug the phone line from the modem, plus, unplug the PC from the wall. Electrical surges can travel over phone lines as well as power lines. They can reduce your PC to toasted marshmallows. Surge protectors provide only a modicum of safety. Your husband will probably tell you that such measures are paranoid (these guys write me all the time), but tell him I know electronic bulletin board operators who've lost PCs to phone line surges. In fact the down payment on my house came partly from a computer consultancy that made most of its money during summer replacing office PCs fried during thunderstorms.

↩ You can put a PC in your sewing room, but you can't put a PC in a woodworking shop. The reason? Sawdust from woodworking tools can get inside the PC and short it out, even set it on fire. Be warned: The same can happen in your sewing room if lots of lint is flying around. But you're neat, aren't you?

# 11

# A TREASURE TROVE OF FREE AND NEARLY FREE CRAFT INFORMATION AWAITS YOU ON COMPUTER SERVICES

*There are some basics you'll need to know to mine computer services for software and information files for needlecrafts.*

One of the most personally enriching ways you can use your computer is to call information services to search for information files and software pertaining to your craft. You can dial CompuServe with your computer and modem and, with just a few keystrokes, find a bevy of files explaining all the different methods of appliqué or how to knit raglan sleeves or buy a loom. Or you can call GEnie and copy to your computer low-cost software for designing quilts. You can even display on your computer's screen pictures of quilts that others have designed. You'll also find quilt block designs that other crafters have created with popular quilt software like Electric Quilt.

This information is stored on the online service in what are called "libraries," as opposed to the public message "forums" explained in earlier chapters. You will usually find a library of files for each public message conference, although sometimes online services have one central library where all the files for the service are stored.

This chapter introduces the terms and concepts used in searching for craft information online. Future chapters will give you step-by-step instructions for finding and retrieving craft information on each of the major computer services.

Online services and Internet are terrific craft information sources—better than the public library. You won't find books or patterns online (those are copyrighted). What you will find are compilations of public discussions that have appeared in the past on the service or Internet about pertinent topics like how to dye fabric for quilting or adjust sewing patterns to fit better. If you own a computerized sewing machine like a Pfaff or a knitting machine, it will be worth your while to get online, for you'll find files containing directions from other stitchers on how to use those complicated machines, as well as files with stitching patterns. Files containing discussions on less-than-mainstream needlecraft topics are also popular. For instance, the weavers on CompuServe have assembled a large, eclectic library on subjects like how to use Kool-Aid to dye wool. ("At different times we've become obsessed with that," explained one weaver.) One file is a collection of anecdotes on "gross things found in wool." These files are easy to find and download, and obtaining them usually doesn't cost you anything more than the basic hourly charge to connect to the service. The individual files are stored on the online service in what are called "libraries".

## There Are as Many Kinds of Computer Files as There Are Types of Knitting Yarn

*T*hink of a computer file as a folder in a file cabinet; that's how it got its name anyway. Like a hanging folder, a computer file contains information about a particular topic. This information may be text that you can read in a word processor, or it may be software. These are some items you'll find in files of craft libraries of online services: a collection of E-mail messages that other crafters have written on a particular topic in the past, like how to clean a knitting machine; a list of mail-order houses for knitting supplies; a piece of software to graph stitch designs for a jacquard loom, for example, or to design loose, wearable art garments; a computer picture, maybe of a quilt that another computer user designed or a jacket she sewed. There might be a picture of another online craft guild member, posted on the service so that other members can see who they're typing messages to.

# Files Have Names (Filenames). If You Learn What the Names Mean You'll Know What to Do with the File

*F*iles are stored on computer services with descriptions that tell you what sort of file they are and what they contain. You may have to request these descriptions specifically (you'll click on a button), or they may appear as soon as you request a list of files.

Files also have names called, miraculously enough, filenames. You can tell what's in a file—whether it's software or whether it's text you can read—by its name. The next few sections list some filenames, what they mean, and what to do with them. This is kind of like learning the Latin roots of words to increase your vocabulary. If you pay attention to these labels, you'll end up with a much better sense of what's available to you on online services. And you'll really know what to do with the files that you download.

## *You Can Read Files That Contain Text Either While You're Connected to the Service or After You Hang Up*

Many of the files that you'll encounter will be basic text files; files that have information that you can read. Their filenames generally end with .TXT, .ASC, .THD, or .DOC. These letters are called file extensions.

**.TXT** is short for *text* as in QUILT.TXT. Any word processor (like Microsoft Word or WordPerfect) should be able to read and show you these files.

**.ASC** is short for *ASCII text*. ASCII text files lack the sorts of formatting doodads (bold, italic, etc.) that word processors allow you to add to a file. Like .TXT files, you can read ASCII files in any word processor.

**.THD** stands for *message thread,* as in QUILT.THD. This means the file is a text file that contains a message thread from one of the services' craft message forums, You should be able to pull this file into any word processor, though you may need to rename it first.

**.DOC** is short for *document* (as in QUILT.DOC). These are also text files that you can read in any word processor. Don't confuse DOC files with a formatted file created by a word processor, like Microsoft Word, for example. In fact, you won't find word-processed files online—no one uploads them.

You can read these text files by either displaying them on your screen while you're connected to the computer service, or you can copy them to your computer (download them) so that you can read them later with your word processor after you hang up. Text files are never uploaded with word-processing formatting because everyone uses a different word processor. Also, the fact that they're posted on computer services in plain text means that they can be read with any type of computer, be it a PC, a Mac, or an Amiga.

## *You Can Display Files Containing Pictures on the Services or Copy Them to Your PC to View Later*

A file that is a computer picture, also known as a graphic file, may have a few different file extensions. Here are the most common ones with clues on what to do with them:

**.GIF** (as in QUILT.GIF) files (called "Jiff") are pictures that are stored in CompuServe's special computer picture format, GIF.

**.BMP** (as in QUILT.BMP) stands for bitmapped file, simply another way of storing a graphics file. Bitmapped files are pictures stored in Microsoft Windows' picture format, BMP.

**.PCX** (as in QUILT.PCX) is a very common color picture format in most computer drawing and design programs.

**.TIF** (as in QUILT.TIF) files (called "Tiff") are picture files commonly created by most computer drawing programs.

There are dozens of other picture formats, but these are the ones you're most apt to see on computer services.

As with text files, you may be able to display a picture file on your screen while you're connected, depending upon the format it's in and the service you're connected to. Or you can copy it to your computer's disk and then display it after you hang up with a paint program, a picture-viewing software utility, or sometimes the software you used to call the service. Because these formats are standard ones, they can be viewed with appropriate software on any type of computer, be it a PC or a Macintosh.

## Virtual Reality Quilt Shows

You can see lots of dazzling quilts, wearable art garments, and other needlework without ever leaving your computer. Stored in the file libraries of the craft forums on computer services are often hundreds of computer pictures of other members' projects and accomplishments. Sometimes the pictures are organized into shows. On GEnie, for example, each month brings a new collection of pictures of some well-known quilt designer who is a guest of the service. GEnie calls it their Virtual Reality Quilt Show.

To view these pictures, usually you need to download the picture file to your PC. These picture files are big, so they'll take a long time to copy to your PC unless you have a high-speed modem. After you log off, you can view the picture with a paint, graphics, or picture-viewing program. Needless to say, the better the resolution of your PC's screen, the sharper the image will be.

On CompuServe you can actually view the pictures while you're connected to the service with certain software, like CompuServe Information Manager or Ozark Software's OzCIS. CompuServe will paint them on your screen within seconds—that is, if you're calling with a 14.4K bps modem. It will take longer if your modem is slower, but it's much easier than the rigmarole of downloading the file.

How do you get your art online? You take a snapshot of your project (or yourself) and scan it with a hand-held scanner. With the scanner's software you store the digitized snapshot as a GIF (the format preferred by CompuServe) or a PCX file and then upload it to the service. If you don't have a scanner, you can mail the photo to the people who run the craft forum and they will scan and post it on the service for you.

CompuServe and GEnie are the best spots to view digitized pictures of needlework. I like CompuServe the best because of its fast connections and the ability to see the pictures online. Digitized needlework is starting to appear on Internet and America Online, too. You'll find some of these pictures breathtaking, and a true source of inspiration.

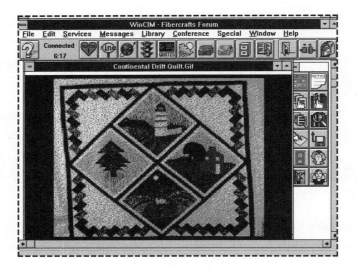

## Files Can Be Programs That Will "Run" When You Type Their Names

Among the many files you'll run across in your online travels will be files with .EXE extensions. This extension is short for *executable* and it signals that the file is actually some sort of program. For example you might see a file called QUILT.EXE.

Once you copy QUILT.EXE from the service to your computer, you have only to type the word **QUILT** (or whatever word, label, or characters precede the extension) at the DOS command prompt (that's C: or D: followed by a flashing screen cursor, like this: C:> or D:>) or to double-click on the file in the Windows Program Manager to run it.

## You've Heard of Shareware, but What Is It?

Shareware is a crazy way to run a business. The idea is that an author posts a piece of software on a computer service with a note saying that you can download it freely and even share it with your friends. If you like it, the author asks you to send money to register it. In return, you may get more pieces of the software or a manual—but not always. Believe it or not, several large software companies got their start this way. Not everyone pays for the software they download and use, of course, but then, not all the software is good.

You'll find many special-purpose crafting programs distributed on computer services as shareware. There are lots of cross-stitch, weaving, and knitting design programs that bear pay-it-if-you-like-it requests. Some of this software is very good. If you decide to use the program regularly, by all means, pay the author. Good work should not go unrewarded.

## *You'll Often Find Files That Have Been Shrunk to Save Space*

The final category of computer files that you should be aware of are shrunken, or, more commonly, compressed files. These are files with extensions like .ZIP, .LZH, .ARC, or .SIT.

These compressed files have been compacted with *archive* or *compression* software. Archive software shrinks a file significantly so that it takes up less space on the computer service and takes less time to upload or download (thus saving you time and money). You're likely to find a lot of these compressed files on online services, and it's easy to compress your own.

The extensions are attached to compressed files by the compressing software and tell you what kind of program you need to decompress the file.

When you download a compressed file, you need to have a copy of the software that was used to compress it in order to decompress it. The craft forums make it a point to tell subscribers which compression software was used to compact the file, and where on the service to find it. Here are the most commonly found compressed files and what to do with them:

> **Files with .ZIP extensions are the most common.** When you find files with .ZIP extensions, as in QUILT.ZIP, you've found a file that has been compressed with a program called PKZIP, from PKWare. PKZIP is by far the most common compression program, and you'll find that most of the compressed files you come across have a .ZIP extension. Before you can decompress ZIP files, you'll need to get a copy of the shareware called PKZIP.
>
> You can find PKZIP on all the computer services, get it from a friend (that's the idea behind shareware), or obtain it for $47 directly from PKWare, Inc. at 9025 N. Deerwood Dr., Brown Deer, WI 53228, 414/354-8699 or 414/354-8559 (fax). You should always keep a copy of PKZIP on your hard disk. It's also handy for hard disk backups.
>
> Once you've installed PKZIP on your computer, you'll most likely do the following (double-check the instructions though):

1 Change to the directory or subdirectory that has PKZIP.

2 Once you're in the right directory, at the prompt type **PKUNZIP** *drive letter:\subdirectory\filename* and press ENTER to run the program and decompress the file.

> If, for example, you type **PKUNZIP C:\SEW\QUILT.ZIP** and press ENTER, you're running the program PKUNZIP and telling it to unzip (also sometimes called extract) whatever has been compressed in the file QUILT.ZIP. You're also telling PKUNZIP that QUILT.ZIP is in the subdirectory SEW on the C: drive. If you need to unZip a file in some other directory, like C:\CSERVE\DOWNLOAD, you'd simply replace **C:\SEW** with **C:\CSERVE\ DOWNLOAD**, or the name and location of the directory in which the file is located.

᠃ **PKZIP is not the only compression software in town.** You'll also find files with these extensions:

**.LZH** (as in QUILT.LZH) means the file has been compacted with the program LHA by Haruyasu Yoshizaki. You should be able to find LHA on your computer service.

**.ARC** (as in QUILT.ARC) means the file has been compressed with ARC-E by Vern Buerg and Wayne Chin. You should also be able to find this software on your service.

**.SIT** (as in QUILT.SIT) identifies Macintosh files compressed with the software called StuffIt. If you've got a Mac you'll need to get StuffIt to decompress these files. If you've got a PC, look for something called UNSTUFF.EXE for DOS which allows you to decompress .SIT files. UNSTUFF is freeware created by Aladdin Systems. If you have trouble finding it, contact them directly at Aladdin Systems, Inc., 165 Westridge Drive, Watsonville, CA 95076, 408/761-6200 or 408/761-6206 (fax) or from online services use AppleLink: ALADDIN; America Online: ALADDIN; CompuServe: 75300,1666; GEnie: ALADDINSYS; or Internet: aladdin@well.sf.ca.us

You may also run into the suffixes .ARJ and .PAK, which signify other, less popular compression programs. You should be able to find all the software you need to uncompress these files on the computer services that carry files compressed with them.

*Note: While these instructions for using PKZIP from DOS are pretty simple, be aware that there are a number of Windows programs out there that will let you run PKZIP from Windows (WINZIP and Drag and Zip, for example). These programs will also decompress files that have been compressed with other programs. These are very handy programs, and you should try to get your hands on them if you run Windows. Drag and Zip comes from Canyon Software (1537 Fourth Street, Suite 131, San Rafael, CA 94901, 415/453-9779). WINZIP comes from Nico Mak Computing (P.O. Box 919, Bristol, CT 06011-0919, 800/242-4775 or 713/524-6394).* ᠃

# You Find Files by Scrolling Through Lists or by Telling Your Online Service to Find Specific Files for You

*O*nline services store files in depositories called libraries. The best way to think of this library metaphor is to think of the different branches of your public library, each with its own collection of books (the books would be files in this case). If your passion is needlepoint, you might find a library in a particular town that has a great needlepoint book collection. In the case of the craft forums, you'd search the various libraries in the forum for the embroidery-related library, and that would be the one containing lots of articles, software, or other files about needlepoint. Figure 11-1, below, shows a sample list of libraries found in the craft forum on CompuServe.

You find the files you're looking for by browsing, or scrolling through, the list of filenames and descriptions that appears on your computer screen when you enter a forum. You can also search for files that match your particular interest, or you can find specific files by using the special tools that most services have to do the searching for you.

**Figure 11-1**
A sample list of libraries on CompuServe. This listing changes weekly as files are added or deleted. Each online service has its own library of files with its own listings.

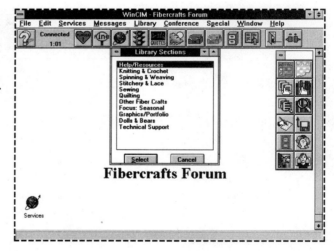

# *File Search Tools Can Really Speed Your Quest for Files You Care About*

All services will offer some sort of file search tool for their particular libraries. For example, if you use WinCim (the Windows front-end to CompuServe), you could enter the Fibercrafts Forum and, once in the forum, click on the "search libraries for file" icon, as shown in Figure 11-2, to find a particular file. Once you make this selection a dialog box appears on your screen and asks you to fill in the blanks.

**Figure 11-2**

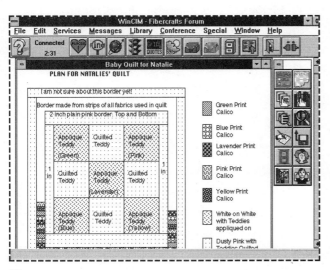

**Figure 11-3**

A typical search might go like this: If you want to find a file that tells you how to use quilting software, you could type "Quilting Software" as your keywords and then click Search (or press RETURN or ENTER). If any files in the forum match this description, the service will come back with a list of them. You'll notice also that you can search particular libraries in the forum by checking or unchecking their boxes.

When typing in the filename, you can use *wild card characters* like * or ?. For instance, if you know a collection of quilt block designs is stored in a file called QBLOCK81. ZIP, but you're not sure about that 81, you can type **QBLOCK*.*** and the service will respond with the names of all the files it has that begin with QBLOCK.

Once the service comes up with a file, or list of files, that matches your search criterion, you should find an option to view a more complete description of the file, or, if it's a text file or computer picture, you may be able to view it while you're still connected to the service as shown in Figure 11-3. The particulars all depend on the service.

# You Get Files from the Service to Your Computer by Asking

*W*hile some computer services let you see picture or text files while you're still connected to them, you'll often find that you need to download files to your computer before you can do anything with them. For example, you can't run software that you find on a service on the service itself; you always need to download it before running it.

So the question is this: How do you get that darn software (or graphic or text file) from that far away computer onto your own? How do you download a file? Basically you tell the computer service the file you want and how you want it sent. You can also tell the service when you want the file sent. (For instance, some services let you *mark* a file so that you can download it later or before you hang up.)

Many years ago, I saw a demo of communications software that used elaborate metaphors to illustrate the file download process. During the download, little rockets flew back and forth across the computer screen, accompanied by messages like "Spaceship File Is Blasting Off!" and "Spaceship File Is Landing!" It was actually an extremely confusing display, and I'm not surprised that the product didn't last more than a month on the market.

What happens during a file transfer is really very simple. The computer service sends the file in the form of bits and bytes over the phone line to your modem. Your modem takes the bytes and sends them to the PC. The PC checks them to make sure that they're all there and in the right order, in the method agreed on in its negotiations with the computer service during the opening moments of the file transfer. If the bytes check out, the PC writes them to its hard disk for permanent keeping (or a floppy disk, if you specified that instead). If they don't, the PC asks the computer service to retransmit them.

> *Note: Every service and software has its own specific way of downloading files. A generic example may not work for you; take a look at the chapters specific to your online service for help in downloading files from them.* ☙

## *"Protocol" Is Just a Fancy Way of Saying "This Is How I Want You to Send Me the File"*

Information moves back and forth over your phone line, between your computer and your online service, by way of something called a *protocol*. Sometimes it's called a *file protocol* or an *error-checking protocol*.

There are dozens of protocols, each tailored for use in specific situations. If you call CompuServe, Prodigy, or America Online with their own special software, you don't have to worry about protocols. The software wisely selects its own. But if you call Delphi or GEnie (or CompuServe with a generic telecommunications software package), you will have to select a protocol each time you copy a file to your PC. These are your choices and the best way to use them.

**CompuServe B+** The fastest and best thing to use when you download files from CompuServe.

**Xmodem** No, this is not a generic modem you buy at Sam's Wholesale Club; it's the oldest file transfer protocol there is. Xmodem is very slow. Use it only when nothing else, including Kermit, works. If you're given a choice, use the *CRC* version instead of the checksum version, because that does the best job checking for errors. It's also faster.

**Capturing computer files is like capturing butterflies.**

**Ymodem** A faster, more modern version of Xmodem. This is my favorite protocol to use when downloading files from GEnie, because it works fast and tends to work reliably.

**Ymodem-G** An even faster version of Ymodem. This protocol doesn't check transmission for errors, though, so use it only when you know your modem is using its built-in v.42 error correction (if it has it) as it's talking to the online service. If you don't know, don't sweat it. Use Zmodem instead.

**Zmodem**   The fastest protocol around; I use it for almost everything, whenever I can. The only time Zmodem will not work well is if there's a lot of noise on your telephone line, in which case it will slow to a snail's pace. You'll know this if your file seems to be moving awfully slowly. If that happens, end the transfer and start over using Ymodem.

**Kermit**   You should probably not bother with this protocol unless none of the other protocols seems to be working out right. Use it when there's lots of telephone noise or when nothing else works. It's indestructible, and it's always faster than Xmodem.

You basically want to pick the file protocol that will get the job done fastest. That may vary, depending on the online service, the kind of modem you have, and whether your phone line is clean or static-y. You will need to do some experimenting to find out which protocol works best for you.

## You Can Automate File Transfers to Save Money

Just as software is available to automate the sending and retrieval of E-mail, some telecommunications software automates the searching and retrieval of files from computer service libraries. Such software is available for CompuServe, GEnie, and Delphi. Before you connect to the service, you tell the software which forums and libraries you're interested in searching, then the software logs on and either conducts the search for you or downloads a catalog of what's available in the library you specified. After the software hangs up, you search through the catalog and make your choices. Then the software logs back on to the service, downloads the files you want, and logs off. It's a great time and money saver. You'll find more information about this software in the chapters about the respective services.

## Things That Go Wrong During File Downloads

When a file transfer botches up don't blame yourself.

The first thing to remember is that if you are able to connect to the online service (which must be the case if you're even able to think about starting a file transfer) the problem does not lie with your modem. Chances are it's the online service itself that's at fault. Try a different protocol, if you are given this choice, or just start the transfer over. Go through this checklist to determine what went wrong.

୬ **Check the filename.** Did you type the filename correctly? Did you specify the proper file library on the computer service? If you typed in incorrect information, the online service may not know which file to send and things will get messed up.

୬ **Check the protocol.** Did you tell the online service and your PC the proper file protocol to use? If the service told you what protocol it planned to use at the start of the file transfer, it was using its default and you may not be able to change it. If you can change it, you'll have to do a bit of detective work with the software's manual to find out how. Watch the screen as the download starts for signs of what protocol is being used at your end. Either way, make sure that your protocol is exactly the same as the one that the service is using.

If you start the file transfer and nothing happens—the progress box on the screen remains blank and doesn't show any bytes transferred—this is probably because your PC and the online service are using different protocols. Or maybe you've told them both to use the same protocol, but they don't agree on how that particular protocol should work. Try again. If it still doesn't work, try the transfer with another protocol.

୬ **Check the progress box.** If there are lots of errors, you've either got a noisy phone line or mismatched protocols. Try the transfer again with the protocol Kermit, which is impervious to phone line noise. Or check to see that the protocols match at both ends. If you're running Microsoft Windows 3.1 or earlier, try running the communications software full screen and don't switch to another application while a file transfer is chugging away.

If the file transfer aborts before it's over, your best bet is simply to try again. Who knows what went wrong? It could be a problem at the computer service, or a problem with the phone line. Most file protocols are set up so that when they encounter a certain number of errors in the data that's received, they quit the transfer. That may be what happened. Try it again.

If you get the error message "Timed Out Waiting for Remote Host" on your screen, your best bet is to try the transfer again. This means that the file transfer gave up waiting for the computer service to start the transfer. Sometimes this happens when the computer service has a hard time getting its act together to start the transfer. Other times it's because your PC and the computer service are slightly out of sync. Or it could mean that your PC and the computer service are using different protocols. (There are lots of different versions of Xmodem, Ymodem, and Kermit floating around. It's not uncommon for a computer service to be running a version that doesn't work too well with the one in your software.) Best solution: Try again.

# CHAPTER 11

# Do You Need to Worry About Computer Viruses?

*A* computer virus is a noxious bit of computer code planted in seemingly harmless software to wreak havoc on an unwitting computer user. Like a biological virus, it has the remarkable talent to self-replicate, copying itself to other computers and software. Some viruses wipe out all your data, others unleash annoying pranks like bouncing the image of a ping-pong ball incessantly over your screen. Once they infect your computer, they can be damnably hard to track down and get rid of. And they can cause a whole lot of damage.

You *cannot* contract a computer virus merely by calling a computer service or bulletin board, scrolling through menus, or reading E-mail messages. You *can* contract a virus by downloading software, because data is being transmitted to your computer and written to your computer's disk. A virus can be hidden in this data.

If you copy files only from commercial computer services don't sweat it. No virus has ever been transmitted through a major consumer information service, thanks to their careful screening of files. Your PC may contract a virus through other risky activity, however. Here are some things to do to keep viruses out of your PC:

Viruses spread easily on computer networks at businesses and schools. Before inserting a floppy disk in your PC that has been in the disk drive of another PC at work or school, run a virus scanning program on it. Recommended is Viruscan by McAfee Associates, Inc., 2710 Walsh Ave., Suite 200, Santa Clara, CA 95051, 408/988-3832. It costs about $25. You can also download it from any computer service. It's stored in a file called SCANV*.ZIP. It comes in both DOS and Windows versions. The Windows version is called WINSCAN.ZIP. Microsoft DOS (version 6) and Windows 3.1 have their own virus programs. Look them up in your manuals for particulars on how to use them. If you have a Mac, get a copy of SAM from Symantec, 10201 Torre Ave., Cupertino, CA 95014, 408/253-9600 or 800/441-7234.

When you download files from Internet or computer bulletin boards, download them to a floppy disk rather than your hard drive. Before decompressing the file and running it, run it through a virus scanner. Some people scan any file they download from any computer service, even commercial ones.

Familiarize yourself with the computer service's virus screening process, and take care not to download files before the service has checked them. Most computer services have a "Recent Uploads Library" where they store new files that customers have posted on the service. This is often the download-at-your-own-risk library for files that haven't yet been checked for viruses.

If in doubt, wait until a file has "aged" on the computer service before downloading it. Files are always listed in libraries with the date they were submitted to the service. Wait a couple of weeks after that date before copying it to your own PC. Let other customers be the guinea pigs to try it first.

If you plan to download files from computer bulletin boards, make sure that you know who the operator is (referrals from friends are great) and that they screen files thoroughly. Never help yourself to files on a bulletin board unless you know the management runs a tight ship.

Scan your PC's hard disk thoroughly for viruses after a technician works on it. Viruses are often passed from infected PCs to healthy ones through computer repair people's diagnostic disks. Similarly, if you buy a PC from a store with the hard disk formatted and the software already on it, scan the disk for viruses. Many companies refuse to buy PCs with pre-formatted hard disks for fear of viruses.

## Posting a File on a Computer Service

*T*o post, or *upload,* in the craft libraries of a computer service, a text file, a picture of your own needlework, or a program that you have authored, you follow a similar procedure as for downloading except that you tell the service what the name of the file is and what library it should be stored in. You also give the service a description of the file. Last, you tell your computer to send a file rather than to receive one.

The methods for uploading files from your computer will differ from service to service.

> Needlecraft files may be the last place for a computer virus, or its non-reproducing cousin, the Trojan horse, to turn up. A Trojan horse is a bit of noxious code lurking inside a seemingly benign piece of software. A common ruse is a program that is ostensibly supposed to paint an American flag on your screen and beep out "God Bless America." It actually wipes out your hard disk instead. This vandal code—that is, code that vandalizes your system—is usually hidden in porno or game files.

*"The people in this forum shepherded me through my decision to upgrade from a mechanical sewing machine to a computerized one. The new machine is so complicated that I would have thrown in the towel long ago.... In real life I hang out with people who think of sewing as being in the same category as chicken ranching. It's reassuring to come here and find others who think of it as an art."—Lorraine Sintetos, textbook writer, Felton, California*

*I can travel almost anywhere nowadays and find a 'CISter' or two. Despite the ever-more-crowded world we live in, so many of us feel very alone much of the time.... The little community we've built here is an antidote for that, and I think we're all a little bit better for it."—Julia Benson, weaver and spinner, Woodstock, Georgia*

*"This is the chattiest, friendliest, most loving forum I've ever had the pleasure to be involved with. I've been a regular in the sewing section of the forum for three years now."—Melinda Krummerich, program/network manager for high-tech optics firm, mother, Baltimore, Maryland*

*"I have not found many people here in Singapore who share my addiction to fabrics, so I was quite lonely. I can talk with others [on CompuServe] who do."—Debbie Moyes, fiber artist, Singapore*

*"What has being online done for me? It has broadened my quilting horizons. I have met national/international teachers, debated the merits of different techniques and tools, cheered others on for being published in quilt books and magazines, applauded the ribbons won and prizes brought home. I have met quilters from Ireland to Singapore who share my love of fabric. I have also received much encouragement and a lot of hands to help with the quilt patterns I design."—Anne Atkinson Browne, quilt designer and coleader of quilting section, Freeport, Maine*

*"When I first came to the craft forum, I didn't know much about computers or about quilting. I used to think of quilting only in terms of patchwork. I had never heard of things like watercolor quilts or landscape quilts. Now I know what people are talking about when they say Hoffman or Liberty."—Diana Walgree, mother of two teenage boys, St. Albans, Vermont*

*"I am an Australian quilter who has made many friends with American quilters. Everyone is so friendly, helpful, and willing to share their time, ideas, and fabric. My husband of twenty-four years, who is a computaholic, helps me download messages and this has given us another common interest." —Cherry Jackson, quilter and teacher, Melbourne, Victoria, Australia*

*"Finding the craft forum has been a turning point in my life.... No matter what time of day it is ... I can jump online and leave a message and will probably get an answer within an hour or so. I come to the conferences regularly and chat with new friends. I love this virtual community, and no matter how high my bill gets, I'm not leaving!"—Jennifer Skolones, facilities maintenance planner, New Haven, Connecticut*

*"I joined CIS when my husband went overseas for five months. I have a ball here and have learned a lot and made so many friends. It's my support group, although people look at me oddly when I say that."—Audra Macmann, weaver, Ohio*

# 12

## COMPUSERVE IS KING
## WHEN IT COMES TO CRAFTS

*It's the hottest online service around. No matter what your interest, you'll find more people who share it and more information about it on CompuServe than on any other service, including Internet.*

I don't think I've ever posted a question on CompuServe, be it about Pfaffs or fimo, that did not elicit oodles of answers from stitchers around the country by the very next day. Dialing into CompuServe's craft forums is like walking down the aisles of a huge craft convention. Tens of thousands of stitchers are online sharing their wisdom, themselves, and their friendship freely. CompuServe's large craft information and software libraries are unparalleled by those of any other online service. Watch the goings-on in its forums for a while, and the myths about online services being inhospitable to women will seem like hogwash.

CompuServe will not say how large its craft forums are. The conference started out as a single message thread about quilting in the livestock forum a few years ago. Today you need only watch the message traffic (over a thousand messages are posted each day) to see how the conference has grown, sprawling into two large public forums that require over twenty people to run, and you realize that these forums are among the biggest public draws on CompuServe. They're bigger than anything on Internet too.

Reading the messages in these mega-craft conferences will expand your knowledge so profoundly it's like earning a graduate degree in textiles. I can't say it too strongly: You gotta get online!

## Stitchers Really Care About Each Other Here

Lest you think that the number of people on CompuServe is intimidating, rest assured that the crafters form a tight-knit community. Members swap fabric, quilt blocks, and notions; they regularly get together in cities around the country to go fabric shopping and attend craft fairs; and they share with each other good news in their personal lives, as well as help each other through tragedies.

When one subscriber in Germany was experiencing a difficult pregnancy, members sent her daily messages of cheer and encouragement. When she went into labor, members held a "virtual waiting room," exchanging E-mail with her husband and getting up-to-the minute progress reports. When the baby was born, her husband snapped a picture, digitized it, and posted it in the forum so that his wife's computer friends could see the baby. "We take care of each other," says Anne Browne, an administrative assistant in Freeport, Maine, who helps run the quilting section of the forum. "It's very odd. We've been through weddings, babies, deaths. Any real-life happening with our members gets shared on CompuServe. There's always someone here to talk twenty-four hours a day."

Many CompuServe crafters are military wives, whose husbands' jobs keep them moving around the country and overseas. In fact, one of the women who helps run the forum is an air force major. Many subscribers are stay-at-home moms for whom the craft forums provide their only conversation with adults during the day. Many are retirees. Many are farm wives. But an equal number are high-powered professional women, including lawyers, doctors, and engineers. Says Browne, "We have a lot of medical people in the quilting area. We think it's because of the nurturing and comfort factor in quilting." There are also a number of men online who quilt or knit.

Figure 12-1
CompuServe subscribers are good at offering advice and sympathy to other members who are struggling to sew wedding gowns. Here is subscriber Tina Norton's gown, as her sister sews on a last button.

"We pride ourselves on being able to find any [needed craft supplies] for anyone very quickly," says Browne. "A woman posted a message saying that she needed a Hoffman cherub print to finish a quilt, and our members found it for her by the next day. I'm constantly amazed at how people share."

Members also engage in organized charity work. A good example is the quilt "Women, Why Do You Weep?" by Carol Myers, an Indianapolis nurse. With the help of CompuServe members, Myers raised over $4,000 for mammograms for poor women. (You can see a picture of it in the Introduction). The name of a cancer victim is printed on each of the 1,000 appliquéd leaves on the quilt; the willow was chosen as a symbol of mourning and also resurrection and strength.

---

**TIP**

*If you own a high-tech sewing or embroidery machine like a Huskygram, or if you own an electronic knitting machine, you owe it to yourself to get on CompuServe, where you'll find more tech support and advice on using these machines than you will just about anywhere else in the world.*

---

## CompuServe's Craft Information Libraries Are Outstanding

*B*ecause of copyright concerns, you won't find many patterns on CompuServe. What you will find, however, are free information files on just about every craft and textile subject imaginable, from lists of mail-order sources for fabric suppliers, to explanations on how to marbleize fabric, to directions on sewing bow-tie quilts and tailoring men's jackets. You'll also find the best online library around for craft software; in fact, you'll find most of the shareware discussed in this book. Here is a list of the libraries in the Fibercrafts Forum, along with some of the topics in the thousands of files:

**Sewing**   Cheapskate decorating tips, duvet cover instructions, lists of millinery supplies, discussions of Huskygram technical issues, comparisons of sewing machines, sources for buttons, tips for sewing velvet, discussions of stabilizers, lots of Pfaff stitch designs and discussions

**Stitchery & Lace**   Lists of cross-stitch stores and supply houses, cross-stitch software, directions on cleaning old lace, Japanese embroidery tutorials, discussions on buying floor stands, tatting patterns, bobbin-lace patterns, cross-stitch tips, lists of lace-making supply houses

**Knitting & Crochet**   How to calculate yarn on a cone, DAK patterns, crochet patterns, video reviews, lace patterns, sock patterns, lists of yarn stores, cast-on methods, discussions of different knitting machines

"We have a constant running battle online about batting. Is cotton better than polyester, and what weight?"—Anne Browne, CompuServe Fibercrafts Forum Sysop

**Spinning & Weaving**   Tying on a warp, spindle spinning, using fiber reactive dyes, powdered dye toxicity, cotton bale fabric information, Damask weaving, Bronson lace weaving

**Quilting**   Festival information, quilting with kids, block patterns, quilting supplies sources, magazine reviews, directions for photo transfer to fabric, appliqué directions and hints, making frames from PVC pipes, quilting software, where to obtain ethnic reproduction fabrics

**Dolls & Bears**   Doll-making supply sources, making bear noses, trimming bears, painting dolls, discussions of bear joints, discussions on and sources for all types of miniatures

**Other Fiber Crafts**   Victorian crafts, pressing flowers, quilling, wreath making

**Seasonal Crafts**  Directions for making ornaments, wreaths, and other holiday decorations

Computer pictures of other members' projects are also online. If you have a high-speed modem (9600 bps or faster), you can display these on your own computer with the click of a mouse button.

Weekly "fireside chats" in which subscribers converse, via keyboard, with guests such as pattern makers, craft book publishers, and fabric vendors are popular. Because CompuServe's staff tries to make sure that every time a subscriber posts a computer-related question, she or he receives an answer from *someone*, the craft forum has become a popular place to post technical computer questions that may not get answered elsewhere.

**Figure 12-2**
CompuServe crafters like to upload scanned photos of quilts and other projects for other members to view and critique.

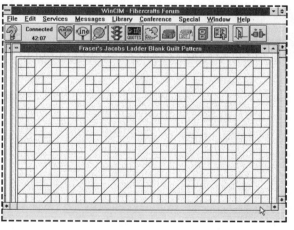

**Figure 12-3**
You'll even find quilt patterns on CIS that you can download and color with any computer paint program.

# Despite Popular Misconceptions, CompuServe Is Not Hard to Use

*I*f you call CompuServe with the free CompuServe Information Manager (CIM) software that comes with your membership, CompuServe is easier to use than Prodigy and America Online. I find CIM's features for reading and retrieving public messages, as well as private E-mail, to be the most versatile, yet simplest, to use of any of the information services' mail features. Searching for files and retrieving them is also easier than on any of the other services. In addition, CompuServe is faster and more reliable in just about every respect than any of its competitors, especially when it comes to sending and receiving mail through Internet.

CompuServe is criticized for high prices, but recent price drops have brought its prices in line with those of competitors America Online (AOL) and Prodigy. (GEnie and Delphi are a bit cheaper—but much harder for a new computer user to use.) If you call CompuServe at high-speed (9600 or 14.4K bps) and use a special software package called a navigator (it automates your use of the service by retrieving just the information you want), CompuServe can be cheaper than AOL or Prodigy. And although CompuServe charges extra hourly fees for accessing some special databases, like medical or investing information (and those fees can be steep), it doesn't charge extra to access the craft forums or libraries. However, you don't get any free hours with your monthly subscription fee of $9.95 like you do with Prodigy or AOL.

## *Take Note: CompuServe Public Messages Disappear*

One drawback to CompuServe is that, because of the volume of messages written in its craft forums, the messages sometimes "scroll off" or disappear from the service a few days to a week after they're written. That means you have to log on at least once a week (or every few days, depending on message traffic) to read any conversations you've been following or else you'll miss the discussion. If there are any public messages that have been written directly to you, you can request that those messages be forwarded to your private E-mail box, where they won't disappear but will stay until you read them. That's convenient, except for one thing: You are charged 15 cents for each message forwarded to your private mailbox.

> **TIP**
> *Be careful of inadvertently accessing CompuServe's premium databases or services for which you may be charged extra per hour. You can easily rack up $100 in charges. If you stick to the craft forums, you have nothing to worry about. Remember, if you accidentally run up a huge online bill, CompuServe customer service can sometimes be extremely forgiving—but only once.*

> *Note: Unlike with America Online or Prodigy, you can call CompuServe with any computer, even that old IBM PC/XT in the basement. You can also call it with any general-purpose communications software like Procomm or the Terminal program built into Windows, although the service will be harder to use than if you use Compu-Serve Information Manager.* ✎

**COMPUSERVE ONLINE SURVIVAL GUIDE**

## How Do I Get Around CompuServe?

*T*he trick to getting around easily in CompuServe is using GO commands. In the old days, when most subscribers logged into CompuServe using general-purpose communications software, they might type **GO CRAFTS** to go directly to the craft forums and skip scrolling through all the menus along the way. All the services on CompuServe have GO commands, and you can still type them directly into CompuServe. However, if you're using one of the CompuServe Information Manager programs, you press CTRL-G, pick "Go" off the menu, or click on the green-light icon on the top icon bar, then type the name of the service you want to go to. CompuServe Information Manager for Windows offers a built-in GO command directory, accessible by clicking on the icon on the program group screen.

## How Do I Get the Special Software for Calling CompuServe?

*T*o get CompuServe Information Manager software, call CompuServe Information Service at 800/848-8199 or 614/457-8600, or write 5000 Arlington Centre Blvd., Columbus, OH 43220. You'll receive, for free, one of the CIM programs (either Windows, DOS, or Macintosh), plus the first month's subscription and $25 in online coupons. You can also get this start-up kit at retail stores, but it will cost you $15 to $40. You can buy manuals for CompuServe separately, but wait until you get online to find out if you need them (you probably won't).

You can download any of CompuServe's Information Manager programs directly from CompuServe for free or a small fee and a usage credit. Use the command GO CISSOFT.

## What If I Need Help Installing the Software or Connecting?

*F*or help installing the software or connecting to the service, call 800/848-8990 from 7 a.m. to 1 p.m. EST. Choose option #3 on the voice mail system.

## How Do I Get Help with CompuServe Once I Get Online?

*C*ompuServe has a number of free forums where you can post your questions to staff online. Labeled as either "Help," "Practice," or "New Member" forums, you can get to them by typing **GO BASICFORUMS** or clicking the "Member Services" icon if you're calling with CompuServe Information Manager.

You'll also find help in the "Introduction/Help" or "Tech Talk" sections of the craft forums. Just write a message stating your problem, and helpful users will spring to your aid.

> ### TIP
> *When you dial CompuServe for the first time, no matter what software you use, head to one of its free get-acquainted or practice forums to become familiar with how the service works, how to read and send messages, and how to download files. You won't be charged anything for the time you spend in the practice forums, and they're a great way to learn to feel comfortable online before the charge clock starts ticking. To get to a practice forum, type GO BASICFORUMS.*

## What's the Best Way to Call CompuServe?

*I*f CompuServe has a local number in your community, the best way to call is to dial that number with your modem. Do not use a CompuServe 800-number if you can help it, as fees for using it are high. If there's no local CompuServe phone number, but a local Tymnet or SprintNet number, dial that instead—but only in the evening. You'll save as much as $10 an hour over daytime rates.

If you call CompuServe frequently, or do more than just send or receive mail, you should abandon the CompuServe Information Manager software, if that's what you're using, and switch instead to a navigator program like TapCIS, OzCIS, AutoSIG, or, if you're a Mac user,

*Note: CompuServe used to charge higher rates for dialing in at fast modem speeds, but no longer does. You should call CompuServe at the highest speed your modem supports (14.4K or 28.8K if your modem has it).* ✎

to CompuServe Navigator. These programs will log onto the service and download your mail, head to forums (like the crafts ones) and download the messages and/or files you want, then quickly log off to save you money online. They and CompuServe work so fast together that they can shave the cost of your calls to pennies.

**TIP**
CompuServe doesn't charge hourly connect fees for accessing a group of services called Basic Services. These include things like news, certain stock quotes, an encyclopedia, Money Magazine's mutual fund database, and several other worthwhile things. If you're using CompuServe Information Manager and want to stick to the Basic Services, click on this picture:

## How Do I Get Other Special Software for Making CompuServe More Pleasant to Use?

*U*sing CompuServe with one of the Information Manager programs is by far the most fun, but that's also the most expensive way to call the service. Once you get yourself oriented online, you *must* download one of over a dozen navigation programs available for making the service faster to use. Here are my picks.

**If you have an 80386 PC or higher running Windows**  You may be a candidate for CompuServe Navigator for Windows from CompuServe. This is a Windows-based automator that will download messages for you and organize them into folders. It requires EGA graphics  or higher, Windows 3.1 running in enhanced mode, and 2 MB RAM. You can download it from CompuServe for $20 (you'll be reimbursed $10 of that on your Compu-Serve bill) by typing **GO NAVSOFT**.

**If you have an old PC or don't mind running things in DOS**   My very favorite navigator is a free program called AutoSig available for downloading. It will run on just about every PC-compatible ever made, and it's not hard to set up. Its only drawback is that its not good at automating searches of file libraries, but hey, it's free. Type **GO PCCOM** to get it.

**If you have a PC with an 80386 processor or higher**   You may want to consider the $40 shareware program OzCIS. OzCIS not only automates online sessions, but also lets you break into the session to go online and enter commands yourself when the need arises. It puts all of CompuServe into convenient pull-down menus. It is DOS-based but will run in a DOS window in Windows. Type **GO OZCIS** to get it.

**If you have a PC with an 80286 processor or higher**   One of the most popular DOS-based navigators for years has been TapCIS by The Support Group (800/USA-GROUP). It's pricey at $79, but this shareware program is easy to set up, it's robust, and you'll find lots of add-on scripts for it online that will do things like automate stock-quote retrieval (though you can do this with CIM too). To download it, type **GO TAPCIS**.

**If you have a Macintosh**   You'll want to use CompuServe Navigator for the Mac from CompuServe. It requires a Mac Plus or higher, System 4.1 or higher, and 650K. You can download it for $50 (you get a $25 usage credit) from CompuServe by typing **GO NAVSOFT**.

All of the navigator software programs have technical support forums on CompuServe to help new users get going. If you run into obstacles using them, you'll find people willing to offer help in the Introduction/Help and Tech Talk message sections of both craft forums, discussed in the next section.

## How Do I Find Other Needlecrafters on CompuServe?

*T*here are two craft forums on CompuServe: The Fibercrafts Forum (GO FIBER-CRAFTS) houses the libraries and public discussions for sewing, knitting, quilting, weaving, and all other needle and fiber arts. The Handcrafts Forum (GO HANDCRAFTS) is devoted to nontextile crafts including clay, woodworking, fimo, rubber stamping, paper crafts, tole painting, egg decorating, and "Other Crafts" like incense making and gingerbread cathedrals. Both forums can be found on the main crafts menu (GO CRAFTS).

**If you're using CompuServe Information Manager for Windows, DOS, or the Macintosh**   Whether you're already online, or you're about to call the service, click on the green-light icon or press CTRL-G and type **CRAFTS** to get to the craft forum main menu. Or type **GO FIBERCRAFTS** to go directly to the forum for textile crafts. (See Figure 12-4.) Or type **GO HANDCRAFTS** to reach the forum for nontextile crafts.

**Figure 12-4**
This is the main menu you'll see for the Fibercrafts Forum on CompuServe if you call with CIM for Windows (WINCIM).

To read the public message forums, click on the "Browse" message icon or choose the "Browse" option in the Message menu. A list of message topics will appear, like the ones listed on the left in Figure 12-5. Choose one by clicking on it. A list of message threads will appear, like those shown on the right side of the figure. To read a thread, click on it.

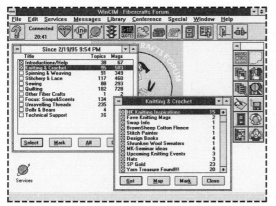

**Figure 12-5**
After you click on the "Browse" message icon in any CompuServe forum, a list of message topics appears. Once you choose a topic, a list of message threads appears.

**TIP**

*The "Unravelling Threads" topic in the Fibercrafts Forum is where members discuss their lives. This is where you'd look for chitchat, recipes, and other over-the-fence talk.*

**If you're dialing in with a general-purpose communications program** Once you get online, type **GO FIBERCRAFTS** or **GO HAND-CRAFTS**. Type **MESSAGES** to get to the message menu and then follow the menus to select topics and choose the message you want to read. You say you're not seeing any menus? Type **OPTIONS**, then choose "2. Forum MODE" and select MENU. If ever you're in doubt about any command, type **HELP**.

## How Do I Send a Private E-mail Message?

*I*f you're using WinCIM, DOS CIM, or the Mac interface, it's a good idea to write private E-mail offline, then later upload it to the service. From the menus at the top of your screen, click "Mail" and then "Create Mail." Type the name and CompuServe numeric address of the recipient. Click "Add" and then "OK." Now enter your subject and type the message. When you're done, click "Outbasket."

To send the mail, you can either click "Mail" and then "Send/Receive All Mail" or (and this is sometimes a better way) click "Mail" and then "Outbasket." When the list of mail appears, click "Send All." This will give you the opportunity to selectively retrieve waiting mail once you get online by clicking the mail button.

If you're dialing in with a general-purpose communications program, type **GO MAIL** and select from the menu "COMPOSE a message." Type your message; when you're done, type **/EXIT** alone on a line. When prompted, type in the recipient's CompuServe numeric address.

## Where Can I Find Needlecraft Software, Patterns, and Clipart for Use in My Needlecraft Designs?

*T*o find needlecraft software and information files, head directly to the Fibercrafts Forum (GO FIBERCRAFTS).

For clipart you'll need to do a bit of searching in other CompuServe file libraries. The easiest way to do that is with CompuServe's Graphics File Finder (GO GRAPHFF). This will search all the applicable graphics-related forums for the kind of clipart you want or for graphics software (such as image viewing or cropping and conversion utilities).

# Needlecraft Software and Information in the Craft File Libraries

**If you're using CompuServe Information Manager for Windows, DOS, or the Mac**  Whether you're already online or you're about to call the service, click on the green-light icon or press CTRL-G and type **CRAFTS** to get to the craft forum main menu. Or, type **GO FIBERCRAFTS** to go directly to the public forum for sewing, knitting, quilting, weaving, and so on, or **GO HANDCRAFTS** to reach the forum for nontextile crafts, like clay, woodworking, fimo, rubber-stamping, and so on.

To browse the craft file libraries, click on the "Browse-Library" button to display a list of  the different libraries or choose this option from the menu. Choose a library; a list of its titles will appear in the order in which they were uploaded to the library. Click on the "Description" button to learn more about a file. Click "Retrieve" to download it.

To search the libraries for specific information or software titles, click the "Search-  Library" button. You can search all the libraries, but it's easiest to search a selected one. To do so, click "None," then type an **X** beside the name of the library you want to search. See Figures 12-6 and 12-7.

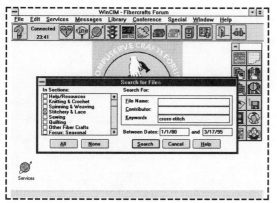

**Figure 12-6**
The easiest way to search for files in CompuServe's craft forums is to select a library, then type in a search word like "cross-stitch."

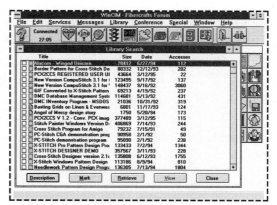

**Figure 12-7**
Once the service searched its stitchery library for all occurrences of the word "cross-stitch," it came up with this huge list of information files and software. To see more of the list, click on the scroll bar on the right. To find out more about a file, select the file with your cursor, then click "Description." To download the file to your computer, select "Retrieve," then click "Mark" to download the file later, when you leave the forum.

**Figure 12-8**
In the Fiberarts Forum library you'll find quilt blocks and appliqué patterns that you can view online. This appliqué pattern for a bulldog was designed and uploaded by a forum member who requested suggestions from other quilters on how to embellish it.

**If you're dialing in with a general-purpose communications program**   Get to the craft forums by typing **GO FIBERCRAFTS** or **GO HANDCRAFTS** after you log on. Choose "LIBRARIES" from the forum menu. Select a library from the list and choose the "BROWSE" option to read through the titles. From here you'll be prompted with menus that will lead you through the file selection and download process.

## Clipart and Graphics Software

To find clipart or graphics software, head to either the general graphics area of the service (GO GRAPHICS) or use the Graphics File Finder (GO GRAPHFF). Searching for and downloading files is the same here as in the craft libraries.

**Figure 12-9**
Whether you're an IBM or Mac user, the easiest way to tap into CompuServe's considerable support, graphics software, and libraries of computer images is to head to the graphics information area (GO GRAPHICS).

# How Do I Get Back to CompuServe's Main Menu If I Get Lost?

*I*f you're using CompuServe Information Manager for Windows, DOS, or the Macintosh and you get lost, click on the earth icon, which you'll spot somewhere in a corner of your screen, or press CTRL-G and type **TOP**. If you're dialing in with a general-purpose communications program, type **TOP** at any prompt.

# How Do I Get General Computer Help on CompuServe?

*C*ompuServe is the *very* best online source for technical help, no matter what your computer or its woes. You'll find hundreds of computer hardware and software vendors online, providing technical support that's often far superior to what you get on the phone after waiting on hold for twenty minutes. You'll also find lots of smart people willing to help you.

Many people (both women and men) head to the craft forums for general computer advice because the computer users in these forums are so good-natured and helpful. But there are many other places on CompuServe where you can get good advice specific to the software or hardware you're having problems with. Sometimes these places are not easy to find. Here's a guide to finding the computer help you need on CompuServe:

**If you own a PC or compatible** Go to the PC Users' Network (GO PCNET) or the ZiffNet service run by the publisher of *PC Magazine* (GO ZIFF). Look around in the public message forums on these services, then post your question in the applicable one. Wait twenty-four hours, then log on again. There will probably be answers waiting for you.

**If you own a Macintosh or other Apple** Go to the Macintosh forum (GO MAC) or to the Macintosh area of the ZiffNet service (GO ZMAC). If you own an Apple II, type **GO MAC-22**.

**If you are having trouble with a particular brand of hardware (like a modem) or computer** Type **GO HARDWARE** to find out what hardware vendors are online providing support, or if there are any forums that deal with that kind of hardware.

> **TIP**
> To search for general computer software, head to the PC-compatible File Finder (GO IBMFF) or the Macintosh File Finder (GO MACFF). You can use either of these tools to search a large selection of CompuServe forums for everything from shareware word processors to spreadsheet programs. However, these tools do not search every file library available on CompuServe (including the craft ones); so if you're looking for a specific program and you can't find it through the File Finders, you may need to check for related forums, like those in the Ziffnet service (GO ZIFF).

**TIP**
*Save money by download-
ing indexes to craft file
libraries to read offline
when the meter isn't ticking. Search for the word
catalog to find the latest
listing for the library.*

If you are having trouble with a particular brand of software (like Windows or WordPerfect)   Type **GO SOFTWARE** to find out what software vendors are online providing support.

To find out if a specific hardware or software vendor is online answering consumer questions   Type **GO UPPORT** to search a directory of the vendors on CompuServe.

## What Is the "Terminal Emulator"?

*I*f you call CompuServe with one of the Information Manager programs, every once in a while the screen will flash with something called the "Terminal Emulator." "It sounds so . . . terminal!" said a quilter friend the first time she ran into it. "I had this vision of being sucked into something big and black." When your computer talks to CompuServe, it must sometimes pretend it's a dumb terminal like the kind that used to be connected to mainframes, hence the term *terminal emulation.* Basically, when you've entered the terminal emulator, the icons disappear and you must type in commands. Usually you'll be given a menu; but if none is in sight and you don't know what to do, try typing **?**, **H**, or **HELP** at the prompt. If that fails, type **EXIT** to retreat from the terminal emulator and get back into the world of icons.

## How Do I Get a List of CompuServe's Latest Prices?

*T*o get a list of CompuServe's latest rates, type **GO RATES** or **GO MEMBER** or click on the member service icon.

> **WARNING**
> *The rates you find listed in the service rates list on CompuServe some-
> times differ from the rates charged for accessing some special databases.
> Before you access any premium database on CompuServe, read the
> database's introductory screens carefully to find the current rates. (Don't
> worry, this warning does not apply to anything in the craft forums.)*

# How Do I Use CompuServe to Get to Needlecraft Goodies on Internet?

*T*here are several ways to tap into the Internet from CompuServe. You can use general-purpose Internet cruising software like NCSA's Mosaic or Netscape, or you can dial a special CompuServe number called a PPP number and access the entire Internet that way. (For more information, type **GO PPP** after you log onto CompuServe.)

You can also use general communications software or any of the CompuServe Information Manager programs. That's the easiest way because you can access Internet essentials through CompuServe's relatively easy-to-use menus. Here are directions to get you started.

**If you're using CompuServe Information Manager for Windows, DOS, or the Mac**   You can reach CompuServe's main Internet menu by clicking "GO" or pressing CTRL-G and typing **INTERNET**.

**If you're dialing in with a general-purpose communications program**   Type **GO INTERNET**.

**Figure 12-10**
Type GO INTERNET or click the Internet icon on CompuServe's Information Manager's main screen to get to CompuServe's main Internet menu. From here you can steer your way to all the important things for stitchers on Internet, from Usenet mailing lists to FTP sites.

# How Do I Send Mail to Internet and Participate in Internet Craft Mailing Lists?

*Y*ou can use your CompuServe mailbox to participate in Internet craft mailing-list discussions. To subscribe to a list, send an E-mail message to the list's subscription address. Remember, your CompuServe mailbox will hold only 100 messages at a time. This means that if you subscribe to several Internet craft mailing lists that generate lots of mail (like QuiltNet or KnitNet), you should check your mail box daily so that CompuServe doesn't start bouncing mail back to the lists when your mailbox overflows. You'll not only miss messages, but the mailing list may cancel your subscription, thinking that your E-mail box is no longer active.

**If you're using CompuServe Information Manager for Windows, DOS, or the Mac**   You write and send private E-mail to someone on Internet the same way that you write someone on CompuServe: by clicking "Mail," then "Create Mail." In the space where you'd type the recipient's CompuServe addresses, you type **INTERNET:***yourfriend'sInternetaddress*. For example, **INTERNET:jane@mcimail.com**.

**If you're dialing in with a general-purpose communications program**   You write and send private E-mail to someone on Internet the same way that you would someone on CompuServe: by typing **GO MAIL**, then selecting from the menu "COMPOSE a message." When it comes time to address the mail, instead of a CompuServe numeric ID, you'd type **>INTERNET:***yourfriend'sInternetaddress*. For example,

>INTERNET:jane@mcimail.com

---

## *Important! Review Your Messages Before Reading Them*

If you subscribe to Internet craft mailing lists, some will send you dozens of messages every day. To save time online (and trim your CompuServe bill), prior to reading or downloading your mail, delete those messages whose subjects don't interest you. You should also subscribe to the digest form of any mailing list, when available, to keep your costs down. (See Chapter 18 for directions.)

### TIPS

*If you use CompuServe Information Manager for Windows, never use the "Send/Receive All Mail" when you go online to read mail. Instead, if you've written any E-mail offline, click "Outbasket," then "Send All" to go online and send those messages. Once you get online, click the mailbox button to list any waiting mail. To delete an Internet message you're not interested in, highlight its title (don't double-click to read it) and click the "Delete" button.*

*To turn your CompuServe ID into an Internet address, add @compuserve.com to the end of your address and turn the comma in the address into a period. For example: the ID 12345,123 would become 12345.123@compuserve.com.*

## How Can I Read Usenet Needlecraft Discussions?

**If you're using CompuServe Information Manager for Windows, DOS, or the Mac**     You can reach CompuServe's Usenet newsgroup menu by clicking "GO" or pressing CTRL-G and typing **USENET**. Click "Usenet Newsreader (CIM)" on the menu.

Now you need to subscribe to the newsgroups you want to read, so click "Subscribe to Usenet Newsgroups." You can search for newsgroups by keywords, or you can subscribe to the ones you want by typing their names, the easiest option. (You'll find a list of the Usenet craft discussion groups in Chapter 18, or see Figure 12-11a.) For instance, you might type in **rec.crafts.textiles.needlework** to read the general needlework discussion.

Once you have finished subscribing to newsgroups, click "OK" and "Close." Now choose "Access Your Newsgroups" from the menu, and the groups you've subscribed to will appear in a menu. Click on the name of the newsgroup you want to read; click the "Browse" button, and a list of message threads in that newsgroup will appear (see Figure 12-11b). To read a particular thread, click on it, then click on the "Article" button to follow the messages in that thread.

**If you're dialing in with a general-purpose communications program**     Type **GO USENET** and follow the menus to subscribe to newsgroups, then read selected newsgroups just as you would with CompuServe Information Manager.

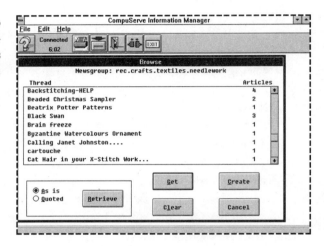

Figure 12-11 a
Once you've subscribed to the
Internet/Usenet discussion groups
you want to read (as you can see, their
names look like names for the subdirectories on your computer's hard disk),
CompuServe Information Manager will
display a list of their titles. To read a
newsgroup, all you do is click on it.

Figure 12-11 b
Once you've selected a newsgroup to read, a list of the topics
of message threads will appear.

# How Can I Use CompuServe to Download
Needlecraft Software and Files from Internet?

*G*enerally, the cheapest and easiest way to search for needlecraft software and information is to head to CompuServe's craft forum libraries. However, you may occasionally hear of a specific file on Internet that you'd like to get. In that case you'd use Internet's File Transfer Protocol feature, or FTP. An "FTP site" is another computer on Internet that the public can access to download files. To get to CompuServe's FTP link, press CTRL-G or click the green-light icon and type FTP as shown in Figure 12-12.

**If you're using CompuServe Information Manager for Windows, DOS, or the Mac**    To get  to CompuServe's FTP link, click the green-light icon or press CTRL-G and type **FTP**. You can use this feature to search files on Internet for occurrences of a word like "quilt," but that can be a fruitless process. Instead, click "Access a Specific Site." In the screen that appears, after "Site Name:" type the address of the FTP site you want to access. For instance, you'd type **gus.crafts-council.pe.ca** to reach the computer of the Prince Edward Island Crafts Council in Canada, where there is a smattering of craft-related files and software.

Leave the other entries on the screen as is (CompuServe will automatically log you on anonymously to the computer with the word "anonymous" and your CompuServe ID using "Anonymous FTP").

Once you're logged on to the faraway computer, you'll see some directories listed on the left side of your screen (see Figure 12-13). Click on one to see what's in it. Any files that you can download will be listed on the right-hand side of the screen. To download one to your computer, highlight it and click the "Retrieve" button.

**TIP**
*Whenever you see a directory listed as "pub" on an FTP server, look inside it because this is usually where the most interesting files available for public downloading are located.*

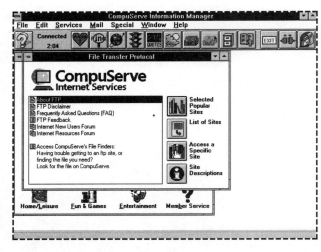

Figure 12-12
To get to CompuServe's Internet FTP link, you'd use the command GO FTP.

Figure 12-13
When you log into a remote computer like that of the Prince Edward Island Crafts Council in Canada, the computer's directories will be listed on the left side of your screen, and the files that you can download will be listed on the right side.

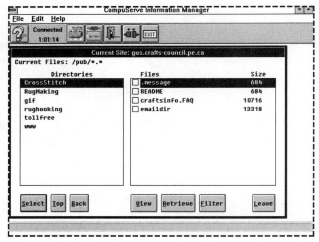

**If you're dialing in with a general-purpose communications program**   You can only use CompuServe's FTP link if you're using one of the CompuServe Information Manager programs.

## How Can I Tap into the World Wide Web from CompuServe?

*G*et to CompuServe's main Internet menu by clicking "GO" or the green-light icon or by pressing CTRL-G and typing **INTERNET**.

If you have a PC-compatible, you'll need to download CompuServe's free NetLauncher software. Click "Direct Internet Access (Dial PPP)." To run the software, you'll need

Windows 3.1 or higher, an 80386 or faster, a 9600 bps modem, and a copy of one of the CompuServe Information Manager programs (either Windows or DOS) already installed. Once you've installed NetLauncher, it will dial a special CompuServe number for you and let you tap into the Web.

If you have a Macintosh, you can use any Internet software like NCSA Mosaic or Netscape to tap into the Web. You'll also need a copy of MacTCP (available in System 7.5) and a copy of MacPPP (available on CompuServe in the Macintosh Communications Forum—to get there, type **GO MACCOMM**). For directions on setting it all up, type **GO PPP-19** on CompuServe.

CompuServe plans to offer access to the Web through it's CompuServe Information Manager programs by the end of 1995.

## How Do I Get a List of Everything That's on CompuServe?

*Y*ou can use GO SERVICES to find a list of all the things available on CompuServe; use the GO commands to get to them. It's a mighty big list, though, and you should copy it to your disk or printer and keep it on hand for reference. While you can search this database by keyword, don't count on finding anything interesting if you use any craft-related words like "quilt" or "sew."

To find the prices for services in this list, you'll need to head to a different part of the service. Type **GO RATES**.

## What Are Some Good Things on CompuServe for My Family?

*O*f all the big online services, CompuServe offers the most high-quality fare for children—as well as their parents. All the online services claim to patrol their public forums to keep out bad languages, illegal material, and pornography, but CompuServe seems to do the best job. True, it does offer access to Internet raunch, but all the online services do these days. Prodigy is the only one that gives parents the option to block it.

Some of my favorite forums are the Pets (GO PETS) and Investors' forums (GO INVFORUM). If you have an ill family member, CompuServe is the very best place to look for treatment and care information. It also offers a superb cancer support forum (GO CANCER). Free access to the day's Associated Press stories and free stock quotes will appeal to news junkies and investors.

# Helping New Computer Users Get Onboard Is a Big Part of a Day's Work for CompuServe's Crafts Forum Assistant Sysop

BY KATHY MORGRET

It wasn't long ago when Kathy Morgret was a deputy county attorney in Montana. She now oversees a new kind of Wild West.

When Susan Lazear and I launched the original Crafts Forum on CompuServe in July 1991, CompuServe's management was skeptical. At the time, a few crafters were meeting regularly in the livestock message section of the Pets Forum. To everyone's surprise, the Crafts Forum quickly grew into one of the most popular areas on CompuServe, with over a thousand messages posted in it daily and a volunteer staff of twenty-five people running it. It's grown so large it's been split into two forums.

I help manage the forums and the volunteers full time. I'm a former deputy county attorney from Montana. I met my husband on CompuServe and moved to Tennessee to join him in 1991. I find that managing an electronic crafts guild from my computer at home is far more satisfying than practicing law.

Most of the volunteers have full-time jobs unrelated to their work on CompuServe, ranging from Air Force major to administrative assistant. Some are retirees. The special thing about the forums is how intimately people get to know each other. Our crafters form a tight community. A lot of our members are housewives with little adult company during the day. CompuServe becomes a break for them from dealing with the kids. We also have online military wives who move around a lot. CompuServe subscribers provide a stable community that will always be there for them. And because CompuServe has worldwide access, members in South Africa, England, Germany, France, Australia, and other countries can tap in.

People help each other through a variety of life crises in the craft forums. They often share the most intimate details of their lives—whether or not they're going to have children, whether or not their spouses care about them.

The craft forums are split into sections like Stitchery & Lace, Quilting, and Sewing. Each section has a volunteer leader, and she (or he) is responsible for reading each day all the messages that are posted in the section. Mostly, we try to make sure that the messages stick to the subject in the message thread that they're a part of. That keeps information and discussions easy for readers to find—which is especially important for subscribers who pick and choose threads to download and read off-line to save money. It's the nature of electronic messaging that messages stray from their topics easily, and whenever that happens we break off messages into separate threads and give them a new subject heading. If a message thread strays too far afield from the crafting topic at hand, we'll move the whole discussion to a general chatting section of the forum so that members can continue their conversation there.

Occasionally discussions become heated, but they seldom erupt into the "flame wars" you sometimes see on other online services. When discussions do start to overheat, we do our best to calm participants down.

The forum's libraries are another area we keep watch over. Every time someone uploads to CompuServe an information file, software, or a graphic, we scan it for viruses, make sure it's not bootleg commercial software, then post it with instructions on what subscribers will need to do in order to run it, read it, or view it. We also make sure that the file is stored in the proper library and catalogued in such a way that subscribers can easily find it with applicable keywords like "tatting" or "quilt."

We also organize real-time chat conferences, both casual ones and more formal ones (the formal ones are the ones with guest "speakers"). Informal ones are held several nights a week and are extremely popular, especially among newcomers to CompuServe. It gives them an opportunity to get fast answers to questions they may have about the service. We usually make available in the libraries transcripts of conferences with guest speakers so that crafters who could not attend can download the transcript and read it later.

Many of the computer users who show up in the craft forums are new to CompuServe, if not to computers themselves. We do our best to make them feel at home and comfortable with the new technology. We think that helping users make efficient use of the service is one of our most important missions.

KATHY MORGRET lives in Tennessee with her husband and two cats.

## How About Other Good Things for Me?

*I*f you run a business, you'll find answers to nearly all your questions in the wonderful Information Please Business Almanac (GO BIZALMANAC). Access is free. Matthew Lesko's Government Giveaway Forum (GO INFOUSA) is both informative and a hoot. If you're a cook, you can access just about every recipe ever conceived in Cooks Online (GO COOKS). Best-selling authors are always turning up online in the Time-Warner Books Forum (GO TWFORUM). *Money Magazine's* mutual fund database is a great place to analyze mutual funds on past performance and investment objectives. Access to it is also toll-free (GO FUNDWATCH).

# WHAT STITCHERS HAVE TO SAY ABOUT PRODIGY

*"I've been a member of the Prodigy cross-stitch BB since August 1991. This network has really helped my shop. I ask my friends here what they'd like to see in stores and what their interests are. They've cheered me on, ordered from me, and have been very supportive. I've also made contacts with designers here and have the inside track on upcoming releases—plus the supplies I'll need so I'll be ready for their designs."—Barb Ryan, needlework store owner, Merrimack, New Hampshire*

**"This board is an extremely active one and seems to be growing by leaps and bounds. With the economy the way it is, there are many shops going out of business and disposable income is not what it used to be. However, this board works hard to keep all the art forms alive . . . This group is nuts. I love them dearly."—Jan Metzger, leader of the Prodigy Crafts Board**

*"Prodigy has really broadened my horizons as a cross-stitcher. I've been introduced to the world of linen, overdyed flosses, silks, new designers and their designs. I've learned about new magazines and reference books about the art of needlework. Not only have my stitching abilities been expanded beyond my wildest dreams, but my wallet has been reduced thanks to all the supplies I've had to get on the advice of Prodigy friends."—Mary Ann Bachmann, mother of four, occupation "domestic goddess," Oakland, California*

**"I have been on Prodigy only since summer but have met many great people. Most of the time I just read and chuckle at the events going on, but often it helps me realize that there are a lot of people out there willing to offer support and love whenever or why ever it may be needed. Happy stitching!"—Betsy Slehofer**

*"My stitching's a very good friend. It's always there, waiting patiently, to be picked up and lovingly handled. It grows in its beauty and gives such happiness to the one who gets to keep it. Prodigy has expanded my world and my stitching interests. I love having others to talk to about my love of this art, as I have no friends who enjoy my addiction to fibers."—Judi Tracy*

**"I only have a few local friends who stitch and actually found them through Prodigy. Because of Prodigy I also discovered a wonderful cross-stitch store not far from my home, suppliers by mail, silk thread, magazines I never knew existed, fabrics I had never heard about, patterns and designers I'd had no clue about, how to fix mistakes in Hardanger, lots of info on framing and matting. I've found here some of the most beautiful electronic friendships one could imagine."—Bobbie Hall**

# 13

## LINK UP WITH THE STITCHING
## SISTERHOOD ON PRODIGY

*You'll find a lot of cross-stitchers, quilters, sewers, knitters, and weavers
on this supereasy-to-use information service.*

rodigy is the *USA Today* of the computer world with its colorful weather maps, surfeit of entertainment news, and video-game-like screens with Crayola-sized letters. While its information content leans toward the superficial (and those panty hose ads at the bottom of screens get annoying), it's a great service to get started on if you've never dialed a computer service with a modem before. It's so easy to use I've heard of three-year-olds navigating it with ease (although I know fifty-year-old newspaper editors who find it bewildering).

Prodigy's needlecraft forums are some of the best. You'll find thousands of stitchers from across the country discussing cross-stitch, crochet, beadwork, knitting, lace-making, sewing, doll-making, spinning and weaving, and smocking/heirloom sewing. Its quilting forum is especially well populated with quilters who range in age from college students to retirees.

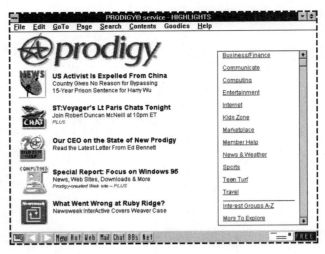

**Figure 13-1**
Prodigy strives to be the TV generation's newspaper substitute with a slick mix of celebrities, news, and sports info. It's a fun service—you'll meet lots of chatty cross-stitchers and quilters online—but you may find yourself yearning for the comparatively rich information content of MTV.

Prodigy also tends to have more consumer information in its sewing and quilting forums than the other computer services do—recommendations on what catalogs to order from, what magazines to subscribe to, what sewing machines to buy. The number of things I've bought on the suggestion of Prodigy crafters outweighs the number of things I've bought on the advice of crafters on all the other services combined.

## Prodigy Quilting Goings-On Can Be Like a Sorority House

$\mathcal{P}$rodigy quilters form a tight community. One popular activity is the "bale party," not a sorority initiation ritual but rather what happens when a group of ten or more quilters pitch in to buy 200 pounds of used kimonos, then divide them up and use the fabric in quilts.

Actually, a lot of goings-on in the Prodigy quilting forum remind one of those in a sorority house. You can have a "secret quilting pal sister" who will send you gifts and notes each month and whose mandate it is to generally "take care" of you. (The other night I logged on and found two ex-secret sisters slugging it out in E-mail, calling each other "selfish.")

At any given time, there are usually twenty-five or more quilt block and fabric swaps going on. Exchanges of cat and dog blocks, Depression-era blocks, and Christmas fabric blocks are popular, as is the "your ugliest fabric" swap. A favorite is the button swap in which members say that because of the large number of participants, "the buttons really fly."

## Sewers, Knitters, Cross-Stitchers, and Weavers Are Equally Vivacious

Quilters are not the only vivacious ones on Prodigy. Cross-stitchers are also online, by the thousands. Messages concerning Aida, floss, and sample round-robins (projects mailed round the country, with each recipient adding to the stitching just like in an old-time sewing bee) can sometimes flood the hobby forum.

Next to CompuServe, Prodigy is the hottest online gathering spot for sewers. You'll find loads of talk about smocking and heirloom sewing, as well as help with particular makes and models of sewing machines like Pfaffs. Patterns for American Girl Doll dresses are a perpetual hot topic. Nancy Zieman of the TV show *Sewing With Nancy* is online answering questions, or else her customer service reps are when she's busy.

Prodigy's knitting klatch is an especially tight, outspoken group. You'll find congregations of weavers, spinners, crocheters, and tatters online too. Crafters on Prodigy are perpetually staging cross-country get-togethers at craft conventions (you can buy lapel pins to wear at craft shows signifying you're a Prodigy craft BBS habitué).

**McCall Pattern**
**2576—Child's Coat.** Cut in 4 sizes, 1, 2, 3 and 4 years
Price, 15 cents.

## Like Tides, Prodigy's Popularity Swells and Recedes

Prodigy is the online service that is probably most responsible for bringing needlecrafters onto the information highway. It was the first online service with a craft forum (everyone laughed at Prodigy for starting it). The free start-up kits that Prodigy mass mailed to computer users about a half-dozen years ago, together with its low prices, brought hundreds of thousands of average Americans online for the first time. (Before this, the online world was populated mainly with computer geeks.) However, as Prodigy prices haven risen over the years, needlecrafters have moved to cheaper services (we're a penny-pinching bunch). As its prices continue to rise and fall, so does its popularity among stitchers. Messages in its needlecraft forums are now in the hundreds per week, where once they were in the thousands.

The upshot is that Prodigy is a great service in which to get your toes wet. But because of its slow speed at updating screens and responding to commands, even at 14.4K bps, no matter how low its prices drop, it will still be expensive. (I embroider while waiting for screens to paint, that's how slowly it creeps.) Unlike other online services, there's no special software you can use to speed up your use of Prodigy, and hence lower your bills. Too, its features are limited—there are no craft software libraries online and no software libraries in general that provide software cheaply. In addition, you won't find the broad range of needlecrafting subjects on Prodigy that you might on other services. You're less apt to spot discussions on, say, Celtic costuming or the best sources for '50s vintage upholstery fabric like you are on CompuServe or Internet. Prodigy also charges extra fees for accessing sports and financial information and for downloading software—and they're steep.

Public messages remain on Prodigy anywhere from a few days to several weeks, depending on how many subscribers are writing. Presently, messages stay on the system a full month or more, so you need only dial in once a month to read the conversations. However, public messages written to you are not forwarded to your private E-mail box if you don't get around to reading them. And Prodigy's lack of foreign links means you won't encounter anyone from overseas online, nor can you log on to Prodigy from that air force base in Germany.

Prodigy also doesn't seem to keep as close an eye on the messages in its public conferences as some other services do. Consequently, shoving matches or "flame wars" occasionally break out, even in places as unlikely as the cross-stitch bulletin board.

## Bottom Line: Cheap Thrills, but You May Not Want to Stay Long

*E*ven with its disadvantages, Prodigy is a fun service. It's the service I dial after a long day, when I don't want to think about much, but instead enjoy being anesthetized by gaudy screens and gossip about celebrities and horoscopes. For me it's a substitute for TV. Prodigy tries to offer something for everyone in the family, from investment advice to columns for teens, from Martha Stewart to guest appearances by NFL coaches. It's the only online service that lets you block off risqué areas (including Internet) from youngsters' eyes. Many parents find, though, that both they and their kids tire of Prodigy's novelty after the first month or two and ache to move on to an information service with more content.

PRODIGY SURVIVAL GUIDE

## How Do I Get the Special Software for Calling Prodigy?

*C*all Prodigy Services at 800/776-3449 (P.O. Box 791, White Plains, NY 10601) and ask for the free Prodigy start-up kit (they'll charge you $4.95 shipping). It will include software that you'll need to install on your computer's hard disk and a user ID and password for logging on. If you use Windows, get the Windows version. (Prodigy is starting to outgrow DOS and can suffer memory problems.)

Any IBM PC, Tandy 1000 or 3000 series, or PC-compatible with 512K, a mouse, and DOS 2.0 or later will connect to Prodigy. Ideally, the computer should have an 80286 processor or higher, or else Prodigy will *really* creep. Your PC can have any type of graphics, although CGA will display the service in black and white instead of color. A hard disk is preferable but not necessary. The only caveat is that if you want to use Prodigy's World Wide Web Browser you'll need to be running Windows and have a 9,600 bps or faster modem.

You can also call Prodigy with any type of Macintosh except the original one.

## What If I Need Help Installing the Software or Connecting?

*C*all Prodigy tech support at 800/284-5933 during the day or evening. Have your network ID ready and be sitting at your computer. Also have on hand your list of computer system specifications from Chapter 1. If you have received an error message, write it down. Prodigy tech support is known for putting callers on hold and routing them all over the Prodigy kingdom depending on the question, so be patient.

## How Do I Get Help with Prodigy Once I Get Online?

*I*f you're online and have questions about Prodigy, click on "Member Help." Or click on "Go to" at the top of the screen and select "Jump to . . ." from the menu. When prompted, type **MEMBER HELP CENTER** and press ENTER. (I personally prefer calling the voice number.)

# What's the Best Way to Call Prodigy?

Since Prodigy's rates are the same no matter what time of day you call, you can call anytime during the day or at night.

# How Do I Get a List of Everything That's on Prodigy?

Click on "Go to" at the top of the screen, then select "A–Z Index" in the menu. Or click on "Contents" at the top of the screen.

# How Do I Get Back to Prodigy's Main Menu If I Get Lost?

Usually the easiest thing to do if you're lost is to click on the "Menu" button on the bottom of the screen. However, depending on where you are on the service, this may just take you back to the last menu you were on. Keep clicking "Menu." Eventually you'll get back to where you started.

# How Do I Get General Computer Help on Prodigy?

Click on "Go to" at the top of the screen, then select "Jump to…" from the menu. When prompted, type **COMPUTER BB,** then press ENTER.

# How Do I Get a List of Prodigy's Latest Prices?

Click on "Member Help" on the introductory screen. Or click on "Go to" at the top of the screen, then select "Jump to . . ." from the menu. When prompted, type **MEMBER HELP CENTER,** then press ENTER. Once you arrive at the Member Help Center, click "Account Billing." Then select "Membership & Fees."

> *Note: Online prices on Prodigy and other information services are constantly in flux. Be sure to call the service and learn all the prices before you sign up.* ৯➤

# How Do I Get Other Special Software for Making Prodigy More Pleasant to Use?

*U*nlike other services, there is no software that will speed up your use of Prodigy's message forums—logging on to retrieve all the messages from the cross-stitch BB, for example, then quickly hanging up so you can read the messages offline.

Utilities are available that will automate the sending and retrieval of *private* E-mail, and if you use Prodigy regularly (especially if you use it to participate in needlecraft mailing lists on Internet), you will want one of these. If you use the Windows version of Prodigy, you'll want to download a program called E-mail Connection for $14.95. If you use the DOS version, you want Mail Manager for $4.95. (One caveat: Prodigy keeps revising its software—in fact, another major revision is scheduled for late 1995. You need to keep updating these utilities in order to keep them working properly with Prodigy.)

To get these, head to the main Prodigy menu and click on the "Computers" box on the right-hand side. At the next menu, click on the "Downloads" box. It may take you a bit of looking around from here to find these packages (Prodigy keeps rearranging the service).

# How Do I Find Other Needlecrafters on Prodigy?

*O*nce you're connected, click on "Go to" at the top of the screen, select "Jump to. . ." from the menu, then type **CRAFTS BB** and press ENTER. See Figure 13-2.

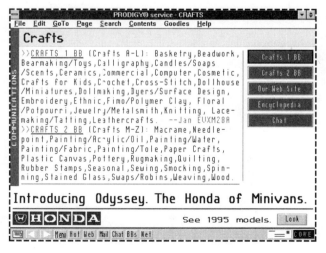

**Figure 13-2**
**At the introductory screen of the Crafts BB, choose Crafts 1 or Crafts 2, depending on your interests.**

Once you've chosen from Crafts 1 or 2, at the BB's introductory screen, click on "Choose a Topic." You'll be presented with a list of the following: Beadwork, Calligraphy, Crochet, Cross-Stitch, Doll-making, Knitting, Lacemaking/Tatting, Needlework, Quilting, Services & Suppliers, Sewing, Smocking/Heirloom, Spinning/Weaving, Swap & Robins. Select one.

Now click on "Begin Reading Notes." Prodigy will display a list of message threads organized by subject. Scroll through these and click on any subject to begin reading.

**Figure 13-3**
As you read messages in a thread, you can click on the buttons at the bottom of the screen to navigate your way through the messages or to write responses.

to read other notes
written on the subject

to write your own
reply to the message

to pick a new
message thread
or topic to read

to read the next
reply in the thread

to read the original
message that started
the discussion

to write a private
E-mail reply to
the message

# How Do I Send a Private E-mail Message?

Click on the "Mail" button at the very bottom of the screen. When your private E-mail box appears, click on "Write" at the bottom of the screen. Type in the Prodigy or Internet address of the recipient. After you've finished typing the message, click "Send" at the bottom of the screen.

## Where Can I Find Needlecraft Software and Clipart for Use in My Needlecraft Designs?

*P*rodigy offers little in the way of downloadable software or pictures. To find the few craft titles it has, head to PC Magazine's ZiffNet computer service (click on "Jump," then select "Jump to . . ." from the menu, and type **ZIFFNET**). You'll pay princely extra fees for this service ($7.50 per month, plus $7.80/hour); and since Prodigy is so slow, getting software here is not advised. You're better off heading to America Online or CompuServe if you want software.

## How Do I Use Prodigy to Get to Needlecraft Goodies on Internet?

*T*o use Prodigy's Internet link, the person in your household who is holder of the "A" account (look at the end of your ID number—if it's something like QRS12A, you've got the "A" account) must sign up online. This is to keep Internet off-limits to children. There are no extra fees to use Internet. To enroll, click on the "Net" button at the very bottom of the Prodigy screen when you're online.

## How Do I Send Mail to Internet and Participate in Internet Craft Mailing Lists?

*Y*ou can send E-mail to anyone on Internet (or any other online service connected to Internet) by typing the recipient's full Internet address at the To: prompt of an ordinary Prodigy private E-mail message. You write the message and send it just like you send an ordinary message.

You can also participate in any of the Internet needlecraft mailing lists described in Chapter 18 simply by sending a sign-up message to the Internet mail list. The E-mail from the mailing list will be deposited each day in your private Prodigy mail box. See Chapter 18 for more information.

**Note:** *To turn your Prodigy ID into an Internet address, add @prodigy.com to the end of the address. For instance, if your Prodigy ID is ABCDEFG, persons on other online services could send you E-mail by addressing it to ABCDEFG@prodigy.com.*

## How Can I Read Usenet Needlecraft Discussions?

You can read and participate in any of the Internet Usenet craft discussions (such as rec.crafts.textiles.sewing) through Prodigy's Internet link. When you're online, click on the "Net" button at the bottom of the screen. When you get to the Internet screen, click on the "Newsgroups" box at the top right-hand corner.

In order to read a newsgroup, you must first "search" for it, then "join" or "subscribe" to it. (This is necessary because there are over 10,000 discussion groups on Usenet.) Start by clicking on "Find Newsgroups." Click on the "Search Newsgroups for Text Pattern" button. Type in your search term—"crafts" will get you a list of the needlecraft newsgroups. Now click "Find now." When the name of a newsgroup is displayed (for instance, rec.crafts.textiles.quilting), highlight it, then click on "Add to Your Newsgroups."

Once you've subscribed to the newsgroups you're interested in, you're ready to read them. Click back through the menus, until you get to your updated newsgroup list. Highlight the one you want to read, then click on "Go to Newsgroup." (See Figure 13-5.) The messages will be displayed. Head to Chapter 18 for more information on Usenet craft newsgroups.

**Figure 13-4**
**Step 1: You can reach the Internet Usenet menu by clicking on "Net" at the bottom of your screen when you're online.**

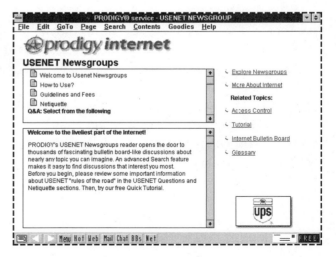

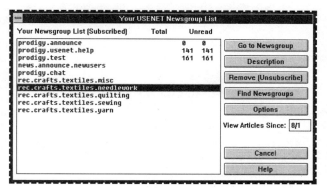

Figure 13-5

Step 2: Once you've clicked on "Newsgroups," Prodigy will display a list of the Usenet discussion groups that you've subscribed to. Listed above are all the needlecraft discussion groups. To subscribe to a newsgroup, click on "Find Newsgroups." Once you've subscribed, you can read the messages in a group by clicking on "Go to Newsgroup."

## How Can I Tap into the World Wide Web from Prodigy?

$\mathcal{P}$rodigy's Web browser lets you explore the riotous world of the Web, where lush computer graphics and hypertext links take you from elaborate quilt block libraries to private knitting nooks, from electronic fashion magazines to sci-fi costume pages. Sadly, it's slow, slow, slow, even with a 14.4K bps modem. It's so slow you may only want to use it to get a taste of the Web (to peek at KosmcKitty's Quilting Web Pages, for instance) and save your Web surfing for other online services that do it better.

To get to Prodigy's Web browser, click the "WEB" button on the bottom of the screen. When you get to the Web menu, click on the box "Browse the Web." You'll get a screen that looks like an E-mail form letter. After the prompt "Document URL:" type the address of the Web page you want to go to (the URL is the page's Internet address). Then press ENTER. (Ignore everything else on the screen.) Your entry should look like this:

Document URL:http://ttsw.com/MainQuiltingPage.html

Everything that follows "Document URL:" is the address, in this case the address of the World Wide Quilting Page. Once you've pressed ENTER, the Web browser will spring into action. After about four minutes of drumming your fingers on the desk, the Quilting Web Page will appear on your screen. (See Figure 13-6.)

If you want to go to a new Web page, head back to the Document URL: prompt and after it type the address of another page. You'll find a list of craft Web pages in Chapter 18.

Figure 13-6
You can reach the World Wide
Quilting Page through Prodigy, but it
may take awhile to get there.

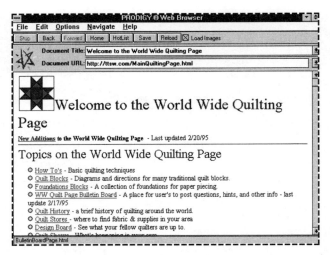

## How Do I Get Craft Software and Information Files Off Internet Through FTP and Gopher?

*Y*ou can also use Prodigy's Web browser to get craft software and information files from Internet. This too takes *much* longer than it should, and you're better off heading to CompuServe's Internet link or that of any Internet provider.

To get files from the Internet, at the Web browser's Document URL: prompt enter the FTP or Gopher address of the computer where you know the software resides. (FTP and Gopher are simply methods that the Internet uses to track down certain addresses.) For instance, you might type the following FTP address:

Document URL:ftp://gus.crafts-council.pe-ca

or this gopher address:

Document URL://gopher.crafts-council.pe.ca:70/

Either of these commands will take you to the Crafts Council file server on Prince Edward Island in Canada.

After a pause, you'll see a list of files that represent the directory of files on the faraway computer you have just tapped your way into through cyberspace. From there you can poke around and download any files that the computer will let you have. Head to Chapter 18 for more information on FTP and Gopher.

## What Are Some Good Things on Prodigy for My Family?

*T*he Money Talk forum offers good discussions about personal investing ("jump" to MONEY TALK BB), while coaches and players are online in ESPNet ("jump" to ESPN). Kids can E-mail penpals and read for-kids features in an area specially for them ("jump" to JUST KIDS). The Homelife BB offers informative conversation about day care, adopting, and home organization ("jump" to HOMELIFE BB). You'll also find the latest Consumer Reports results online ("jump" to CONSUMER REPORTS).

## How About Other Good Things for Me?

*Y*ou'll find directions for simple craft projects ranging from origami party decorations to craft projects for kids in the HomeLife BBS ("jump" to MAKE IT!).

**Figure 13-7**
**"Jump" to MAKE IT! and you'll find new craft projects every week that are sure to brighten up your life.**

*"My father had to talk me into getting online and now I never get off! The needlework forum has been especially meaningful to me because I recently moved to Utah, and the cross-stitch forum has given me an opportunity to meet new friends with a common interest of cross-stitching. By participating in the bulletin boards, I was able to find resources and share patterns on subjects I was unable to find through conventional means. I am trying to cross-stitch pictures of all the places we have lived (I am an air force wife) and couldn't find patterns for some of the states. Through AOL, I was able to get what I needed."—Joanne Carlson, Layton, Utah*

*"What I like is having another place besides my guild to get questions answered. I can get tips and advice and I don't have to wait long for a response. So far I've gotten advice on a spinning project, a knitting project, and am currently getting tips on buying a used drum carder (for spinning)."—Cooki Messmer, Portland, Oregon*

*"I haven't the time to join a guild, so I feel this is my guild. I travel a good bit and use these forums to keep connected. Recently, I spent six months away from home, working; having this connection to weaving and spinning kept me sane." —Duncan Terrell, Royal Oak, Michigan*

*"I'm a new spinner and an old knitter who just got a wheel for Christmas. What I like about America Online is that it's just like having a guild meeting right in your living room whenever you want. You don't have to wait till next month to get encouragement or information. People are friendly and never rude."—Peg Strang, Avon, Ohio*

*"The thing that I've gotten most from AOL's forum is a sense of community, something seriously lacking in everyday life. People seem to genuinely care about others. The only thing you are judged on is the quality of your ideas, not the way you look or the color of your skin."—Cher Underwood, Chicago, Illinois*

*"AOL has done wonderful things for me. It has allowed me to communicate with designers and friends. Stitch Chat has provided me with useful tips on projects as well as needlecraft accessories. Round robins have put me in touch with new people while gaining a unique needlework piece. Last but not least, the secret pal swap has added a new dimension (and mystery) to needlecrafting. Everyone I have met online has been very friendly and helpful."—Susan E. Carlson, Hawaii*

*"I've been a member of both America Online and Prodigy and both have strengthened my love for needlework. Through each of these services I have come in contact with people who have helped me purchase hard-to-find items, and that in turn has encouraged me to expand my stitching techniques and take on unfamiliar forms of embroidery. I've been able to meet so many kind, wonderful people who share a love for this beautiful art."—Noelle Walters, Enfield, Connecticut*

*"I can't imagine being without America Online needlecraft folders! I sign on at least once a day to check my mail. It's addictive. I actually had withdrawals during vacation!"—Letha Welch, Grafton, Wisconsin*

# 14

## NEEDLECRAFT KLATCHES BLOOM ON HIP AMERICA ONLINE

*Between MTV and SPIN magazine sites, small communities of quilters, crocheters, and weavers flourish on this vibrant service.*

merica Online is as colorful as American pop culture itself. You'll find *SPIN* magazine listed on the same menu as *The New York Times*. MTV's often raucous forum is located just an icon click away from the sober world of National Public Radio. The service is full of surprises too—like the database that lets you search the Bible by keyword, or the electronic cookbooks with recipes from celebrities. The service is eye catching, with jazzy screens and a feel-good interface. It's no surprise that AOL has blossomed into the nation's premier home computer information service. Its low hourly fee—which is the same no matter what time or at what speed you call, and no matter what you access (with a few exceptions)—has helped.

AOL's needlecraft forums do not hum with activity to the extent of those on CompuServe, Prodigy, and GEnie. In comparison, they're sparsely populated. Some complain they're chilly.

This is probably because they're scattered and tucked in out-of-the-way spots on the service. *Woman's Day* magazine hosts a moderately well-attended forum filled with craft patterns from magazine editors (including lots of crochet ones) and lively discussions on knitting, sewing, and homey arts like decoupage and handmade wallpaper. But you need to poke around in the magazine section of the service to find it.

The quilters on AOL only recently have banded together and agitated for more AOL cyber–real estate for themselves, establishing their own public forum with their own software library. Other crafters like weavers, spinners, and sewers still remain isolated in the backwaters of the service in an area called "The Exchange," which they share with other hobbyists. They do not have a software library of their own.

Part of the reason that AOL doesn't devote as much of its service to needlecrafts as other online services do may be because its management is unaware of the interest. *Inside Media* reports that when AOL's CEO Steve Case was asked what it would take to get more women online, he replied "shopping." Meanwhile, AOL's competitors, who don't offer any more shopping than AOL does, estimate that 35 to 40 percent of their subscribership is already female.

It is possible that by the time you read this, the needlecraft forums will be located in entirely different spots. AOL is a service that, like rock' n' roll, is always changing with the times.

## AOL Offers Some Unique Advantages

*F*or consumers, America Online is presently among the best deals in information services. It offers lively forums, a good selection of consumer information, and comparatively low prices. Its navigation software is also supereasy to use.

Messages stay in public forums nearly forever, so you can easily read all the messages on, say, machine knitting, from the past year or two. In contrast, CompuServe's forum messages vanish in days; Prodigy's last a few weeks. Because AOL's messages stick around, it's easy to search for advice and discussions on a particular topic, even if those discussions date back several months.

AOL also offers an Internet link that's easier to use than those on other services. If you're at all curious about Internet, this is the place to test the water. Low connect rates, the ability to automate E-mail retrieval, and no extra charges for receiving lots of mail from Internet make AOL an ideal service to use if you plan to sign up for those wonderful needlecraft mailing lists described in Chapter 18.

Last, AOL offers a free trial that's too good to pass up. Call their 800-number and they'll send you the software free, plus the first month's subscription free and a few hours of access. It's worth trying. Just remember to cancel your subscription before the first 30 days are up or they'll start billing you.

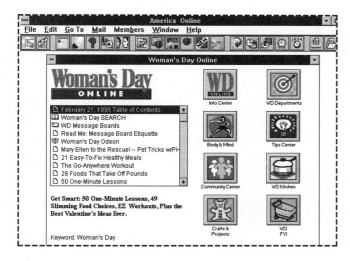

**Figure 14-1**
*Woman's Day* on America Online offers a rich selection of sewing and craft tips, patterns, conversation, and features from the magazine.

## AOL Has Its Weaknesses Too

Like all mass media on the cutting edge, America Online often appears to teeter on the brink of chaos. The service can be agonizingly slow to access in the evening, due to high numbers of subscribers overloading the system. Message retrieval and screen updates also can be slow. While AOL offers one of the easiest-to-use Internet links around, the link suffers continuing problems. Even receiving E-mail from friends on Internet can be ticklish at times, with messages getting lost in cyberspace for days (although they get to you eventually).

When parents complained that it was too easy for kids (or them) to stumble into the virtual reality sex chat conferences by accidentally clicking the wrong screen button, AOL responded by offering a way for parents to lock their kids out of the chat area. This only works, however, if parents discover the problem themselves, then figure out how to activate the lock. Too, you can't prevent kids from wandering into sexually oriented forums or the porno-rife, uncensored Internet. I hear more complaints from women about being propositioned on AOL than I do from women on other services. (You can prevent propositioning by activating the parental-control chat lock.)

AOL doesn't offer any international links, though some subscribers tap in from overseas by calling long distance. This means that if you're looking for an online service you can dial into from, say, an air force base in Germany, you're better off heading to CompuServe or GEnie.

## How Do I Get the Special Software for Calling America Online?

*T*o get AOL's software, call them at 800/827-6364 or write to America Online, 8619 Westwood Center Dr., Vienna, VA 22182 and ask for the free start-up kit. Your kit will include software that you'll need to install on your computer's hard disk. If you use Windows, get the Windows version rather than the plain DOS version. Of course, if you use a Mac, you should request their Mac version.

To call America Online, you can use any Macintosh or a PC-compatible with an 80286 or higher processor and hard disk. The software will not work with older IBM PCs and compatibles. America Online has discontinued support for the Apple II.

## What If I Need Help Installing the Software or Connecting?

*I*f you need help with the software or making your first connection, call America Online customer support at 800/827-3338 from 6 a.m. to 4 p.m. EST. Have on hand your list of computer specifications and the make and model of your modem.

## How Do I Get Help with America Online Once I Get Online?

*T*o get help while online, you can press CTRL-K and type HELP, or click on "Member Services" from your main menu and choose the appropriate icon for the help you require.

## What's the Best Way to Call America Online?

*C*all the local phone number that supports the highest modem speed of your modem, since AOL's hourly charge is the same no matter at what speed you call. Also, because AOL costs the same no matter when you call, you can call anytime, day or night. To find a list of AOL access numbers in your community, press CTRL-K, type REFERENCE, then click on "AOL Local Access Numbers."

You can also keep your online costs down by using AOL's FlashSession feature to send and retrieve mail automatically. To set up a FlashSession, press ALT-M while you're offline, select "FlashSessions… ," then click on the "Walk Me Through" icon. You can also select "FlashSession" from the drop-down menu under Mail.

To tell the software to log on, gather your mail, then log off, press ALT-M and select "Activate Flash Session Now," or use the drop-down menu under Mail. (It may take the software awhile to do this, so be patient.)

To read your mail, once the software has logged off, press ALT-M and select "Read Incoming Mail," or use the drop-down menu under Mail. If any mail was retrieved, the software will display a list of messages. Click on the one you want to read.

Unfortunately, there's no way to get AOL's software to log in to public forums, like the quilting one, and gather messages for you to read offline.

> **TIP**
>
> *If you're not amenable to receiving propositions from "cyberstuds" while online—unsolicited messages like "Hi! R U blond?" that pop up suddenly while you're in the midst of sifting through the quilt block library— activate the parental lock, also known as a "bozo filter." You'll find it in the Members pull-down menu at the top of your screen. Click "Parental Control."*

## How Do I Find Other Needlecrafters on America Online?

Needlecraft communities are fragmented on America Online. You'll want to check out three spots: the Needlecraft/Sewing Center, the Quilting Board, and *Woman's Day* Online.

### *The Needlecraft/Sewing Center*

The Needlecraft/Sewing Center offers small but ardent discussions on sewing, knitting, crochet, cross-stitch, and weaving. To get to it, log on, press CTRL-K or choose "Go To" and type the keyword **EXCHANGE.** Click the "Crafts & Sewing" icon in the menu that appears, then click "Needlecraft/Sewing Center." You'll be prompted to choose from the Knitting Board, the Needlecrafts Board, the Sewing Board, and the Weaving & Spinning Board. Highlight one and click on it. Click "Browse Folders." You'll get a list of message threads that you can scroll through.

Now select one of the threads that interests you. Click "List Messages" and a list of messages will appear. You can scroll through this list and read any message by clicking on it. Click "Next Message" to read the next message in the conversational thread. To start reading a new thread, close the current message by clicking on the top left-hand corner of its window. Select a new message from the list.

## The Quilting Board

The quilting message center has been growing by leaps. Members swap blocks and fabric, get together at Paducah, and discuss the latest Hoffman fabrics with the urgency of missionaries. To get there, log on and press CTRL-K, then type **QUILT**. Select "Quilting Board" from the menu and click "Browse Folders." Highlight and click on the message thread you want to read, then click "List Messages." Now scroll through the list of messages that appear and read the ones you want by highlighting and clicking on them. Click "Next Message" to read the next message in the conversational thread.

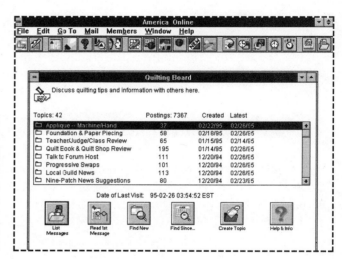

**Figure 14-2**
You can get to the Quilting Board on America Online by pressing CTRL-K and typing QUILT. You can read any of the message threads in the topics displayed on this screen by clicking the "List Messages" icon. A list of messages stored under that topic will be displayed.

## Woman's Day Online

You'll find scintillating craft discussions in the forum run by *Woman's Day* magazine. The Incredible Sweater Machine, sold through the Home Shopping Network, was a recent star in a conversation between new converts to machine knitting. Where to find patterns for crocheting Dutch shoes was another urgently discussed topic. Needless to say, you'll meet lots of knitters and crocheters here. There are sewers online too. And you'll spot crafters discussing arts you seldom encounter outside the pages of *Woman's Day*, such as braiding rugs from plastic bread bags and recycling slipcovers into garment bags. It's a conference alive with ideas.

To get there, get yourself online, then press CTRL-K and type **WOMAN'S DAY**. Click the "Crafts & Projects" icon. Select the Craft Message Center or the Home Decorating Message

Center. Now click "List Categories." In the Craft Message Center you can choose from "Knitting & Crocheting," "The Sewing Circle," and "Other Crafts." Choose one, then select "List Topics" and scroll through the list for a topic that interests you. If you click "List Messages," a list of messages will appear.

> **TIP**
> *Do you collect antique sewing tools? If so, there's a discussion for you on America Online. To get there, press* CTRL-K, *then type the keyword EXCHANGE. Click on the icon for the "Collector's Corner." Select the "Antiques & Memorabilia" board. Click "Browse Folders" and select the topic "Antique Sewing Items."*

## How Do I Send or Receive Private E-mail?

To send a private E-mail message while online, press CTRL-M or select "Mail" from the drop-down menu and then "Compose Mail." Once a dialog box pops up, in the To: field type the recipient's AOL subscriber ID or his or her full Internet address. Type a subject and your message, then click the "Send" button.

To compose mail offline, close the Welcome window that prompts you for a password and then press CTRL-M or use the drop-down menu under "Mail" (selecting "Compose Mail"). In the To: field type the recipient's AOL subscriber ID or his or her full Internet address. Type a subject and your message and then click the "Send Later" button to send it when you log on. You can then use the FlashSession feature (discussed earlier in this chapter) to send and receive your mail automatically.

## Where Can I Find Needlecraft Software, Patterns, and Clipart for Use in My Needlecraft Designs?

You'll find needlecraft software and/or patterns in three different libraries on AOL: the *Woman's Day* pattern library, the quilting library, and the general computer software library. You won't find as much here as you will on CompuServe or GEnie, but you will find some of the more popular shareware programs described in this book.

## *The Woman's Day Libraries*

These are the most interesting libraries on America Online because they include a selection of patterns from the pages of *Woman's Day,* including downloadable diagrams and even stencils. You'll find patterns for wooden chickens, cross-stitch greeting cards, Victorian cats, silk scarves, Amish aprons, and even something called a "Bandanna Bear Wreath."

To get to the *Woman's Day* libraries, get yourself online, then press CTRL-K and type **WOMAN'S DAY** (or type **WOMAN'S DAY** into the Keyword feature). Once there, click the "Crafts & Projects" icon and you'll uncover two main libraries: "Sew What?" and "Crafts Corner." "Sew What?" is where you'll find the Amish aprons and silk scarves. Click the "Crafts Corner" icon for the wooden chickens. In both libraries you'll find textual directions for a pattern stored in a different section of the library from its graphic portion (diagrams, stencils, etc.). After you download the text portion of a pattern, be sure to click the "Graphics Library" icon to see if your file has any accompanying graphics; download them too.

**Figure 14-3**
From the *Woman's Day* craft libraries you can download directions for all kinds of craft projects, from brooches made with hot-glue guns to gingerbread boy sweatshirts. First download the written directions, then check to see if there are accompanying graphics. Shown here is a pattern for a Victorian cat. The pattern appears on your computer screen as it downloads.

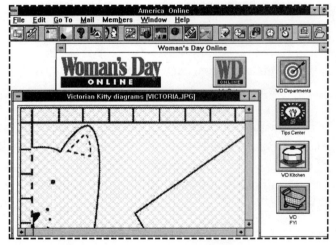

## *The Quilting Library*

AOL's Quilting Board offers a growing library of quilt block patterns (in .BMP format), quilting software, and even quilting FAQs from Internet. To get there, log on to AOL, press CTRL-K, and type **QUILT.** Select "Quilting Library" from the menu, and a list of files will appear. You can scroll through them, read their descriptions, and download any you want by highlighting the appropriate one and then clicking the "Download Now" button.

## *The General Software Library*

A small collection of needlecraft software, including knit programs, sewing pattern–making demos, and quilting software is nestled in the general software library. To get there, press CTRL-K and type **COMPUTING.** Select "Applications Forum," then click "Software Libraries." In the selection of libraries, select "Home & Leisure," then click "Crafts." A list of programs will display. To display more of the list, click the "List More" button in the bottom right-hand corner.

To download a file, highlight the name of the file and click "Download Now," or "Download Later" if you prefer to download it with AOL's Download Manager just before you log off.

## *The Clipart Library*

To search the clipart libraries for noncopyrighted images to use in designs, press CTRL-K and type GRAPHICS. Click "Resource Center" in the pop-up menu. At the next menu, click "Imaging Resource Center." You can choose either 24-bit image scans (like PCX, TIF, or bitmaps) or GIF scans. Once you select an image format, choose a library to browse through, from names like Wildlife and Cartoons. To download an image, highlight the name of the file and click the "Download Now" icon. Sorry, you can't see the image before downloading it.

# How Do I Get Back to America Online's
# Main Menu If I Get Lost?

*T*here's more than one way to get back to AOL's main menu. Click the "Main Menu" button at the bottom of the screen. Or click the "Welcome!" triangle in the bottom left-hand corner. Or click "Windows" and choose "1. Main Menu" from the window list.

**Figure 14-4**
**If you get lost, find your way back to this main menu by clicking on the "Main Menu" button or the "Welcome!" triangle in the bottom left-hand corner of your screen.**

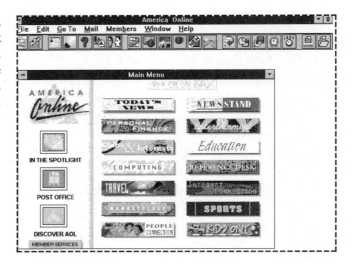

# How Do I Get General Computer Help on America Online?

*P*ress CTRL-K and type **COMPUTING**. From the forum list that appears, pick the topic that you want information on.

# How Do I Get a List of America Online's Latest Prices?

*W*hile online, press CTRL-K and type **BILLING**. Look under "Explain Billing Terms" for the rates you're being charged. You'll also find answers to your other billing questions here.

# How Do I Get Other Special Software for Making America Online More Pleasant to Use?

*U*nlike the other online services, there's presently no special software that you can use in conjunction with America Online's software to speed up your use of the service. You can, however, automate the sending and retrieval of private E-mail by using AOL's FlashSession feature, discussed earlier in this chapter.

# How Do I Use America Online to Get to Needlecraft Goodies on Internet?

*A*OL offers the easiest-to-use Internet tools of any online service. They're simple to navigate, fun to explore, and, best of all, you don't need to know anything about Internet to use them. To get to AOL's main Internet menu, log on, press CTRL-K, and type **INTERNET**.

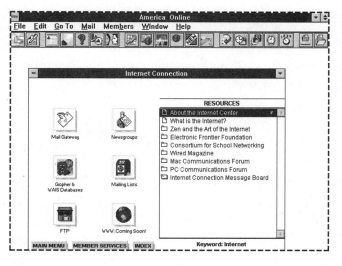

**Figure 14-5**
You can point and click your way down the information highway from America Online's Internet link (the main screen is shown here). Notice the Gopher icon? Click on it to begin your search of the world's computers for all occurrences of the word "quilt."

# How Do I Send Mail to Internet and Participate in Internet Craft Mailing Lists?

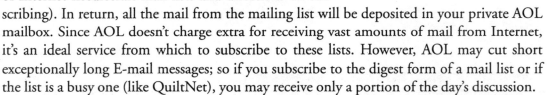

*F*irst of all, ignore the special "Internet Mail" and "Mailing List" icons on AOL's Internet menu. Ignore the search features too. It's easier to send an Internet E-mail message another way. Write your message as you normally would (start by pressing CTRL-M while online). The only difference is that you type the recipient's Internet address in the message's To: field instead of the person's screen name. You then send the message as you'd send any other message.

Similarly, to join any of the wonderful craft Internet mailing list discussions, you send a private E-mail message to the list's Internet address (see Chapter 18 for a list of Internet needlecraft mail lists and directions on subscribing). In return, all the mail from the mailing list will be deposited in your private AOL mailbox. Since AOL doesn't charge extra for receiving vast amounts of mail from Internet, it's an ideal service from which to subscribe to these lists. However, AOL may cut short exceptionally long E-mail messages; so if you subscribe to the digest form of a mail list or if the list is a busy one (like QuiltNet), you may receive only a portion of the day's discussion.

You should use AOL's FlashSession feature to retrieve your mailing list messages each day, reading and responding to them offline to cut down on your time online. Directions on using FlashSession are discussed earlier in this chapter.

# How Can I Read Usenet Needlecraft Discussions?

*O*nce you're online, press CTRL-K and type **INTERNET.** Click the "Newsgroups" icon when it appears on your screen.

In order to read Usenet craft newsgroups, you need to "add" or "subscribe" to each one the first time you read it. The easiest way to do this on AOL is to click the "Expert Add" icon that appears when you click on "Newsgroups." Once you've selected "Expert Add," at the prompt type *one* of these newsgroup names (see Chapter 18 for a description of each):

rec.crafts.textiles.needlework

rec.crafts.textiles.sewing

rec.crafts.textiles.quilting

rec.crafts.textiles.yarn

rec.crafts.textiles.misc

rec.crafts.beads

rec.crafts.marketplace

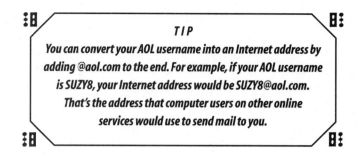

**TIP**
*You can convert your AOL username into an Internet address by adding @aol.com to the end. For example, if your AOL username is SUZY8, your Internet address would be SUZY8@aol.com. That's the address that computer users on other online services would use to send mail to you.*

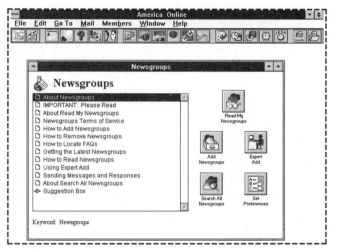

**Figure 14-6**
To reach those famous Internet Usenet crafts and textile discussions, get to AOL's Usenet menu by pressing CTRL-K, typing **INTERNET**, then clicking the "Newsgroups" icon. From here you'll need to subscribe to each newsgroup you want to read. The easiest way is to click "Expert Add" and type the name of the newsgroup you want to join.

**Figure 14-7**
Once you've subscribed to a newsgroup, you can read it by scrolling through a list of message threads and clicking on the ones you want to read.

Now click the "Add" button, and when AOL reports that you're subscribed to the group, click "OK."

To read the newsgroup you selected, go back to the main Newsgroup window by closing the present window (click on the upper left-hand corner), then clicking "Read Newsgroups." Scroll through the list of newsgroups on the screen and highlight and click on the one you want to read.

Click "List Unread" and a list of message threads will appear. You can scroll through this list, click on threads you want to read, and move forward and back through the thread by clicking the arrow buttons.

Once you've finished reading, click "Mark All Read" so that the next time you log on to AOL, the Usenet reader will display only new messages that you haven't read.

You need to go through this process for each Usenet newsgroup you want to subscribe to and read. This takes time, but remember you only have to go through the process once. The next time you log on you can go straight to your chosen newsgroups and read the new messages.

## How Do I Browse the World Wide Web with America Online?

*T*o get to America Online's Web browser, once you log on, mouse-click the Internet bar on the main menu, or press CTRL-K and type INTERNET. Click on the picture that looks like a globe. Type the address of the Web page you want to get to into the long blank box on the top of the screen.

## How Do I Get Craft Software and Information Files Off Internet Through AOL's FTP and Gopher Features?

*I* find AOL's FTP and Gopher links to Internet to be a bit perilous and slow to use when it comes to searching and retrieving files off Internet. It can take forever to get something off Internet through AOL—and if it's a long information file like a needlecraft FAQ, it sometimes arrives chopped short. Given the choice, I prefer CompuServe's Internet link when retrieving files. CompuServe's is so much faster that it ends up being considerably cheaper. AOL's Internet link, on the other hand, is more pleasant to use than that of any other online service. If AOL is your service, here's how to use it to retrieve files from the Internet.

## *Using FTP to Search for Internet Needlecraft Files*

FTP (File Transfer Protocol) is a way of searching for and retrieving information and software from other computers in the far-flung Internet kingdom. You don't have to know any far-flung computers in particular, or even what FTP is, in order to use it. FTP is the only way you can get software off Internet via AOL.

To use FTP, start by getting yourself online, then press CTRL-K and type **INTERNET.** Click the "FTP" icon, then click "Search for FTP Site." Now type in a search term like "quilt" or "hobby." A list of gibberish will appear. For instance, you might see an address like

ftp.cc.uch.gr

This is the Internet address of a computer at the University of Crete in Greece that has some hobby files you can download. Write it down.

To reach this Grecian computer, click "Go to FTP" and then "Other Site." Now type

ftp.cc.uch.gr

and click the "Connect" button. Be forewarned that it may take awhile for AOL to connect to that far-off computer and that sometimes you'll get an error message telling you the computer is busy and to try later. Don't give up. Patience helps a lot when it comes to Internet. (After all, just because the government built the Internet to survive a nuclear war doesn't mean that it's fast or even easy to use.)

If you're lucky, AOL will connect to the Crete computer. When it does, a list of its file directories will appear. This list of file directories may look fairly incomprehensible (not only are some in Greek, they're written in a code called UNIX), but you can look through them, and even download files that seem interesting simply by highlighting them and clicking the "Download Now" button at the bottom of your screen. Once you've downloaded various files, you can look through them offline to see what you've got and whether they're useful.

## *Using Gopher to Search for Internet Needlecraft Files*

Gopher is another way to search for and retrieve software and information files through Internet, although you can only use the Gopher feature on AOL to get information (as opposed to software) files. Like FTP, you don't need to know anything about Gopher in order to use it on AOL.

To use Gopher, start by getting online, pressing CTRL-K, and typing **INTERNET.** When the choice appears, click the icon "Gopher and WAIS Databases" and you're almost there.

Gophers are computers on Internet that help you look for files. AOL lists some popular Gopher computers, but you won't find any crafting information with these. You're better off clicking "Search All Gophers," which will search all the Gopher computers in the world for you.

When prompted, type in a word like "quilt" and click "Search." Gopher will go to work digging up files that match your request.

Eventually good-old Gopher will come up with a list of news and information files described with the word "quilt." Scroll through the list and click on the ones you're interested in, one at a time. In response, Gopher will get the files for you and display each on your screen. To save a file to your hard disk, click on "File" in the upper left-hand corner of your screen, select "Save," and type in a filename.

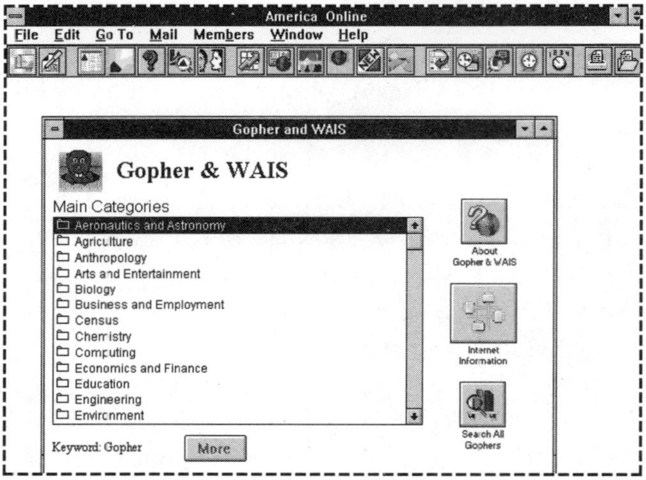

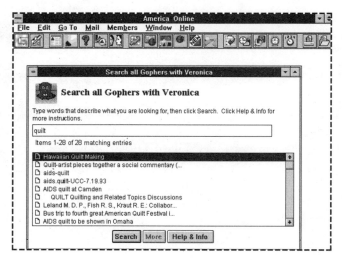

**Figure 14-8**
Once you get to the main Gopher screen, skip the kid's stuff and click on "Search All Gophers" to search all the computers out in cyberspace for quilt patterns and sewing advice.

**Figure 14-9**
Gopher came up with this list of articles when I searched all the computers in the world for occurrences of the word "quilt." Each article is located on a different computer, in a different part of the world (it's hard to tell where). When you click on any article, Gopher will display the text on your screen and you can read it as if you were seated in front of that far-off computer.

## How Do I Get a List of Everything That's on America Online?

Press CTRL-K and type **REFERENCE**. Click on "AOL Directory of Services" and you'll see a list of services. You can then search the Directory of Services for those that might interest you.

## What Are Some Good Things on America Online for My Family?

America Online offers a great kids-only section where your child can exchange E-mail with other kids and read features intended to expand their minds. Press CTRL-K and type **KIDS** to reach this section. Here, you'll find educational features such as the *National Geographic* and parent and teacher forums, but let's get real: how often are your kids going to want to tap into *National Geographic* online, and how often are *you* going to want to read the parent and teacher conference?

In the Pets Forum you'll find online advice from vets, trainers, and breeders (press CTRL-K, then type **PETS**). I learned how to train my dog here and got advice that saved my cat's life. A pet-loss support network offers compassion to those who've lost a friend. Amateur investors will find financial advice in the forum run by the American Association of Independent Investors (press CTRL-K, then type **AAII**).

## How About Other Good Things for Me?

If you're the kind of news junkie who ends up detoured at the magazine rack for thirty minutes whenever you walk into a grocery store, you'll be in heaven on America Online. It offers full-text stories from the current issues of many leading magazines, including *Time, Elle, Atlantic Monthly, Omni,* and *Scientific American,* plus hobby magazines like *Popular Photography* and *American Woodworker.* Also online are stories from the day's *New York Times,* the *Chicago Tribune,* Reuters news wire service, and other wire services and newspapers. Plus, you don't have to pay anything extra to read them. (Back issues of thousands of publications are available on CompuServe, but you have to pay *lots* to search and read them.) Sorry, *The National Enquirer* is not among the mix.

# WHAT STITCHERS HAVE TO SAY ABOUT DELPHI

*"[Delphi] is a place to go where it never matters how you are dressed or what your hair looks like....I am always thrilled when someone enters my quilt shop and asks, 'Are you Katy-Did?' (that's my online handle). That's happened to me more times than I can count."—Kathleen Pappas, quilt shop owner, Montrose, CA*

*"My online friends are my link to sanity....With the help and encouragement of other onliners I have been able to venture into unknown areas. Quilting, fabric dyeing, silk painting, beadwork, and silk ribbon embroidery are just a few."—Evelyn Portrait, "domestic goddess," Lynn, MA*

*"I've made some wonderful friends in the cross-stitch forum on Delphi. My life would be empty without them. What have I learned? How to move forward in my craft and take chances while learning new stitches."—Mary Kay Barker, Garland, TX*

*"I have learned more about quilting online than I'll ever be able to learn by reading books. Here you can ask if someone has tried a method that you want to learn and they will help you through learning it. This group can also cheer you up when you're feeling down."—Dorothy Smith, Sayville, NY*

*"I am a full-time secretary at a university, providing substantial support for my disabled husband and myself. I have found that most guilds meet at times when my family responsibilities prevent me from attending. Through the Textile Arts Forum I can get valuable information on techniques, suppliers, and upcoming events. Swaps, round-robins, database files, and photos give me 'guild meetings' I cannot attend otherwise. I have also found other women who fill caretaker roles in the household. Delphi has given me a valuable link with the outside world and a very loving and supportive sisterhood."*
*—Nancy Forrest, secretary, Richmond, VA*

*"I've posted more messages than I can count that start with 'I need some ideas on...' and have gotten marvelous suggestions and advice. I've met about ten members of the Textile Arts Forum in person. Each has been a delight to be with. In May we had a get-together in Baltimore and for the first time in recent memory, I felt like I belonged in the group, rather than being someone on the outside looking in. I'm a stay-at-home mom and this group is my lifeline to the outside world—my opportunity to communicate with those who share my interests. I can't remember what I did without it."—Christine Utting, mother, Stoverstown, PA*

*"Although I live in a highly populated area I do not have many friends who are cross-stitchers or who understand the thrill of taking a blank piece of fabric and creating something beautiful. I have made many friends online who share the love of the needle. I have learned various techniques that others are using that I was not aware of and have been educated on types of fabrics, new threads, and about many new designers."*
*—Bonnie Ingalls, management analyst for Defense Dept., Sterling, VA,*

*"This is truly a family of wonderful, amazing friends. I would be lost without them."—Debra Brinkman, accountant, Colorado Springs, CO*

*"We all get online for the knitting, the quilting, and so on, where we get solid doses of information, advice, and encouragement about our interests. But in the process we get much more. The caring, camaraderie, and sense of family that have sprung up with people we otherwise might never have encountered in our lifetime represent the real legacy of the Textile Arts Forum. In terms of feeling connected to one's best and highest self and to the best impulses of humankind...TAF has been the mother lode."—Rita Levine, knitting and crocheting co-host, Textile Arts Forum, Pittsburgh, PA*

# 15

## CROSS-STITCHERS, QUILTERS, AND OTHER FIBER-FOLK HAVE A BLAST ON DELPHI

*Its low cost and a congenial atmosphere have made
this small service a favorite port of call for needlecrafters.*

Delphi differs from other major online services in several regards. Its main attraction is its low price. You can converse with stitchers around the country for evening bargain rates of about $1 to $2 an hour, a privilege that will cost you several dollars an hour more on the other commercial services. Delphi's automation software can bring its costs down even more. "My monthly bills are under $30," says Susan Druding, who dials in every day to run the Textile Arts Forum. She says her monthly bills are considerably higher on other services for far fewer hours online.

Delphi also differs from other online services in that you don't use special software to call it like you do Prodigy or America Online. You use a general communications program like Procomm Plus or WinComm. That makes Delphi harder to use than its competitors because you don't get screens with pictures; instead you get menus and prompts at which you type commands.

Another way in which Delphi differs is that most of its craft forums are not run by Delphi but rather by average people who pay for the privilege of hosting their own forums. As a result, the craft forums are cozy and quirky, as well as popular.

## Cross-Stitchers Like Delphi's Free-Ranging Chatter

*D*elphi's cross-stitch forum is run by Debs Butler, an administrative assistant in Charlottesville, Virginia. The forum is fairly new as this book goes to press, yet already it is frequented by about 75 stitchers who are writing each other as many as a thousand messages a week.

"It's a little family," says Butler. "They say, 'You're like our mom.'" She laughs that at age 34 she's probably the youngest person in the conference. "I can go on this board and tell them I've had this kind of crappy day, and I'll receive all sorts of support and sympathy. My dog was sick several months ago and members still ask me how he's doing."

As with most of the online services, many Delphi participants live in rural areas and are cut off from urban life. Many are military wives whose families lead a transient life. When a member doesn't appear online for several days, other members call her by phone.

Messages veer into topics not related to stitching, and members like it that way. Forums on other services are stricter about keeping messages related to cross-stitch. "We do what stitchers like to do," says Butler, "talk about stitching and talk about our lives." (Butler's forum doesn't offer software and information files, but it may in the future.)

While members frequently get together in other cities to visit embroidery shops and each other, they haven't yet organized the swaps and group projects that stitchers on other services have. They do have a popular "secret sister society" like Prodigy's, in which members are assigned a pal to send gifts.

Figure 15-1
Delphi's Textile Arts Forum is one of the liveliest spots for stitchers in cyberspace. To get there, type CUSTOM 135 from Delphi's main menu.

# National Online Quilters Also Talk It Up

*Y*ou don't have to frequent electronic craft forums for long before you realize that Cheryl Simmerman, who heads the free-spirited gaggle of quilters on Delphi, is something of a legend among quilters. The Battle Creek, Michigan, secretary and mother goes by the online name of "Loonsey." She and her cohorts on Delphi have donned the imposing name of National Online Quilters, but no name could be more misleading. In actuality, they are a happy-go-lucky bunch who write under cute nom de plumes like "Peashooter" and "Flipper." Their messages bubble with slang like "fab" for "fabric" and "mega-sale," as well as emotional pleas like, "When I got home, I couldn't find the recipe! WAAAA! Could you PRETTY please sent it to moi again?"

According to Simmerman, the National Online Quilters wandered from computer service to computer service until finally choosing Delphi as the only place that would give them the freedom to converse as they pleased. Like members of the cross-stitch forum, they did not want to be constrained by rules that kept their discussions strictly to business. (One day I scrolled through a couple hundred messages and, frankly, couldn't find a single one that had anything to do with quilting. But they were sure fun to read.)

> "My only rule is that they have to be nice," says Simmerman, "and they've got to be able to express the joy of the quilt board—and of life itself. No whining. I don't put up with that."

One trait these quilters have in common is that they love to computer CB. Two nights a week, as many as 40 or 50 converse via keyboard, sometimes for hours at time. The night I joined in, little was said about quilting, but a lot was said about husbands who ignore their wives' advice when buying computers, and other aggravations in life. Delphi is a good place for computer CBing because its low evening rates are lower than those of any other computer service.

Members swap fabric and quilt blocks and have staged charity fund-raisers. They've even made a cooperative quilt (some members made blocks, one did the appliqué, one machine quilted, and so on), which brought $500. The money was used to send a chronically ill child to summer camp. A dozen members also got together and rented a lakefront house where they spent a week quilting.

"We've had members whose children have run away from home or been ill, and we provide a lot of emotional support to each other on the board," says Simmerman. She adds brightly, "Three or four of us have kindergartners and we're currently providing each other with emotional support to deal with that."

A small file library of digitized pictures of quilts and block patterns is available, along with some quilting software. And, Internet crafting discussions and databases are also available, something you won't find in the craft forums on any of the other major computer services. Simmerman says these hold little interest for her quilters, who come mainly for the conversation.

When stitchers in the Textile Arts Forum were asked why they preferred Delphi over the needlearts forums on other services, the answers were nearly unanimous. "People, people, people!" cried a machine knitter with the logon "CyberFyberOtter." "Great people," agreed another. A third said, "We've got really smart people here, and our host [Susan Druding] is wonderful."

## The Textile Arts Forum Is Low Key, Warm, and Eclectic

Delphi's very popular Textile Arts Forum is a departure from its other stitching forums. It's a more traditional electronic crafting bee in the sense that, except for an occasional foray into non-craft discussions, members are encouraged to stick to talking about their handiwork. It's run by Berkeley, California, weaver, spinner, teacher, and businesswoman Susan Druding.

"We've got a mixture of grandmothers, young mothers, students, and even a woman who's writing her doctorate in communication on women in cyberspace," says Druding. The forum also hosts a handful of men, most of whom, says Druding, read messages but refrain from posting their own. Most crafters in the forum are quilters, cross-stitchers, and spinners. "For some reason we have an awful lot of spinners," says Druding. Lots of machine and hand knitters also frequent the forum, whose members number in the hundreds. Approximately fifty to a hundred messages are written in it per day.

Crafters stage round-robin-like exchanges that tend to be more informal in nature than those on other services. "The spinners have round-robins, but you don't need to be a spinner to participate," says Druding. "Everyone passes on whatever they can, whether it's a bit of something they're working on or a question about spinning. The other day I got a packet that contained a sample from a woman who's spinning paper, a Japanese technique she studied in Indonesia. You spin paper and silk and dye it with safflower to get a golden or pink tone. I got some yarn a member spun from the wool of a rare type of sheep together with angora, and I got a sample of metallic thread spinning from another."

Members meet informally at craft shows around the country. They're planning charity sewing for hospitals and Habitat for Humanity.

While the Textile Arts Forum has an ample craft software and information library, one of the things that makes it stand out is how easy Druding has made it to get at everything. Internet Usenet craft messages and Gopher servers (computers in other parts of the world from which you can retrieve software and information) can be tapped into from one simple menu. The forum also provides access to the craft-related "pages" on the World Wide Web (an adjunct to Internet), where information is organized like pages in an encyclopedia. (See Chapter 18 for more information on Usenet and the World Wide Web.) Unfortunately, from Delphi's Internet link you currently cannot see the Web's extraordinary graphics and sound; you must read the pages in dull text. (This will probably be changing in the near future.)

## Bottom Line: Delphi's a Very Good Deal for Stitchers

Delphi's sparse offerings in some areas inspire most of its crafters to maintain subscriptions on other services like CompuServe and GEnie. Even so, you can't beat its low cost, and automation software is available to bring your online bills down even lower.

Still, Delphi doesn't offer the kind of family fare that Prodigy, CompuServe, or America Online do, and you won't find the same broad range of forums, databases, news, travel, or entertainment features that these services carry. You find some of those things, but they're expensive to access and meager in scope.

Delphi pushes its custom forums and its Internet link. Its several hundred custom forums span from the truly worthwhile, like those for nursing and woodworking, to the blatantly raunchy. Delphi may be the online version of Wal-Mart, but you may want to think before letting young members of your family tap in.

*The only foray into quirkiness that's permitted in the Textile Arts Forum is its "Textile Arts' Weight Loss and Exercise Support Group." Forum leader Druding says she suspects many members need it, considering how much time they spend sitting at the computer or the loom.*

**DELPHI ONLINE SURVIVAL GUIDE**

## How Do I Get the Special Software for Calling Delphi?

One of Delphi's advantages is that you can call it with any computer. To call it with an all-purpose communications program like Procomm, the Terminal program in Windows, or the software that came with your modem, you dial Delphi just as you would a computer bulletin board. Once connected, you log in with your password and service ID, and type commands at its menus.

There are a couple of ways to sign up for Delphi. You can call Delphi Internet Services Corporation at 800/695-4005 (1030 Massachusetts Ave., Cambridge, MA 02138) and ask for a free start-up kit. Or you can call 800/695-4002 using your computer modem. When you get a connection, press ENTER several times. When you get a prompt asking for a password, type **FREE**. You'll then get a few free hours to play with the service.

If you're using an 80386 PC or higher, with 4 MB RAM, and you're running Windows, Delphi will send you the free navigation software InterNav. InterNav will automatically log you on to the service and help you maneuver the treacheries of its private E-mail feature, though you'll still need to tap your way around the rest of the service yourself. (As this book goes to press, Delphi is writing better navigation software to supplant InterNav, so be sure to ask about it when you call.) You can download InterNav for free by heading to the "Using Delphi" service. To get there from the main menu, type USING.

See the section on other special software (pages 325–326) to learn about autopilot programs to automate your use of the craft forums.

*Note: As this book goes to press, Delphi Internet Services is redesigning both its content and forums, as well as the software that can be used to call it. Sometime soon you should be able to connect to Delphi with a traditional Internet navigator like Netscape, which will let you enjoy the wild graphics of the World Wide Web and cruise the Internet more easily.* ᗧ

**Figure 15-2**
Delphi's free InterNav navigation software for PCs running Windows makes it easy to log on and get oriented on the service. To really enjoy the service, though, you'll want to upgrade to an autopilot program or use the special version of Netscape when it becomes available for Delphi.

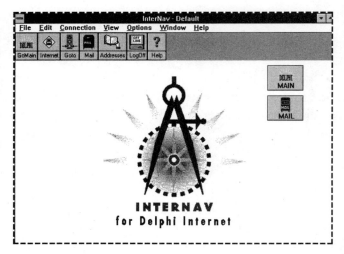

# What If I Need Help Installing the Software or Connecting?

*I*f you need help installing the software or connecting, call Delphi technical support at 800/695-4005 from 8 a.m. to 11 p.m. EST on weekdays or 12 p.m. to 11 p.m. on weekends.

# How Do I Get Help with Delphi Once I Get Online?

*I*f you need help with Delphi, post a message in any of its crafts forums and you'll surely get the help you need. You can also head to Delphi's member help forum from the main menu (to get there type **MAIN**) by typing **SERVICE** and then **FORUM** to read or write public messages. To send customer service a private message, type **PRIVATE**.

# What's the Best Way to Call Delphi?

*W*hen you sign up you'll be given five free hours online. To start out, choose the 10/4 plan, which gives you four hours of evening access for $10 per month. You pay $4 per hour for each additional hour online. After the first month, if you decide you like Delphi, switch to the 20/20 Advantage plan. That gives you 20 hours of evening access for $20 each month, plus a one-time $19 sign-up fee. Internet access costs an additional $3 per month. After that, access is $1.80 an hour.

Your best bet is to dial Delphi only in the evening when SprintNet and Tymnet access is free. If you call during the day, you'll be billed an additional $9 per hour. If you have no SprintNet or Tymnet numbers in your community, you can link into Delphi for free if you have an Internet connection.

To keep your online bills low, you should call at the highest speed you can (14.4K bps is supported) and use one of the navigation programs described in the next section.

# How Do I Get Other Special Software
# for Making Delphi More Pleasant to Use?

*I*f you're using a PC or Macintosh, you can download a shareware navigation program from Delphi that will automate message retrieval from the crafts forums. One popular Delphi navigator for PCs is called Rainbow. It will run on any PC or compatible in existence, even old 8088s and 8086s (the original IBM PCs). To get a copy of Rainbow, type **CUSTOM 250** at the main Delphi menu. Rainbow is $35 shareware, available from Colston & Associates, Inc., 125 N. 14th St., Suite 204, Fort Smith, AR 72901, 501/783-4688, or you can write DavidColston@delphi.com.

Other popular navigator programs are the D-LITE navigators. To get a copy of any of the D-LITE navigators, type **GO COMPUTING** at Delphi's main menu (type **MAIN** to get there), then **D-LITE**. You'll find DOS, Windows, and Macintosh versions. The PC and Mac versions are $29; the Windows version is $39. You can get more information about the program from the D-LITE forum on Delphi or by writing Circular Logic, at perry@ delphi. com, or P.O. Box 162, Skippack, PA 19474, 610/584-0300.

## How Do I Find Other Needlecrafters on Delphi?

*Y*our first stop should be the Textile Arts Forum (to get there, type **CUSTOM 135** from Delphi's main menu). You can also access the forum through another forum that you might enjoy called the Hobbies & Crafts Forum (type **GO HOBBIES**).

Once you get to the Textile Arts menu, type **FORUM** to read the public messages. Type **READ 1** to read the first message; press ENTER to read the ones that follow (Druding recommends reading the first four messages in the forum to get started). To read the fifty most recent messages, type **HIGH NEW**. To search for messages containing a particular word, like "tatting," type **DIR FULLTEXT TATTING** and press ENTER.

The commands to read messages in the other needlework conferences are the same. To get to the National Online Quilters Forum, type **CUSTOM 220** from the main Delphi menu. To join the cross-stitch forum, type **CUSTOM 291**.

**TIP**
*Computer CBing is very popular on Delphi, especially in the needlecraft forums. (I get the impression that stitchers feel more comfortable CBing here than they do on America Online where uninvited propositions are routine.) While you're in any of the needlecrafts forums, someone may well ask if you'd like to chat. To talk to them, head back to the main menu of the forum that you're in (type EXIT) and type CONFERENCE. To respond to their typed messages, all you need to do is type back. When you've finished chatting, type EXIT to return to the forum's menu.*

# How Do I Send a Private E-mail Message?

To send a private E-mail message, type **MAIL** at the main Delphi menu, then type **MAIL** again at the next menu. To begin writing your message, type **SEND,** then type the Delphi ID of the recipient. After you've finished typing the message, press CTRL-Z to send it.

# Where Can I Find Needlecraft Software, Patterns, and Clipart for Use in My Needlecraft Designs?

While you won't find as much needlecraft software and information files on Delphi as you will on CompuServe or GEnie, it's so cheap to download files from the service that if you can find what you're looking for, you may do well to download it here. The largest file collection is in the Textile Arts Forum (CUSTOM 135). At the forum's main menu, type **DATABASES,** then choose a category from the list. To browse through file descriptions in that particular library, type **READ.** Type **SEARCH** to search for particular files. The service will ask if you want to download any of the files it finds. (If you're calling with a general communications program, be sure you know the command to start a file download. It's usually something simple like pressing PGDN or ALT-D.) You'll also find a small selection of software and information files in the National Online Quilter's Forum (CUSTOM 220).

# How to Find Clipart and Graphics Software on Delphi

To find clipart and graphics on Delphi, at the main Delphi menu type **COMPUTING,** then type **GRAPHICS** to reach the graphics arts forums. You'll find a selection of shareware graphics software that you can download. Note, though, that the clipart library is an extra $4 an hour to access, and the content of the free graphics library is somewhat disappointing. For clipart to use in needlework or designing, you may be better off with GEnie or CompuServe.

# How Do I Get Back to Delphi's Main Menu If I Get Lost?

To return to the main menu, type MAIN at any menu. You can get to anything on Delphi from this menu.

Figure 15-3
The trick to not getting lost on Delphi is to be able to find your way back to this main menu. Type MAIN to get here. Type EXIT to get out of any menu or operation you may be stuck in.

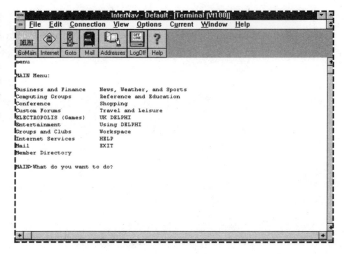

## How Do I Get General Computer Help on Delphi?

To get general computer help on Delphi, type **COMPUTING** at the main menu to reach the computer help forums. When you arrive, you'll find public forums devoted to Amigas, Apples, Ataris, Macintoshes, Commodores, Tandys, and PC-compatibles.

## How Do I Get a List of Delphi's Latest Prices?

To get a list of Delphi's latest prices, type **USING** (for "Using Delphi") at the main menu and then type **RATES**.

## How Do I Use Delphi to Get to Needlecraft Goodies on Internet?

Thanks in large part to Susan Druding, it's extremely easy to tap into much of the needlecraft information on the Internet. The main menu of Druding's Textile Arts Forum includes all the Usenet craft-related newsgroups, interesting art and needlecraft-related sites (like the Los Angeles County Museum of Art), and even World Wide Web needlecraft sites. You can also tap into Usenet newsgroups and search Internet via Gopher through the National Online Quilters' custom forum main menu.

## How Do I Send Mail to Internet and Participate in Internet Craft Mailing Lists?

*D*elphi is a good service to use to tap into Internet craft mailing lists like those described in Chapter 18 because there are no extra charges to receive large amounts of mail from Internet (as there are on CompuServe). With Delphi you can download mail more quickly than you can on GEnie and Prodigy.

**TIP**
To make your Delphi subscriber ID into an Internet address, add @delphi.com to the end. For instance: JaneJones@ delphi.com

You send an Internet message on Delphi just as you'd send an ordinary private E-mail message. First you get to the mail menu (type **MAIL**), then type **MAIL** a second time to select E-mail, and then type **SEND** to compose the message. Next, enter the recipient's Internet address using the following syntax: To:**IN%** *"recipient@theiraddress.com"*. For instance, to send a message to Polly Smith on Prodigy, you'd type To:**IN%** **"pollysmith@prodigy.com"**. (Notice how the Internet address is placed inside quotation marks.) That's it. Now go ahead and send your mail.

## How Can I Read Usenet Needlecraft Discussions?

*Y*ou can read any of the Usenet craft newsgroups from the main menus of the Textile Arts Forum (CUSTOM 135) or the Quilters Online Forum (CUSTOM 220). Once at the main menu of either of these forums, type **USENET** to get to the newsgroups. (The Textiles Arts Forum also offers access to the very important discussion group alt.food.chocolate. Yumm.)

## How Can I Use Delphi to Download Needlecraft Software and Files from Internet?

*T*hrough the Textile Arts Forum (CUSTOM 135) on Delphi you can search Internet computers for craft-related material and tap directly into some craft computers, like that of the Prince Edward Island Crafts Council in Canada. At the forum's main menu, type **USENET** and press ENTER. You'll spot an option that will let you search Internet for keywords related to files (like "quilt" or "knitting"). Choose this option and run a search based on the topic that interests you. When your search retrieves a bunch of files, you can download any files you'd like.

You can also reach Internet by typing **INTERNET** at the forum's main menu to get to the Internet Navigator. Once there you'll be presented with a menu of some selected Internet craft information libraries and files.

You can do some Internet surfing from the main menu of the National Online Quilters forum (CUSTOM 220). To do so, type **INTERNET** at its main menu and you'll be able to access a Gopher server that will let you search the Net for software and other files.

## How Can I Tap into the World Wide Web from Delphi?

*Y*ou can access craft-related World Wide Web pages from the Textile Arts Forum (CUSTOM 135), but you won't get the splashy graphics that everyone loves about the Web. Rather, all you'll get (at least as this book goes to press) is droll text. When Delphi becomes accessible through the popular Web walker and Internet navigator Netscape, you'll be able to get the pictures too. To get to the Web pages, type **INTERNET** at the textile forum's main menu, then choose "World Wide Web Sites" from the next menu.

## How Do I Get a List of Everything That's on Delphi?

*T*here's really no way to get a list of all of Delphi's offerings. The most interesting places on the service are the hundreds of subscriber-created custom forums, and you can get a list of them. At the main menu type **CUSTOM**, then type **DIRECTORY** at the next menu.

## What Are Some Good Things on Delphi for My Family? For Me?

*D*elphi is a more adult-oriented service than other major online services, so you may want to think twice before getting your kids an account. For adults, it's a convivial place, where lots of lively people log on every night to talk to friends. The custom forums offer an ever changing roster of attractions and conversational topics. You'll find Rotarians online, several forums for nurses, a club called "Statuesque and Rubenesque," and one for the spiritually inclined called "Club Tibet." In Callahan's Saloon subscribers spill out their troubles in frothy public E-mail. All of these forums can be found through the Custom Forum menu (type **GO CUSTOM**).

You won't find much investment advice on Delphi, and the stock quotes are expensive (seven cents apiece). Nor will you find large databases full of marketing demographics or newspaper stories. You will find a wide selection of stories from Reuters and UPI news wires. Available services may change, as Delphi is in the process of revamping the service and its information content, so stay tuned.

*"Every now and then my hair color takes over and I cannot be held accountable for my actions."*
*—spotted in E-mail signature in Crafty Crafts mailing list on Internet*

*"Spent so much on the loom, I've got nothing weft"*
*—spotted in E-mail signature in Crafty Crafts mailing list on Internet*

# WHAT STITCHERS HAVE TO SAY ABOUT GENIE

"I love GEnie because of the caring I have found, not only among the quilters but in other areas of the service as well, like the cooking, genealogy, and medical roundtables. As a result of the quilters on GEnie, I've had a quilt in several national shows, learned new techniques, and progressed to a new level in quilting."—Julie Gray, Cape Coral, Florida

**"I am on GEnie almost every night keeping up with what is going on. The group [in NeedleArts] is very special because we can be open with our thoughts, ask beginner questions, or just listen and learn from each other. This is a very caring group of people."—Jane Hill, Wright-Patterson Air Force Base, Ohio**

"I've tried all the other services, and even with their glitz and graphics I don't think any of them can hold a candle to the wealth of information on GEnie. The friendships I have made and the support I have received, through smiles and tears, will last for many years to come."—Judy Smith, Washington, D.C.

**"The friendship of the women (and men!) on this board is truly outstanding, and the swaps and progressives are great fun. I also love the idea that no matter where I travel I can find someone to fabric shop with. My offline friends marvel at all we do here. This group is truly on the cutting edge of the art, and we all have time to answer each other's silly questions. I love this group! I wouldn't trade it for anything!"—Linda Fee**

"I teach and lecture about quilting around the country, and I always tell my students about my online guild on GEnie. I tell them this is the guild I attend every morning—and that I wear pajamas to meetings!—Brenda Groelz, Phillips, Nebraska

**"As a quilting teacher, I feel that GEnie helps me learn about new techniques and gives me instant access to show information. It's been great making new quilting buddies all over the world."—Karen Combs, Columbia, Tennessee**

"The wonderful, sharing people in the quilting area on GEnie make this service the very best! This is the ultimate quilting bee!"—Gloria Hansen, Hightstown, New Jersey

**"When I have a question about a project or pattern, help is only a day away (or less). —Dianna L. Whitmer, Kodiak, Alaska**

"I've learned more about quilting and sewing-machine arts from this board than I'd ever imagined. Whenever I have a question, it gets answered. Whenever I am frustrated by my lack of progress on a project, I get help and empathy. And whenever I am excited about a breakthrough, I get enthusiastic support. All without having to drive to a meeting!"—Mary Ison, Glenn Dale, Maryland

**"I've participated in swaps, led a mystery quilt group, and done an online lecture. They have all been learning experiences. I have made new friends, some of whom I've met face-to-face. Online is the place to be!"—Ellen Rosintoski**

"Here we are challenged, we are nurtured, we have strength, we are allowed to be weak, we are allowed to be wrong. So many quilt guilds are catty and political. We have no time for that."—Cozy Bendesky, Pennsylvania

# 16

## QUILTERS AROUND THE GLOBE
## CALL GENIE HOME

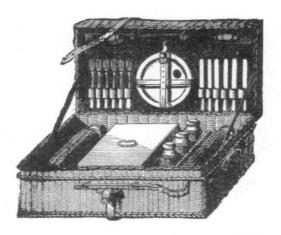

*It's not as glamorous as CompuServe or America Online—or as big—but it's one
of the hottest electronic salons for quilters and other sewers.*

Ceneral Electric's GEnie gets knocked a lot in the press. In terms of jazzy screens and Internet access it simply hasn't kept up with the America Onlines of the world. In fact, calling this consumer information service with your computer can be a hair-pulling ordeal—like logging in to an insurance company's mainframe. Still, it hosts one of the most popular quilting and sewing communities in cyberspace, thanks to the hard work of a troop of volunteers who spend dozens of hours each week uploading quilt patterns, organizing charity events, and creating the world's first multimedia needlework magazine.

"Since I've been online, I've watched the quilt-makers grow to such an extent it's almost unbelievable," says Joy McFadden, the Sacramento, California, quilter who runs GEnie's NeedleArts Roundtable. "The unconditional support that everyone gives everyone to encourage them to do the work that they'd like to do is unbelievable. It's something you don't see anywhere else. I've watched so many quilters start their own businesses, get published in national quilt magazines, and enter and win national shows—things they wouldn't have done had their friends on the board not given them the self-confidence to go out and do it." McFadden says that the attractions of the forum include its intimacy and its down-to-earth ways. "The offline craft guilds can be so political," she says. "There's no politics here."

## Enthusiasm Keeps the GEnie NeedleArts Forum Vibrant

Volunteers work hard to keep GEnie's needlecraft forum, the NeedleArts Roundtable, on the humming edge of sewing. McFadden says she sometimes spends over 16 hours a day uploading quilt block patterns, writing online newsletters, and organizing "virtual reality quilt shows," among other tasks. "Being a mother is my hobby, GEnie is my life," she jokes. Many other quilters and needle artists assist her, including the "Official NeedleArts Tech Angel" Sandy Wheeler, who contacts every new member when they log on to find out if they're having any problems with the service. *Quilter's Newsletter Magazine* is online. So are representatives of the needlework programs Electric Quilt, Quilt-Pro, and Cross-Stitch Pattern Maker, offering technical support. Several well-known quilt artists are also there, including designer Jan Cabral. "This is where the serious quilters hang out," says Brenda Groelz, of Phillips, Nebraska.

Charity events are a favorite activity. Quilters raised $14,000 for Midwest Flood Relief in 1993, which was dispersed to quilting guilds in flooded areas so that their members could replace lost supplies. During the Gulf War, members pitched in to assemble 12 quilts in patriotic themes, with everyone sewing blocks or lending expertise. One of the quilts was presented to General Norman Schwartzkopf. The story goes that he is so fond of it that he will not permit it to be displayed at quilt shows unless a GEnie-ite drives to his house and picks it up to hand deliver to the show. He will not allow it to be shipped.

Another popular activity is the "virtual reality quilt classes" in which teachers and students communicate via computer CBing: The teacher types instructions, which appear on the students' computer screens; the students type questions back, which appear on the teacher's screen, and so forth. Quilting techniques from hand appliqué to strip piecing are taught this way. GEnie even hosts an annual needlearts show and contest, in which members upload digitized images of needlework projects and compete for prizes. (If you don't have a way to digitize your project, never fear. You can mail a photo of it to a member of GEnie's needlearts digitizing team, and they'll scan it and upload it to the service for you.)

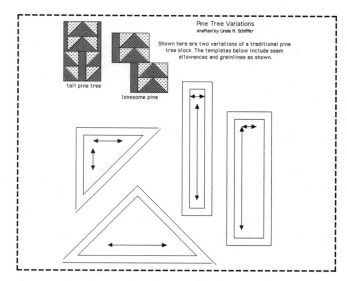

**Figure 16-1**
One of GEnie's unique attractions is its libraries of hundreds of quilt block designs like this one, available for both PCs and Macs. You don't need any special quilt software to use them. All you have to do is print them out. If you use Electric Quilt or Quilt-Pro, you'll find quilt blocks for use specifically with those programs too.

---

*Note: When Gail Ford had a hard time finding clipart to use in her needle-art designs, she created her own library of clipart. Her clipart is ideally suited for use with the Pfaff PCD software or with many other needlecraft programs. You'll find it online in GEnie's NeedleArts Software Library. Look for files SEWCLIP1.ZIP and SEWCLIP2.ZIP.*

---

## GEnie Has Special Attractions for Quilters

*I*n addition to the approximately two thousand quilters you'll meet online on GEnie, talking about everything from charm block swaps to convincing their daughters to clean their rooms, you'll also find some extraordinary quilt block libraries.

PC users will find quilt block designs stored in popular graphics formats like GIF that can be used with any basic drawing or design program including CorelDRAW!

If you use the quilt design program Electric Quilt, you especially need to get online, not only because Electric Quilt Co. offers technical support there, but because you can choose from a library of thousands of block and template patterns to download and use with the program. You'll also find shareware utilities for use with Electric Quilt, like Windows icons and a viewer that lets you view designs created in Electric Quilt even if you don't own a copy of the program.

*If you're a Macintosh user, GEnie is the place to go. You'll find hundreds of quilt blocks, along with templates and directions for assembling them, for use with SuperPaint or any Macintosh paint program.*

Figure 16-2
You'll find the first multimedia needlework magazine on GEnie. It's called *Virtual Threads* and it's assembled by stitchers on GEnie. (It's free and takes about 10 minutes to download.) Inside you'll find crochet and quilting patterns, directions for smocking and shadow appliqué projects, lots of pictures, patterns you can print out, book reviews, recipes, and more. You maneuver through this information-packed magazine by clicking on elements on the screen.

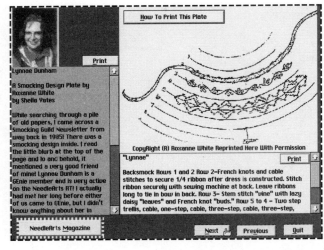

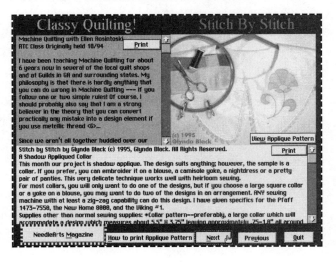

## GEnie Has a Lot for Other Stitchers Too

Quilting isn't the only game on GEnie. If you're a cross-stitcher or Pfaffie, a knitter or "wearable artist," or whether you're just interested in learning fimo, you'll find lively discussions on just about everything. They're not as well attended as those on CompuServe, but they're interesting and extremely useful nonetheless. Pfaffies will find a huge library of Pfaff stitch designs—something you won't find on other services.

For doll makers, there's a doll progression in which participants mail doll projects around the country for each person to add a personal touch. (Members are jokingly warned that some of the dolls can get pretty crazy looking, resulting in one's family wondering what kind of company you are keeping in your late-night calls to GEnie.) Another GEnie tradition is concrete gooses—the kind used as lawn or door decorations and outfitted appropriately with the passing of the seasons. You'll find patterns for dressing your concrete goose in the NeedleArts' library.

> **TIP**
> *When downloading a file from GEnie, choose Zmodem. It's the fastest file transfer protocol on the list. If it doesn't work, choose Ymodem.*

There's a monthly online needlework newsletter filled with book and product reviews by GEnie subscribers and reasonably well-stocked file libraries of needlework software and information files from Internet. There's also a database of fiber arts guilds around the world and a database of stitching magazines and books.

Public messages stay online forever, in one form or another. It's fun to capture to your computer all the messages from a particular topic for the past few years, then hang up and curl up in an armchair and read them.

## GEnie May Be Your Most Economical Way to Get Online

GEnie's rock-bottom connect prices, together with free software that's available for automating message retrieval from public conferences like the NeedleArts one, make GEnie one of the most cost-effective ways to tap into the information highway. GEnie stitchers say their connect bills average under $15 a month, even though they call every day to read the NeedleArts Roundtable and to exchange E-mail with friends on GEnie and even on other online services and Internet. That's about as cheap as you can get for using an online service so regularly. GEnie subscribers also like the fact that the message forum is well organized and they can get to the subjects they want quickly and skip the ones they don't. International links to Germany and Japan make GEnie popular with military families.

As for GEnie's lack of flashy screens à la America Online, most GEnie stitchers say they don't miss them. In fact, most subscribers started out on Prodigy or America Online and found they preferred GEnie's no-frills service. Says quilter Gale Hey of Kennewick, Washington, who has called GEnie home for years, "I just don't feel that cute graphics add anything to the online experience except time and cost."

## GEnie Can Trigger Headaches, Demand Patience

*T*he problem with GEnie, as everyone who uses it is quick to note, is that it can be a pain to use. Like chewing tinfoil, dialing GEnie is not something to look forward to, no matter what software you use to call it. Learning how to use the service requires patience and time. What's more, it can take repeated attempts just to get a modem connection.

Despite GEnie's abundance of software and information files for needlecrafters, searching and downloading these files can require the patience and persistence of an international chess whiz. GEnie doesn't offer the tools that other online services do to make searching fast and downloading easy. (For a story I wrote for a computer magazine, I clocked how long it took to search and download a certain program file on every major information service. While it took minutes on all the other services, it took an incredible two hours on GEnie, due to service glitches.) On the positive side, the NeedleArts Software Library is far better organized than other libraries on GEnie, so it may not take you two hours to download just one program.

Sending and receiving private E-mail is also trouble fraught at times. GEnie's link to Internet is extremely limited.

Every year or so a rumor goes around the computer industry that GEnie is about to fold. If it did, it wouldn't surprise some. As far as content and ease of use, GEnie's about eight years behind its many competitors. But if it did disappear, it would be a loss for stitchers, as well as other computer users in search of a truly low-cost way to talk to friends online.

Let's hope that what Mark Twain said of himself applies to GEnie as well: "The rumors of my demise are greatly exaggerated."

GENIE ONLINE SURVIVAL GUIDE

# How Do I Get the Special Software for Calling GEnie?

*Y*ou can call General Electric Information Services at 800/638-9636 (401 N. Washington St., Rockville, MD 20850) to get special navigation software and a sign-up kit to call GEnie. To run the software you need a PC that's a 386 or later (with VGA and Windows 3.1 or later) or a Mac Plus, Mac Classic, or later Mac with at least 4 MB of RAM.

If your computer is older or a different model (like an Amiga), you'll need to use a general communications program to call GEnie the first time, but that's not hard. GEnie's navigation software is primitive. Once you get online and familiarize yourself with the service, you'll want to download a copy of one of the free or shareware navigation programs like Aladdin (for PCs and Amigas) or Online Servant (for Macs) and use that instead. See pages 340–341 for directions on how to get these programs.

As this book goes to press, General Electric is creating new navigation software for calling GEnie, but don't hold your breath; past efforts haven't been too rewarding.

# What If I Need Help Installing the Software or Connecting?

Call GEnie's Client Services at 800/638-9636.

# How Do I Get Help With GEnie Once I Get Online?

*Y*ou can send a private E-mail message to NEEDLE& or JODY. Or, type **GENIEUS** at a main menu (type **TOP** to get there). If you're using the free navigation software sent to you when you signed up, choose "Online" from the top bar then "Move to Page/Keyword" and type **GENIEUS**.

# What's the Best Way to Call GEnie?

*G*Enie prices to call the service during the day traditionally have been much steeper than to call at night ($9 an hour or more!). As the online service wars continue, that may change. GEnie also charges more per hour for connecting at higher speeds (2400 bps access is cheapest). Additionally, it levies tolls for calling through certain computer long-distance calling services like SprintNet. Even calling a GEnie 800-number results in a high toll. The best strategy is to keep aware of GEnie's current prices (type **RATES** online) and know all the particulars regarding fees for the GEnie phone number you're calling (type **PHONES** online). Extra connect charges apply to certain GEnie databases (like Dun & Bradstreet). Overall, however, you're charged the same hourly fees to access everything on the service, including E-mail.

No matter what kind of computer you use, it's advisable to call GEnie with a navigation program like Aladdin or Online Servant. These programs will download messages from the public conferences you specify, then log off and let you read and reply to messages offline. Using them is *much* easier than calling GEnie with any other communications software and fighting GEnie's prompts yourself. To obtain them, see the directions in the following paragraphs.

## How Do I Get Other Special Software for Making GEnie More Pleasant to Use?

*I*f you use a PC, an Amiga, or an old Atari, you'll definitely want to get a copy of the free Aladdin software for calling the service. (Do not confuse this software with the program you got free in the mail when you signed up.) From any main conference or information menu, type **ALADDIN** (you may need to choose the Exit command off the menu you're presently on to reach a menu where this command will work). Or, if you're using the free navigation software sent to you when you signed up, choose "Online" from the top bar then "Move to Page/Keyword" and type **ALADDIN**. You'll see a menu listing the different versions of ALADDIN that you can download, including Amiga, PC, and Windows.

---

**TIP**

*GEnie frequently changes its service, as well as the Aladdin software that's used to navigate it. To guard against glitches, keep your copy of Aladdin current by occasionally checking the Aladdin Roundtable (type ALADDIN at any main prompt) to see what's happening.*

---

Aladdin will run on just about any PC, no matter how old. If you're a PC user, skip the Windows version and go for the DOS one. It's much better.

If you use a Macintosh, get a copy of the $20 shareware program Online Servant, also available on GEnie at page 606,3. It's file #1611. You can obtain more details on it by writing ONE.CLICK.

## How Do I Find Other Needlecrafters on GEnie?

$\mathcal{F}$rom any main conference or information menu, type **NEEDLE** (you may need to choose the Exit command from the menu you're presently on to reach a menu where this command will work). Or, if you're using the free navigation software sent to you when you signed up, choose "Online" from the top bar then "Move to Page/Keyword" and type **NEEDLE**. This will take you to the main menu of the NeedleArts Roundtable. Choose "NeedleArts Bulletin Board" to get to the messages. From here you'll find dozens of message topics, including sewing, smocking, toy making, cross-stitching, fiber arts, wearable arts, beading, quilting, and crafts for kids.

**If you use the free software** If you're using the free navigation software that came with GEnie when you signed up, click on a topic and you'll find message strings relating to that topic. (Hint: click on "Mail" at the top of your screen, then "List All." This will display all the messages that are in the conference. The next time you log on, you'll want to choose "List New" to display only the messages that have been written since the last time you logged in.) To answer a message, click on the reply button.

**If you call with a general communications program** If you're calling with a generic communications program, first get a list of topics by typing **INDEX**. Then save the list to disk or print it out.

Next, you'll need to set the topic category you want to read. Choose a category from the list and type **SET** *x* **ENTER** (*x* is the category number from the list).

Now type **READ**, followed by the number of the *topic* you want to read. Again, you'll need to refer to the list of topics. As you read through the messages, GEnie will prompt you, asking you whether you want to reply to a message or move on to the next one.

---

### TIP

*GEnie gives each user three different subscriber names. The subscriber ID you use to log on is a gibberish string of letters and numbers like XYZ12345. Your subscriber name (like PAM, for example) is the name that people use to send you E-mail. (It's also the name you use to turn your GEnie address into an Internet one, as in pam@genie.geis.com.) Your third name is a nickname. When you tap into a conference like NeedleArts, you can change your subscriber name to any nickname you wish. To do so, log on with a general communications program. When you get to the bulletin board area of the roundtable, type NAM and press ENTER, then type the nickname you want and press ENTER again. That will set your nickname permanently for that forum.*

---

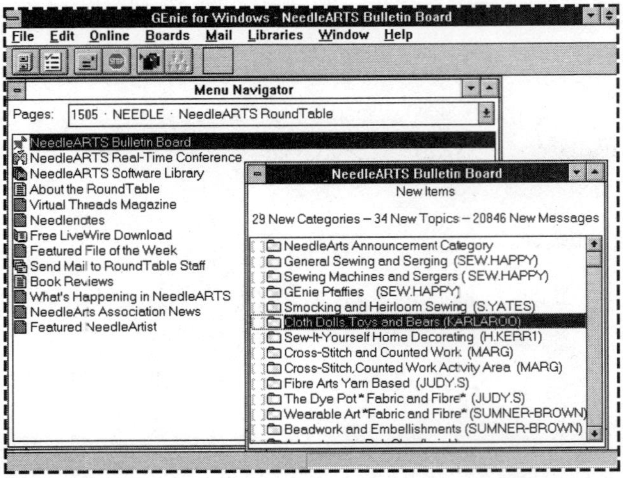

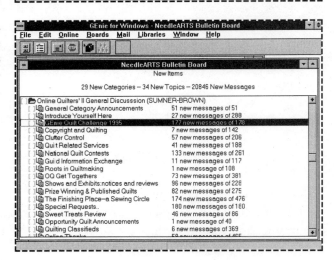

**Figure 16-3**
If you can't find a discussion on GEnie that you're interested in, you're on the wrong planet.

**Figure 16-4**
Pick your way through the discussion threads in the NeedleArts Roundtable using GEnie's free navigation software.

# How Do I Send a Private E-mail Message?

*F*rom any main conference or information menu, type **MAIL** (you may need to choose the Exit command from the menu you're presently on to reach a menu where this command will work), then choose "6. Compose and Send GE Mail Online" at the mail menu. Or, if you're using the free navigation software sent to you when you signed up, choose "Mail" from the top bar then "Create New Mail."

Enter the recipient's GEnie ID or Internet address at the To: prompt (remember to add **@#inet** to the end of the address if it's an Internet address). When you're through typing the message, click "Send Now" if you're using the free navigation software. If you're using a general communications prompt, type **\*S** alone at the beginning of a line to end the message and send it.

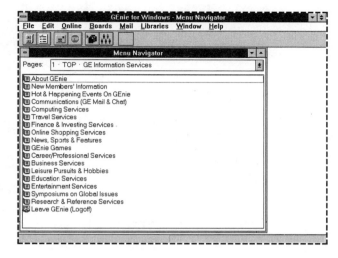

**Figure 16-5**
**Sending a private E-mail message with GEnie's free navigation software is fairly easy. If you call with a general communications program, it's a bit more ticklish. You need to remember to type *S to send the message. GEnie can take awhile to respond to your commands.**

# Where Can I Find Needlecraft Software, Patterns, and Clipart for Use in My Needlecraft Designs?

## *The NeedleArts Roundtable Software and Clipart Libraries*

These libraries are your best source for clipart, as well as needlecraft software and information files. You'll find clipart of hearts, sewing birds, baskets, floral borders, and other art suited to needlework. To get there from any main conference or information menu, type **NEEDLE** (you may need to choose the Exit command from the menu you're presently on to reach a menu where this command will work).

If you're using the free navigation software sent to you when you signed up, choose "Online" from the top bar then "Move to Page/Keyword" and type **NEEDLE**. This will take you to the main menu of the NeedleArts Roundtable. Choose "NeedleArts Software Library." If you're using the GEnie navigation software, a list of the different libraries will appear. To begin browsing one, click on a name. The libraries range from text and information files to "yarn-based design files." You'll find all the clipart in Design/Paint/Clipart, including Gail Ford's special needlecraft clipart libraries stored as SEWCLIP1.ZIP and SEWCLIP2.ZIP.

If you're using a general communications program, when you enter the NeedleArts library a list of menu choices will appear. Pick "8. Set Software Library." This will display a list of the libraries. Choose the one you want, then select "Browse" or "Search." Browse will display a description of each file in the library. (Going through a library with Browse can be a slow process.) By choosing "Search" you can search the library by typing in words like "flying geese quilt."

GEnie will prompt you, asking if you want to download a file. When you say yes, it will ask you what file transfer protocol you want to use. Pick Zmodem. If that doesn't work, try Ymodem. You may have to issue a command to your communications software to receive the file (a simple command found in its help file or manual), or try using the PGDN key or a "Download" or "Receive" menu command.

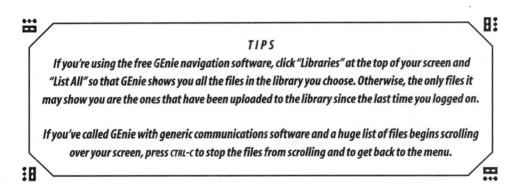

**TIPS**

*If you're using the free GEnie navigation software, click "Libraries" at the top of your screen and "List All" so that GEnie shows you all the files in the library you choose. Otherwise, the only files it may show you are the ones that have been uploaded to the library since the last time you logged on.*

*If you've called GEnie with generic communications software and a huge list of files begins scrolling over your screen, press CTRL-C to stop the files from scrolling and to get back to the menu.*

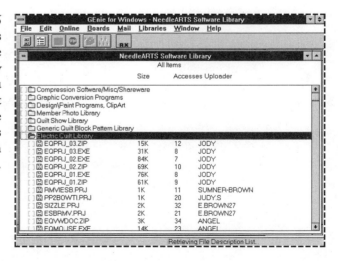

**Figure 16-6**
When you enter the NeedleArts Software Library, depending on the software you're using GEnie may display a big list of files. It's up to you to sift through the list and figure out which files you want. This figure shows a list of quilt block patterns that you can download and use with Electric Quilt design software.

## *More Graphics Libraries*

To get to a more general graphics library, type **GRAPHICS** at any main menu. Or, if you're using the free navigation software, choose "Online" from the top bar then "Move to Page/Keyword" and type **GRAPHICS**. From the menu choose "Graphic Images Software Library," then click "Lexicor Library." You'll find GIF and JPG images, although the library isn't huge and, unlike CompuServe, you can't view the files until after you download them.

# How Do I Get Back to GEnie's Main Menu If I Get Lost?

*F*rom any main conference or information menu, type **TOP** (you may need to choose the Exit command from the menu you're presently on to reach a menu where this command will work). Or, if you're using the free navigation software sent to you when you signed up, choose "Online" from the top bar then "Move to Page/Keyword" and type **TOP**.

# How Do I Get General Computer Help on GEnie?

*F*rom the main menu (type **TOP** to get there), type **COMPUTING**. If you're using the free navigation software sent to you when you signed up, choose "Online" from the top bar then "Move to Page/Keyword" and type **COMPUTING**. You'll get a menu listing public

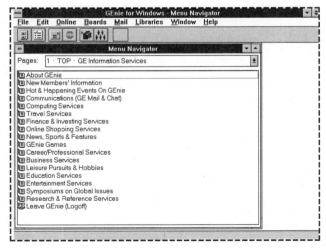

Figure 16-7
This is what GEnie's main menu looks like when you call the service with the free Windows navigation software. Type TOP at most any prompt to get here.

conferences for Apples, Ataris, Commodores, Macintoshes, PCs, and Amigas. You'll find help in any of these forums.

## How Do I Get a List of GEnie's Latest Prices?

*F*rom any main conference or information menu, type **RATES** (you may need to choose the Exit command from the menu you're presently on to reach a menu where this command will work). If you're using the free navigation software sent to you when you signed up, choose "Online" from the top bar then "Move to Page/Keyword" and type **RATES**.

## How Do I Use GEnie to Get to Needlecraft Goodies on Internet?

*A*s this book goes to press, GEnie has just unveiled its new Internet access, including Usenet newsgroups, Web surfing, Gopher, and FTP file access. However, using it is tough and most elements aren't working. Considering GEnie's track record, don't hold your breath on getting flashy Internet access anytime soon. To get to GEnie's main Internet menu, go to page 5000.

You can send mail to friends on other online services, and also on Internet through GEnie's Internet E-mail gateway, with *moderate* reliability. You can also participate in Internet mailing lists and receive Internet FAQs by mail. You can even read some Usenet craft newsgroups through E-mail. (See Chapter 18 for more information.)

## How Do I Send Mail to Internet and Participate in Internet Craft Mailing Lists?

*U*sing GEnie to send and receive E-mail via Internet is a bit more convoluted than it is on other online services. That's because when you send an E-mail message to someone on Internet, you must add to their address the suffix **@inet#**. For instance, if the recipient's Internet address is **angela@mcimail.com**, to send Angela a message from GEnie, you would address it to **angela@mcimail.com@inet#**.

Similarly, if Angela wants to send you mail through Internet, she would suffix your GEnie subscriber ID with **@genie.geis.com**. If your GEnie ID is **melissa**, your Internet address would be **melissa@genie.geis.com**.

Otherwise, you would write and send the message as you'd send any other private E-mail message on GEnie. You would insert the Internet address in the TO: field.

Many quilters participate in the Internet mailing list QuiltNet from GEnie, but they need to be careful that when they send mail to the list for broadcast, they are sending it to the proper address (appending the **@inet#** suffix to the mailing list's Internet address).

See Chapter 18 for more information on subscribing to QuiltNet and other craft mailing lists.

## How Do I Get a List of Everything That's on GEnie?

*F*rom any main conference or information menu, type **INDEX** (you may need to choose the Exit command from the menu you're presently on to reach a menu where this command will work). Or, if you're using the free navigation software sent to you when you signed up, choose "Online" from the top bar then "Move to Page/Keyword" and type **INDEX**.

## What Are Some Good Things on GEnie for My Family?

*T*he family member who can't bear to part with his Commodore will find other "classic" computer owners online (type **COMPUTING** at any main prompt). The Outdoors Roundtable offers lively banter on bicycling, hiking, and more (type **OUTDOORS** at any main prompt). In fact, you'll find a public conference devoted to just about every hobby and leisure pursuit you can imagine, from stamp collecting to model railroads (type **LEISURE** at any main prompt). The Star Trek conferences are especially popular on GEnie.

## How About Other Good Things for Me?

*T*he Small Business and Home Office Roundtable is probably the best such public message forum of its kind available online for small-time operators (type **HOSB** at any main prompt). The investment forum is also good (type **INVEST**). In the Arts & Crafts Roundtable you'll find lots of information about rubber stamping, polyclay, and folk arts (type **CRAFTS**).

# MICROSOFT NETWORK WELCOMES QUILTERS, SEWERS, AND OTHER FABRIC JUNKIES

*This sizzling new online service for Windows 95 users offers an oasis of sparkling graphics and cheer for textile=holics.*

Microsoft Network promises to be one of the leading online services of the '90s. It's rich with beautiful graphics, lightning fast so you're not drumming the keyboard while screens update, and it offers meeting spots for quilters and other crafters.

To access Microsoft Network, you need Windows 95 and a powerful PC (ideally a 486 or faster). If you've got the right equipment, your reward will be an online service that's as easy to use as Windows, with the look and feel of the Windows' desktop.

Microsoft Network offers sophisticated E-mail tools that until now have been virtually unheard of in the mass-market online world: You can add photos, artwork, and sound to E-mail messages by dragging and dropping these extras into your messages (quilters will love that). You can link spreadsheets, charts, and software to your messages so that recipients can

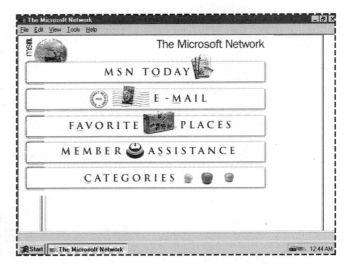

**Figure 17-1**
Microsoft Network may become
one of the leading online services
of the twenty-first century.

download them simply by clicking on an icon in the message. You can also visit multiple areas of the service at once and cut and paste text between the areas as you write messages. Internet access is part of the bargain too.

For stitchers Microsoft Network offers several needlework forums. Although the service is still very new (only a handful of stitchers are online as this book goes to press), expect the traffic to be heavy. Overall, the service's fare is family oriented, with public forums spanning topics from hobbies to the arts and sciences and family issues. Its success will depend on how fast Windows 95 gains popularity; its price of $1 to $2.50 is a bargain that is sure to attract many subscribers. Overall, it's a beautiful looking service, and I wouldn't be surprised if it becomes a favorite meeting spot for stitchers.

## How Do I Log on to Microsoft Network?

*Y*ou need a modem and Windows 95 installed on your computer. To sign on, you can either click the "Online Registration" button on the "Welcome to Windows 95" screen that appears when you turn on your computer, or you can click "Start" at the bottom lefthand corner of the screen, head to "Programs," then select "The Microsoft Network." You'll be prompted for your credit card number, your address, and a password. Once you have filled out the on-screen forms, your software will log you on to the service and you'll be ready to go.

For further information contact Microsoft Corporation (800/386-5550, 1 Microsoft Way, Redmond, WA 98052).

Administrative support is available from 8 a.m. to 5 p.m. PST weekdays at 503/245-0905. Technical support is available from 6 a.m. to 6 p.m. PST weekdays at 206/635-7110.

# How Do I Find Other Needlecrafters on Microsoft Network?

Once you're logged on to Microsoft Network, click "Categories" on the main screen. Choose "Interests, Leisure & Hobbies" (see Figure 17-2). Point and click on the "Arts & Crafts" icon, then the "Stitch" one. At the next screen you can choose from Quilting, Sewing or assorted Needle Arts discussions (see Figure 17-3). You'll find pictures of other crafters' projects, applicable software and Internet newsgroups, and messages from other crafters.

**Figure 17-2**
Click on the "Hobbies" icon in the Categories menu to get to the crafts and textile forums.

**Figure 17-3**
Microsoft Network lets stitchers communicate in a BBS style but with powerful tools like the ability to add graphics and even sound to messages.

# 18

## INTERNET IS FOR THE WIRED CRAFTER

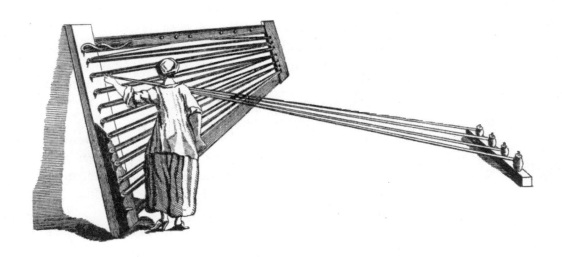

*This anarchic, postmilitary, computer genius hangout has become a land of riches for quilters, weavers, couturiers, and anyone who wants to make Lava Lamps.*

Everyone is talking about Internet these days. From elected officials to TV hosts, it seems like everyone is logged into the "Net," as modem jocks call it. The Net is suddenly very chic. It's where Al Gore picks up his E-mail. Internet E-mail addresses are popping up on business cards all over. Books on it are selling like hotcakes, and there's more than one trendy magazine devoted to it.

But the question is this: Do *you* need to become a Net surfer?

Internet is not a computer information service in the traditional sense; it is an anarchic web of computer links between universities, corporations, and government offices. It is the haunt of sewing educators, fiber artists, and costumers. It's also filled with college faculty and students who are most likely to have free access to it through their university computers. However, more and more average folk are showing up on the Net, especially in the needle-craft discussions. The worldwide computer party line that is the Internet has grown increasingly accessible to the general public over the past couple of years.

Internet offers crafters some of the most free-ranging, eclectic discussions about needle-crafts in the online world. You'll read about everything from how to braid onions and garlic to how to sew costumes for reenactments of the Boer War. You'll find information files, called "FAQs" (frequently asked questions), with answers to all the questions a crafter could ever have, from recommendations on good books about ethnic clothing to lists of mail-order sources for bugle beads. In fact, the best thing about Internet is not all those high-powered databases you hear about (with a few exceptions, most of them are university databases with highly specialized subjects). The best thing is that you'll meet all kinds of people who will generously share their wisdom with you. The Internet also offers private E-mail that you can send to practically any-one, on any computer network in the world, be they in Chicago or Uzbekistan.

All the commercial online services offer subscribers access to Internet in varying degrees and for varying prices, with both changing all the time. All of the services also permit sub-scribers to send and receive private E-mail from Internet. This means you can use the Internet to send E-mail from your online account with one commercial service, like Compu-Serve, to friends on a completely different service, like Prodigy. And your friends can send mail to you, too. (See "How to Send E-Mail to Needlecrafters on Other Online Services" in the Appendix for specific directions.)

Most of the services (if not all by the time you read this) provide access to Internet's lively public discussions, called "Usenet newsgroups." A few (Delphi, America Online, Compu-Serve, and Prodigy) actually let you use Internet to tap into other computers around the world. You can dial into America Online, for instance, and, using its Internet link, tap into home economics class lists stored on a computer in a vocational school in South Africa or download quilt-making software from computers in Australia.

One of Internet's big advantages for consumers is that it can be considerably cheaper to use than commercial online services. Companies that provide access to the Internet, called "Internet providers," are springing up in communities around the country. You can now get low-cost access to the Net for $15 to $25 per month, including anywhere from 10 hours to unlimited monthly access time. That's a bunch cheaper than the $25 to $75 per month many people ring up using CompuServe, or the other big-name services. Many businesses are also providing their employees with free access to the Internet through the company computer network. (See "How to Find an Internet Service in Your Community" in this chapter for more information on selecting an access provider.)

This chapter is a guide to all the different kinds of needlecraft information you'll find on Internet. But one caveat: The Net changes faster than the weather. Almost every time I write about this section of the information highway I find that the roadmap has changed significantly by the time my story appears. In addition, the variety of craft information and discussions has been mushrooming, and there will surely be more than what's in this chapter by the time this book gets into your hands.

Frankly, I think it's very ironic. Internet was designed for the Pentagon and defense contractors to talk to each other about attack helicopters. Now look what it's become: a haven for needlecrafters, whose most aggressive act is driving too fast to get to a craft store sale. Who says civilization isn't progressing?

## Use Internet to Send Electronic Mail to Anyone, Anywhere, Even on Other Online Services

*I*f this book inspires you to do nothing more than send E-mail over Internet, I will consider my mission accomplished. If you can send E-mail, you can tap into the wealth of information on the Net.

You can use Internet to send E-mail to just about anyone in the world, even people on computer services you don't subscribe to. As illustrated in this chapter, you can also use it to send messages to computers connected to the Internet and get them to send you information.

You can use Internet to send mail to your son or daughter at college or at a military base overseas. You can even send E-mail to your spouse at work if his or her office computer is connected to the Net. Internet is the postal service of the computer world. Delivery usually occurs in minutes, although it can take a day or more if the message is going overseas or to South America.

> *Note: How private is the E-mail you send over Internet? Not very. Your E-mail will zigzag through computers all over the country (and possibly the world), taking an often circuitous route to its destination. Anyone who runs the computer that routes it can read it. Still, it beats the U.S. Postal Service in many ways, not the least of which are price and speed.*

The chapters on the commercial online services provide specific directions on how to send Internet mail from each of the services. It's really not hard. All you'll need to know is the recipient's Internet address and your own (your Internet address will be different from your personal address or ID on the computer service you subscribe to) so they can write you back. Though there are some variations, here, in order, are the basic parts of an Internet address:

- ✒ Your name or subscriber ID on the computer service you belong to, for example, Martha Jones or Toodles.

- ✒ The "at" sign (@), followed by the name of your service, like Netcom, CompuServe, Prodigy, and so on, with the service name followed by a period.

- ✒ A period, followed by a code specifying whether the computer is a commercial online service (com) or a school (edu), military (mil), or government (gov) computer network.

- ✒ Finally, sometimes a period followed by a designation for a particular country, like "uk" for United Kingdom or "us" for United States if the message is traveling outside the country of its origin.

*Note: As long as your E-mail isn't destined for some obscure country, it doesn't matter whether you type the E-mail address in upper or lowercase letters.* ✒

For example, if your name is Martha Jones, you subscribe to Prodigy, and your Prodigy ID is martha, you would tell people your Internet address is "Martha at prodigy dot com." It would look like this:

martha@prodigy.com

See "How to Send E-mail to Needlecrafters on Other Online Services" in the Appendix for more directions and advice on sending E-mail between major online services.

## For Truly Empowering Needlecraft Information, Subscribe to Internet Mailing Lists from Your Home or Office PC

*W*hen most people think of Internet, they think of tripping the light fantastic on some gossamer modem highway, bopping from computer to computer, keying in mystic, hackerish commands. In reality, you'll discover the most valuable crafting information and enjoy the most scintillating conversations in relatively simple Internet mailing lists. And you don't need any special software to tap into them. Heck, you don't even need to know much about Internet to hop on the I-Way.

Internet mailing lists are quasi-private group discussions on specialized topics, like the making of wearable art, running a home-based craft business, or sewing fantasy costumes. It might help to think about Internet mailing lists as a kind of forever-growing chain letter traveling between interested people. Someone raises a topic, a huge bunch of people weigh in with their thoughts or comments, and soon that one comment has generated hundreds or thousands of messages.

Mailing lists are similar to the discussions that arise on an office computer network. Someone raises an important issue in an E-mail message and copies that message to a dozen or more employees. Those people reply via E-mail, copying their messages to everyone in the mailing list, and soon you have a discussion of the issues involved that is more incisive than any debate during an office meeting.

A mailing list may have hundreds of participants. Rather than going to some specific area of a computer service, participants find messages waiting for them each day in their private E-mail box on their online service. That service may be CompuServe, Prodigy, America Online, GEnie, or even business E-mail providers like AT&T Mail or MCI Mail. Many office computer networks also qualify. In fact, the majority of crafters who subscribe to Internet's needlecraft mailing lists are tapping in through their office PCs. Isn't that amazing? You can take a break from your overload of work E-mail and enjoy reading a few messages about knitting socks.

To join a mailing list, you send an E-mail message from whatever online service you subscribe to (or your office computer network if the network allows you to send Internet mail) to a computer on the Net. That subscription request will be read and processed either by the computer or by an individual running the mailing list. It depends on the list. Once you've been added to the subscriber roster, the computer will send you all the messages from other participants on the list daily. To participate in the discussion, you write an E-mail message and send it to the computer, and the computer distributes it to all the list's subscribers.

**TIP**

*Mailing lists generate anywhere from a couple of messages a day to hundreds a week. This can be a problem only if the online service you subscribe to charges for each piece of E-mail you receive over Internet. In that case, you'll need to ask that the mailing list computer send you a compilation of the messages, or a "digest," each day rather than mailing each complete message to you individually. (Directions on how to do that will be E-mailed to you when you subscribe to the mailing list.) This digest will come to you as one huge E-mail message with the full text of all the messages written that day to the mailing list. You should also set up your communications software to automatically log on, download the messages, and then log off, so you can read and reply to the messages offline.*

---

*Lirene, an American quilter who lives in Nagoya, Japan, dials America Online in the United States. But, as much as she'd like to, she doesn't participate in the quilting discussions on that service. That's too expensive at $1/minute in long-distance charges. Instead, she saves money by subscribing to Internet's wearable arts mailing list, where conversations span a wide range of sewing topics, from how to buy a dress mannequin to the copyrights on sewing patterns.*

 *The messages are deposited each day in her private E-mail box on America Online. She logs on, downloads the messages, and then hangs up. She reads and responds to the discussion "offline," when she isn't connected to the computer service by an expensive long-distance call. "I like the wearable arts mailing list because the message traffic isn't too heavy," says Lirene, "and there is some really useful information in it."*

# How to Find an Internet Service in Your Community

*S*elling direct Internet access to computer users is the latest cottage business craze, and it should come as no surprise that not all Internet services are created equal. To find out if there's an Internet service in your community (a local one means a local phone call), start by asking at computer users' clubs or computer stores. For more information, send an E-mail message to **info-deli-server@netcom**, typing **send pdial** in the body of the message. You'll get a list of some Internet services in reply.

Here's what you should ask when you call to inquire about the different services:

What are the charges? Is there any set-up fee? Are there monthly or hourly charges? Are there any extra charges for sending or receiving E-mail? Is there toll-free access, or are there extra charges for calling through some service like SprintNet or Tymnet? Are there any extra fees for high-speed access?

What kind of software will I get? Will I have to pay extra for it? What kind of documentation will I get? (I know one computer user who, when he signed up with a service, received some ridiculous freeware utility on a floppy disk with a hand-printed card explaining how to copy it to his hard disk—that was the software and the extent of its documentation.)

Will I get Web access?

Will I also get E-mail, FTP, gopher, and Usenet access?

Is there a tech support number I can call for help installing the software and making the connection? When can I call?

Will I encounter busy signals when I call during peak hours, like evenings and weekends?

What is the service's connection capacity to Internet? (It should be a T1 line for local service, T3 for regional.)

> *Note: Everyone's favorite Internet service these days is Netcom via its NetCruiser interface. Set-up fee is $25, with a monthly fee of $19.95 and unlimited usage in the evening (800/501-8649).*

How about those Internet-in-a-box deals you see in bookstores? Are they worth it? *PC World* testers judged Spry's $149 Internet in a Box the best deal, even with its relatively high price tag. It offers good Internet tools, discount coupons for several service providers, and Ed Krol's "The Whole Internet User's Guide and Catalog" (O'Reilly & Associates, Sebastopol, CA), which is my first pick for the best Internet book around. Would *I* personally buy it? Probably not. I'd rather discover Internet through lower-cost methods, like experimenting with a major online service or subscribing to a low-cost service in my community.

# Ten Tips About Joining Internet Craft Mailing Lists

Mailing lists are really where the action is on Internet. Participating in their discussions is different from joining discussions on commercial computer services, though. For one, the messages come to you; you don't have to hunt for them. Here are some tips to get you started with mailing lists:

1   **To subscribe to a mailing list you will send an E-mail message to a particular Internet address.** Either a computer or a human will process your message. Always read and follow the directions closely for subscribing. If your subscription message is returned as undeliverable, check the E-mail address you used and reread the directions carefully. Most messages are returned because the address was typed wrong. Also, check the words you used in the body of the message. One misplaced or misspelled word, or even an extra space, could be the cause of the rejection. Always try again.

2   **Once subscribed to a mailing list, you will receive a welcome message with directions on how to participate in the discussion.** Read the directions, then *print them out and save them for future reference. This is important!* You will need these directions in order to unsubscribe to the list (like when you're on vacation and don't want E-mail to overrun your mail box). You'll also need the directions to get back-dated messages from the computer running the mailing list, and for other chores.

　　The welcome letter will also tell you what kinds of messages are appropriate. For instance, it is forbidden to broadcast commercial solicitations or announcements to a mailing list. If you lose the list's directions, try sending a message with just the word "help" or "info" in its body to the original Internet address that you subscribed to.

3   **All mailing list messages are sent to and from Internet,** so be sure you're familiar with the Internet E-mail link you used to subscribe to the list.

4   **Be aware that mailing lists have several different E-mail addresses.** There's the E-mail address you sent your original subscription request to. When you post a message to everyone on the list, you send it to another address. The person who runs the mailing list also has her own administrative E-mail address. *Know what these addresses are and what they're used for.* You won't want to send administrative commands to the address for E-mail, thus broadcasting the commands to everyone on the list. That welcome message you (hopefully) printed out will spell out which address is which.

5   **When you reply to a message from a mailing list, your communications software may not necessarily send it to the right address** if you just click on its "Reply" command. Know the proper address for mailing list replies and make sure your software is sending it there. Also, if you want to respond via private E-mail to a message, avoid embarrassment and make sure that the message is going to the recipient's private E-mail address and not being broadcast to everyone on the mailing list!

6   **Always sign your messages with your name and your own personal Internet E-mail address** so that others can easily spot your address if they want to answer you personally. That way they won't have to go looking for your address in the long routing information (called a "header") at the top of the message. In fact, many mail readers delete that header.

7   **Remember that many crafters who subscribe to these lists are receiving the mail at their offices.** Be courteous and broadcast to an entire mailing list only mail that will be of interest to the majority of subscribers. Do not send personal notes, thank-yous, or requests for followup information to everyone on the list. Preface the subject of your message with a word that indicates it's from the list—like "wearables:" or "knit:"—and make the rest of the subject clear and meaningful. That way, office PC users will be able to distinguish their mailing list E-mail from their business mail, and all recipients can easily sort through the messages they want to read.

8   **If a message you send to the mailing list comes bouncing back to you, check the E-mail address and try sending it again.**

9   **Sometimes the computers that run mailing lists offer additional information on the subject,** including back messages, message digests, and sometimes files and FAQs. The welcome letter that arrives when you subscribe will tell you how to send commands to the mailing list computer so that it will send you this information.

10   **Remember that volunteers run the mailing lists, often investing lots of time, and sometimes money.** Please try to make their lives easier by first following the directions in the welcome sheet before contacting them and asking for help. Follow the rules they set for the discussion, and always be polite.

Participating in the wonderful Internet mailing list discussions is really much easier than it might appear. If you can send and receive an E-mail message from your computer you're most of the way there.

Below are descriptions of all the Internet needlecraft mailing lists and directions on how to subscribe to each. The only thing you'll need to know before you use them is how to send an Internet E-mail message from your computer or the computer service you're subscribed to. (Head to the chapters on individual online services for directions on how to do that.) You don't have to be anyone special to subscribe to these lists, all you need to do is send an E-mail message to the computer (or person) that traffics the mail.

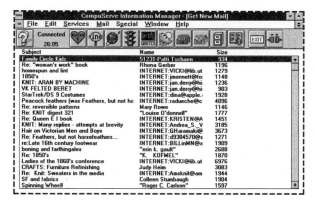

**Figure 18-1**
This is what my CompuServe E-mail box looked like each morning after I subscribed to a batch of needlecraft mailing lists. Messages on Aran knits, 19th century women's clothing, and furniture refinishing arrived in my mailbox throughout the day. It took just minutes for me to download all these messages (about 50) so that I could read them offline (when the time charge clock wasn't ticking), using CompuServe Information Manager.

> **Note:** *Many Internet craft-related mailing lists are run from office computers, often with the employer's approval, but sometimes with the boss "looking the other way." For that reason, some of these lists are transient in nature, disappearing overnight, or suddenly moving to another Internet location.*

## *Knitters Pick Up Stitches and Friends on KnitNet*

Warm-hearted, witty banter is the fare on KnitNet, the premier spot for knitters on the infobahn, run by a programmer-analyst named Jill at supercomputer maker Cray Research. Subscribe to KnitNet and your E-mail box will be filled with daily vivacious musings on Fair Isle knits, Shetland versus Merino wool, the peculiar hand-knitting practices in *Addams Family Values,* and the replicator versus hand-knitting controversy regarding the starship *Enterprise.* A recent conversation analyzed the technical plausibility of mystery novel scenarios in which knitting needles are the murder weapon. (For some reason I get the feeling that many of the people on this list are librarians.) Patterns and pattern advice are also part of the repartee. Perfect coffee-break material! Message volume is high, so you may want to order the digest form.

To sign up, send an Internet E-mail message to

listserv@geom.umn.edu

The only line in the message should be

subscribe knit *YourFirstName LastName*

For example,

subscribe knit Polly Smith

To send a message to everyone on the mailing list, address it to

knit@geom.umn.edu

To request that the mailing list computer send you one big E-mail message each day rather than 40 or 50 separate ones, send a message to

listserve@geom.umn.edu

The only line in the message should be

set knit mail digest

## Machine Knitters Share Secrets in Their Mailing List

Machine knitters are united by anxieties unknown to most of the human race. Problems like how to generate Aran knits on a machine that sometimes behaves like a pasta maker with sheep fur for brains or how not to be regarded as a kook by neighbors who hear you scream in the night, "Do that one more time, snookums, and I'll knit the darn cables on a pair of #2 needles myself!"

To sign up for the Machine Knitters mailing list, send an Internet E-mail message to

amys@iquest.net

Leave the subject line blank (or type a period), and type in the body of the message

sub machknit *YourFirstName LastName*

If you have trouble subscribing, you can also send a personal E-mail message to the list's owner Amy Stinson at the same address.

## How to Search the Internet for More Stitching Tips

You can easily search the Internet for things that interest you by heading to one of the many "searchers." My favorite is Excite! at **http://www.excite.com/**. Another good searcher is DejaNews at **http://www.dejanews.com/**. While Excite! is good for searching the Web, DejaNews will search archives of Usenet messages for ones that interest you. (Usenet is that large collection of public messages that swirls through the Internet.)

To sign up, send an Internet E-mail message to

listproc@seas.gwu.edu

The only line in the message should be

subscribe k1p1_list *YourFirstName LastName*

To send a message to everyone on the mailing list, address it to

k1p1_list@seas.gwu.edu

## *QuiltNet Offers Quilters Yet Another Way to Socialize Wildly*

Quilters are an awfully chatty bunch. As such, they have found more ways to socialize on the info highway than physicists, mathematicians, and *Star Trek* fans put together. QuiltNet is one place they visit for a daily sprinkling of fact, gossip, and hearsay on all the things quilters love to talk about. (Attention Trekkers: making *Star Trek* quilt blocks is a common topic.) QuiltNet's high volume of mail and large number of participants have made it one of the biggest mailing lists on Internet, so be sure that you subscribe to the digest version or your mailbox will be swamped with messages. (If your interest is in quilt swaps, see the next mailing list.)

To sign up, send an Internet E-mail message with the subject "quiltnet" to

listserv@ukcc.uky.edu

The only line in the message should be

sub quiltnet *YourFirstName LastName*

Once the computer receives your request, it will send you an electronic form letter asking you to verify your subscription, to which you must reply within 48 hours. You'll find a confirmation code in the text or subject line of this form letter. Make a note of it; you may need it later. Use your communications software to reply to the message. The only line in the message should be

ok

If the message is returned to you, send another reply. The only line in the message should be

ok *confirmation code*

To send a message to everyone on the mailing list, address it to

quiltnet@ukcc.uky.edu

Because of the high volume of E-mail that swirls around on QuiltNet, you may want to request that the QuiltNet computer send you a daily digest of the messages rather than individual messages. To do this, send a message to

listserv@ukcc.uky.edu

The only line in the message should be

set quiltnet digest

However, be aware that some online services will chop a message digest short if it's too long for their mail processors to handle.

> *Note: When responding to digested E-mail, be especially careful that the E-mail address your software is sending the message to is the one you intended.*

## *Quilters Swap Goodies Through the Quilt-Exchange List*

In addition to being vivacious, another sign of serious quilters is that they love to give gifts. Not surprising, since the gift of a quilt is probably the ultimate gift of time, art, and craftsmanship.

As with the commercial online services, quilters on the Net exchange a flurry of blocks, notions, and birthday gifts on a regular schedule known as a "swap." The Quilt-Exchange list was formed when messages about swaps flooded the mailboxes of everyone on QuiltNet, and it has the schedules for Internet-wide swaps of gifts, notions, blocks, and fabric, along with any messages pertaining to the swaps. (If you sign up, be careful, or you'll run your credit card past its limit in three months.)

To sign up and start buying enough presents to outfit every quilt guild in Iowa, send an Internet E-mail message to

listserv@ukcc.uky.edu

The only line in the message should be

sub q-xchg *YourFirstName LastName*

Once the computer receives your request, it will send you an electronic form letter asking you to verify your subscription, to which you must reply within 48 hours. You'll find a confirmation code in the text or subject of this letter. Make a note of it, because you may need it later. Reply to the form letter by sending the message

ok

If the message is returned to you, send another reply. The only line in the message should be

ok *confirmation code*

To send a message to everyone on the mailing list, address it to

q-xchg@ukcc.uky.edu

You may prefer to receive a daily digest of the E-mail messages rather than each individual message. To do this, send a message to

listserv@ukcc.uky.edu

The only line in the message should be

set q-xchg digest

## The Nontraditional Quilting List Offers Quilters a New Way of Seeing

Quilt artists wary of the high volume of messages they'll receive if they sign up with QuiltNet should try the Nontraditional Quilting list. This list is for daring quilters who prefer not to get hundreds of E-mail messages that "discuss their hubbies and kitties at length," quips founder Marie-Christine Mahe. (She has a point. QuiltNet members like to discuss whether the "cat goddess and the quilt goddess are in harmony.") "This of course makes us into curmudgeons," says Mahe, "but then we have a much higher signal-to-noise ratio [than the other lists] and real quilting info." A show of quilts designed around an Internet theme and assembled by subscribers to this list has been touring the country. The Nontraditional list likes to keep its membership low.

To sign up with the Nontraditional list, send an Internet E-mail message to

listserv@yalevm.cis.yale.edu

The only line in the message should be

subscribe notrad-l *YourFirstName LastName*

You won't become a subscriber as soon as your message is received. Instead, once the computer receives your message, it will send you information about the list and ask if you really want to join. You'll need to answer "yes" before you're actually added to the list.

To send a message to everyone on the mailing list, address it to

notrad-l@yalevm.cis.yale.edu

## Interquilt Helps Quilters Through Bad Hair Days and UFOs

You can never have too much of a good thing. That's true of fabric, yarn, quilt projects, and also of E-mail with other quilters. InterQuilt strives for an even more casual atmosphere than the other quilt mail lists. "If you've had a bad hair day, tell us about it," the welcome letter encourages. "You MUST LIKE to receive mail! You MUST ENJOY reading Thank-yous and chitchat!" The list concentrates on topics that obsess all quilters—fabric, shows, shops, patterns, and UFOs (or "unfinished objects" in Internet craft parlance). The only rule is "No whining." Membership cards with the InterQuilt logo and your name in laser foil are available. Pretty cool.

To join, send a personal E-mail note with "IQ" in the subject line to Melissa Bishop at

mbshop@needles.com

or visit their Web site at

http://kbs.net/tt/

This list does have a membership fee—$21 per year. Once you've paid your fee (Tangled Threads, 475 Mill Rd., Coram, Long Island, New York 11727-4137; 516/736-0320), Melissa will send you directions on how to send messages to the other members.

*Note: This mailing list is maintained by a person, not a computer, so please don't send any messages with commands that are normally processed by a computer.*

## *Electric Quilt Users Share Tips Through Their Own Mailing List*

Electric Quilt is the premier quilt design software with leagues of fans. Subscribe to this mailing list, and you'll learn tech tricks you'll never see in any computer magazine, like how to create 50,000 Dresden plate variations in 15 seconds, and how to design isometric blocks with soul. Every technical question and problem you could possibly have will be answered here within hours. You might want to request the digest version, because message traffic gets heavy.

To join, send an Internet E-mail message to

mailserv@grove.iup.edu

The only line in the message should be

subscribe info-eq

To send a message to everyone on the mailing list, address it to

info-eq@grove.iup.edu

## *Sewers with Serious Style Keep in Touch Through Wearable Arts*

If you approach sewing as an art rather than a chore, you'll *love* Diana Close's Wearable Arts mailing list. Here you'll find chitchat that spans from where to find ethnic clothing patterns to how to give garments just the right quilted touch without leaving them hanging heavy with batting. You'll meet costumers, wearable artists, and lots of ordinary sewers with grand visions and good advice. You'll receive around ten E-mail messages a day.

To sign up, send an Internet E-mail message to

wearable-request@lunch.engr.sgi.com

The only line in the message should be

subscribe

To send a message to everyone on the mailing list, address it to

wearable@lunch.engr.sgi.com

## *Ragdoll Makers Share Hopes, Dreams, and Whimsical Spirit in This Offbeat List*

If you've ever begged off a dinner invitation at a chi-chi restaurant so that you could finish sewing hair onto a Raggedy Ann, take heart. There are others like you. Lots of them. They commune regularly in this almost counter-culture mail list that encourages members to share idle, warm conversation, even if it's unrelated to doll-making. While other Internet lists would excommunicate you if you mass-mailed thank-yous to the whole list, doing so is de rigeur here. The list is sub-titled "an elinor peace bailey [& others] fan club"—you know, that crazy doll lady whose "little people" look like they just walked out of cyberspace. Come join the fun!

To join, send a personal note with "dolls" in the subject line to Melissa Bishop at

mbshop@needles.com

or visit their Web site at

http://kbs.net/tt/

This list does have a membership fee— $21 per year. Once you've paid your fee (Tangled Threads, 475 Mill Rd., Coram, Long Island, New York 11727-4137; 516/736-0320), Melissa will send you directions on how to send messages to the other members.

*Note: Please don't send any messages containing computer commands! Melissa maintains the list manually.*

## *Pfabulous Pfaff Pfreaks Pfind Pfellowship Pforever*

Like a worldwide cult whose members combine cunning stratagems with blind devotion, Pfaff owners are like no other sewing machine owners in the world. They revel in the arcanities of P-memories and M-memories, and if you put them in a room together they'll reminisce for hours about their most memorable revelations regarding the rainbow buttons. If you join this Pfabulous Pfaff Pfan Club list, you'll be initiated into the rites of the Pfaff's "uncharted territories." You'll discover that there are secret Pfaffers even in the highest levels of NASA. No Pfaffer should miss out. Remember, that's Pfaffer like "Trekker," not Pfaffie like "Trekkie."

To join, send a personal note with "Pfaff" in the subject line to Melissa Bishop at

mbshop@needles.com

or visit their Web site at

http://kbs.net/tt/

This list does have a membership fee—$21 per year. Once you've paid your fee (Tangled Threads, 475 Mill Rd., Coram, Long Island, New York 11727-4137; 516/736-0320), Melissa will send you directions on how to send messages to the other members.

> *Note: Please don't send any messages with computer commands! Melissa maintains the list manually.*

## *Bernina Groupies Swap Bits, Stitches, and Secrets*

If you see the world through a Bernina rather than a Pfaff presser foot, you'll enjoy this list. Here you'll find members who strive to answer such philosophical questions as "If my stitches are balanced, but the universe is not, do I really care?" Find out why people who own incredibly expensive computerized sewing machines and large thread collections are the best people to have as friends—especially when you need to machine-quilt an 8 × 12 bedspread!

To join, send a personal note to

berninaoffice@ttsw.com

To post a message to the list, send it to

berninaoffice@ttsw.com

A human, Sue, maintains this list, so please be polite and don't send computer commands—tell her in the body of your message that you want to subscribe.

## *Viking Owners Band Together in the Viking Venerations List*

If you're a Huskygram user or your sewing machine is a Viking, get in touch with other Viking owners through this newly formed list. To join, send an E-mail message to

majordomo@acpub.duke.edu

The only line in the message should be

subscribe viking-l

## *Historical Costumers Swap Secrets in Their Mailing List*

Ever wonder what Elizabeth I had in her closet? Ever pore over those ads for patterns to make authentic reproductions of Scarlett O'Hara's wardrobe, thinking how much fun it would be to wrestle with whalebone corseting and 60 yards of velvet? If so, you may be a candidate for the Historical Costume mailing list. Here costume designers, and others who just get a kick out of sewing Bronze Age frocks, pontificate on historical topics. Discussions run the gamut from the best sources for 16th-century-style shoes to whether Victorian etiquette required that men and women part their hair differently, and other subjects guaranteed to take you beyond Butterick's.

To sign up, send an Internet E-mail message to

h-costume-request@lunch.engr.sgi.com

The only line in the message should be

subscribe

To send a message to everyone on the mailing list, address it to

h-costume @andrew.cmu.edu

**Wisely, this list does not permit discussions about Halloween costumes.**

## Fantasy Costumers Commune in Cyberspace
## Through Their Own Mailing List

At some point in their lives all sewers yearn to design a dragon costume, complete with a shimmering tail. If your time has come, you'll delight in the Fantasy Costume list, with its weekly discussions about creating fantasy, sci-fi, or "serious" Halloween and Mardi Gras costumes. You'll find a constant flow of information about techniques, supply sources, and ideas for making a man or woman into a creature as large as the imagination. E-mail traffic is light, so be patient if you don't receive messages right away.

To sign up, send an Internet E-mail message to

f-costume-request@lunch.engr.sgi.com

The only line in the message should be

subscribe

To send a message to everyone on the mailing list, address it to

f-costume @lunch.engr.sgi.com

## Indulge Your Love of Fine Old Garments with the Vintage Clothing List

Costumers, and anyone who's idea of *real* clothes shopping is sifting through racks at an estate sale, will enjoy this mailing list. The Vintage Clothing list is devoted to finding, preserving, and restoring clothes and jewelry from the Victorian era through the sixties. It's one of the few areas on Internet where advertisements are welcome, but only if you're selling antique clothing or jewelry. Recommendations on resale and antique shops are also welcome. Message traffic is light, so don't be surprised if it takes awhile for your first messages to arrive.

To sign up, send an Internet E-mail message to

listserv@brownvm.brown.edu

The only line in the message should be

subscribe vintage *YourFirstName LastName*

To send a message to everyone on the mailing list, address it to

vintage@brownvm.brown.edu

## FURSUIT Offers Furry Costumers Meaningful Friendships

If your job entails sewing and maintaining costumes for the likes of the San Diego Chicken, or if your idea of a satisfying weekend is turning 20 yards of acrylic plush into a gorilla suit, you owe it to yourself to join FURSUIT. FURSUIT is described in its charter as "a small furry fandom focused group concentrating on constructing our own furry bodysuits/heads/appliances/etc. Anthro critters of any kind as well as Mythicals are welcome." There are entry requirements to joining: You must have either created or worn a furry costume at a convention, or "done something that indicates your motivation towards furry costuming." To subscribe, send a personal E-mail message to Robert King at

> fursuit-list-owner@mcs.com

or

> Robert_C_King@att.com

## Rug-Hookers Share Wisdom Through Woolgatherings E-zine

Rug-hookers learn and practice their craft in isolation, observes Canadian rug-maker Deborah Merriam. Her informal online newsletter, or *E-zine* (for "electronic magazine"), provides a way for rug-hookers around the world to keep in touch. The Rug-Hookers newsletter is deposited every other Sunday in subscribers' E-mail boxes via Internet. You can submit tips, questions, and just conversational messages to appear in this free-roving publication and other rug-hookers will respond. Subscribe to *Woolgatherings* by sending Merriam an E-mail message at

> dmerriam@gpu.srv.ualberta.ca

---

**TIP**

*Feeling guilty about subscribing to Internet mailing lists through your office computer? You shouldn't. The best way to learn a new technology is to play around with it, using it to indulge in the things you enjoy. That's how computer whizzes become so good at what they do: They play with computers. And you can become a computer whiz too, just by hunting for all the great needlecraft information on Internet. Trust me, this will add $10,000 to your annual salary.*

---

## *The Weaving List Offers Reams of Wise Counsel to Fiber Artists*

Weaving doesn't have to be lonely. Sign up for this list and you'll receive a dozen or more E-mail messages each day from other weavers and spinners around the world on all aspects of their art, from dyeing to buying weaving supplies.

To sign up, send an Internet E-mail message to

weaving-request@his.com

The only line in the message should be

subscribe

To send a message to everyone on the mailing list, address it to

weaving@his.com

## *An Eclectic Crowd Mingles on the Crafty Craft List*

If you'd rather read a more low-key craft mailing list than the ones listed above, where tips about refinishing furniture commingle with horror stories about cutting fake fur, you'll enjoy this one. I call it The Big Vax list, because it appears to be managed by an old-fashioned mainframe computer called The Big Vax at Alfred University. You can post a question on just about anything (candle-making, fur dyeing, bedroom painting), and lots of people will give you advice. The folks here are *very* friendly.

To sign up, send an Internet E-mail message to

listserv@bigvax.alfred.edu

The only line in the message should be

subscribe crafts-L

To send a message to everyone on the mailing list, address it to

crafts-l@bigvax.alfred.edu

*Note: The Crafty Craft list was born when members of the Internet mailing list for cat owners (FELINE-L) overwhelmed the list with discussions about cat-oriented craft projects. When I innocently wrote a message to the Crafty Craft list mentioning that I was collecting fabrics printed with cats to one day make into a quilt with a cat theme, I was flooded with messages from other quilters who were doing the same thing.* ✍

## Get Advice on Running a Craft Business Through This List for Entrepreneurs

Do you dream of turning your extensive collection of cross-stitch charts of the Staten Island ferry into a home business? If so, consider joining this mailing list for craft entrepreneurs. Message traffic is so light that weeks may go by without a message, but be patient, says founder Teri Miller. Miller credits the list with helping her establish a successful business selling craft goods on the info highway. If you have questions about how to establish your own business, by all means post them to the list and others will reply.

To sign up, send a personal message to the Internet address

crafts-business-request@hustle.rahul.net

Miller answers all requests herself because she feels that a computer-generated response is so impersonal.

To send a message to everyone on the mailing list, address it to

crafts-business@hustle.rahul.net

Miller says that if you have problems subscribing to the list you should drop her a note at

shannah@rahul.net

and she'll gladly add you to the list.

> *"I posted a message asking if anyone could direct me to a source for a special yarn that I had run out of half-way through a pattern. The yarn was no longer available due to a fire at the Italian factory. In just a few hours, a knitter named "Mary" in the United Kingdom offered to look for the yarn at the Harrowgate knit show. A week later, it was on my desk! KnitNet is amazing!!! I've been knitting for more than forty years, and it tickles me to know that knitting is my on-ramp to the information super-highway. I've never had more fun."*
> *—Margery Noel, a clinical psychologist in Santa Fe, NM*

## QuiltArt Offers Friendly Chat and Good Tips

Occasionally the QuiltNet mailing list fills up with subscribers and cannot accept any new ones. When that happens, the next favorite place for quilters on Internet is the QuiltArt mailing list. The main topic of discussion is ostensibly art quilting, but talk veers into any territory dealing with quilt-making. To sign up, send an E-mail message to listserv@netcom.com

In your message type:

subscribe quiltart-list *yourE-mailaddress*

To send a message to everyone on the list address it to

quiltart-list@netcom.com

## *Share Inspirations with Other Midwestern Quilters*

Meet quilters from the central United States, including Texas and southern states, in this laid back list for midwesterners. One recent topic was nature appliqué quilts inspired by the midwest. Traffic is light, so don't be surprised if weeks pass before you see messages. Better, write a message to the list to introduce yourself and strike up a conversation. To sign up on the Midwest Quilters' list, send an Internet E-mail address to

listserv@ricevm1.rice.edu

The only thing you should type in the body of the message is the line

subscribe mwquilt

To send messages to everyone on the mailing list, address your message to

mwquilt@ricevm1.rice.edu

## *The Cheapest Way for You to Join Needlecraft Mailing Lists May Be to Sign Up for MCI Mail*

If you don't have access to a low-cost Internet link, whether through a university or local Internet service, and you blanch at paying the high hourly fees of the big, commercial online services for Internet access, consider joining MCI Mail.

MCI Mail is an E-mail-only computer service. You won't find databases or public forums on it, and you can only use it to send and receive E-mail. But low cost has made it the preferred E-mail service for members of the computer industry for years. And its Internet link means you can use it for participating in needlecraft mailing lists, as well as obtaining FAQs and other goodies from the Internet.

For just $10 per month you can receive as many Internet messages on MCI Mail as you want. There are no hourly connect fees so you can stay online as long as you need to. And, because you tap into MCI Mail through an 800 number, if you live in a small town or rural area you won't have to pay any additional hourly long-distance or computer network fees as you might with CompuServe and America Online. For your $10 monthly charge, you can send 40 E-mail messages each month to anywhere in the world. You can also send faxes. (I use MCI Mail to send faxes rather than use my fax-modem so I can save on long-distance charges.) The fee for sending additional messages is very low.

MCI even offers a lower-cost plan that lets you receive as many messages as you want for $45 per year, though you're charged for each E-mail message you send. It's not hard to tap into MCI Mail with a general communications software package like Procomm Plus for Windows or DCA's Crosstalk Communicator. MCI Mail may just be all the Internet access you need. MCI Mail is available in just about every country in the world. To subscribe, call 800/444-6245, or 202/833-8484 outside the United States.

## Usenet's Crafts Newsgroups Are Wellsprings of Advice and Creativity

*U*senet newsgroups are analogous to public discussion groups on commercial computer services. You can leave messages to other computer users around the globe, and they can respond to you. The messages follow each other in topics or threads.

There are thousands of newsgroups on Internet, ranging in topic from collecting hockey memorabilia to cancer support. Since Internet discussions are the only communications forum in the world where people are free to say exactly what they want at all times, conversations can sometimes grow rude. (It's little surprise that all the computer slang for appalling behavior has arisen on Usenet—*flame*, for instance, means to tell someone off, *spam* means to mass-mail E-mail sales pitches to everyone connected to the network—something that's forbidden.) Pornography is another Internet bane. Since no one polices the Net, anarchy reigns. But fear not: The needlecraft newsgroups on Usenet are fairly sedate (although not without an occasional flame). Thousands of crafters tap into them, and, since Internet has no geographic bounds, you're as likely to spot correspondents from India as from Indiana.

At the same time, Internet's craft newsgroups offer less advice and chitchat than the craft forums on CompuServe, GEnie, or Prodigy. Generally, each newsgroup posts about 20 to 40 messages per day, compared to the hundreds posted in the topic areas on commercial services. And, unlike the craft forums on commercial services, the Internet forums are more businesslike. Crafters generally ask their questions and leave. The intense, personal friendships that arise on other services are much less commonly formed on the Net.

Indeed, the Net has a special etiquette. (When you log on through a major service like America Online, the service spells it out for you.) You're advised to watch the conversation carefully for a few weeks before jumping in. Otherwise, you might commit some faux pas, like reiterating something that someone else has recently said, or writing a message that's far afield from the subject at hand. The ostensible reason is to "save bandwidth"—in other words, not waste precious computer resources on frivolous chat. However, peer pressure also plays a role in governing what is and is not permissible to say online; everyone wants to look cool on Usenet.

Usenet craft conversations excel at filling you in on the esoteric. You'll find discussions on crafts that you may never have heard of, or at least never thought of pursuing (like making soap from carrots). You'll learn about unusual crafts like making dolls from apples, upholstering chairs with geometric rayons from the Fifties, or creating your own Lava Lamps.

I've listed here the Internet craft newsgroups most interesting to needlecrafters. Their names are organized like the names of the subdirectories on your computer's hard disk. The "rec" prefix means that they're part of the "recreational" newsgroups, while the "crafts" part of their name means they're crafts-related. The rest of the words in their address will give you additional clues to their nature.

You can participate in all the Usenet discussions from CompuServe, GEnie, Prodigy, Delphi, and America Online, although the procedure for doing so will differ with each service. Check the chapter on the service you subscribe to for more information. You can also tap into these discussions through the Fibernet BBS. See Chapter 19 on computer bulletin boards for more information.

In general, you'll need to find your way to the service's Internet link before you can tap in. Once there, you'll select the Usenet feature, sometimes called the "Usenet newsreader." You'll need to "subscribe" in Internet parlance to the newsgroup you want to read by typing in the name of the newsgroup at some prompt or on a menu. After that, you can immediately begin reading and replying to messages, called "articles."

One more note: When people write messages, they often repeat large chunks of the message they're answering. You'll also see long lines of gibberish heading the tops of many messages. The gibberish is just routing information, listing all the places the E-mail traveled before it got to its destination on Usenet. Simply scroll through the junk with your DOWN ARROW or PAGE DOWN key to get to the message.

Here, then, is the list of Usenet groups on the Internet. Welcome aboard and have fun!

**rec.crafts.textiles.needlework**  Cross-stitchers and needlepointers meet in this discussion group, where the general topic is anything pertaining to any form of decorative stitching done by hand. Practitioners of all forms of embroidery are welcome. Conversation ranges from canvas selection to floss to framing.

**rec.crafts.textiles.sewing**  Anything involving sewing is fodder for chitchat in this newsgroup, where topics range from the different brands of sewing machines to how to make drapes. Sources of supplies are frequent topics, as are favorite notions and peeves about different fabric manufacturers.

**rec.crafts.textiles.quilting**  This group is one of many cyberspace havens for quilters. Topics include anything that interests quilters, from rotary cutters to quilted garments. Quilt block exchanges are frequent.

**rec.crafts.textiles.yarn**  Here's where you go to discuss knitting, crochet, weaving, rug-hooking, and anything else having to do with yarns and fibers. Dying, spinning, and discussions on fibers are also part of the conversation. Most of the people in this discussion group seem to be weavers and spinners.

**rec.crafts.beads**  This is one of the best spots in cyberspace to discuss bead-making, stringing, and acquisition. You'll learn about everything from Hishi beads to where to buy rhinestones in bulk.

**rec.crafts.textiles.misc**  This area is used to discuss any craft or craft-related subject not covered by the other craft newsgroups. Recent topics include crafts for children, insurance for crafters, mouse nativity sets (!), soap-making, and where to buy high heels for dolls.

**rec.crafts.marketplace**  Use this group to post an E-mail "classified" to sell those 400 jars of buttons cluttering your closet. Although the Internet normally forbids advertisements, this group was created to give individuals and small craft businesses that can't afford to advertise elsewhere a place to sell their wares.

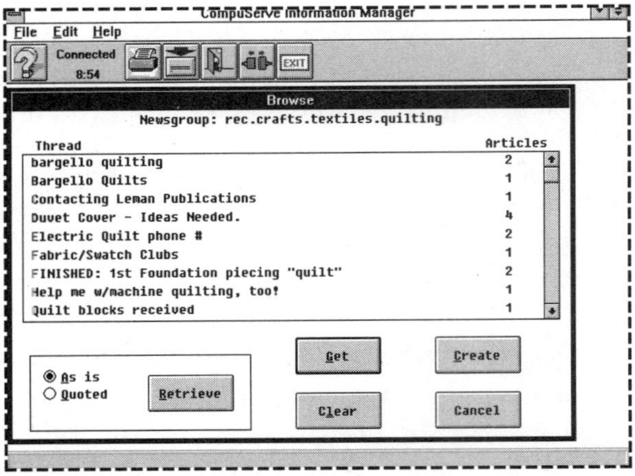

**Figure 18-2**

This is how you would see Internet's quilt discussion group through CompuServe. Listed in the window are the topics of message strings in the discussion. To read individual messages, you'd highlight the subject with your mouse and click on it. To read the next message in the string, you click on one of the arrows under "Articles."

## You Can Read Usenet Craft Newsgroups Through E-mail

Let's say the only access you have to the Internet is an Internet address, and your office computer doesn't let you read Usenet newsgroups. If so, you can still read some of the craft discussions by subscribing to a special service run by the Electronic Library Project at Stanford University. (You can't post messages in the newsgroups, however.) To join, send an E-mail message to

netnews@db.stanford.edu

Type nothing but the word

help

in the message. In response, the Stanford computer should send you directions on how to sign up for this free service. Basically, all you need to do to subscribe is to send another message to that same address, with the keywords that you want the computer to search the Usenet messages for. For example:

subscribe stitch linen

period 2

end

This series of commands would trigger the computer to send you all Usenet messages that include both the words "stitch" and "linen." And it would send them to you every two days. The flaw in the system is that the service won't send you all the messages posted in a particular newsgroup like **rec.crafts.textiles.needlework.** That's why it's still better to tap in to Usenet groups through a commercial online service or Internet provider.

## "Frequently Asked Questions" Bring You the Needlecrafting "Wisdom of the Net"

*E*ver find yourself at 2 A.M. with a needle and thread, puzzling over how to get the points in an appliqué tree branch perfectly pointed? Why not fire up your PC, dial into the Net, and snare some sage advice from appliqué experts in the bitstream? It's not hard, thanks to a wonderful invention called the FAQ, which stands for "Frequently Asked Questions."

FAQs are compilations of common questions, posed by needlecrafters in Usenet or mailing list messages, and answers to those questions from kind, knowledgeable, and eloquent people. People collect these messages, organize them into a coherent form, and distribute them on Internet as FAQs. They're distributed as both E-mail messages and as files that you can download.

You'll find all kinds of FAQs: From sewing and quilting, to knitting and cross-stitch. FAQs hold items like book reviews, addresses of mail-order sources for both esoteric and common materials, and fabric store recommendations. They'll also have questions and answers about topics like baby quilt ideas, bleeding fabric, batting, copyright information for quilters, dye safety, fabric storage, how much to charge for your work, metallic thread, paper-piecing techniques, sashiko, and stain removal tips. You get the idea.

FAQs are distributed in several ways. They may be distributed with the Usenet newsgroups from which their advice originally sprung, or else stored on a computer connected to Internet where anyone can retrieve them. Several of the needlecraft mailing lists also offer FAQs that are usually updated on a monthly or semimonthly basis.

FAQs are free. They exist through the continued generosity of computer users around the world. If someone sends you a FAQ, drop them an E-mail note of thanks. You might also send a note of gratitude to the person who maintains the FAQ, since keeping one up-to-date and circulating requires no small investment of time. FAQ authors usually forbid their FAQs from being posted on commercial online services, so you'll usually find them only on Internet.

You'll find a listing of all the needlecraft FAQs below. Each listing also includes the easiest way to obtain the FAQ.

## *Sewing and Textiles FAQs*

There are five general sewing and fiber-related FAQs. One includes a long list of mail-order sources for materials ranging from natural fiber fabric to heirloom sewing supplies. Another has the addresses of recommended needlecraft magazines, a discussion on how to buy a serger, and some excellent advice on restoring Grandma's treadle sewing machine. A two-part FAQ has a compilation of reviews of books on sewing and pattern drafting—hundreds of them, it seems. The fourth is a historical costuming source list, and the fifth is a general crafts supply source list.

You can find these FAQs posted as long E-mail messages in three different Usenet news-groups: **rec.crafts.textiles.sewing**, **news.answers**, or **rec.answers**. Look for messages with "faq" in their subject line. (When you subscribe to these newsgroups on CompuServe, you'll only get the last 20 messages posted in the groups, so you may need to hang around a while until the FAQs are posted again.)

If you still can't find the FAQs, you can obtain them through E-mail by sending an Internet message to the address

mail-server@rtfm.mit.edu.

Type these lines in the text of the message:

send usenet/news.answers/crafts/textiles/faq

send usenet/news.answers/crafts/textiles/books/part1

send usenet/news.answers/crafts/textiles/books/part2

send usenet/news.answers/crafts/historical-costuming

send usenet/news.answers/crafts/finding-suppliers

Each line will trigger the computer to send you the FAQ mentioned in that line as an E-mail message. If you want only certain FAQs, include only their lines in your message.

"*When life deals you scraps, make quilts.*"—*part of the signature to an E-mail message on QuiltNet.*

## Quilting FAQs

There are nearly fifty quilting FAQs, ranging in topic from how to make watercolor quilts to how to light your workspace. Members of the Internet mailing list QuiltNet assemble the FAQs. At present, the only central computer on which the FAQs are available is the World Wide Web Quilting Home Page (discussed later in the chapter). To get them you must send an E-mail message to the librarian of the particular FAQ you want, and she will send it to you.

For an index to the FAQs and their librarians, send an Internet message to the address

mail-server@rtfm.mit.edu

In the text of the message type this single line:

send usenet/news.answers/crafts/quilting-faq-index

In return, the computer will send you a message listing all the current E-mail addresses of QuiltNet members who maintain FAQs. To obtain a particular FAQ, send an E-mail message to the person responsible for it. And please remember to be polite since the members, not a computer, will be answering the message. It may take a few days to receive the FAQ, so be patient.

Current quilting FAQs cover many different subjects, including appliqué hints (especially for circles); baby quilt ideas; batting; beginner's projects; bleeding fabric; books; borders; catalogs; copyright information for quilters; design walls; dye safety; environmental issues and quilting; ergonomics for quilters; exchanges; fabric manufacturers' addresses; fabric storage; guild information; guild program and project ideas; history of QuiltNet; how much to charge for your work; how to avoid wavy edges; lighting your workplace; magazine addresses; magazine reviews; metallic thread; New Jersey quilt resources; paper piecing; pricing quilts; quilt show reviews; QuiltNet guild card info; QuiltNet member biographies; recommended quilt stores; remembrance quilts; sashiko; sewing machines; sewing room ideas; software for quilt design; stabilizing bias edges; stain removal tips; teacher reviews; tea dying; thimbles (how to make your own and the address of a craftsman who makes custom thimbles); tying a quilt; and watercolor quilts.

## Cross-Stitch FAQ

At present there's just one cross-stitch FAQ, but it's a doozy. At almost one hundred pages in length, it answers nearly every question a stitcher could possibly have, from how to choose and clean fabric, to how to choose between flower thread and pearl cotton, and whether to use a hoop or a frame. It includes a chart that converts between DMC and Anchor threads and one listing the fiber content of hundreds of embroidery fabrics. You'll find tutorials on Assisi work, blackwork, drawn and pulled thread, shadow embroidery, hardanger, and waste canvas. It even includes simple computer graphic stitching charts. The guide is rich with tips and advice from other stitchers.

You can find a copy posted as a four-part message in the Usenet newsgroup

rec.crafts.textiles.needlework

or in

news.answers

or

rec.answers

(When you subscribe to these newsgroups on CompuServe, you'll only get the last 20 messages posted—so you may need to hang around a while until the FAQs are posted again.) You can also obtain a copy of the FAQ by sending an E-mail message to the Internet address

mail-server@rtfm.mit.edu.

Type these lines in the text of the message:

send usenet/news.answers/crafts/cross-stitch/part1

send usenet/news.answers/crafts/cross-stitch/part2

send usenet/news.answers/crafts/cross-stitch/part3

send usenet/news.answers/crafts/cross-stitch/part4

The computer will send you all four parts as long E-mail messages. If you'd like only a specific part, simply type the line that identifies that part.

## *Knitting FAQs*

You can get ten superb knitting FAQs via E-mail from the KnitNet Internet mailing list. (See the discussion of KnitNet earlier in this chapter.) To get them, send an Internet E-mail message to

ddancer@net.com

The subject line of the message should contain one of the following entries, specifying which FAQ you want (don't include the parenthetical explanation in your message):

Baby FAQ        (free baby patterns created by KnitNet members)

Beads FAQ       (directions and suggestions on how to use beads in knitting)

Books FAQ       (a list of knitting books, publishers, and sources)

Ends FAQ        (ways to finish off your yarn ends, especially in multicolored work)

Events FAQ      (knitting festivals and workshops)

Klein FAQ       (free patterns to knit Klein bottle–shaped hats and möbius scarves—only on Internet!)

LilyChin FAQ    (messages written by members of the mailing list about a Lily Chin presentation)

Scarves FAQ     (free scarf patterns and material suggestions)

Stores FAQ      (a directory of knitting stores, yarn manufacturers, and mail-order supplies sources)

Patterns FAQ    (noncopyrighted patterns that have been shared on KnitNet)

Here are some additional tips:

☙ You don't have to include any information in the body of the message (the computer will ignore it). However, if your communications software requires that you type something in the message before you can send it, type anything, even a period.

☙ You don't have to be a subscriber to KnitNet to obtain the FAQs.

🔊     Do not ask for more than one FAQ in a message.

🔊     If you don't receive any of the knitting FAQs by the next day, send an E-mail message with the subject "FAQ Trouble" to

ddancer@netcom

🔊     Write a personal message explaining what went wrong since a human, not a computer, will answer this message.

🔊     Doll FAQ has knit patterns for doll clothes. This FAQ is available by writing a personal note to

cmcmill@gsvms2.cc.casou.edu

## Spinning Wheel FAQ

Elizabeth Zimmermann, knitting doyen and host of the old TV show *Busy Knitter,* despaired in a book written just 20 years ago that in her entire life she had never known any knitter but herself to spin. How things have changed! Today spinners crowd the info highway. (Look for them in Usenet's **rec.crafts.textiles.yarn** newsgroup, in CompuServe's Craft forum, under "Weaving and Spinning"; in KnitNet; or in the FiberNet computer bulletin boards described in the next chapter.)

Whether you're a knitter or weaver, you *absolutely must* get a copy of The Spinning Wheel FAQ. It explains the difference between the various kinds of wheels, offers advice on how to buy a new or used wheel, and includes reviews of major brands. I've seen this FAQ only on Diana Lane's Textile Home Page on the World Wide Web. (Directions on how to get there appear later in this chapter.) If you can't get there, try sending an Internet E-mail message to the FAQ's author Chris Jordan at **caj@jb.man.ac.uk.** She'll be glad to send it to you via E-mail.

## *Rug-Hooking FAQ*

The Traditional Rug-Hooking Resources FAQ is another information treasure chest that is, sadly, too hard to come by. Authored by Deborah Merriam, publisher of *Woolgatherings* (see the mailing list section earlier in this chapter), it includes answers to any question a rug-hooker might have, offering advice on cleaning, hanging, maintenance, restoration of priceless rugs, and a myriad of other things. It includes an incredible rug-hooking materials source list and bibliography that most rug-hookers would trade their oldest child for. It's posted around the twentieth day of each month as a two-part message in Usenet's **rec.crafts.textiles.misc** discussion group.

You can also snare a copy of it off the Prince Edward Island Craft Council computer in Canada. You'd either use FTP commands or access it through the World Wide Web (directions on how to do both appear later in this chapter). To obtain it via FTP, use the Internet address **gus.crafts-council.pe.ca**. Log in to the computer as "anonymous" and type in your full Internet address as a password. Change to the directory by typing **cd pub/rugmaking**, then type the command **get faq.part1.z** and press ENTER. Once you've received the first part of the FAQ, type **get faq-part2.z** and press ENTER to get the second part.

> *Note: It took me several tries to get this FAQ off the Prince Edward Island computer, because their Internet link is slow and often unreliable. If all other attempts to obtain it fail, you can always write Merriam at **dmerriam@gpu.srv.ualberta.ca**.*

## How to Get Files from Internet

Occasionally, a Usenet or mailing list discussion may have a reference to software or an information file that you can get through Internet. The instructions usually give some totally incomprehensible directions including what look like computer hard disk path descriptions. For example, you might find something like this: "You can anonymous FTP gus.crafts-council.pe.ca in the files /pub/crosstitch/cross1.Z." Huh? you say.

FTP stands for "file transfer protocol." It's a service provided by some computers on Internet. If the computer service you subscribe to offers FTP, you can tap into computers around the world that also provide FTP service and download files stored on those computers. FTP doesn't cost you any more in connect charges than what it would normally cost to connect to the service. CompuServe, America Online, Prodigy, and Delphi offer FTP, and GEnie is likely to offer it soon.

I like CompuServe's FTP the best because you don't have to know a lot to use it, and it usually works pretty fast. It transfers files to your computer in a reasonably short period of time. I don't like Delphi's FTP because you need to learn a lot of esoteric Internet commands before you can use it. (What that means is that you have to buy and actually read one of those Internet books that are the size of the New York phone book!) I don't like America Online's FTP either, because it's slow and often unreliable.

Finally, if your community has low-cost Internet access services, like Netcom, you can probably find one that offers an FTP service that's even better and maybe even easier to use than those found on commercial online services.

To obtain a file through FTP, on a service like CompuServe or AOL, you first need to access the service's FTP menu. On CompuServe, type **GO FTP** and press ENTER. Once the FTP menu appears, you type in the address of the computer you want to access. In the example at the beginning of this section the address would be **gus.crafts-council.pe.ca**. (On services like Delphi where you have to enter the command yourself, you'd type **ftp gus.crafts-council.pe.ca** at their Internet prompt and press ENTER.) When the remote computer asks you for your logon name, you type **anonymous** (hence the name "anonymous FTP"). When it asks for a password, you type your Internet address. (CompuServe's FTP enters these responses for you.) Since the services are changing their offerings rapidly, by the time you read this, other services may offer access to FTP that's as easy as CompuServe's.

**Figure 18-3**
The main menu of CompuServe's FTP services. You type GO FTP to get there. You click on icons on the right side of the screen to start tapping into computers as far away as Java to retrieve files.

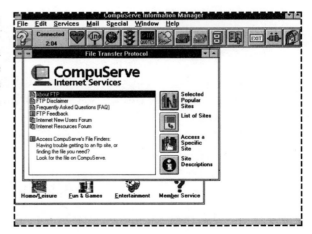

From there, things are pretty much smooth sailing. First, you type the specific directory path where the file you're looking for is located (assuming you know it), and a list of the files in the directory appears. (Depending on the system through which you access Internet you may have to type **CD**, followed by the directory path, and then press ENTER before you'll see a list of files.)

If you don't know the name of the directory you want, you'll have to log on without it, and then fish around in the directories that the FTP server lists. You move through these directories like you move through the directories on your hard disk, typing **CD** to change directories, and **DIR** to list directories. One hint: If you see a directory named "pub," go for it; that's usually where the craft software is located.

Unfortunately, there's usually not much in the way of file descriptions, so you should pretty much grab those files with intriguing names and check them out later, once you've copied them to your computer. Before you start your file transfer, and, depending on your Internet access, you may have to type **BIN** at the remote computer's prompt for it to transmit the file to you. If you don't, it may end up on your PC as mush. If you're calling through an Internet service that provides you with just an austere command prompt, you'd enter the command **get** followed by the file's name to get a file.

If you're on CompuServe and you're using CompuServe Information Manager for Windows or the Mac (if you're using CIM for DOS you won't be able to access the FTP service on CompuServe), you'd click on the box beside the name of the file with your mouse, so that an X appears in it, and then click on the Retrieve button.

The next two sections include the addresses of computers on Internet that have some interesting needlecraft files.

*TIP*

*Having a hard time getting what you want on Internet? Did the E-mail you sent come bouncing back to you? Always try again, for Internet can be a testy bugger. Reread the directions. Make sure you typed the E-mail address correctly. Try a variation of the command that the directions suggest (directions for how to do things on Internet are notoriously unreliable).*

## *The Prince Edward Island, Canada Crafts Council Server*

To reach this computer, FTP to

gus.crafts-council.pe.ca

or connect by Gopher (see the section "A Few Words About Gopher") to

URL://gopher.crafts-council.pe.ca:70/

Once connected, you'll find a wee collection of craft info.

*Note: Be patient when you try to connect to this server. I've tried to connect through a number of different Internet services and have had trouble getting and staying connected. You might try late at night when the online traffic has died down. If you're lucky, they'll have resolved the problems by the time you read this.* 🐘

## *SunSITE Northern Europe*

To reach this computer, FTP to

doc.ic.ac.uk

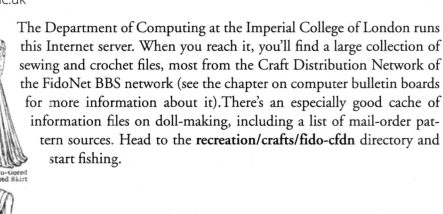

Seven-Gored
Tucked Skirt

The Department of Computing at the Imperial College of London runs this Internet server. When you reach it, you'll find a large collection of sewing and crochet files, most from the Craft Distribution Network of the FidoNet BBS network (see the chapter on computer bulletin boards for more information about it). There's an especially good cache of information files on doll-making, including a list of mail-order pattern sources. Head to the **recreation/crafts/fido-cfdn** directory and start fishing.

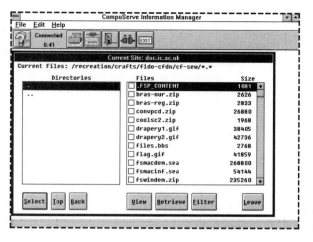

Figure 18-4
The Northern European SunSITE as accessed through CompuServe and Information Manager. You select the directory in the column on the left. Then you see the files in the directory listed on the right. You select the directory in the column on the left (no directories are visible now). To copy a file to your computer, you select it in the list and then click Retrieve.

# A Few Words About Gopher

*Y*ou may have heard of something called *gopher*. Internet's Gopher is the quickest way to feel like Alice in Wonderland in the modern age. A Gopher server is a special computer that you log on to through another computer service (like CompuServe or AOL) and it performs a search for you on other Internet-connected computers around the world. It then presents you with a menu of the computers on which it has found information of the sort you're seeking. From there you can tap into those computers to get at the information. You can even go a step further and tap into more computers through the computer you've just tapped into. And on and on.

One night I ran a Gopher search for occurrences of the word *sew* on Internet, and just kind of hitchhiked from computer to computer around the world. Tapping into a computer at a newspaper in Australia I found schedules for a craft show. While digging around in the computer of a U.S. fabric manufacturer, I found technical papers authored by a competing fabric manufacturer. (They seem to be in some kind of race to create computer simulations of cotton fiber, in order to learn more about where cotton gets its strength.) Wandering into the computer of a vocational school in Maine, I located some home economics class schedules. Finally, I located about a dozen mathematical papers about "sewing" together the complex, multidimensional geometric shapes that mathematicians like to play with.

Wandering into all those computers was perfectly legal; in fact they are set up so that the public can have free access to their information. If you're like me, you'll probably end up spending an entire evening dredging up nothing but pointless information. But then, that's the nature of Internet.

I think the best place to use as a spring-board for Gophering is America Online. While America Online's Internet access is pretty crummy, it's easy to use, with self-explanatory icons and menus through which you can leisurely click your way around the electronic highway. AOL's Internet offerings will give you a feel for what this Gopher stuff is all about, and you don't have to know anything to use it.

Here's a Gopher address to get you started. It's for the Textile & Fiber Arts Gopher at Rice University, which is a great source of information on historical costuming, including FAQs with sources, tips, and bibliographies for pattern and period fabrics. To get there, type

gopher://riceinfo.rice.edu/11/.subject/Textiles/Hist.cost

**Figure 18-5**
The disappointing results of a worldwide search through America Online's Gopher service. It's not AOL's fault, but the most interesting thing that turned up in a search of the word "sew" on all the world's computers was a news story about a surgeon re-attaching a patient's head.

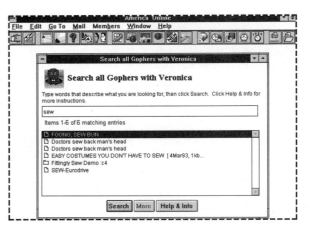

*TIP*

*Stymied about what to type in the subject line of an E-mail message you're sending to a computer to subscribe to a mailing list or obtain a FAQ? Type anything. The same goes if your online software prompts you for a name. The computer won't care. On the other hand, I like to type the purpose of the message into the subject line ("subscribe to knitnet") so that if the receiving computer sends back some weird reply full of computer gibberish and error messages, I have some way of knowing what my message was originally supposed to do.*

# The World Wide Web Takes You
# Places You've Never Dreamed Of

*G*opher is on its way out (thankfully, some say), soon to be replaced by a new form of net-cruising called the World Wide Web. Bopping around Internet through the World Wide Web, looking for needlecraft stuff, is more fun than helping a friend clean out the public lockers she had to rent to store all her yarn.

Using the World Wide Web is a lot like playing a computer game. You point and click on icons or highlighted text on the screen. As you explore, quilt blocks or photos of other knitters' sweater projects materialize almost magically in gorgeous color, or you're whisked to patterns or databases of specialized textile supply stores.

The Web is a lot like Prodigy with its mouse-happy interface and splashy screens, but it's worlds better because it's so much faster and the information content is rich. (Prodigy now offers access to the World Wide Web.) And, most of the Web is created by real people like you or me, not big corporations. (Anyone with access to an Internet service in their community can set up a World Wide Web page.) For needlecrafters, the World Wide Web is almost like having a mini-online service especially for us.

In order to tap into the Web, you need a special kind of Internet connection, and usually special software. Most of the major online services, including Prodigy, are experimenting with providing Web access. If you work or study at a university, you can probably tap into the Web. Talk to your network administrator. Many Internet service providers offer Web access. The one most recommended is Netcom via its NetCruiser interface (800/501-8649). (If you send an E-mail message to **info@netcom.com** you'll get pricing and access information for Netcom, and you'll find out whether there's a local Netcom node in your community.) In addition, there may be an Internet service in your community that offers even lower cost access to the Web.

Finally, you're going to need a high-speed modem (14.4K bps or faster), a fast computer (486 or Mac), and, ideally, high-resolution graphics like Super-VGA. The Web will shuttle lots of computer graphics to your PC, and you'll want that process to be as fast as possible to keep your frustration level low.

Is Web access worth it for all the hassle involved in tapping in? I think so, and I tend to be a curmudgeon when it comes to weighing hassles vs. benefit in wrestling with my computer to make it do something new. And once you have the Web working, you won't have to learn anything else to travel the Net. It's perfectly self-explanatory.

Still not convinced? Here's what you'll find on the Web.

*"I could spend all day every day in front of the computer playing [on the Web]," says Emily Way, who runs Emily's Online Knitting Magazine on the Web.*

*I could too!*

## *Knitters and Crocheters Will Find Heaven on the Textile Home Page*

The Web is organized into pages, a lot like the pages in a magazine. These pages display pictures, information, lists of contents, and highlighted words or phrases. To get to them you type into your Web crawling software an address like **http://www.textiles.org**. From there you click on highlighted text or graphics to move around. When you click on the highlighted text (and sometimes the pictures) you'll be whisked to related information, sometimes located on another, distant computer. As you cruise the Web you'll find more pages of information, text, and graphics that you can learn from and explore.

Knitter Diana Lane runs a delightful World Wide Web page for knitters, crocheters, cross-stitchers, and other yarn-based needlecrafters. Her page is sometimes known as Diana's Knitting on the Web, or the Textile Home Page. Her page can route you to especially valuable conversations from KnitNet (how to knit with beads, how to knit shawls); patterns (one for Dr. Who's scarf and the infamous möbius scarf and Klein bottle hat patterns); the Internet knitting FAQs; and a cross-stitch library. You can also "flip pages" to reach other Internet resources and textile-related pages, like the Prince Edward Island Craft Council page.

In your Web browser, type

http://www.textiles.org

**Figure 18-6**
Diana Lane's World Wide Web Textile
Home Page offers an oasis of knitting
tips, talk, and patterns in the swirling
bitstream. Click on any highlighted
word or phrase on the screen and you'll
be whisked to that information.

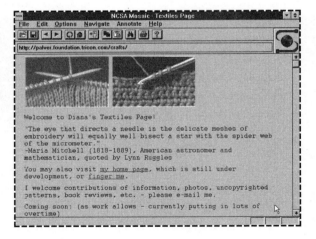

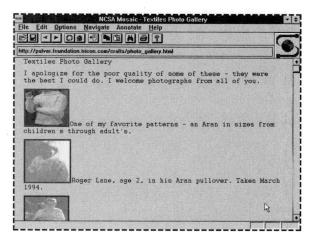

**Figure 18-7**
You'll even find photos of projects in the Textile Home Page. Overall, this is much better than Prodigy, wouldn't you say?

From the Textile Home Page you can flip to *Emily Way's Online Knitting Magazine*. Or in your Web interface, type

http://www.io.org/~spamily/kit/

This fascinating page has lists of knitting stores around the world, recommended books for knitters, patterns, tips, and other goodies. Highly recommended!

## *Quilters Can Access All of Internet's Quilting Resources with the Quilting Home Page*

The Quilting Home Page, run by tireless Sue and Eric Traudt (the former known by the logon name KosmcKitty on some online services), provides one-stop shopping to access everything that Internet has to offer quilters. You'll find all those hard-to-get quilting FAQs, plus information on quilt stores, quilt history, quilt design, and more. The Quilting Home Page offers hyper-text links to tap into the page's store of information and even other art-related services on Internet like the Textile or the Fine Art home pages. In your Web browser, type

http://ttsw.com/MainQuiltingPage.html

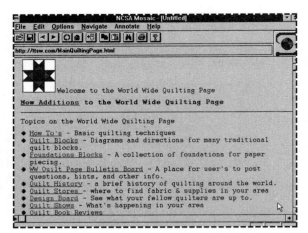

**Figure 18-8**
Head to KosmcKitty's Quilting Home Page to find all the best quilting info and resources on Internet. It's just like tapping into Einstein's brain, that is, assuming he was a quilter.

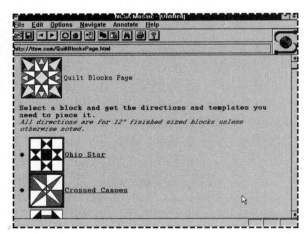

**Figure 18-9**
From the Quilting Page, you can select from a list of blocks, and the service will print directions and measurements to make them. All you have to do is save them to disk and print them.

## *The Cross-Stitch Home Page Offers Software and FAQs*

Head to Kathleen Dyer's Cross-Stitch Page for FAQs, cross-stitch shareware, and perhaps best of all, access to the complete archives of FidoNet's Crafting File Distribution Network. There you'll find all sorts of wonderful and strange patterns and advice, ranging from directions on how to crochet wedding gowns for Barbie to tips on sewing nursing bras. In your Web browser, type

ftp://ftp.crl.com/users/ro/kdyer/xstitch.html

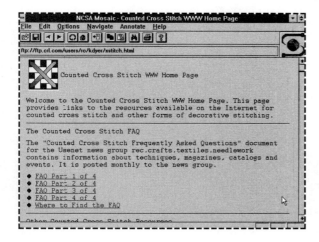

**Figure 18-10**
The Cross-Stitch Page is a perfect place to go to get that wonderful Cross-Stitch FAQ or to obtain craft-related files normally reserved for FidoNet BBSers.

## Other Needlecraft-Related Pages on the Web

Other craft pages you might find useful are

**The Prince Edward Island Craft Council Page.** Type

URL://gopher.crafts-council.pe.ca:70/

This page offers a pretty good directory of craft materials suppliers that is easy to search, plus a database of articles on running a craft business.

**Jacque Caldwell's Home Page: "A Serious Knitter on the Web."** Type

http://www.aus.com/~jacque/

to find out what Jacque is up to.

**The Vintage Clothing Mailing List Page.** Type

http://www.cs.brown.edu/people/smh/vintage/vintage.html

This page offers book reviews, lists of stores and sources for vintage clothing, and archives of past messages from the list.

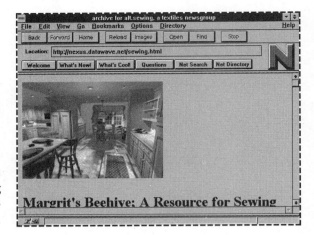

**Figure 18-11**
When last I visited Margrit's Sewing
Beehive on the Web it was under con-
struction. Here is Margrit's kitchen.

**Margrit's Sewing Beehive: A Resource for Sewing & Textile Information.** Type

http://nexus.datawave.net/sewing.html

**The QuiltNet Mailing List Home Page.** Type

http://sjcpl.lib.in.us/MFNet/MFNetLife/QuiltNetMail.html

**The World Wide Web Fashion Page.** Type

http://www.charm.net/~jakec/

**Chris Powell's Fashion Page.** Type

http://www.sils.umich.edu/~sooty/fashion.html

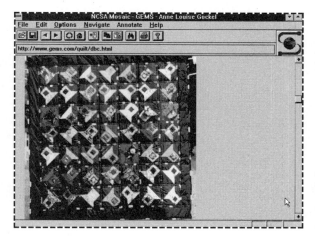

Figure 18-12
At the Internet Friendship Quilt Gallery you'll see many beautiful quilts sewn by Internet-surfing quilters for cyberspace friends. This quilt was made for Diane Barlow Close, in thanks for her hard work in founding the Usenet quilting discussion group and numerous Internet needlecraft mail lists. Look closely and you'll see that the blocks are made of computers. To get to the Friendship Gallery, aim your Web crawler to http://www.gems.com/quilt/fr-gal.html

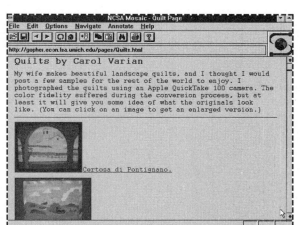

Figure 18-13
The husband of quilter Carol Varian of Michigan was so in awe of his wife's quilts that he created for them their own colorful cyberspace gallery on Internet. To get there type into your Web crawler http://gopher.econ.lsa.umich.edu/pages/Quilts.html

**The Fine Art Forum Directory of Art-Related Web Resources.** Type

http://www.msstate.edu/Fineart_Online/art-resources.html

This page is a springboard into all the art-related information and databases found on Internet.

**University of Kentucky Art Source.** Type

http://www.uky.edu/Artsource/artsourcehome.html

## Craft Stores and Suppliers on the Web

A growing number of merchants are setting up shop on the World Wide Web. While it's never a good idea for you to send your credit card number through the Internet, either by including it in an E-mail message or typing it into a Web page, the Web's colorful graphics make it a good place to browse. Call the advertisers' 800 numbers to order.

**The Internet Center for Arts & Crafts.** Type

http://www.xmission.com:80/~arts/index.html

You'll find a small selection of craft stores and suppliers online in this "cybermall."

**Craft King.** Type

http://www.xmission.com:80/~arts/ck/ck_main.html

This is a mail-order source of craft supplies.

**Stitcher's Source.** Type

http://www.xmission.com:80/~arts/stitch/mainstit.html

This Web page is another mail-order source of stitching supplies.

**The Craft Video Listing Page.** Type

http://branch.com:1080/infovid/c313.html

This Web page is an electronic catalog of hundreds of needlecraft how-to videos you can order online.

**Crafter's Showcase.** Type

http://www.northscoast.wm/unlimited/product_directory/cs.cs.html

This page is an electronic sales catalog, with photos of handmade items from California crafters, like angel dolls and wooden carousels.

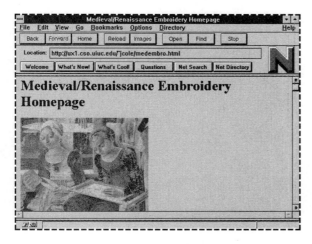

**Figure 18-14**
Embroiderers will want to check out this Web page, where photos of medieval stitchery combine with intelligent discussions and authentic designs that you can print out.

# More Needlecraft World Wide Web Pages

Needlecraft-related offerings on Internet have been growing like hothouse daisies. The following information-rich Web pages appeared online in less than a two-month period as this chapter went to press. That's why they're tucked in at the end of the book. By the time you read this, there will doubtless be many more.

## *The Internet Textile Server*

The Internet Textile Server, at

http://www.textiles.org/

should be your first stop on the infobahn for information pertaining to any needleart, from spinning to quilting. The server offers links to Internet textile FAQs, Usenet needleart newsgroups, needlecraft software sites, and much more.

## *Medieval/Renaissance Embroidery Homepage*

Embroidery enjoyed a golden age between the twelfth and seventeenth centuries, thanks to commissions by the church and royalty of many extraordinary garments and wall hangings. Learn more about embroidery in this age and see some amazing embroidery designs at

http://ux1.cso.uiuc.edu/~jcole/medembro.html

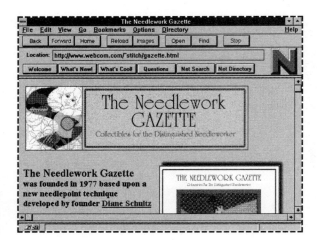

**Figure 18-15**
Expand your needlepoint stitch repertoire
by heading to the Wonderful Stitches page.

## Wonderful Stitches Page for Needlepointers

Also called The Needlework Gazette, this Web page features instructions for and photographs of different needlepoint stitches each month, plus more for needlepointers:

http://www.webcom.com/~stitch

## Arachne's Web Server for Lace Makers

This page at

http://www.arachne.com/

for lace makers offers lists of suppliers, pictures of bobbin lace in progress, and other hard-to-find info for lace makers as well as crocheters. The emphasis is on sixteenth and early seventeenth century lace.

## Hooked! The Traditional Rug Hooking Home Page

Pictures of hooked rugs, the Woolgatherings E-Zine, and the Traditional Rug-Hooking FAQ can be obtained on this gathering spot for rug makers at

http://gpu.srv.ualberta.ca/~dmerriam/hooked/html

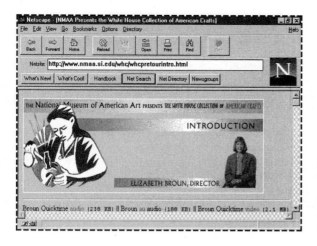

**Figure 18-16**
Tour the White House Collection of America Crafts via the comfort of your home computer. Pictures of breathtaking quilts are part of the tour.

## National Museum of Art, the White House Collection of American Crafts

If you didn't see the exhibit of quilts and other American crafts at the Smithsonian's National Museum of Art, you can catch part of the exhibit on this page at

http://www.nmaa.si.edu/whc/whcpretourintro.html

You can even view a video clip of Hillary Rodham Clinton introducing the exhibit. The National Museum of American Art's main page is at

http://www.nmaa.si.edu/masterdir/pagesub/tourthegallery.html ·

## Australian Textiles

Australian quilters have developed a distinctive artistic voice. Some say it's because light south of the equator is so intense and hence fabric colors are more vibrant. This page displays dozens of innovative art quilts by well-known Australian fiber artists:

http://ausarts.anu.edu.au/www/textiles.html

## Traditional Andean Textiles

Learn more about the distinctive weaving and clothing designs of the Andes at

http://rain.org/~pjenkin/textile.html

The page also includes a link to another Web page on alpacas, which will be appreciated by weavers.

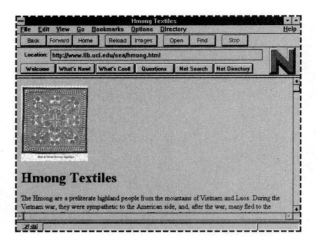

Figure 18-17
Be inspired by Hmong appliqué and embroidery. This page displays many beautiful creations by Hmong stitchers.

## Hmong Textiles

The distinctive whorling appliqué designs and embroidery of the mountain people of Vietnam and Laos are among the most beautiful stitchery in the world. This page displays dozens of incredible images of Hmong art:

http://www.lib.uci.edu/sea/hmong.html

## The Bayeux Tapestry

This embroidered chronicle of the Battle of Hastings of 1066 is history's most famous piece of needleart. Now you can view the entire 230-foot-long tapestry on your computer, via thirty-five digitized segments. You can also see close-ups of curious and amusing scenes stitched in the margins. Visit the Bayeux Tapestry page at

http://blah.bsuvc.bsu.edu/bt

## The Tangled Threads Home Page

Check in on the Pfabulous Pfaff Pfan Club, Inter-Quilt, or the Ragdoll Makers' Mailing List at the home of Tangled Threads. You'll also see some doozies of dolls online (including one that looks not unlike Bette Midler), plus you can shop for elinor peace bailey doll patterns through an "elinor online gallery." Head to

http://kbs.netusa.net/tt/

## Marilyn Imblum Leavitt's Cross-Stitch Web Site

Cyberspace home of one of the world's greatest needlework artists—she designs all those angels we love under the Lavender & Lace name. You can see every one of her designs here in an online gallery at

http://www.tiag.com/

## Medieval/Renaissance Embroidery Home Page

You'll wish you had the time to embroider like this. Visit them at

http://ux1.cso.uiuc.edu/~jcole/medembro.html

## Society for Creative Anachronism Arts & Crafts Page

Learn how to make chain mail and other medieval garb, as well as learn about lace-making techniques on the pages of the Society for Creative Anachronism at3

http://www4.ncsu.edu/eos/users/s/sfcallic/SCA/Crafts.html

## Turtle's Quilting Playground

View quilts, download quilt patterns, and access the Usenet quilting newsgroup on this festive page at

http://fly.hiwaay.net/~bnick/turtle.htm

## Suzanne Marshall's Quilts

Suzanne Marshall's innovative quilts based on designs of old tapestries are a must-see for net surfers at

http://wucmd.wustl.edu/quilts/srm.html

## Margaret's Quilts

Margaret displays her beautiful quilts and blocks at

http://eec.psu.edu:80/~scott/quilts.html

**Figure 18-18**
JoAnn's Quilting Page offer links to many
other quilting hot spots on the Internet.

## JoAnn's Quilting Page

On her page JoAnn writes that she's unimpressed by the World Wide Web and would rather spend her time quilting. It was her husband who programmed her quilt page, she says, apparently over her protests. It's a wonderful page, though, with links to many other things on Internet for quilters. Visit JoAnn at

http://www.charm.net/~jcain/joann.html

## Bertha's Craft Page

Bertha must get every craft catalog in the universe. Lucky for us, she's chronicled them all on her home page at

http://penny.mhn.org/~bertha/

## Nina's Quilt Index Page

Find your way to lots of good things that Internet has to offer quilters by heading to Nina's page at

http://www.cfn.cs.dal.ca/~ae862/quilt.html

## Oklahoma City Memorial Quilt Project

As quilters on Internet assemble quilts for victims of the Oklahoma City bombing, they display the blocks and record their progress at

http://www.xmission.com/~arts/ok/

## Friendship Quilters of San Diego

Quilters in San Diego are a lively bunch, full of activities and ideas. See their quilts at

http://turnpike.net/metro/quilter/index.html

## Michiana Free-Net Quilting Book Reviews

Read reviews of the latest quilting books at

http://sjcpl.lib.in.us/MFNet/MFNetLife/QuiltBooks.html

## Hard-to-Find Needlework Books

There's a bookstore in Newton, Massachusetts, that specializes in obscure needlecraft books. Visit their Web page at

http://www.ambook.org/bookstore/needlwork/

or download their catalog from FTP site

ftp://ftp.netcom.com/pub/ht/htfnb

## Directory of Online Craft Stores

To find dozens of craft stores and crafts people who sell their products on the Internet, head to this World Wide Web page at

http://www.mecklerweb.com/imall/2crftsnd.htm

## Amish Quilts for Sale

There's something anachronistic about Amish quilts being sold in cyberspace. You can view many of these lovely quilts at

http://www.folkart.com/~latitude/amish/amish.htm

## Antique Sampler Reproductions

Order kits and patterns to stitch reproductions of samplers in European museums at

http://www.xmission.com/~arts/special/special.html

These are elaborate kits, costing as much as several hundred dollars.

## FutureNet Crafts

Tap into a variety of British needlecraft publications, including Cross Stitcher, at

http://www.FuturNet.co.uk/crafts.html

## Craft Magazines

Subscribe to a variety of craft magazines, from *Crochet Fantasy* to *McCall's Needlework* at

http://www.netline.com/magnet/magnet.subject.html#13

## Yarn & Stitches

You can order needlecraft supplies from this store in Dallas, Texas:

http://www.shoponline.com:80/shop/YandS_home.html

## Whiffle Tree Quilts

Whiffle Tree is a quilt store in Silicon Valley. You'll see lots of really cool quilts on their page at

http://www.danish.com/WTQ/

# More Favorites as of March 1996

## The Tailoring & Sewing Page

You'll find instructions on pattern drafting and fitting here.

http://www.panix.com/~aqn/tailoring/index.html

## Underwire & Bras FAQ

Underwire will never get the best of you again. Learn how to sew undergarments like a pro.

http://www.funhouse.com/babs/FAQ.html/

## Tangled Threads' Antique Sewing Machine FAQ

Have you ever considered restoring your grandma's treadle? Check here.

http://kbs.netusa.net/tt/faq/index.html

## Nancy's Notions

Nancy offers some of her favorite sewing tips, plus tips from her viewers.

http://www.nancysnotions.com/

## The Costume Page

You'll find links here to costuming info and advice all over the Internet—like directions for how to sew medieval wedding gowns, military costumes, and 19th-century corsets.

http://users.aol.com/nebula5/costume.html

## Godey's Lady's Book

Take a peek at the online version of that oh-so-elegant ladies' magazine of the 19th century. Includes fashion plates.

http://www.history.rochester.edu/godeys

## Rob Holland's Virtual Quilter Newsletter

Rob is a smart and opinionated guy who knows everything there is to know about computers and quilting. You'll find his latest software reviews and commentary at this colorful site.

http://www.tvq.com

## The Cat Quilts Database Page

An online gallery of quilts, wearable art, and embroidery patterns sewn in a cat theme.

http://www.execpc.com/~judyheim/catqlts.html

# How to Find Craft Shareware on Internet

Searching Internet for craft software can be an onerous chore. It's much easier to log on to one of the major online services and browse through their craft libraries. But if Internet is the only way you have to get online, you don't have much choice in the matter.

If you have World Wibe Web access, start your hunt by pointing your Web crawler to the Virtual Shareware Library at

> http://gnn.com/gnn/wic/comput.53.html

This mega-archive will search the world's major shareware archives for anything your heart desires, including DOS, Windows, and Macintosh software.

If you prefer gopher or FTP, tap into the shareware archive at Indiana University by FTPing to

> cica.indiana.edu

or gophering to

> ftp.cica.indiana.edu

Head to the "pub" directory for software that the "public" can download.

Macintosh users can also avail themselves of the huge shareware archive at the University of Texas. Point your Web crawler to

> http://wwhost.ots.utexas.edu

A note of warning: These Internet shareware libraries come and go. One week's hot FTP spot for craft software is next week's "unknown address." Happy hunting!

# 19

## A GUIDE TO THE BEST NEEDLECRAFT-RELATED COMPUTER BULLETIN BOARDS

*Yes, there are even computer bulletin boards for stitchers. Log
on to these homey "computer rec rooms" on the info
highway and you'll meet others who share your interests.*

Computer bulletin boards are the People's information services. Hundreds of thousands of them dot the information highway like eccentric little roadhouses. They have names like the Dead Zone, Eagle's Nest, and Marty's Playroom. A computer bulletin board system, or BBS, is a personal computer just like you or I have, except that it's set up so that people can dial into it with their computers. Callers can send or receive private E-mail, participate in public discussions, and peruse information and software libraries like those on the large commercial online services.

In the past, BBSs have endured a reputation as hangouts for teenagers and computer hoodlums. But the stereotype is undeserved, for many BBSs are truly family affairs. They provide as much good information, conversation, and software as the CompuServes of the world. While most BBSs are run as a hobby from someone's family room or basement, and thus are free to call, some are small businesses that charge a fee.

Rarely do BBSs offer needlework forums or libraries. You're more likely to find bulletin boards devoted to motorcycles or video games. The BBS world is a conspicuously male one, and this may be the reason stitchers have not crowded them like they have commercial services. Possibly it's because of our frugality; too many long-distance calls to BBSs can result in phone bills that require a forklift to deliver.

Nevertheless, a few delightful BBSs exist for needlecrafters. One advantage they have over the larger commercial services, like Prodigy and America Online, is that you can use any computer or modem to call them (even that old relic from the time of the Carter Administration).

## Calling a BBS May Be Your Best Computer Learning Experience

You call a BBS with general communications software, like Procomm Plus, WinComm, and so on. Chances are that some brand of communications software came with your modem, so you should check for this first before going out to buy another package.

Because you don't call BBSs with specially tailored navigation software (like WinCim or the Prodigy or AOL front ends), it's a little more complicated to connect to and navigate BBSs than it is online services like America Online. But a well-chosen BBS may be your best telecomputing learning experience.

> *Note: I'm embarrassed to admit how many hundreds of dollars in long-distance charges I racked up in my first months of modem ownership. I found the BBS world to be a fascinating one and made friends that I still consider soul mates. At the time, there weren't many BBSs in my community, but that was years ago. Today there are probably hundreds in yours.*

I strongly advise you to get your toes wet online by calling one of the bulletin board systems described below. When you connect, you'll find friendly folks who'll be anxious to help and will answer all your computer questions. If you prefer to keep your calls local, ask your computer store or users group if they have a list of BBSs in your community, or check for a listing in a local computer newsletter or magazine.

If you have a PC, does that mean you can't call BBSs run on a Macintosh, and vice versa? Of course not. Through a modem, your computer can talk to any other computer in the world.

## *BBS Echoes Let You Commune with Minds on Other Continents*

Some BBSs participate in an unusual techno-phenomenon called "echoes." When a BBS echoes something, it takes a public conversation that's happening on the BBS and transmits it to other BBSs so that computer users on those boards can participate in the discussion. This process, called echoing, can make BBS conversations truly global. Some BBSs echo (or send) discussions all over the world, even into the Middle East, Taiwan, and seemingly remote islands. One such echo, called FidoNet, is extremely popular and has a network of thousands of BBSs around the globe.

One echo specially created for crafters is called FiberNet. FiberNet is broadcast from a large BBS in Henning, Minnesota. It's run by Theresa Parker (who is a weaver) and her husband, Ron, and it's supported by a list of benefactors that reads like a who's who in the weaving world. FiberNet echoes to BBSs in Alaska, Indiana, Illinois, and California. It also provides BBS callers in those areas with a way to participate in the Usenet textile discussion groups on Internet.

Like FiberNet, FidoNet and another popular BBS echo called RIME also echo some crafting discussions. They offer their callers downloadable repositories of knitting, crochet, and sewing patterns.

The FidoNet craft echoes are extremely popular, offering special conferences for sewers and quilters, in addition to a general craft conference. There's also one devoted to home crafting businesses. The discussions "echo" to BBSs as far away as Japan, Germany, and Australia. The FidoNet collection of patterns is known as the Crafting File Distribution Network. It offers some sewing and knitting patterns, but its strength lies in its crochet patterns, of which it has the largest collection available anywhere online. You'll find patterns for everything from snoods to baby booties. You can obtain the files through the "echo" on your local FidoNet BBS, but you can also obtain them through Internet (for directions see "How to Get Files from Internet" in Chapter 18).

There is probably a FidoNet or RIME BBS in your community. Again, check with your local computer store, club, or magazines for a local BBS list. Here's a list of Fido BBSs that carry the craft "echo" discussions:

| | | | |
|---|---|---|---|
| 206/427-1123 | Shelton, WA | 702/386-7979 | Las Vegas, NV |
| 212/594-4425 | New York, NY | 708/356-7107 | Lake Villa, IL |
| 214/250-4479 | Dallas, TX | 716/256-3687 | Rochester, NY |
| 214/243-0378 | Addison, TX | 716/473-5204 | Rochester, NY |
| 218/729-7026 | Duluth, MN | 716/548-7343 | Byron, NY |
| 304/743-1143 | Milton, WV | 716/695-0583 | N.Tonawanda, NY |
| 309/829-0169 | Bloomington, IL | 717/888-5421 | Athens, PA |
| 310/543-0439 | Redondo Beach, CA | 719/599-4568 | Colorado Springs, CO |
| 403/285-7338 | Calgary, AB (Canada) | 804/531-9214 | Norfolk, VA |
| 407/725-6646 | Palm Beach, FL | 805/641-0641 | Ventura, CA |
| 407/728-7386 | Palm Bay, FL | 810/795-5829 | Sterling Heights, MI |
| 410/592-2568 | Baltimore, MD | 813/955-7138 | Sarasota, FL |
| 414/552-7848 | Kenosha, WI | 817/897-7085 | Glen Rose, TX |
| 502/886-7146 | Hopkinsville, KY | 909/923-1031 | Ontario, CAN |
| 503/288-5443 | Portland, OR | 910/659-0576 | Winston-Salem, NC |
| 508/788-1603 | Framingham, MA | 912/369-5093 | Hinesville, GA |
| 517/627-4461 | Grand Ledge, MI | 912/953-5184 | Macon, GA |
| 607/844-3744 | Dryden, NY | 913/284-0359 | Sabetha, KS |
| 615/672-4747 | Whitehouse, TN | 918/534-1603 | Dewey, OK |
| 615/691-1887 | Knoxville, TN | | |

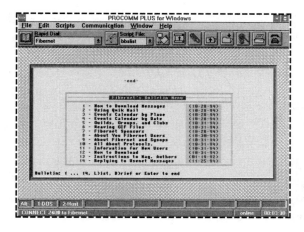

**Figure 19-1**
FiberNet can be as valuable a source of information for the weaver or knitter as Internet.

## If You Call Out-of-Town BBSs, There Are Ways to Keep Your Phone Bills Down

When I first started calling BBSs, the only way to control long-distance costs was to call late at night or on weekends. Now there are special long-distance calling services that let you call faraway BBSs at night for one modest monthly fee. Many such services have come and gone through the years, some good, some rip-offs.

One is G-A Technologies' Global Access service (800/377-3282). When you sign up for their service, you can call the Internet and different BBSs in most U.S. cities for about $4 per hour if you call in the evening. (Daytime rates range from $7 to $13 per hour, depending on the board and the time of day.)

*Note: Computer users always want to know if you can use these services to make cheap voice long-distance calls. Unfortunately, no. The long-distance connections that these companies provide use a special signaling technique on the phone line that facilitates the passage of a large volume of computer calls but won't carry your voice.*  ✒

## *Use BBS Readers to Lower Your Time Online*

Aside from signing up with a special long-distance service to cut your BBS phone bills, you might also try using something called *readers*. BBS readers are special-purpose communications programs that you use to call the board. Like the automatic mail readers for big online services, BBS readers connect to the BBS and pick up any waiting E-mail or message strings (that you designate in advance) from selected forums, and then they log you off so you can read and respond to messages offline, thus saving time and long-distance charges. To find out if there's a reader available for the BBS you like to call, check the announcements on the board, or ask the person who runs it.

# How to Call a BBS

Here's a quick, step-by-step procedure for calling a BBS

1   Fire up your general communications program, be it Procomm, Quicklink, or the software that came with your modem.

2   Find the program's dialing directory or phone book. It will probably look like a list of phone numbers and it may have odd computer settings listed beside each.

3   Once you find your dialing directory or phone book, type in the phone number of the BBS you want to call. You'll probably be given the chance to change the communications settings, but the default settings are probably OK. If you wonder whether you've got the right communications settings, make sure that you have terminal emulation set for ANSI/BBS, and that you have 8-N-1 settings: 8 data bits, no parity, and 1 stop bit. I always like to set the modem speed (its bits-per-second rate) to 2400 bps the first time I phone a new BBS—it's often easier to connect at this lower speed than at a higher one. Once you know that the BBS exists (they flicker in and out of existence like candles) and that your modem will connect to it, you can always call back at a faster modem speed if the BBS supports it.

4   Be sure to save any new phone book or directory settings, and double-check that the phone number was recorded properly in the directory. Some communications programs (Procomm for Windows, for example) tend to lose newly entered numbers if they're not entered and saved just right.

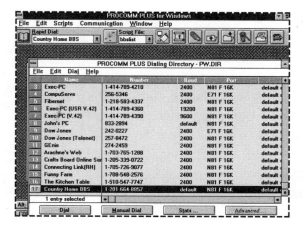

Figure 19-2
Telecom program dialing directories have grown complicated in recent years. The dialing directory for Procomm for Windows looks like you could use it to launch the space shuttle.

5   Once you've got your directory updated, it's time for the modem to dial the phone number. Find and select the number in the dialing directory. Make sure that your modem is turned on and that the correct BBS is selected, and then choose "Dial" or some equivalent command that tells your software to dial the phone number.

*Note: When calling a BBS for the first time, call during normal waking hours so that, if you have a wrong number, you don't wake someone up.*  🐾

6   If all is well, and your modem is set up to make noise, you will probably hear a bunch of eerie noises: beeps, screeches, and a kind of "shwoosh!" as your modem connects. When and if the sounds stop, press ENTER (or RETURN), which will tell just about any board that you're there and ready to proceed. Sometimes you'll need to press ESCAPE too. (You may have to wait a few seconds before anything happens, and you may have to press ENTER a second time, so be patient.)

7   If a message like "NO CONNECT" pops onto the screen, that means that one of the modems hung up or simply couldn't connect. No problem yet, though—try again. If after a few more tries you still can't connect, try dropping the modem speed from 2400 to 1200 bps. This is a desperate act, but it sometimes works. If you still can't connect, boost the speed back up to 2400 bps, and try disabling your modem's V.42/V.42bis error correction

and compression. (Another desperate act. You'll need to sift through the modem's manual to figure out how to do that.) If that doesn't work either, and you don't have another modem to try, give up and find another board.

8   Once you've got your modem connected to the BBS, you'll see some sort of introductory screen, and you'll be asked to log on with your name, a password, and maybe some additional information like your address and interests. (Be sure to write down your password and username so you don't forget them.) The BBS may also ask you nosy questions like your birth date and phone number, but you don't have to answer honestly. The BBS may also ask you lots of techy questions about your terminal and the

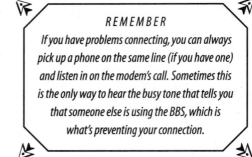

**REMEMBER**

*If you have problems connecting, you can always pick up a phone on the same line (if you have one) and listen in on the modem's call. Sometimes this is the only way to hear the busy tone that tells you that someone else is using the BBS, which is what's preventing your connection.*

kind of connection you have, and you may have no idea how to answer. Again, you can probably ignore the questions or fudge answers to them, but it's probably better to just accept any settings that the BBS uses as its default. They'll probably work.

**Figure 19-3**
This is what you'll see when you log on to the BBS called The Crafts Board Online Service in Northport, Alabama. When you log on to a BBS for the first time, it will ask you nosy questions. Then, when it's done, it will display a welcome screen or main menu. Use this menu to find your way to the messages and files. Whenever you get lost, simply find your way back to this menu to reorient yourself. You'll be able to access it from any other menu.

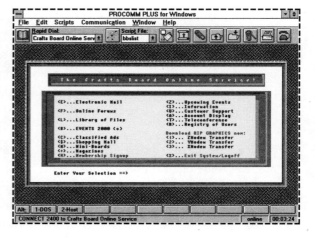

BBSs are usually divided into a public message area and a file library. Generally, there is a menu for each that is accessible from the BBS's main menu. You'll find many different libraries and many forums. Unscrambling the menus and finding your way around may be like trying to take a civil service test in Hungarian. But be patient with the BBS, and remember that nothing you type into it will hurt it.

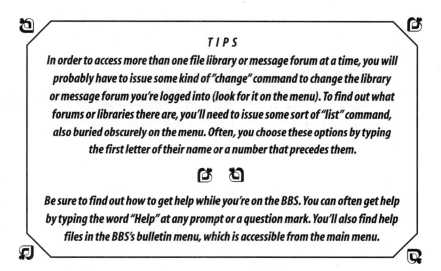

**TIPS**

*In order to access more than one file library or message forum at a time, you will probably have to issue some kind of "change" command to change the library or message forum you're logged into (look for it on the menu). To find out what forums or libraries there are, you'll need to issue some sort of "list" command, also buried obscurely on the menu. Often, you choose these options by typing the first letter of their name or a number that precedes them.*

*Be sure to find out how to get help while you're on the BBS. You can often get help by typing the word "Help" at any prompt or a question mark. You'll also find help files in the BBS's bulletin menu, which is accessible from the main menu.*

**Figure 19-4**
All craft BBSs have a public message area where you can discourse with other stitchers on the subtleties of your art. This is the main message menu on the Connecting Link of Traditional Rug-Hooking BBS in Ontario, Canada. Not very self-explanatory, is it? Here's a hint: Whenever you're on the main message menu of a BBS and you can't figure out where the messages are, try "changing area"—as shown in the command entry. That will take you to the different public message forums.

419

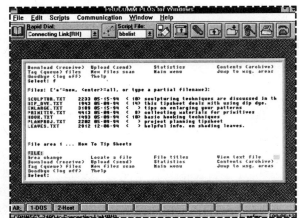

**Figure 19-5**
All craft BBSs have a file area where you can download software, patterns, pictures, and tips. This is a list of rug-hooking tip sheets available on the C.L.O.T.H. BBS.

While you're playing with your favorite BBS, keep these additional tips in mind.

⌐ℯ    Some BBSs have a sysop (sysop stands for system operator) page that let's you signal for the owner of the board. Once you've got the sysop's attention, you can chat with them in computer-CB fashion. Often the sysop is not around, but if you do happen to reach them, they may break in and type "Hello!" onto your computer screen. In that case, all you have to do is type an answer.

⌐ℯ    Always be polite and act like a guest when visiting a BBS, because that's what you are. Remember that you and your computer may be tapping into someone's family room, interrupting Perry Mason reruns, or some such thing.

## These Are the Top BBSs for Needlecrafters

*N*ow that you're ready to do some adventuring of your own, here's a list of some of the top BBSs for needlecrafters. There are lots of BBSs out there, so once you've checked out this bunch, I encourage you do some exploring on your own.

## FiberNet

FiberNet, based in Henning, Minnesota, is a free BBS for spinners, weavers, and knitters—although most of its five hundred regular users are knitters. Its benefactors include a long list of well-known weavers, plus Interweave Press, the Handweaver's Guild, the Wool Forum coalition, and Golden Fleece Publications. Its library of weaving patterns and software is modest, but its public discussions are lively, ranging from knitting socks to baking bread to worming sheep with tobacco leaves. It also has the very popular Usenet craft textile discussions from Internet.

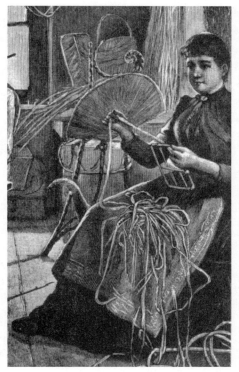

FiberNet
Route 1, Box 153
Henning, MN
Proprietors: Theresa and Ron Parker
Phone: 218/583-4337 (BBS); 218/583-2419 (voice)
Price: Free. If you send $5 to the above address, along with a description of your computer, the Parkers will send you a disk containing FiberNet's special offline mail reader and more information about the board.

FiberNet discussions echo to these BBSs.

☞ Patti Johnson's Alaska Pirate Society BBS, Anchorage, AK, 907/248-9364 and 907/248-9365

☞ Steve Read's Some Sunny Day BBS, Connorsville, IN, 317/825-5044

☞ Ellen Bloomfield's The Funny Farm BBS in Lake Villa, IL, 708/548-2576

All of these boards also have other craft-related offerings.

## Arachne's Web

Arachne's Web BBS is named after the peasant girl in Greek mythology whose weaving rivaled that of Minerva and who was eventually turned into a spider by the incensed goddess. It's quite a nice BBS, where a steady stream of weavers and spinners discuss their crafts. Its library is larger than that of FiberNet, with book lists, demos of weaving programs, accounts of weaving festivals written by members, and instructions on how to do things like spin silk cocoons. One day soon it will be linked into FiberNet.

Arachne's Web
Fairfax, VA
Proprietor: Phil Loftus
Phone: 703/425-7748
Price: Free

## The Funny Farm

The Funny Farm is another free board run just outside Chicago by spinner, knitter, and VGA Planets addict Ellen Bloomfield. Ellen welcomes all crafters, including weavers, cross-stitchers, and quilters. She aims to provide a "safe place where those who are afraid of computers can feel at home." And indeed she does. The Funny Farm offers craft-related software, electronic messages, and access to FiberNet.

The Funny Farm
Lake Villa, IL
Proprietor: Ellen Bloomfield
Phone: 708/548-2576
Price: Free

## The Crafts Board Online Service

The Crafts Board Online Service, run by Holland Communications in Northport, Alabama, is a popular hangout for crafters who earn a living with their hands. Some of its unique holdings include a vast and detailed database of craft festivals and a database of the "movers and shakers" in the craft industry. It also offers discussion forums ranging from sewing to quilting and lace-making. It's not free, but its price of 25 cents an hour is pennies compared to the rates of the big services. It has about 50 paying members.

The Crafts Board Online Service
Holland Communications
3617 McFarland Blvd., North
Northport, AL 35476
Phone: 205/339-0722 (BBS); 205/333-8045 (voice)
Price: 40 hours for $10; 90 hours for $20; 140 hours for $30

## Connecting Link of Traditional Hooking (C.L.O.T.H.)

Rug-hookers who want to learn more about their craft, or who are looking for patterns or simply like-minded crafters, will enjoy this BBS run by Shirley Poole and her rug-hooking supplies store, The Burlap Room. Here you'll find conversations on dyeing and puritan frames, details of Canadian rug-hooking schools and workshops, plus lists of materials suppliers. You'll also find online tip sheets and free patterns (a pony, leaves, poppies, and a cardinal were recent offerings). There are not many people in the world who hook rugs in the traditional manner; this is one way to find more.

Connecting Link of Traditional Hooking (C.L.O.T.H.)
46 Little Lake Dr.
Barrie, Ontario, Canada L4M 4Y8
Proprietor: Shirley Poole
Phone: 705/726-9077 (BBS); 705/726-8516 (voice)
Price: Free

## The Stitcher's Source

Southern Californians and FidoNet-addicts will appreciate this one-stop source for needlecraft supplies and craft files from the FidoNet network, where they'll also find echoes of craft conversations from Fido. The Steeles sell all manner of needlecraft supplies at cut-rate prices, and if you log on you can download or request a free mail-order catalog.

The Stitcher's Source
Phone: 714/589-1718
Proprietors: Lesa and Mark Steele
Price: Free

# 20

## CAN YOUR CRAFT BUSINESS MAKE MONEY ON THE INFORMATION HIGHWAY?

*Books with titles like How to Make a Fortune on the Information Highway are flooding bookstores. Will the infobahn increase your cash flow?*

Commercial information services like Prodigy and the Internet are wonderful places to network with other sewers and needlecrafters—to get advice, make business contacts, find out what others think of your product. But despite the cultural hyperbole in the air (and in business magazines), the infobahn may turn out to be a rotten place to mass-market, mass-mail, or close a sale of any kind.

For starters, people don't like getting E-mail with offers to sell them things. And they don't like reading it in public message forums either. You can't blame them, because they are paying through the nose to read those messages. Nor do they want to sit at their computer sifting through junk mail. Too, the Internet is paid for by our tax dollars. Money from the federal government and universities that might otherwise go for scientific research is what keeps Internet afloat. No one wants to see this precious national resource become clogged with junk mail and billboards.

Finally, commercial online services like CompuServe strictly forbid subscribers from posting public messages for the purpose of selling or promoting products. It says so in the membership agreement the service mails you when you sign up.

Nonetheless, craft supplies and patterns are sold almost daily on most of the online services and Internet as well. (I've purchased everything from quilt bats to fabric paint and patterns on Internet.) How can this be?

## The Myth of Online Shopping

Shopping by computer through online services has been touted as the wave of the future. Major department stores like J.C. Penney and automobile makers like General Motors are online pumping wares. Most of the major online services offer online malls with products ranging from flowers to art deco furniture. Do computer users buy things in these malls? The computer services claim they do, but I don't know anyone who does. The fact is these "cyber-malls" are a lucrative form of revenue for online services. Of course they'll claim the malls are splendid sales venues.

As a shopper consider this: Would you rather shop by flipping through a catalog over lunch and dialing an 800-number or by fighting your way through computer screens to look at fuzzy pictures, then tapping out your order in an E-mail message? Most of us would take catalogs any day. At any rate, there are presently no needlework mail-order stores on any of the major information services, though a few recently have sprung up on Internet in an increasingly commercial area known as the World Wide Web. The verdict is still out on whether any money is being made.

## How About Setting Up a Computer Bulletin Board?

Some craft companies mentioned in Chapter 19 have set up their own computer bulletin board systems. Computer users can call in, download catalogs and software, and participate in craft discussions. For most store owners and home craft entrepreneurs, though, a BBS will demand more time and resources than it's worth (the BBS needs a phone line, a computer and modem, and the special software to run it). Too, needlecrafters don't seem overly enthusiastic about making long-distance calls with their modems to BBSs just for chitchat, especially when they can log on to a major online service more cheaply.

# A World Wide Web Page Is a More Feasible Idea

*S*everal craft mail-order companies have set up shop on the World Wide Web, the branch of the Internet where computer users get those vibrant, video-game-like screens and click on pictures to surf the Net. Web pages are colorful cyberspace depots of text combined with graphics and hypertext links (they're described in Chapter 18). You can display quilt blocks on them, photos of dolls, knitting projects. Anyone can log in to them for free from almost any Internet service, and many major online services as well.

There's now a cybermall exclusively for craft companies, where retailers and artisans can display and sell wares. Called The Internet Center for Arts and Crafts, the mall will create a Web page for you and put your mail-order catalog on it for $1 per day. You can display photos of products on your page, along with their descriptions and buying information. When customers are ready to buy, they send you an E-mail message or call you on the phone.

Setting up your own Web page through an Internet service like Netcom isn't too expensive either. A page costs about $20 to $30 a month to maintain, although you'll need someone who's technically adept to help you set it up. These hurdles are easily overcome and, unlike with a BBS, once a Web page is working, it's relatively maintenance free. (Contact some of the Internet services in Chapter 18 for more information on getting your Web page.) To contact The Internet Center for Arts and Crafts send an Internet message to **arts@xmission.com**.

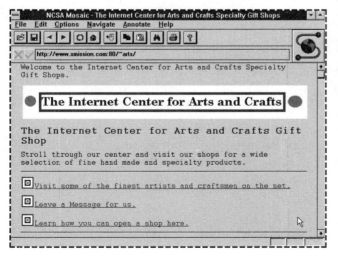

**Figure 20-1**
For just $1 per day you can advertise on the World Wide Web through this little cybermall, The Internet Center for Arts and Crafts. To get there, point your Web crawler to http://www.xmission.com:80/~arts/.

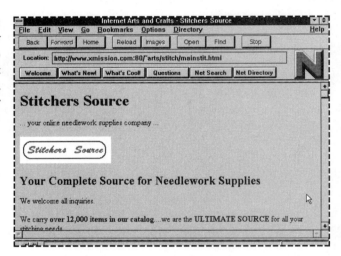

Figure 20-2
An artist named Bess Anni sells quilts, bunnies, and pillows through this Web page operated through The Internet Center for Arts and Crafts. You can't see it here, but if you scroll down this page you'll find digitized photos of the quilts and bunnies.

Figure 20-3
Stitcher's Source doesn't offer any pictures on their Web page, also operated through The Internet Center for Arts and Crafts, but you can download their mail-order catalog. You call them to order.

Will you be able to display your whole catalog on a Web page or on a series of linked Web pages? That depends on your ambition and the size of your catalog. The craft companies currently advertising on the Web usually display only five to ten photos of products on their pages since anything more would take a considerable investment of time to set up.

Then there's the credit card problem. Internet is not a good place for your customers to be typing their credit card numbers, since E-mail messages bounce from computer to computer around the country (or the world) before getting to their destination. Messages can become easy prey to hackers. You'll want to include an 800-number on your Web pages and advise customers to call it to place orders.

Can you sell enough goods through your Web page to cover the monthly fee for maintaining it? Perhaps not, though time may prove me wrong. Look at Web pages as public relations. If

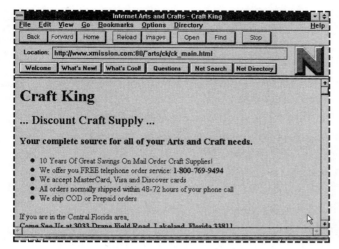

Figure 20-4
Another resident of The Internet Center for Arts and Crafts, Craft King mail-order supply house, doesn't display pictures or offer an online catalog but instead asks you to call them and order a catalog.

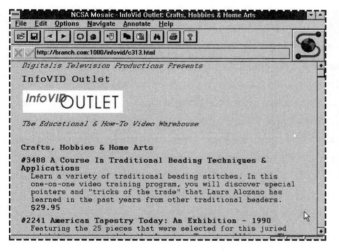

Figure 20-5
InfoVID, which sells craft videos, is one of the few companies that lets you read their entire mail-order catalog on the Web. The catalog is huge (only a snippet is shown here) and must have been quite a chore to put online, but it's cheap advertising and, considering how information-rapacious craft fanatics who haunt Internet are, may pay off in sales.

you're an artist, they'll give you the chance to display your creations to the entire electronic world—or merely the chance to have fun with technology and express yourself digitally.

## Consider Posting Classified Ads Where Appropriate

Most of the online services, and Internet as well, have designated places in the public message areas of their craft forums where members can post for-sale ads for free. Do needlecrafters read these? Yes, they do, because who isn't looking for a good deal on a used quilt frame or wouldn't leap at the chance to unload someone of an old box of needlework patterns for the cost of shipping?

The online etiquette for posting for-sale ads differs with each service, and you should find out what the rules are before you write your ad. The Internet populace frowns on prosperous companies posting advertisements in **rec.crafts.marketplace**, which is a Usenet discussion group devoted to nothing but ads relating to crafts. Internet habitués prefer instead that advertisers be struggling crafts people with no other means to promote their wares.

Some online services prefer that writers stick to advertising only one-time attic-sale items in their classified sections. For example, say you want to get rid of your grandmother's Ashford loom or clean all those Simplicity patterns out of your closet. If so, you might head to America Online to post an ad in the for-sale folder in the "Needlecraft/Sewing Center." And of course, these services permit you to write only one "electronic classified." Write more than that and you may get a note of reprimand from the service or angry messages from other subscribers. Persistence and obnoxiousness are not rewarded in cyberspace.

Etiquette is an important part of trying to sell something online. There are very strict rules for how to do it—some are clear, others unspoken—and these rules differ according to the service, as well as in various areas of Internet. Breaching one, even unintentionally, can result in people "flaming" you (sending you angry E-mail) or even in losing your account. Some needlecrafters on Internet are so fearful of being mistaken for a salesperson that, whenever they recommend a product, they end the message with a disclaimer like "I am not affiliated with the manufacturer in any way. I am not getting paid to write this. In fact, I have never had any contact with the manufacturer whatsoever! Not in this life, not in any other! Honest!"

Before you write *any* message selling a product, know the etiquette on the online service or in the portion of Internet where you plan to place your ad. Watch what other people post over the course of at least a few weeks. If in doubt, contact the person who runs the forum, newsgroup, or mailing list and ask them if your ad would be appropriate.

*Note: A "spam" is an E-mail sales pitch that is mass-mailed to everyone on Internet, even people tapping in from commercial services. If there is one thing almost every Internet-ite agrees on, it is that people who spam are a noxious bacteria. Some recent spams include ads for gold jewelry, computer security devices, and cancer cures.*

# Get Yourself Listed in Internet FAQs
# If You Sell Craft Products Mail Order

*I*nternet FAQ files, or "frequently asked questions," are text files that contain compilations of answers to questions that people frequently ask on Internet. Chapter 18 describes the dozens of needlecraft-related FAQs available. Among the most common questions that people ask online are the names and addresses of mail-order sources for particular needlecraft products, like ribbon for silk ribbon embroidery or fabric for sewing outerwear. They also ask about magazines and craft-related software products. If you sell any craft supplies mail order, or if you publish a newsletter or magazine or software package, it behooves you to get your business listed in the right Internet FAQs.

To do so, first find out what FAQs are available and get copies of them. (See Chapter 18 for listings of these FAQs and for directions on how to get them.) Then, find the private E-mail address of the volunteer responsible for maintaining the FAQ (it will be listed at the beginning of the file) and send the person a note asking if your product or company can be included in the listing. It goes without saying that you should include your business's name, address, phone, and a brief description of the products you sell (you'd be surprised at how many people forget to include these things when they write E-mail). Should the librarian respond that your company is not appropriate for the FAQ, don't feel rejected. Politely ask if they know of any FAQ that might be more appropriate.

## Needlecraft Products Are Sometimes Sold Through Networking

*I*n her book *A Woman's Guide to Online Services*, Judith Broadhurst explains that women frequently find employment through online services, not by tapping into big databases of classified ads (although they exist) or posting job-wanted ads, but by networking with professionals in their field through public message forums and private E-mail. You get to know people online, they get to know you; and over the course of months or even years, professional friendships develop. At some point they may mention that they are looking for an employee with certain skills, or you may mention that you are looking for a new job. Voila! A match is made, but the communication that created it is subtle.

Just as with job hunters and employee seekers, the pairing of buyer and product in the online world can involve networking that uses equally subtle communication. I once mentioned on Internet that I was having a hard time finding elinor peace bailey doll patterns. The next day I received a message from a fellow elinor fan reporting that she "might" have a few that she would be glad to get rid of. When I mentioned that I had five quilt tops lying around waiting for bats, I received a message from another casual friend who told me she "might" be able to get some of the bats I wanted at wholesale prices. I mentioned that I was interested in trying a knitting machine, and another acquaintance let drop a hint into the conversation that she "might" be able to give me a good deal on one. There are common threads to these transactions: The sellers were all people I knew; they weren't just leaping out of a bush making a cold sales pitch. And they were all able to offer me truly good deals, though they didn't try to sell me anything beyond hinting in a private message that they "might" have what I was looking for.

I'm not saying that if you have a craft store you should get online and start "hinting" to everyone on Internet that you can sell them Drizzle Tints at cut-rate prices. Rather, should you run across an enclave of cyberspace sewers who are discussing the difficulty of finding this paint in their communities, and should you *happen* to have some that you are willing to unload at "pal" prices (not 20 percent above wholesale, but true pal prices), you may want to refer to the situation in a message—subtly of course. They'll probably love you for it.

## Setting Up Shop Online

*B*arb Ryan runs a cross-stitch store in Merrimack, New Hampshire, and sells craft supplies by mail order. Many of her over 1200 mail-order customers are stitchers she's contacted through online services. "It took me five years of answering random questions on the craft boards of America Online, Prodigy, and Delphi to establish a good reputation," says Ryan.

If Ryan has any cardinal rule it's to never E-mail any unsolicited sales pitches. "I only E-mail people in response to a message they post mentioning that they're looking for a particular product. Then I tell them that if they can't find the product locally, I'll be glad to ship it to them," says Ryan. "I don't give them a sales pitch." Her second golden rule is to ship products the same day they're ordered. "This establishes the most important and critical relationship in online sales: prompt follow-through." After the initial sale, she remains silent and doesn't try to sell the customer anything more. She waits for the customer to come back to her.

Frances Grimble, a nationally known sewing writer, has been selling copies of her book on sewing and restoring vintage fashions for the past few years on Internet. "We gave a copy of it to a writer who makes costumes and asked her to write an objective review. She posted the review in the historical costuming and vintage clothing mailing lists," says Grimble. "We've since posted the review to several other applicable mailing lists, as well as sent copies of the review by private E-mail to people who have publicly asked for book recommendations or help with this kind of sewing."

But even though the book, *After a Fashion,* is now mentioned in FAQs and on Web pages, and is frequently recommended by Internet sewers in discussion lists and newsgroups,

Grimble's only sold eighteen copies on Internet, a minuscule percentage of the thousands of copies of the book that have been sold. "It's not a wonderful way to sell books," says Grimble.

Because of the casual nature of E-mail, selling online can pose other challenges. For instance, customers may tell you in an E-mail message that they want to order an item, then mail you a check weeks or months later and not tell you what it's for. It's important to keep good records of online customers and print out their messages, as well as keep a file of E-mail addresses. Get to know customers' real names in addition to their computer logons, and always try to get a phone number so that you can verify any orders that aren't clear.

While it's important to convey a professional image in any business, it's especially important online. More than a few crafters have mailed off checks for supplies that never materialized. Always provide customers with a voice number they can call should they have questions, as well as a street address. Business cards and brochures go a long way in establishing legitimacy (if you frequent the craft forums on Internet, consider inserting a business motto in your E-mail signature with an offer to mail a brochure to anyone who asks). If you're selling mail order, become a member of a mail-order association that requires members to adhere to a code of ethics, and advertise this fact in your brochures.

But the most important thing, according to Ryan, is to become someone customers trust. "Even via modem people can tell if you're sincere, if you really want to help them versus if you're more interested in digging into their wallets," she says. "I've had stitchers ask me to sell them something sight unseen, and I'll talk them out of it if I think it's not worth their time or money. That makes them come back."

## People Who Can Provide Information Are Always Welcome

When I first started using computers, way back when Peace Corps workers in West Virginia were first trying to convince mountain women to stop using polyester plaids in their patchwork, there was this ethos: If another computer user needed information and you had it, you did all you could to help, whether that meant tapping E-mail messages into the night or making long-distance calls. The computer community grew, and technology advanced as a consequence, with as much thanks to generosity as to capitalism and research grants.

That generosity ethos has been eroding, sadly, partly because we're all getting 500 E-mail messages a week and can't possibly answer them all. But the truth remains that people who take the time to provide helpful information to others in need are always welcome on the E-way, no matter if they're individuals or businesses. Needlecrafters as a group are especially hungry for information.

I wish more companies in the craft and sewing industry would get online, answering stitchers' questions, discussing their products, and talking about the industry in general. Sewing machine manufacturers especially owe it to themselves to get "wired." Nancy Zieman of the *Sewing With Nancy* program and *Nancy's Notions* catalog has customer reps on Prodigy. They're not pumping products, merely answering sewers' questions about presser feet and seam tape. What wonderful public relations! Everyone loves them for it. *Quilter's Newsletter Magazine* editors participate in a quilt forum on GEnie and they're part of the reason that forum has flourished into one of the most popular electronic quilting bees around. I'm sure many quilters have subscribed to *QNM* because of it. I bet many quilters had never heard of *QNM* until they logged onto GEnie. Reps from the sewing magazine *Sew News* are on America Online.

Most of the online services offer evening "chats" in which experts on some craft technique, be it machine appliqué or ribbon embroidery, discuss their art or their product with a live "auditorium" of computer users who are logged in around the country. The experts answer questions and even teach techniques through this futuristic conferencing medium. Online services are always looking for guests for their weekly chats. If you have something to share or teach, contact the person who runs the craft forum on any of the commercial online services discussed in this book. They'll be more than glad to welcome you on board.

A few companies have representatives who log on to online needlecraft forums regularly to spot questions from subscribers about their products. They then jump into the conversation and answer the questions. (It's generally forbidden on online services to try to strike up a conversation about your own product. It's better to wait until someone else asks a question about it. That's when you chime in with an answer. But keep it succinct and dispassionate. No one wants a sales pitch.)

## The Real Reason to Go Online Should Come from Your Heart

Selling products is not the reason to go online. You should go online to make friends, to share your knowledge with others, to expand your artistic horizons, and to give of yourself. The information highway has temporarily deteriorated into a Goldrush Alley where delusional corporate conglomerates think they can make a ton of money by opening up the Internet to people who want to sell cubic zirconium. The madness will pass. The cybermalls will be boarded up in a few years. But that hardly matters, because you, as an artist, are after something more elemental, a thing more important than lucre: helping yourself and others express what's in one's heart. *That* is the reason to go online.

## *How Online Services Helped Me Launch My Sewing Newsletter Business*

### *By Karen Maslowski*

WHILE SEARCHING FOR a new career several years ago, I joined the Professional Sewing Association here in Cincinnati and offered to write their monthly newsletter. This ended up being my job for the next five years. The PSA started putting on professional conferences designed to further members' business skills. As publicity chair for the first conference, called "Beyond Pin Money," I posted a message about it on the sewing boards of America Online and Prodigy. The response was terrific! We ended up with attendees from all over the country. We had also run a classified ad in *Sew News*, but most of the names on the mailing list we used to promote the conference came from addresses we gathered through the online services.

I eventually started my own quarterly newsletter for sewing professionals called *Sew Up a Storm: The Newsletter for Sewing Entrepreneurs*. I posted messages on Prodigy and America Online offering a free sample issue to anyone who responded. I distributed over 700 copies. While not everyone who requested an issue subscribed, I now have a mailing list of sewing professionals, which is like gold, for this is an audience of home-based businesses and isolated professionals. There are a lot of sewing entrepreneurs out there, but they can be very difficult to find.

I've made some incredible professional contacts on online services, not to mention friendships with sewers I've never met face to face. Not only have many of my subscribers come from Prodigy and America Online, but more than half my writers have too. Right now I'm writing a book on how to make money sewing, and over a third of the hundred-plus professional sewers I've interviewed I've met on Prodigy.

The bottom line is this: My publishing business could never have gotten off the ground without these online services. And the Professional Sewing Association wouldn't have had such wonderful success with its first conference efforts either. We have Prodigy and America Online to thank for our being able to link up with a difficult-to-reach audience.

*Karen Maslowski's Internet E-mail address is*
*SewStorm@aol.com.*
*You can also reach her at SewStorm Publishing,*
*944 Sutton Rd., Cincinnati, OH 45320-3581.*

*"Practice random acts of kindness and senseless beauty."—*
*motto frequently spotted in E-mail messages*
*in needlecraft discussions throughout Internet*

# APPENDIX A

# CONSUMER ADVICE

## How to Keep You and Your Family
## Safe on the Information Highway

*T*ales about "stalkers" on the info highway—sociopaths who send innocent people harassing E-mail and even intrude on their private lives—are becoming regular fare on tabloid TV news shows. Should you worry about your safety on computer services?

Some of the threat is, I think, overblown. In ten years of covering the online beat for magazines and patrolling every computer service, I've never been harassed. But I know both women and men who have.

If you frequent only the needlecrafts forums on computer services, your chances of coming into contact with an ugly character are almost nil. That's not to say that there aren't bad guys out there or that you shouldn't take precautions. You need to be especially careful if your children are using the computer. Child molesters posing as children are known to frequent computer services, trying to lure youngsters to clandestine meetings.

"Every maximum security prison has a computer lab these days," says Detective Frank Clark, the electronic crimes expert of the Fresno, California, Police Department, "and I'll give you one guess as to what those criminals do when they're released: They try their hand at computer fraud." Often they use computer services to enlist unsuspecting kids as helpers with credit and calling card fraud.

Here are Detective Clark's tips for keeping your family safe on the info highway:

## Protect Yourself

**Be street smart.** Just like on the street, not everyone you encounter online is as caring or sincere as they make themselves out to be. Not everyone is who they say they are.

**Stay alert for swindles.** Many subscribers to commercial computer services have been bilked by con artists, some posing as multiple people with different E-mail IDs. In one scam, a thief posed as a woman suffering a horrific disease. The same thief also pretended to be the woman's roommate and friends. All these fictitious people sent E-mail to the unsuspecting victim, telling him how desperately in need of money their friend was. Overcome with compassion, this gentleman sent some money to the fictitious woman. He later became suspicious, contacted police in the woman's city, and learned of her long rap sheet for fraud.

**Never send anyone money, and never give out your credit card number.** The rules for avoiding telephone scams apply online. Never send money, unless it's to a business that you've contacted first, either by U.S. mail or by phone, and that you know is legitimate.

**Never tell anyone your computer service password.** If someone contacts you by E-mail, claims to work for the online service, and requests your password, report them to the service immediately. Chances are very good that they're planning to steal online services by charging them to your account.

**Never give out personal information about yourself or your family to strangers online.** Don't give out your address or phone number either.

**Avoid E-mail arguments that include name-calling and threats.** Verbal brawling or "flame wars" via E-mail are part of the game in some electronic forums. They can grow nasty and get out of hand. Don't pick fights, and don't join them. While all you see is words on the screen, don't forget that the characters behind those words may be very odd!

᠍᠍ **Never reply, either via private or public E-mail, to obnoxious messages.** Ignore them as you would obscene phone calls.

᠍᠍ **Use the "Bozo eliminator" available on certain services to free you from creeps.** Some services, like Prodigy, let you delete E-mail messages from consistently obnoxious people without having to read them or even knowing they've been sent to you. This same feature is available for certain Internet mail readers. Contact your Internet service provider for more details.

᠍᠍ **Contact the police and online service if you are a victim of crime.** Not all police departments are online savvy, but they'll try to help you in any way they can.

## Protect Your Child

᠍᠍ **Never use the computer as a baby sitter.** Keep the PC in the family room, not your child's bedroom, and supervise your child's use of it. Too many parents leave their kids alone with the computer for hours at a time, naively assuming that they can't get into trouble.

᠍᠍ **Know more about PCs than your kids do.** Too many parents are computer-ignorant. They don't know what's going on out there or what their kids can get into with a computer. If you need to know more about computing, take some classes through your local PC user groups, vocational schools, or community colleges.

᠍᠍ **Never let young children dial computer services or bulletin boards by themselves.** Keep an eye on your children just as you would in any other situation away from home. I know one father who dials BBSs with his son but selects the boards carefully to make sure they're not offensive. He also asks his friends to leave his son messages so that the boy can have some safe E-mail to read each time he logs on.

᠍᠍ **Talk to your teenagers regularly about the people they exchange E-mail with on BBSs and computer services.** Teach them caution. Tell them just because an E-mail correspondent claims to be another 16-year-old, that doesn't mean they are. Impress on them the foolhardiness of meeting any stranger they exchange E-mail with. In too many cases, children who have gone to meet someone they exchanged messages with on a BBS—someone they thought was another child—have been molested. In one case the child was murdered.

🙽   **Block access to the computer "chat" or "CB" rooms if the service permits.** (America Online and Prodigy do.) The computer CB feature is also known as the "sexchat" feature on most services.

🙽   **Be aware that there is pornography online, especially on Internet but also on most commercial computer services, so keep watch on the files your child downloads.** At this writing, pornographic pictures and messages are either available online or accessible through Internet links on all the commercial computer services. Prodigy's Internet link is the only one that can be "locked" by the family's master account holder.

🙽   **Remember that no computer service is completely safe.** Your kids can get into trouble on any of the services, be it the family-oriented Prodigy or the more raucous Internet. So keep an eye on them when they're using the computer.

## How to Get Your PC to Communicate Over Hostile Rural and Suburban Phone Lines

*M*any rural and suburban dwellers find that their high-speed fax-modems have trouble negotiating the phone lines in their neighborhoods. The symptoms are dropped connections, bursts of chaotic strings of computer characters on the screen, and an incessant inability to connect at speeds faster than 4,800 bps.

The most telling symptom is that your modem works fine for years, then one day it stops making high-speed linkups. You contact the phone company, and they tell you that they have "modernized" their equipment. Most likely this means that the phone company has installed multiplexers in its switching offices. Multiplexers funnel hundreds of calls onto one heavy set of phone lines, greatly reducing the signaling bandwidth available to each call. With less bandwidth, the modem's signal gets squeezed, and the modem acts like it's broken.

Another possibility, especially if you live in a rural area, is that your modem's signals are being distorted by repeaters. Repeaters are amplifiers that the phone company installs on the phone line to boost signals that travel long distances to the nearest switching office. Repeaters boost voice signals above background noise and can interfere with delicate modem signals.

If your modem is acting flaky, and you think either multiplexers or repeaters may be the cause, try these things:

🙽   Test the modem at another location like a city office building. If it exhibits the same connect problems as it does at home, the modem is probably at fault. If it behaves normally, the phone lines are probably to blame.

୬✎   Contact your phone company and try to find someone who can talk technical. (This may be hard.) Ask them to send out a technician to remove the repeaters from your phone line. Don't let the phone company charge you for this. While this may not solve the problem, it has provided relief for some.

୬✎   Call a local computer store and ask to borrow several different brands of high-speed modems to try on your phone line. Different brands handle the intrusion of repeaters and multiplexers with widely different quality. Avoid Zoom Telephonics modems, Practical Peripherals, and Bocas. Try Hayes, Multi-Techs, and Microcoms. You may find that a specific brand will work just fine at high speed on your line.

୬✎   If all else fails, ask your local phone company if they'll install a private data line that bypasses the multiplexer. Some phone companies will charge you hundreds of dollars for one, while others may charge just a modest installation fee and tack a few dollars extra onto your phone bill each month. Still others will argue that they don't want to give you some special service that your neighbors don't have. Whatever your phone company's policy, you'll probably have to make a lot of phone calls to get a direct line to the phone company's switching office. You'll probably also have to whine a lot, and you'll certainly have to talk to engineers, because the sales reps probably won't know what you're asking for. Still, computer users who have these direct lines say it's worth the hassle to get one.

# How to Choose a Long-Distance Phone Company When a Computer Is on the Phone

*D*oes it make a difference to your modem which long-distance company you use? Yes, but only if you're making long-distance calls to BBSs, online service regional numbers, or are sending faxes across the country.

When you place a long-distance call, the call doesn't go straight to its destination. Your voice or modem signal zigzags all over the country, hopping from one regional switching office to another, like a budget airline flight. The exact path will depend not only on where you're calling, but also on the time of day and the amount of traffic on the phone network. There are so many variables that one carrier may provide consistently "clean" sounding calls whenever you call Cleveland, but give you fuzzy lines when you call Dubuque.

In the past, BBS junkies preferred AT&T (first choice) and Sprint (second choice). There were even a few studies in telecom magazines confirming that these two services provided modems with the cleanest connections. But these days, all the long-distance carriers are deploying better switching and line technologies. The only caveat is that some of the small, obscure carriers don't always provide noiseless long-distance. But even that is not likely to be a problem, because built-in error-correction in modems has made modem communication nearly indestructible, even when there's hissing on the line.

So, unless your fax-modem makes lots of long-distance calls during which you notice odd computer characters popping up on the screen, don't worry about which long-distance carrier you use. The one you have is probably fine.

## How to Keep Your Online Bills Under Control

Your monthly online service bill doesn't have to be as high as the heating bill for a glass house in the Arctic. The best way to keep your bills low is to find out exactly what you'll be charged for *before* you sign up for an online service. The ads may sound like all you'll be billed is a monthly fee, but there are other costs involved, and they can mount up fast. Those costs might include:

§ **An hourly connect fee for accessing all or certain parts of the service.** Connect fees are sometimes as much as 100 percent higher during the day. Some services may charge higher hourly connect fees for calling at higher modem speeds like 9600 or 14.4K bps, than they do when you dial in at 2400 bps or lower. Find out what parts of the service you can access for the flat monthly fee and what parts you're going to have to pay extra for. CompuServe, Prodigy, GEnie, Delphi, and America Online presently charge hourly fees to access their needlecraft forums. One solution might be to read messages on the services at a lower bps rate, and download files or perform searches at the highest rate your modem supports. Besides being faster, it's cheaper to download at a higher rate than at the lower rates.

§ **Extra database charges.** Business and investment databases and special services on CompuServe, Prodigy, and GEnie carry extra fees. Those fees may include an access fee, a search fee, an extra hourly toll, and a data fee (you're charged for the number of screens or records you display). *Be sure you understand all the fees that apply before tapping into any database!* When using certain databases you can easily rack up close to $100 or more in an hour's search if you're not careful.

❧ **Extra hourly connect or telecommunications fees for calling the service through an 800 number, or through Tymnet or Telenet.** Prodigy and America Online don't presently charge you to call their services through the low-cost computer dialing services Tymnet or Telenet. However, CompuServe and Delphi do, although Delphi charges (at a whopping $9 per hour) only if you call during the day. CompuServe also charges extra if you call their 800-number, rather than a CompuServe network number. Find out the cheapest way to call the computer service from your community, and make sure you call when rates are lowest. If you have a choice of numbers in your area, be sure that you choose one that carries no toll charges if at all possible.

❧ **E-mail charges.** E-mail charges vary from service to service. Some examples of extra charges that may apply include a fee for receiving more than a certain number of messages each month, fees for receiving mail from Internet and other online services, and fees for mailing program files.

When you sign up for a service, use it judiciously for the first month, until you get your first bill. Then you can get a good idea of how many dollars your hours (or minutes) online are going to translate into. Online service fees go up and down with the rapidity of airline fees, so it's important that you keep abreast of the current fee structure of any service you subscribe to.

Aside from managing your online time, your most important stratagem for keeping online bills low is to call the service with navigation software that logs you on, automatically gathers your mail and forum messages, and then logs you off to write your answers offline. See the chapters on the various online services for recommendations on what software to buy, as well as more service-specific tips on keeping your online bills down.

## How to Send E-mail to Needlecrafters on Other Online Services

*Y*ou can send electronic mail to literally anyone in the world, on almost any online service. You can also send mail to many computer bulletin boards. The easiest way to send mail between online services is through Internet.

The chart on the following page lists some procedures for addressing mail through Internet to someone on another online service.

| Online Service | Addressing Procedure | Example |
| --- | --- | --- |
| America Online | Type the user's America Online ID, followed by @aol.com | smithy@aol.com |
| CompuServe | Type the user's CompuServe ID number, followed by @compuserve.com Be sure to change any comma in the ID to a period. | 10000.01@compuserve.com |
| Delphi | Type the user's Delphi logon, followed by @delphi.com | tom@delphi.com |
| GEnie | Type the user's GEnie logon, followed by @genie.geis.com | t.smith@genie.geis.com |
| Microsoft Network | Type the user's Microsoft Network ID, followed by @msn.com | JoanSmith@msn.com |
| Prodigy | Type the user's Prodigy ID, followed by @prodigy.com | zzzz123@prodigy.com |
| AppleLink | Type the user's AppleLink ID, followed by @applelink.apple.com | tom@applelink.apple.com |
| BITNET | Add .bitnet to the end of the user's BITNET address. | tom.smith@acme.bitnet |
| MCI Mail | Type the user's numeric MCI Mail ID (not their real or network name) followed by @mcimail.com Delete the hyphen from the ID. | 1234567@mcimail.com |

# INDEX

# Give Us a Piece of Your Mind

Did *The Needlecrafter's Computer Companion* meet your expectations? (Why or why not?)

.................................................................................................................................................................

.................................................................................................................................................................

**How could this book be improved?**

.................................................................................................................................................................

.................................................................................................................................................................

**Any suggestions for other computer books for non-computer people?**

.................................................................................................................................................................

.................................................................................................................................................................

❏ **Add me to your mailing list**　　　　❏ **Send me your catalog**

**HOW TO REACH US**

**Name**

**Title**

**Company name**

**Address**

**City**　　　　　　　　　　**State**

**Zip**　　　　　　　　　　**Country**

**Phone**

**Fax**

**E-mail**

**no starch press**
1903 Jameston Lane
Daly City, CA 94014-3466
415-334-7200
Fax: 415-334-3166
nostarch@ix.netcom.com
74012.2506@compuserve.com

## "IF YOU BUY JUST ONE COMPUTER BOOK THIS MONTH, MAKE IT HEIM'S."

Steve Bass, *PC World contributing editor*

*I Lost My Baby, My Pickup, and My Guitar on the Information Highway: A Humorous Trip Down the Highways, Byways, and Backroads of Information Technology,* by Judy Heim

By award-winning *PC World* columnist Judy Heim. Find out how to turn your PC into a "This Space for Sale" sign; read an excerpt "From *The Secret Programmer's Handbook*"; learn "What to Do the Morning After You've Spilled Your Guts in an E-mail Message to 80 Million People Around the World." As funny a look at the underside of the Information Highway as you'll ever read. ISBN 1-886411-00-X, $9.95 (USA).

## WHO YOU GONNA CALL?

*The Computer Phonebook,* by Robert Baker

It's 3 a.m. Your printer just munched an entire ream of paper and you've got a migraine. Or you've been using an application for a year now and want the latest bug fix. What to do? Who to call? Haul out the *Computer Phonebook,* with address, phone, fax, e-mail, BBS information, and more for over 15,000 hardware and software manufacturers. Updated annually, this book is a steal at only $9.95 (USA). Believe us, you'll need it when you least expect it—and it will be there. ISBN 1886411-03-4.

## ARE THERE REALLY CATS ON THE INTERNET?

*Internet for Cats,* by Judy Heim

The facts are undeniable: cats are surfing the Internet more and more everyday. To find out where and how, check out Judy Heim's latest book, *Internet for Cats*. You'll find out where to go on the Internet for free veterinary advice, how to interpret cat graffiti, and even where to search out a little cat romance. You might consider this book offbeat, weird, or goofy, but we think it's just the facts. Twenty-five original cartoons by cover artist Alan Okamoto add to the fun. ISBN 1-886411-07-7. $8.95 (USA).

☎ No Starch Press books are available in fine bookstores everywhere, or to order call **1-800-420-7240**

# No Starch Press

1903 Jameston Ln

Daly City CA 94014-3466

# ABOUT THE SOFTWARE AND
# HOW TO INSTALL IT

You must have a hard disk to install the programs packaged with this book. You may run the LETSGO install program from either DOS or Windows. To install under DOS, make sure that a DOS prompt (like C:>) is showing on your screen. Place Disk 1 in your A or B floppy drive and, at the DOS prompt, type **A:LETSGO** or **B:LETSGO**, depending on the location of your disk, and press ENTER. Follow the instructions on the screen to complete the install. You may choose to install individual programs by checking or unchecking them. Note that the program type, either DOS or Windows, is listed next to the name of the program. If your system runs only DOS, you should install only the DOS programs (you won't be able to run the Windows programs). If you're running Windows, you should be able to run all of the programs.

> *Note: If you get an error when you type **A:LETSGO** or **B:LETSGO**, make sure your floppy drive can read high-density disks. For double-density or 5.25" disks, please return your original disks to No Starch Press. Be sure to tell us the type of disks you require, and include your mailing address and phone.*

If you are running Windows, insert Disk 1 in your drive and choose "Run" from the Program Manager's "File" menu. Type **A:LETSGO** or **B:LETSGO**, depending on the location of your disk, and press ENTER. Follow the install program's instructions on your screen, checking or unchecking the programs you wish to install.

> *Note: Some of these programs were not tested to run under Windows 95. Should you encounter problems with any program under Windows 95, please contact the software publisher directly.*

Once you have copied the programs to your hard disk, read the following instructions to see if any further install is necessary.

# Crossmagic™ for DOS Shareware

*K*eep track of your burgeoning collection of DMC or Anchor floss, plus all your Balger filaments, beads, and fabrics with this nifty cross-stitch database. If you like it, mail in the registration and you'll get a souped-up version.

**Minimum System Requirements:**  512K RAM; hard disk; color VGA

**Installing:**  LETSGO creates a subdirectory named c:\needle\crosmagc on your hard disk. To finish installing Crossmagic under DOS, change to the CROSMAGC directory by typing **cd c:\needle\crosmagc** and press ENTER. Then type **INSTALL** and press ENTER. To install under Windows, open File Manager and double-click on the file named install.bat in the CROSMAGC directory. Follow the installation instructions on your screen (which will create a new directory, XMAGIC), and install the program. You can cancel the install by pressing CTRL-C. Once installation is complete, you may delete files in the working directory c:\needle\crosmagc; the program is in c:\xmagic.

   To run the program from DOS, change to the XMAGIC directory by typing at a DOS prompt **cd c:\xmagic**; press ENTER. Now type **XMAGIC** and press ENTER to start the program. To run the program from Windows, open File Manager and double-click on the file xmagic.exe in the XMAGIC directory, or choose "Run" from the "File" menu and type **c:\xmagic\xmagic**.

**To Order or for Help Installing:**  Model Systems, P.O. Box 40047, Glenfield, Auckland 10, New Zealand.

# Cross-Stitch Designer for Windows Shareware

*C*ross-Stitch Designer (also known as Pattern Maker) is a Windows program that lets you design cross-stitch patterns like the professionals. It's one of the best on the market. You can also use it for designing needlepoint, knits, and other charted needlework. Because the version included with this book is an evaluation version, patterns can be only 50 × 50 grids square. Mail in the registration fee, and you'll be sent a version that will create much larger patterns.

**Minimum System Requirements:**  Windows 3.1; Microsoft-compatible mouse; VGA

**Installing Under Windows 3.1:**  LETSGO creates a directory on your hard disk named CSD40. To complete the Cross-Stitch Designer install, choose "Run" from the Program

Manager's "File" menu. In the dialog box type **c:\needle\csd40\setup** and click "OK." A dialog box will open, asking you to select or confirm the installation directory. Choose "OK" to continue. The program files will be copied to a directory on your hard disk, named XS40SHR. When the installation routine asks you whether it should add icons to Windows, click "Yes." Now double-click the Cross-Stitch Designer icon in Program Manager to run the program. When your installation is complete, you may delete the files in the CSD40 working directory.

> *Note: Be sure to read the files readme.txt and manual.wri in the CSD40 or*
> *XS40SHR directory for more information about using the program.*

Cross-Stitch Designer is shareware. If you continue to use it after the fifteen-day trial period, you should mail in your registration (contained in file register.txt in the XS40SHR directory).

**To Order or for Help Installing:** HobbyWare, P.O. Box 501996, Indianapolis, IN 46250. Phone 317/595-0565; GEnie: NeedleArts Roundtable; CompuServe ID: 71543,1504.

## Fittingly Sew™ for Windows Demo

*T*he *Fittingly Sew* demo gives you a taste of the program's ability to let you generate custom slopers for clothing design in minutes. Use computer-aided design tools to fashion the slopers into original patterns. This demo requires considerable hard disk space: 2.25 megs.

**Minimum System Requirements:** 80286 or higher; Windows 3.0 or higher; 1 MB RAM; Mouse; 800K free disk space

**Installing:** LETSGO creates a directory named FSWINDEM on your hard disk. To finish installing Fittingly Sew, select "Run" from Windows' Program Manager's "File" menu, type **c:\needle\fswindem\fsdemins** and press ENTER. When Fittingly Sew is finished installing, you can run the demo by double-clicking its icon in Windows' Program Manager.

**To Order or for Help Installing:** Bartley Software Inc., 72 Robertson Rd., Box 26122, Nepean, Ontario K2H 9R6, Canada. Phone 613/829-6488; 800/661-5209 (North America); E-mail: 72133.3102@compuserve.com

# KnitWare™ Sweater Design for DOS Shareware

*D*esign sweater knit patterns in a variety of custom sizes and styles with this premier knit design program.

**System Requirements:** 8286 or higher; DOS 3.3

**Running the Program:** LETSGO creates a directory named KWS on your hard disk. To run KnitWare from DOS, change to the KWS directory by typing **cd c:\needle\kws** at the DOS prompt and press ENTER. Then type **KWS** and press ENTER. To run KnitWare from Windows, choose "Run" from the "File" menu in Program Manager, type **c:\needle\kws\kws** in the box labeled "Command Line" and press ENTER. Be sure to read the files kwsorder.doc and kwsread.me both found in the subdirectory c:\needle\kws.

**To Order or for Help Installing:** Morningdew Consulting Services Ltd., 7604 Morningdew Rd., R.R. #5, Victoria, B.C. V8X 4M6, Canada. Phone: 604/652-4097

# Personal Patterns Jackets for DOS Demo

*H*undreds of custom-fit jacket patterns can be yours with Personal Patterns Jackets. This demo lets you print patterns for jacket fronts. For the complete patterns you'll need to buy the full program from Water Fountain Software, Inc.

**Minimum System Requirements:** DOS 2.0; CGA, MCGA, EGA, VGA, or Hercules graphics; hard disk

**Running Under DOS:** LETSGO creates a directory on your hard disk named JACKETS. To run the program, type **cd c:\needle\jackets** from the DOS prompt. Once in the JACKETS directory, type **JKTDEMO** and press ENTER to launch the program. Follow the instructions on your screen. If you are running Windows, launch File Manager and double-click on jktdemo.exe in the JACKETS subdirectory, or choose "Run" from the "File" menu in Program Manager, type **c:\needle\jackets\jktdemo** and press ENTER. Be sure to read the file jktman.txt in the JKTDEMO subdirectory for more information on the program.

**To Order or for Help Installing:** Water Fountain Software, Inc., 13 E. 17 St. 3rd floor, New York, NY 10003-1924; phone 212/929-6204

# Quilt-Pro™ for Windows Demo

Quilt-Pro ranks beside Electric Quilt as one of the best quilt-design programs on the market. Take this limited demo for a spin to find out if it's for you. If you like it, you can order the full version from Quilt-Pro Systems.

**Minimum System Requirements:** Windows 3.1 or higher; Microsoft compatible mouse; hard disk

**Installing Under Windows:** LETSGO creates a directory on your hard disk named QPRO, with several subdirectories. Read the readme.txt file in this directory before continuing.

To complete the Quilt-Pro install, select "Run" from the Program Manager's "File" menu, type **c:\needle\qpro\install** in the dialog box, and press ENTER. Follow the instructions that appear on your screen. Once Quilt-Pro is installed, you may launch it by clicking on its icon in Program Manager. You can then delete the files in the working directory c:\needle\qpro.

**To Order or for Help Installing:** Quilt-Pro Systems, P.O. Box 56092, The Colony, TX 75056; CompuServe ID; 73577,717; GEnie; Quilt-Pro; Prodigy; XCDA74B; Internet; 73577.717@compuserve.com; or phone 214/625-7765.

# VQuilt™ for DOS Shareware

This simple quilt-design program doesn't tabulate yardage, but it's great for designing blocks, and it works better than some programs you see advertised in quilt magazines.

**Minimum System Requirements:** 80286; DOS 3.0; 550K RAM; color VGA; Microsoft-compatible mouse; hard disk

**Installing:** LETSGO creates a directory on your hard disk named DEMOVQ. Before you can run VQuilt you will need to run its install program. To do so under DOS, type **cd c:\needle\demovq** and press ENTER. Type **INSTALL** and press ENTER. To start VQuilt from DOS, type **cd c:\vqltdemo** from the DOS prompt and press ENTER. Once in this directory, type **VQLTDEMO** and press ENTER.

To install VQuilt from Windows, select "Run" from the Program Manager's "File" menu and type **c:\needle\demovq** in the box labeled "Command Line." Choose "OK". Then select "Run" from the "File" menu in Program Manager, type **c:\vqltdemo\vqltdemo** to run the program.

**To Order or for Help Installing:** Computer Systems Associates, P.O. Box 129, Jarrettsville, MD 21084-9998. Phone 410/557-6871; fax 410/557-7928; E-mail: GEnie: P.HISLEY; CompuServe: 73177,162; Internet: pnh@clark.net

# X-STITCH Pro™ for DOS Shareware

*B*ill Love's X-STITCH Pro is your best buy for low-cost DOS-based cross-stitch design software. This program runs on just about any PC. You can copy and evaluate the program for free. If you like it, be sure to send in your shareware registration.

**Minimum System Requirements:** DOS 3.3; 512K RAM; hard disk; SVGA graphics; mouse

**To Order or for Help Installing:** Pilgrim Works, P.O. Box 16615, Greenville, SC 29606

**Running the Program:** LETSGO creates a subdirectory on your hard disk named c:\needle\xspro. To run the program from DOS, change to the XSPRO directory by typing **cd c:\needle\xspro** at the DOS prompt; press ENTER. Now type **XP** and press ENTER. To run the program from Windows, choose "Run" from the "File" menu in Program Manager. Type **c:\needle\xspro\xp** in the box labeled "Command Line" and press ENTER, or open File Manager and double-click on xp.exe in the XSPRO directory. Be sure to read the files read.me (for additional program requirements) and regist.doc (for licensing and registration information), both found in the XSPRO directory.

# About the Disks

*The Needlecrafter's Computer Companion* comes with two, high-density IBM PC disks that contain some of the most popular DOS and Windows needlecraft software. (For a Macintosh disk with similiar programs, send a check or money order for $1.50 for shipping and handling to No Starch Press, 401 China Basin St., Ste. 108, San Francisco, CA 94107-2192. Please include your name, address, phone number, and a copy of your sales receipt.) These programs are either shareware or demo programs. A demo is a stripped-down version of the full program. Shareware is try-before-you-buy software (it's not free); and although you can copy it and give it to anyone you like, if you use it you should buy it by mailing in the registration fee.

The programs are in a compressed file that must be installed (see the preceding instructions). The installation program requires that you have a hard disk in your computer. Be sure to read the file nostrch.txt on Disk 2 for any changes to these instructions. See the preceding pages for brief descriptions of the programs on the disks.

> *Note: Unfortunately, because we are not the publisher of the software on these disks, No Starch Press cannot help you with problems installing or running it on your machine. Please contact the software publishers directly for help with the software. For help with the LETSGO installation program or to replace defective disks, please contact No Starch Press at 401 China Basin St., Ste. 108, San Francisco, CA 94107-2192; 415/284-9900; fax: 415/284-9955; E-mail: info@nostarch.com.*